"Wake Up, Mr. West"

"Wake Up, Mr. West"

*Kanye West and the Double
Consciousness of Black Celebrity*

JOSHUA K. WRIGHT

McFarland & Company, Inc., Publishers
Jefferson, North Carolina

LIBRARY OF CONGRESS CATALOGUING-IN-PUBLICATION DATA

Names: Wright, Joshua K., 1978– author.
Title: "Wake up, Mr. West" : Kanye West and the double consciousness
of black celebrity / Joshua K. Wright.
Description: Jefferson, North Carolina : McFarland & Company, 2022.
Includes bibliographical references and index.
Identifiers: LCCN 2021058374 | ISBN 9781476686486 (paperback : acid free paper) ∞
ISBN 9781476644400 (ebook)
Subjects: LCSH: West, Kanye. | Rap musicians—United States—Biography. |
African American celebrities—Biography. | BISAC: MUSIC / Genres & Styles /
Rap & Hip Hop | SOCIAL SCIENCE / Ethnic Studies / American /
African American & Black Studies
Classification: LCC ML420.W452 W75 2022 | DDC 782.421649092 [B]—dc23
LC record available at https://lccn.loc.gov/2021058374

BRITISH LIBRARY CATALOGUING DATA ARE AVAILABLE

ISBN (print) 978-1-4766-8648-6
ISBN (ebook) 978-1-4766-4440-0

Front cover: Kanye West performing at Lollapalooza Chile
in Santiago on April 3, 2011 (photograph by Rodrigo Ferrari)

Printed in the United States of America

*McFarland & Company, Inc., Publishers
Box 611, Jefferson, North Carolina 28640
www.mcfarlandpub.com*

To
The Reverend Obie and Dr. Arthuree Wright
Mrs. Iris L. and Arthur S. McLaughlin
Peanut

Table of Contents

Preface:
Let's Have a Toast
for the Douche Bags

Americans are obsessed with celebrities. Millions of people devote hours each week to following their favorite celebrities' lives—liking their latest pictures, videos, and posts—on Facebook, Instagram, and Twitter. Celebrities include entertainers, athletes, writers, politicians, media members, models, public intellectuals, and influencers. Michael Levy, a noted clinical psychologist and author of *Celebrity and Entertainment Obsession: Understanding Our Addiction* (2015), argues that, as a society, Americans have become psychologically addicted to these high-profile figures in the same way as one becomes addicted to drugs and alcohol. Consequently, celebrities can affect cultural trends, politics, consumerism, academics, and social movements. When professional athletes in the National Basketball Association (NBA) and actors Tom Hanks and his wife Rita Wilson tested positive for the coronavirus (COVID-19) in March 2020, Americans took note. Schools closed, businesses shut down, and people self-quarantined throughout the nation. The *Baltimore Afro-American*, a black-owned newspaper, placed the actor Idris Elba on its cover next to the caption "Black People Do Get Coronavirus" to raise awareness and debunk the myth that blacks could not contract the disease.

In America's black community celebrities have always had a special status because their success and mainstream acceptance have helped uplift the race. For example, when the late actor Chadwick Boseman donned his Black Panther costume, millions of black boys and girls felt like superheroes. When Senator Kamala Harris became the first black female vice presidential nominee, Black Entertainment Network (BET) aired a commercial that stated, "When one of us makes history, we all do." Black celebrities are heroes, role models, trendsetters, and social activists. Likewise, their downfall can stain the race. Since the turn of the 20th century, black celebrities

1

have often had to choose between the role of spokesperson for their race or builder of a personal empire endorsed by individuals outside of and with little vested interest in the black community.

This implicit responsibility could impact every aspect of their lives from choosing where to live, whom to marry, whom to vote for, and how to use their platform. Their privileged status does not make them immune from the "black tax," or the added cost of being black in America. All black people pay this tax and are susceptible to what black writers call "the white gaze" regardless of how much education they have, how much money they make, or how famous they become. From the turn of the 20th century through the present, most black celebrities have experienced what W.E.B. Du Bois called the double consciousness because of this tax. The double consciousness is the psychological challenge of "always measuring oneself through the eyes" of a racist white society.

Since the early 20th century black celebrities have walked a tightrope across two worlds: one white and one black. They dealt with a double burden of being "too black" for some mainstream audiences and "not black enough" for some black audiences. Many exceptional blacks in America, regardless of fame, have experienced this burden at some point in their lives. Kanye West, also known as Ye, is no stranger to the double consciousness. For years his unapologetic blackness and sharp critiques of America's race problem evoked praise from blacks and a mixture of adoration, fascination, and criticism in (white) mainstream America. However, in recent years he has been accused of selling his *soul* for a coveted seat at the "white man's" table.

Kanye West has impacted American popular culture and zeitgeist more than most entertainers of his generation. In his preface for *The Cultural Impact of Kanye West* (2015), Julius Bailey wrote the following:

> For Nobel laureate Toni Morrison, the child wears the mask of the comedian attempting to make sense of the world, yet for the adult, the tragedy is realized in our inability to take possession of the world. Kanye asserts from his first album to *Yeezus*, a complex child-like, yet sophisticated nihilistic analysis where there are no social guidelines to help us cope with inequities and racism.... A careful look at Kanye's work recapitulates the Du Boisian question of being seen as a problem and, in Richard Wright fashion, brashly revolts against the Black man's acceptance of an identity that is a menace to society.... In Kanye's hands, Twain's Huck Finn would have "nigger Jim" talk as if he were able to claim his agency over the author.[1]

After transitioning from one of the top music producers in hip-hop to a solo artist, Kanye West transformed the sound of hip-hop and pop music in the early 21st century. Kanye's reach extends far beyond music. He is arguably one of the most influential creatives in the fashion industry, helping open doors for other unconventional black designers. His business ventures with Adidas and Gap made him one of only 17 black billionaires worldwide in 2020. *Rolling Stone* and *Time* magazines labeled him a genius. Kanye has lectured at Harvard and Oxford Universities and received an honorary doctorate from the School of the Art Institute of Chicago. Jeffrey McCune, a professor at Washington University, began offering a popular course titled "Kanye West: Black Genius and Sonic Aesthetics" in 2017.

Since 2009 Kanye's personal struggles with bipolar disorder, an opioid addiction, and his mother's tragic death have overshadowed his accomplishments. His high-profile marriage to Armenian-American socialite and reality television star Kim Kardashian and her wealthy white family, coupled with his fascination with white male role models and European fashion brands, led some to accuse him of suffering from what Frantz Fanon, a French West Indian philosopher, referred to as the "colonized mind." When Kanye called out elite white fashion houses and Nike for racism and classism, some wondered if he was only enraged because they denied *him* a seat at their exclusive table. After he called slavery a choice for black people and publicly aligned himself with President Donald Trump and conservative activist Candace Owens, a large segment of black America canceled him and relegated him to the sunken place, a terrifying metaphor for psychological oppression.

What does Kanye West teach us about the black celebrity's struggle to achieve wealth, the American Dream, and mainstream acclaim domestically and abroad while a maintaining a strong connection to the larger black American community and his or her own sense of black identity? This study uses the extremely complicated tale of Kanye West to address broader issues of celebrity, race, class, and identity within America's black community. While Kanye West is my primary case study, throughout the book his narrative is placed in the context of past and contemporary black celebrities who have experienced this double consciousness. The celebrity's story is relevant because it is a microcosm of being black and exceptional in America.

What specifically inspired me to write about Kanye was the controversy surrounding his 2018 TMZ interview and budding relationship with President Donald Trump. At the time, I was two years into co-editing a special issue on Kanye for *The Journal of Hip-Hop Studies*. As a full-time university professor, I learned that a number of people under the age of 21 do not know much about Kanye West. They know his sneakers, a few songs, and his wife, Kim Kardashian, and her famous family. Kanye has become a caricature for many younger millennials and members of Generation Z and a disappointment for many older black Americans. Consequently, I found a considerable lack of depth in many private and public conversations about him. This study attempts to provide a nuanced perspective and historical context to facilitate more constructive dialogue on Kanye West.

The list of previous literature on Kanye West primarily consisted of non-scholarly articles in periodicals and social media. Academics contributed essays on Kanye West in Julius Bailey's 2014 edited book *The Cultural Impact of Kanye West*. However, the contributors barely explored double consciousness. Sarah J. Jackson analyzed the media's depiction of Kanye's comments about President George W. Bush following Hurricane Katrina in her 2014 book *Black Celebrity, Racial Politics, and the Press: Framing Dissent*. Despite these exceptions, there are a limited number of scholarly books and publications dedicated to Kanye West. Since 2008, a small but growing number of graduate students have written dissertations on him, namely: Hazel Bell James Cole's "George Bush Doesn't Care About Black People," (2008); ShaDawn D. Battle's "'Moments of Clarity': Veiled Literary Subversions and De-Colonial Dialectics in the Art of Jay Z and Kanye West" (2016); and April Marie Reza's "Yeezy Taught Me: Race, Gender, Class & Identity Through Rap Music" (2018). I co-edited "'I Gotta Testify': Conversations on Kanye West, Hip Hop, and the Church," along with VaNatta Ford and Adria Goldman for a 2019 special issue of the *Journal of Hip Hop Studies*. Non-academic books on Kanye West include his late mother's memoir *Raising Kanye: Life Lessons from the Mother of a Hip-Hop Superstar* (2009) and music journalist Mark Beaumont's biography *Kanye West: God & Monster* (2015). It was announced in April 2021 that Netflix had purchased the rights to a new Kanye West docuseries, including decades of unreleased footage and interviews, for $30 million. Unfortunately, I was already finished writing the book before the docuseries debuted.

My research included academic articles, biographies, and editorials on Kanye; analyses of his entire musical catalog; interviews provided by Mr. West and individuals in his inner circle; and attendance at his live performances. I incorporated some of the methodologies used by noted scholars Omise'eke Natasha Tinsley, Joan Morgan, and Michael Eric Dyson. Their acclaimed books discussed black celebrities Beyoncé (*Beyoncé in Formation: Remixing Black Feminism*), Lauryn Hill (*She Begat This: 20 Years of the Miseducation of Lauryn Hill*), and Tupac Shakur (*Holler If You Hear Me*), respectively. Beyond undertaking an in-depth look at Kanye West's life and career, I reviewed the writings of Du Bois, scholarly critiques of the double consciousness, and biographical sources on a variety of historical and contemporary black celebrities. I delved into several interconnected issues related to Kanye West's public image, such as interracial marriage, black conservatism, black spirituality, mental illness, social stratification, civil rights, and political activism. I also surveyed 131 individuals over 18 to analyze their opinions on Kanye West and black celebrity and how the double consciousness influences their lives.

This study consists of three parts, each with three individual chapters. Here is a brief overview of each section.

Part I. Welcome to the Good Life: Kanye West and the Souls of Black Folk

This first section sets the stage for the book by defining the double consciousness concept and examining its effect on black celebrity in America. Chapter one looks at the role race has played in defining Kanye's public persona and his most polarizing moments. Examples include his verbal assaults on President George W. Bush and Taylor Swift, his attempt to rebrand the Confederate flag, the infamous 2018 TMZ interview, and his public support of President Donald Trump. Such episodes manifest why Kanye West is among the world's most intriguing and outspoken black celebrities of the 21st century.

Chapter two situates Kanye's narrative within a broader historical context of trailblazing black celebrities who preceded him in the 20th century. Vignettes feature Bert Williams, Jack Johnson, Lena Horne, Josephine Baker, Dorothy Dandridge, Sidney Poitier, Bill Cosby, Richard Pryor, O.J. Simpson, and other past celebrities who paid the dues for this freedom Kanye has. The third chapter focuses on the success, tragedy, and the double consciousness of Kanye's most adored muse, Michael Jackson. Kanye modeled much of his career after that of his idol. Michael Jackson was the first black artist to almost transcend race. Nevertheless, he still experienced overt racism in the mainstream and contended with questions about his blackness in his own community as he opened doors for his peers and future entertainers like Kanye West. Jackson's personal and professional issues foreshadow some of Kanye's recent struggles.

Part II. Everything I Am: Becoming Kanye

The chapters in this section focus on Kanye West as a man, son, husband, and father. Kanye's music, image, and worldview as a black man result from the influences around him. He is just as much a product of his familial upbringing and his hometown—Chicago, Illinois—as he is a product of fame, celebrity, and his marriage to Kim Kardashian. Chapter four begins with an intimate look at Kanye's family. His mother, Dr. Donda West, was a child of the civil rights struggles and generations of black progress in

Oklahoma. She became the English department chair at Chicago State University, an HBCU, and a Fulbright scholar in Nanjing, China. His father, Ray West, was an outspoken student leader in college and a member of the Black Panther Party after a comfortable childhood out of the norm for most blacks. Kanye's parents divorced, after which his mother played a more prominent role in his life. Her influence is evident in his early music. Her tragic death in 2007 left a void in his life that was unfilled until he married into the wealthy Kardashian-Jenner family. Many of Kanye's critics blame his mother's death and his celebrity interracial marriage for his strained relationship with the black community and his mental breakdown.

Chapter five explores the racial politics behind Kanye's relationship with Kim through the lens of past and present black celebrities who have dated and married outside of their race. Some black stars appeared to date non-black partners for assimilation and advancement. While some were guilty of selecting non-black partners to advance socially or because mainstream beauty standards influenced them, this was not the case with everyone. Consequently, these celebrities faced questions about their blackness, and their biracial children had the challenge of identifying with one race or the other. This chapter concludes with a conversation about Kanye's eldest child, North, and the double burden she confronts as a biracial celebrity in America.

Chapter six examines the role that Chicago plays in Kanye's life. Chicago was a prime destination for southern blacks during the Great Migration. The city's residents embodied a unique sense of overcoming struggle, entrepreneurship, political activism, culture, and artistic expression passed down the generations. Kanye's uber-successful entrepreneurial spirit is a byproduct of his hometown. The music of Chicago's black community—soul, house, gospel, jazz, rap, and drill—permeates his discography. Much of Kanye's mythology is linked to the city's soul artists he associated with early in his career. Furthermore, Kanye has made it part of his mission and political agenda to raise awareness about the city's gang violence and gang leader Larry Hoover. As fame and success have moved him further away from his beloved "Chi," many black Chicagoans fear that they have lost their hero to stardom, the Kardashians, and his craving to be adored by white America.

Part III: The Miseducation of Kanye West: Politics, Prayer, and Platforms

This final section of the book explores the double consciousness role in relation to Kanye's politics, spirituality, and how he compares to other present-day black celebrities in America. Chapter seven delves into Kanye's pivot from beloved superstar and innovator in the black community to a detested mouthpiece for President Trump and conservatism. Although Kanye's evolution was confounding for most of his liberal fans, his lyrics have included conservative themes since his career began. Some critics believe that Kanye's strategic bid for president in 2020 to steal votes from Joe Biden, the Democratic nominee, was orchestrated or exploited by President Trump and the Republican Party. Conversely, others see his politics as a manifestation of Kanye's need for notoriety and craving for a seat at the "white man's" table. Either way, Kanye West's politics provide a fascinating analysis of black conservatism. We can draw parallels between Kanye's support of Trump and Sammy Davis, Jr.'s, relationship with President Richard Nixon in the 1970s. The ridicule that both men faced manifests the experiences of other black celebrities and non-famous blacks who were labeled "Uncle Toms" for publicly promoting political values that are out of sync with the masses in black America.

Chapter eight dissects Kanye's religious conversion and return to his roots in the black church as he transitioned into making only gospel music and Christian rap. Kanye's move to gospel came on the heels of a tumultuous two years in the press following his support of Trump, criticism of former president Obama, comments on slavery, and a mental breakdown. Kanye's Sunday Service Choir and worship services placed him back at the center of the black Christian experience that has relied on praise and worship to overcome racial injustice in America. I analyze the significance of Kanye's 2019 Howard University Homecoming Sunday Service in Washington, D.C. This service highlighted the factors that made him so beloved and polarizing in the black community for over a decade. I discuss what can be inferred from Kanye's choice to hold Sunday Service at Howard, given the school's stature within the black community and the African diaspora. Finally, I assess the complicated relationship between Kanye's newfound faith, conservatism, and his appeal among southern white evangelical Christians.

Chapter nine compares Kanye West with other contemporary black celebrities who have become more political and adopted overtly pro-black stances akin to their counterparts' behavior in the 1960s and 1970s at the risk of their mainstream appeal. This new phase for the black celebrity, which began in 2016, reached a plateau during the protests over the shootings of George Floyd, Breonna Taylor, Ahmaud Arbery, and Jacob Blake in 2020. As the country was facing two pandemics, the coronavirus (COVID-19) and systemic racism, black entertainers were at the forefront of social activism. Why have these celebrities become so outspoken and culturally aware in recent years? Does this prove that the black celebrity no longer fears mainstream disapproval for their activism and unapologetic cultural pride or needs white America's validation to be successful? The chapter also explores the significance of cancel culture and how it influences Kanye and his peers to speak out or remain silent. Are black stars allowed to make missteps and evolve as multi-dimensional human beings without being viewed as "sellouts" to their race?

Introduction:
Kids See Ghosts

"You know it's hard to be black in a world controlled by white folks. Du Bois said we have a double consciousness. We try to be black; meanwhile, you got a white ghost harboring over your head saying, 'if you don't do this, you won't get no money. If you don't do this, no one will think you're beautiful. If you don't do this, no one will think you're smart.' That's the ghost. You're trying to be black, and the ghost is telling you to be a ghost." *Amiri Baraka*[1]

In the summer of 2020, social media was abuzz with viral videos of Kanye West crying on stage at a political rally in Charleston, South Carolina. Kanye stood there wearing a bulletproof vest. The numbers "2020" were shaved into his hair. A celebratory moment that was supposed to launch his campaign for the upcoming presidential election turned into a disaster. Folks were asking whether Yeezy had finally snapped and "gone crazy." Did he need to be hospitalized again? Kanye would emphatically deny all mental health rumors during exclusive interviews with Nick Cannon and Joe Rogan three months later. One of the first people to visit Kanye, days after the rally, to check on his well-being was comedian David Chappelle. Kanye and Chappelle have been close friends for years. They met on the set of Chappelle's Comedy Central sketch series, *Chappelle's Show* (2003–2006), in 2003. This was Kanye's first nationally televised performance. Chappelle described Kanye upon their meeting by saying he reminded him of a young Cassius Clay in the 1960 Summer Olympic village. Kanye just knew he was destined to win the gold. Chappelle says the minute he realized Kanye was destined for stardom was when someone called Kanye as he was watching pre-recorded sketches with Chappelle in the editing room. According to Chappelle, Kanye told the person on the phone that he could not talk because "my life is dope and I do dope shit" and then he hung up.[2]

Kanye was a two-time guest in the second season of *Chappelle's Show* and featured in the 2005 documentary, *Dave Chappelle's Block Party*. Chappelle is one of the few people who can genuinely relate to Mr. West. Bambi Haggins notes in *Laughing Mad: The Black Comic Persona in Post Soul America* (2007), Chappelle enjoys a dual credibility formed in predominantly middle-class black and white spaces that allows him to engage in important social critiques with diverse audiences. This is a privilege that Kanye knows quite well. Like Kanye he was raised by a single mother with a Ph.D. He built a career off being a provocateur who inspired, entertained, and offended large segments of black and white America. At the peak of his stardom, Chappelle, who, like Kanye, has been labeled a genius, had mainstream media and some in black America questioning his sanity.[3]

For nearly three years *Chappelle's Show* was the most provocative television show in America. The first season DVD set, which sold two million copies in the first week, became the best-selling DVD in television history. The series' sketches, known for being outrageous, irreverent, and raunchy, forced viewers to think about racism's absurd foolishness. Chappelle dealt with Clayton Bigsby (the blind white supremacist who did not know he was a black man), the racial draft, the Niggar family (a suburban white family in the 1950s), and the fictional ordeals of the first black person to use a "whites only" toilet.

Chappelle's Show received a vast amount of critical praise, including two NAACP Image Award nominations and three Primetime Emmy Award nominations. Dave Chappelle signed a $50 million contract in August 2004 to film the third and fourth seasons. The following May, with the premiere of season three approaching, he walked off the set and never returned. Speculation about his disappearance ran rampant. He was "crazy," on drugs, or hidden away in a mental asylum. As it turned out, Chappelle had quit the show and taken a self-imposed exile in South Africa, unbeknownst to anyone except his brother William. After he returned to America Chappelle broke his silence with a live interview on *The Oprah Winfrey Show* on February 3, 2006. "I felt in a lot of instances I was deliberately being put through stress because when you're a guy who generates money, people have a vested interest in controlling you."[4] He compared himself with other notable black celebrities—like Martin Lawrence—accused of "going crazy" once they achieved a certain level of mainstream success. While Chappelle admitted to feeling paranoid, he denied the rumors of being in a mental health institution. In his trademark sarcastic tone of voice, he asked Winfrey, "Who leaves America and goes to Africa for medical attention?"[5]

Chappelle attributed his reasons for leaving the show to the fact that he was doing sketches that were funny, yet socially irresponsible. He believed that he was being encouraged by the white executives at the network to make this brand of comedy. One sketch led him to this revelation.[6]

The sketch's premise was that every race had its pixie, which symbolized an internal racial complex. Chappelle's pixie was a pint-sized man in blackface wearing a bellboy's uniform.[7] Despite the negative connotations of blackface, he chose this horrifying image as the N-word's visual presentation. However, when writing the sketch, he failed to realize that the way viewers watch television is entirely subjective. Also, everyone is not able to comprehend the depth of black satire.[8] When Chappelle previewed the sketch before a live audience, he was bothered by the reaction of a white man in the room.[9] He assumed that the gentleman was laughing at him derisively. "I don't want black people to be disappointed with me for putting that out there," he said. "No, you didn't want to be disappointed in yourself," replied Winfrey.[10] In modern terms, Chappelle, the great-grandson of Bishop William David Chappelle, did not want to be canceled by his own community.[11]

Winfrey shared a similar experience she had years earlier when taping an episode with Ku Klux Klan (KKK) members and skinheads. She intended to use the interview to expose the atrocities and ignorance of those white supremacist groups. However, when she saw people in her audience applauding the bigots on the stage between commercial breaks, she realized that some people interpreted this applause as an affirmation of the bigotry. Winfrey pledged never to allow herself to become a part of societal problems and not the solution. She realized that she had a responsibility, not only to the black community but also to herself, to use her platform responsibly.[12]

Dave Chappelle chose to visit South Africa because he thought it was the best place to rediscover his true self. Hollywood made him feel like a prostitute who had to compromise his integrity for fame and fortune. He shared a story with Winfrey concerning an awkward moment while appearing in the film *Blue Streak* (1999). The film's writers and producers unsuccessfully tried to make him wear a dress. In his mind, Hollywood had a history of feminizing black men. "Show business has to do with compromise and wearing the mask. Black folks, we wear that mask. We walk in that boardroom; you gotta put that mask on. It's like we're bilingual. [When] we speak job interview, and we speak what we speak around each other."[13] Chappelle was referring to Paul Laurence Dunbar's noteworthy 1896 poem "We Wear the Mask."[14] Winfrey asked him if he felt like he had become a sellout in the black community. He replied, "I felt like they [Hollywood] got me in touch with my inner coon."[15] Perhaps this was the impetus for Chappelle's more recent stand-up specials, which have addressed everything from the lynchings of Emmett Till and George Floyd to the election of President Joe Biden.

In recent Netflix specials and interviews Chappelle jokes about the benefits of being Dave Chappelle. "The police don't fuck with me," he says, referring to police brutality in black communities. Rich whites tell him secrets that poor whites and non-white minorities are not privy to. Black celebrities in America, like Chappelle, are often given a symbolic seat at mainstream America's table. Fame has allowed these individuals entrance into a different social stratification that is foreign to the masses of black Americans. In rare cases, these men and women transcend race. A notable example of this is manifested in Sammy Davis, Jr.'s, guest appearance on a 1972 episode of *All in the Family* (1971–1979).[16] The Norman Lear sitcom centered on Archie Bunker (Carroll O'Connor), a fictional blue-collar worker in Queens, New York. Archie was a staunch racist whose vocabulary consisted of words like *spades, Zulus,* and *jungle bunnies* to describe blacks. In this episode, Davis left his briefcase behind in Archie's taxicab. When Archie returned home, he could not stop bragging to his family about whom he met that day. Archie thought he was paying Davis the highest compliment by describing him as "a good-looking white man dipped in caramel."[17] When Davis arrived at Archie's home to claim his briefcase, Archie called him the greatest credit to his race. Davis thanked him and sarcastically said that he was sure Archie's race was proud of him too. Archie's admiration was a classic example of the psychological disconnect suffered by whites who love black entertainment and culture but not black people.

All in the Family provided a stark example of the fine line that black celebrities walk in America. In one sense, Davis appeared immune from racism; however, he knew it was always around him. Miles Davis, the quintessential jazz trumpeter, addressed this dilemma in his 1962 interview with *Playboy* magazine. When asked if he still faced prejudice, Miles Davis shared a story about a white electrician coming to his home to make repairs. The electrician assumed he was "the help" and turned red as a beet upon learning that he was sadly mistaken.[18] In his 2008 stand-up comedy special *Kill the Messenger,* Chris Rock joked that all the black residents in his neighborhood were among the most significant figures in the history of their professions. By contrast, his nearest white neighbor was just a dentist. He was not a world-renowned oral surgeon or a celebrity doctor like Dr. (Mehmet) Oz. He was just a dentist.

In the early 20th century, a black person's celebrity did not earn her or him a pass from racism. Marian Anderson, the nation's best-known classical singer in the 1920s and 1930s, debuted with the prestigious New York Philharmonic in 1925. She amazed audiences in Europe so much that Finnish composer Jean Sibelius dedicated his song "Solitude" to her. None of this mattered to the Daughters of the American Revolution (DAR) who prohibited her from performing at their venue, Constitution Hall, in 1939 after Anderson was invited by Howard University to headline a concert.[19] Nat King Cole dealt with similar discrimination. The gifted jazz musician and vocalist from Washington, D.C., became the first black man to host an American television series in 1956. Cole, who always projected the perfect image of black middle-class respectability, sang at the 1956 Republican National Convention. Cole's fame was insignificant when he and his wife purchased a home in the exclusive neighborhood of Hancock Park in Los Angeles. Members of the property owners' association reached out to his manager to suggest that he reconsider his purchase. When he refused to heed the warning, the Ku Klux Klan (KKK) burned a cross on their property to welcome them to the neighborhood.[20]

Brother Outsider

The Academy Award-winning film *Green Book* (2018) reintroduced the public to the late Dr. Don Shirley, a queer black man who became the world's most accomplished classical/jazz pianist and composer. *Green Book* depicted Shirley, portrayed by Mahershala Ali, as wholly removed from the black community due to his exceptionalism. According to the film's script, Shirley's racist white driver, Frank "Tony Lip" Vallelonga, introduced him to the music of Little Richard and taught him to eat fried chicken. The fictionalized Shirley came across as a figure in Langston Hughes's 1926 poem "The Negro Artist and the Racial Mountain." In the poem Hughes lambasted the black person of means who intentionally dissociated him/herself from other blacks and black culture and fully embraced whiteness. This individual gloated over being the "only" black in their neighborhood, school, church, or social setting.[21]

Green Book focused on Dr. Shirley's tour of the Jim Crow South in 1962. Shirley suffered repeated incidents of severe racism and homophobia. Despite choosing to make that trip, he was unprepared for the hatred he encountered. The same fancy white clubs that rolled out the red carpet for him to perform would not allow him to use their bathrooms. One of the film's most poignant scenes was Shirley and Vallelonga's argument as they stood outside in the rain. As the pair stood on a dark, wet highway, Shirley cried out that his life consisted of living alone in his fancy castle above New York City's Carnegie Hall. He traveled the world playing music for rich white people who wanted to feel cultured by listening to a Negro play *their* music. But as soon as he exited the stage, he was just another nigger to them. "I suffer that slight alone because I am not accepted by my own people because I'm not like them either. So, if I'm not black enough and I'm not white enough, and I'm not man enough, then tell me, Tony, what am I?"[22]

Shirley's family rejects his characterization in this film written by white men and told from their perspective. Although the real Dr. Shirley may not have dealt with such isolation, there are many famous blacks who know the feeling of not fitting in. David Robinson was among the best basketball players in the National Basketball Association (NBA) in the 1990s. He won two world championships with the San Antonio Spurs and was a member of the 1992 U.S. Olympic basketball team, better known as The Dream Team. Robinson, a graduate of the prestigious Naval Academy in Annapolis, Maryland, spoke to *Sports Illustrated* columnist Jack McCallum about growing up feeling perpetually trapped between two worlds: the student and the athlete, the black world and the white world. Robinson was often the only black student in his classes. His peers were friendly up to a certain point. The social glass ceiling was evident when they would invite him to parties. He was always designated as the referee when they played spin the bottle because his classmates assumed that white girls should only kiss white boys. Things did not improve when Robinson hung out with his black friends. He said that if the guys got to trash-talking while on the basketball court, someone would call him an "Uncle Tom" for speaking or acting a certain way. The black kids often said Robinson was not black enough. The actions of the white kids reminded him that he was not white enough either.

My father, who is retired, routinely watches *The Price Is Right* (1972–present) and *Let's Make a Deal* (1963–present) in the morning. Wayne Brady, the host of the latter series, can relate to Robinson's experience. As a child of West Indian descent, Brady was bused to a predominantly white school in Orlando, Florida.[23] He grew up believing that he was too poor, too ghetto, and too dark-skinned to fit in with his white classmates. Simultaneously, he felt uncomfortable around black kids in his neighborhood because they viewed him as a rich white boy. One of Brady's first big breaks came as the sole black comic in an improvisation group called House Full of Honkeys. His next break came as the lone black comic on *Whose Line Is It Anyway?* which Drew Carey hosted.[24]

Wayne Brady's mainstream success came at a cost. The younger black comics on HBO's groundbreaking series, *Def Comedy Jam* (1992–1997), viewed him as a "sellout" doing "white" comedy for "white" audiences. This criticism inspired Paul Mooney's famous sketch on *Chappelle's Show*. "White people love Wayne Brady because he makes Bryant Gumbel look like Malcolm X," said Mooney in the role of Negrodamus.[25] Mooney and others did not realize how much the white executives at the networks sanitized Brady's public image. He routinely fought with ABC to have black guests on his show. He fought with the network over his attire. If Brady did not wear a suit, network executives feared he would look too "urban" for their audience.[26] The stress from trying to appease both worlds—one white and one black—hurt his mental health and ruined his second marriage.

Defining the Double Consciousness

Wayne Brady and David Robinson both experienced the double consciousness. W.E.B. Du Bois introduced the concept in his 1897 *Atlantic Monthly* article "Strivings of the Negro People."[27] Du Bois was the leading black intellectual at the turn of the 20th century and a founder of the National Association for the Advancement of Colored People (NAACP).[28] Du Bois taught at Wilberforce University, an HBCU in Ohio, before joining the faculty of Atlanta University (now Clark Atlanta University). He traveled to England to participate in the first Pan-African Congress in 1900. Three years later he published a series of autobiographical and historical essays addressing the question, "what does it mean to be black in the world?" This series, titled *The Souls of Black Folk*, became his seminal work and popularized the double consciousness for a wider audience:

> It is a peculiar sensation, this double consciousness, this sense of always looking at one's self through the eyes of others, of measuring one's soul by the tape of a world that looks on in amused contempt and pity. One ever feels his two-ness, an American, a Negro; two souls, two thoughts, two unreconciled strivings; two warring ideals in one dark body, whose dogged strength alone keeps it from being torn asunder.... He does not wish to Africanize America, for America has too much to teach the world and Africa. He wouldn't bleach his Negro blood in a flood of white Americanism, for he knows that Negro blood has a message for the world. He simply wishes to make it possible for a man to be both a Negro and an American without being cursed and spit upon by his fellows, without having the doors of opportunity closed roughly in his face.[29]

Academics have debated the legitimacy of the double consciousness and Du Bois's connection to it for decades. Jazz critic Albert Murray said the idea of dual identities incorrectly presumes that the American identity is white.[30] Was this burden of duality a problem impacting all blacks, or something incorrectly proposed by the black bourgeoisie? Adolph Reed, Jr., argued in *W.E.B. Du Bois and American Political Thought* (1999) that Du Bois never clearly defined the concept.[31] Du Bois held a scientific understanding of double consciousness, according to Reed, that expressed a dichotomy between what he believed to be the primitive nature of blacks and the civilized soul of European culture.[32] In 2003 Ernest Allen, Jr., called the double consciousness a false notion that the Talented Tenth, a term Du Bois gave to the privileged black elites and intellectuals expected to lead the race, were burdened by a divided cultural awareness and the needs of the black masses.[33]

George Ciccariello-Maher writes that Du Bois's initial explanation of double consciousness was severely limited, one in which the segregationist veil was seen idealistically and could be solved by the attainment of a liberal arts education. Ciccariello-Maher believes that Du Bois's writing initially expressed optimism because he was writing for predominantly white audiences. "For we must not forget that the veil is an actual institution—formal and informal racialization and segregation—that creates the two 'worlds,' Black and White, on either side of the color line…. Double-consciousness, on the other hand, as an outgrowth of the veil exists in that consciousness confined to the dark side of the veil," wrote Ciccariello-Maher.[34] Du Bois, unlike his primary rival of this era—Booker T. Washington—did not grow up enslaved in the South. He was born free in the majority-white town of Great Barrington, Massachusetts. His experiences differed from that of the masses. Du Bois, the first black student to earn a Ph.D. from Harvard University, was one of the most educated Americans of his era. He was a cosmopolitan who traveled the world and completed his graduate studies at Harvard University and in Berlin, Germany.

Du Bois's sojourn in the South as a student at Fisk University in Nashville, Tennessee, and an instructor at Atlanta University contributed to a reversal of his optimistic outlook expressed in "Strivings." In chapter thirteen of *The Souls of Black Folk,* his essay "Of the Coming of John" discussed a nonfictional plow-hand named Black John given the opportunity to live in the city and enter the white world thanks to his educational opportunities. Education and privilege did not provide an escape from racism. Instead, it made Black John aware of the veil that denied him and other blacks the privilege given to whites. Amanda Taylor, the Assistant Vice President of Diversity, Equity, and Inclusion at American University in Washington, D.C., says that white privilege does not mean whites automatically have easy lives. But their race will not be a barrier to success.[35]

The criticism of W.E.B. Du Bois notwithstanding, the notion of a double consciousness has become widely accepted by many scholars and the masses when discussing race. Lauren Wilkinson's acclaimed Cold War–era spy novel, *American Spy*, about Marie Mitchell, the lone black FBI intelligence officer assisting in bringing down the communist black president of Burkina Faso, is a tale of the double consciousness.[36] Mitchell must complete her assignment even though she secretly admires what the president is doing for the black people in his African country. She is torn between these two worlds around her. The double consciousness is not restricted to the black American community. Karen Ishizuka's *Serve the People: Making Asian Americans in the Long Sixties* (2018); *Be Water* (2020), ESPN's 30-for-30 documentary film on Chinese actor Bruce Lee (born Lee Jun-fan); and the PBS docuseries *Asian Americans* (2020) document the struggles of people of Asian Americans to be accepted by fellow Asians and white Americans.

During the civil rights movement, racist whites saw Asian Americans as the "model minority" group because they were not militant like the "negroes" and were "grateful" for everything that America offered them. Asian American parents instructed their children to keep their mouths shut, never complain, and be that "good" minority. Good Asians in the 1950s and 1960s identified first as Americans and downplayed their Asian heritage.[37] Bad Asians agitated and aligned themselves with the protests of blacks and Latinos. This full embrace of mainstream American values came at a price. In the film *Crazy Rich Asians* (2018), Rachel Chu (Constance Wu), a Chinese American economics professor, was not viewed as "real" Chinese by her fiancé's family in Singapore. According to Jeannie Mai, a co-host on the syndicated television talk show *The Real*, this "model minority" myth and "real" Asian tropes have divided Asian Americans amongst themselves and other minority groups in America.[38]

Following the fatal shootings of six Asian-American women spa workers in Atlanta, the *New York Times* published a statement by Rebecca Wong, a 17-year-old, Asian-American teenager in New Jersey. Wong wrote about her parents' efforts to disassociate themselves from their native community and culture. She refused to learn Catonese in hopes of becoming "more American" and successful. The violence in Atlanta, committed by a troubled white male and the anti-Asian sentiment resulting from the Coronavirus reminded her that no matter how hard she tried to fit in, she would always be Asian.

The Latinx community is also familiar with the double consciousness. A scene from the 1997 film *Selena,* starring Jennifer Lopez as the slain Mexican American singer Selena Quintanilla-Perez, depicts Selena's father, Abraham, lecturing her and her brother about the struggle they must endure to be accepted by both native Mexicans and white Americans. "We gotta prove to Mexicans how Mexican we are, and we gotta prove to the Americans how American we are," he says.[39] I interviewed professor Oliver Rosales; media personality Elena Romero; Isaac Hernandez, a manager for information technology at the Federal Deposit Insurance Corporation; and immigration rights activist Daniella Vargas for my podcast series, *Woke History*, on August 15, 2020. They could all relate to the words of Selena's dad. Hernandez, a Puerto Rican born in Brooklyn, New York, who describes himself as "unapologetically Latino," often finds himself as "the other" in professional settings. As the only Latino, he must master the ways of the dominant group. At the same time, his current privileged status and American upbringing make him stand apart from native-born Puerto Ricans when he visits the island.

Frantz Fanon, a French West Indian philosopher and member of the revolutionary Algerian National Liberation Front, incorporated double consciousness elements into his first book, *Black Skin, White Mask* (1952), and his final book, *Wretched of the Earth* (1961).[40] His residency in France inspired his writing. He began *Black Skin, White Mask*, with a story about a white girl on a train whose reaction to seeing a black passenger is, "Look mama, a negro." At that uncomfortable moment, the passenger became mindful of his "otherness." For Fanon, humanity was the bond between the self and others. I am only human if others recognize my humanity. Slavery and colonialism had ingrained an inferiority complex in the minds of some blacks living overseas. For Fanon, the white slave master did not look at the black slave for self-recognition. He looked at the black because he needed a workforce. Consequently, the black individual was dehumanized. The slave became fixated on the identity of the white master. He or she desired to be regarded as a subject, not as an object. He or she yearned, at all costs, for the white man's approval of the equal value of his intellect. "For the black man, there is only one destiny, and it is white," wrote Fanon.[41]

Two Words

Kanye West alluded to the double consciousness on his debut album *The College Dropout* (2004) with DeRay Davis's comedic portrayal of a school administrator in the album's opening skit. The fictional administrator asked Kanye to provide words of encouragement to his students. Rather than give an uplifting and respectable speech, Kanye proceeded to rap about selling drugs as a ticket to get off welfare and move from the ghetto. The irate school administrator admonished Kanye for behaving like "a nigger" and embarrassing him in front of the white people in the audience. In his 2009 dissertation "A Critique of Du Boisian Reason: Kanye West and the Fruitfulness of Double-Consciousness," George Ciccariello-Maher said of Kanye, "His exposure to the effects of the veil was always more pronounced than had been Du Bois', emerging by way of a radical family heritage."[42] Kanye's famous "Pinocchio Story" performance during his 2005 Hollywood Bowl concert was a visual presentation on his own double consciousness.

Kanye West has gone from being praised in the black community for his thought-provoking lyrics on race and social issues to being canceled and having his blackness questioned. In her article "Kanye's Frantz Fanon Complex," J.A.M. Aiwuyor criticized Mr. West for having the colonized mindset Fanon spoke of in *Wretched of the Earth* (1961). "Kanye has an obsession with getting acceptance, but not the 'colored' kind," wrote Aiwuyor.[43] Kanye West, at times, appears engaged in an internal struggle. For all his boasting about being free—unbought and unbossed—surely he must realize the financial benefits of mainstream acceptance.[44] Kanye would not be a billionaire without such acceptance. Concurrently, he is hurt by being dismissed by large segments of black America who view him as "crazy," a "sellout," or an "Uncle Tom." There is great irony in Kanye choosing to name his 2018 collaborative album with Kid Cudi *Kids See Ghosts*. In the words of Amiri Baraka, "We try to be black; meanwhile, you got a white ghost harboring over your head."[45]

PART I

Welcome to the Good Life

Kanye West and the Souls of Black Folk

ONE

"Pinocchio Story"

> "Wake up, Mr. West. Wake up, culture. Everybody thinks they're so woke but they're following the rules of what woke is supposed to be." *Kanye West*[1]

"I am not a guy who gets scared easily," David Letterman confessed as he stood before a live audience for the Season 2 debut of his Netflix series, *My Next Guest Needs No Introduction* (2018–present), and the 19th anniversary of his quintuple bypass surgery. One would think that little would intimidate Letterman at this point in his celebrated career, but this was no ordinary guest who was about to grace his stage. This guest recorded and produced some of the most influential music of the 21st century. This guest has repeatedly compared himself to icons like Pablo Picasso, Paul the Apostle, Walt Disney, Steve Jobs, and Malcolm X. This guest verbally sparred with everyone from internationally famous pop stars to world leaders. This guest audaciously proclaimed that he could end racism and classism with fashion, prevent homelessness with *Star Wars*-inspired dome-like structures, and end hunger with his ideas on farming.[2] Most importantly, this was the guest who made *Jesus Walk*. Letterman's next guest was Kanye Omari West, and he needed no introduction! This opening chapter examines the most notable controversies and commentaries that have defined Kanye's public persona and made him one of the most intriguing and outspoken celebrities of the 21st century.

Kinda Like a Big Deal

Kanye West is arguably the most important musical artist of his generation! As a producer he has flawlessly mastered the art of sampling and interpolating sounds from diverse genres to construct musical masterpieces. A fascinating example is his 2013 song "Blood on the Leaves" which blends Nina Simone's "Strange Fruit," Jay-Z's "Heart of the City," TNGHT's

"R U Ready," and C-Murder's "Down for My N*ggaz." Kanye's albums serve as a sonic blueprint for the events in his life and motivation for listeners in similar predicaments. At his best, his albums are reminiscent of Marvin Gaye classics, which pierced the listener's soul and emotions.

This statement is part hyperbole and part fact. In the late 1990s Kanye West was a little-known hip-hop producer from South Side, Chicago. His name was being mispronounced as Kane. Kanye's profile was boosted by producing "Izzo," "Takeover," and three other tracks on Jay-Z's (Shawn Carter) 2001 album, *The Blueprint*. After being rejected by countless record labels, unable to foresee his potential as more than just a producer, Kanye secured his place in history with a collection of groundbreaking rap albums. From that point forward, a "Monster" was born.

Kanye's gift for making music has earned him an NAACP Image Award, a Dove Award, five MTV Video Music Awards, nine BET Awards, nine *Billboard* Awards, two American Music Awards, 74 Grammy nominations, and 22 Grammy wins. He has sold more than 21 million albums and garnered more than 100 million digital downloads worldwide. Overall, he has 10 number-one albums on the *Billboard* Hot 200 chart, which tracks album sales for all genres: *Late Registration* (2005), *Graduation* (2007), *808s & Heartbreak* (2008), *My Beautiful Dark Twisted Fantasy* (2010), *Watch the Throne* (2011), *Yeezus* (2013), *The Life of Pablo* (2016), *Ye* (2018), *Jesus Is King* (2019), and *Donda* (2021). There are the four number-one singles on the *Billboard* top 100 and another 19 top 10 singles. MTV presented him with the Michael Jackson Video Vanguard Award, their highest honor, in 2015 for his outstanding contributions to the art of making music videos.

As a producer and a rapper, Kanye West has inspired multiple paradigm shifts in the sound of popular music. Without his audacity to defy hip-hop's toxic masculinity parameters, we do not get Drake (Aubrey Graham) or Travis Scott (Jacques Webster II) dominating the charts since the 2010s. Before their ongoing feud, Drake publicly regarded Kanye as his biggest inspiration. In 2008 MTV voted Kanye the "Hottest MC in the Game." This recognition was a quite a feat because he is not a genuine lyricist in the vein of emcees like Rakim, Black Thought, or Rapsody. Kanye has always relied on co-writers to assist him in crafting his most inventive lyrics. For example, he used eight co-writers for his 2009 single "Love Lockdown."

Early in Kanye West's career, critics compared his rap lyrics' depth to that of the late Tupac Shakur.[3] Bono (Paul Hewson), the lead singer of the rock band U2, cited Kanye's "Black Skinhead" as one of the 60 songs that saved his life.[4] But Kanye's reach extends far beyond music. Following in the footsteps of Andre 3000 (Andre Benjamin) and Pharrell Williams, he made it acceptable for heterosexual black males to wear tight-fitting cloth-ing, pink polos, and brighter colors without being considered gay. Kanye is arguably one of the most influential creatives in the fashion industry, help-ing to open doors for unconventional black designers such as Virgil Abloh, the first black artistic director at Louis Vuitton; Jerry Lorenzo; and Salehe Bembury. Bulky "dad shoes," slides and Croc-like runners made with foam produced from algae are must-have items because of Kanye's endorse-ment.[5] His 2013 Red October Yeezy II sneaker for Nike is priced at $9,000–$40,000 on the current resale market. The Adidas Yeezy 350 V2 model rivals Nike's Air Jordan I and XI, the Converse Chuck Taylor, and the Adi-das Superstar as the most sought-out sneaker on the market.[6] On April 26, 2021, the sneaker investing platform RARES purchased a prototype of the Nike Air Yeezy 1 that he performed in at the 2008 Grammys for a world record-breaking $1.8 million.

Kanye West's deal with the German multinational sportswear cor-poration Adidas made him the world's highest-paid hip-hop celebrity in 2019. On March 17, 2021, *Bloomberg* reported that Kanye, who was shock-ingly $53 million in debt four years earlier, was worth $6.6 billion, making him the wealthiest black person in American history. *Forbes* would refute Kanye's net worth; nevertheless, he is one of only seven black billionaires in America and seventeen worldwide.[7] Kanye, America's second wealthiest black man, receives an 11 percent royalty of Yeezy revenue and has full own-ership of his brand. Besides designing sneakers, he signed a 10-year deal with Gap to launch Yeezy Gap, a collaborative fashion line.[8] Gap released its first product, a blue $200 puffer jacket made from recycled nylon, on his 44th birthday.

Rolling Stone and *Time* magazines labeled Kanye West a genius. Busi-ness maverick Elon Musk called Kanye the person that inspires him.[9] Besides delivering lectures at Harvard University and Oxford University, he received an honorary doctorate from the Art Institute of Chicago in 2015. Jeffrey McCune, a professor at Washington University, offers a popu-lar course titled "Kanye West: Black Genius and Sonic Aesthetics." Kanye's polarizing statements and behavior have garnered the attention of three U.S. presidents: George W. Bush, Barack Obama, and Donald Trump. His actions and tweets receive daily scrutiny on social media and in the press, domestically and globally. Kanye has accomplished all of this without read-ing music, being a naturally gifted lyricist, holding a college degree, or receiving long-term formal schooling in fashion design. His success results from sheer hard work, God's blessings, and a "can't tell me nothing" swag-ger. In the words of rapper Pusha T (Terrence Thornton), Kanye West is "kinda like a big deal."

As Kanye walked onto the stage to embrace David Letterman, silence quickly transformed into exuberant applause from the pleasantly surprised audience. One young woman leaped in the air as if she was just gifted a new car by Oprah. Kanye sat across from Letterman decked out in a fresh pair of high top Yeezy boots. His hair was bleached blond. The bottom row of his front teeth was covered by a gold and diamond encrusted bridge. His face was chubby, showing the signs of the weight gain he experienced due to the medication he was taking for his bipolar disorder. The nearly hour-long episode featured excerpts from their live interview and Letterman's private tour of Kanye's immaculate $60 million estate in Calabasas, California, which he designed with Belgian architectural designer Axel Vervoordt.

Kanye's conversation with Letterman touched on a wide range of topics, from mental health to politics. He spent a considerable amount of time describing his bipolar disorder, which was diagnosed in 2017. After making fans in Sacramento, California, wait 90 minutes for his concert to begin on November 19, 2016, Kanye went on a 30-minute profanity-laced tirade after only performing three songs, dropped his mic, walked off the stage, and abruptly concluded the concert. Two days later police officers were called to the home of his trainer, Harley Pasternak. Kanye's erratic behavior forced paramedics to transport him to the Ronald Reagan UCLA Medical Center for evaluation. He was hospitalized at the Resnick Neuropsychiatric Hospital at UCLA for eight days.[10]

Kanye told Letterman individuals like him are stigmatized and dismissed as "crazy."[11] Until recently, mental illness was a taboo subject in the black community. Taraji P. Henson's fictional character Cookie Lyon on the FOX series *Empire* (2015–2020) referred to her son's bipolar disorder as a "white person's disease." Blacks are 20 percent more likely to experience serious mental health disorders than whites and are 40 percent less likely to receive care.[12] Blacks often fail to seek professional medical attention due to the stigma of appearing "crazy" or weak, lack of health insurance, finances, or a belief that prayer will solve their problems. According to the National Alliance on Mental Illness (NAMI) only one in three black Americans who need mental health care receive it.[13] Kanye West has been among a growing number of black celebrities including Simone Biles, Naomi Osaka, Kendrick Lamar, Mary J. Blige, and Big Sean (Sean Anderson) to speak publicly on their mental health struggles. Some view this willingness to admit vulnerability as a new form of black power.[14]

Kanye spoke to Letterman about his father, Ray West, a fiery man known for his visual art skills, sharp tongue, and inability to remain passive. He credited his mother, Dr. Donda West, with his love for words. She had a Ph.D. in English education and chaired the English department at Chicago State University. The tenor of the interview grew uncomfortable as Kanye shared his views on the #MeToo movement. In the past, he had drawn the public's ire for defending Bill Cosby and R. Kelly (Robert Kelly) in the wake of their criminal charges for sexual misconduct.[15] He continued to argue on their behalf, causing Letterman to challenge him. The conversation grew even more contentious when Kanye compared liberal Democrats to high school bullies picking on less popular kids for wearing the wrong (red MAGA) hat to school. Kanye's thoughts on repealing the 13th Amendment in the U.S. Constitution for its role in mass incarceration only received tepid applause after he chastised the audience for not clapping.[16]

It did not take Kanye West's Letterman appearance to reveal that he was unconcerned about making others feel comfortable. On his album *Yeezus* Kanye interpolated King's "free at last" to describe a woman's bare breasts. Then there was "On Sight," in which Kanye equated John Carlos and Tommie Smith's raised fists at the 1968 Olympics with a graphic pornographic act. The self-proclaimed "greatest artist that God has ever created" might be known more for his public outbursts and perplexing behavior than his admirable accomplishments. Podcast host Joe Rogan describes Kanye as a person who deconstructs things and finds flaws in the system. He deconstructs music, fashion, Christianity, politics, and American society. His inability to play well with others and adequately communicate his thoughts is a large part of his lore.

Better Stand Still Emmett Till

One of Kanye's most memorable concerts was a performance of his *808s & Heartbreak* album at Los Angeles' Hollywood Bowl on September 25, 2015. The concert was an extraordinary spectacle featuring a full orchestral string section, background singers, an electronic band, a woman painted in gold, and 14 women clothed in white robes. By the end of the night, the concert transitioned into a TED talk on being black in America. Kanye ended his set with an enthralling presentation of "Pinocchio Story."[17] As the conductor led the string section into song, a spotlight reflected Kanye's silhouette off a staircase on the stage. He walked slowly across the stage; his movements appeared robotic due to a heavy burlap outfit that bandaged his face and body like a mummy. In the song Kanye compared himself to the fictional children's character Pinocchio, a wooden puppet created by an Italian woodcarver named Geppetto. Pinocchio dreamt daily of becoming a "real" boy, but he was controlled by Geppetto and, ultimately, the world around him. A reminder of Pinocchio's oppression was his nose, which grew longer whenever he told a lie. Kanye related to Pinocchio by describing himself as an individual controlled by the music industry and the mainstream media. But unlike Pinocchio, he was punished for speaking *his* truth.

Kanye West is a black man born near Atlanta, Georgia, one of the prominent locations for civil rights activism and black wealth in America. He was reared in Chicago, a prime destination for blacks fleeing Southern terror during the Great Migration. He is the son of two radical black parents and the grandson of elders who suffered segregation's harsh realities. His father joined the Black Panther Party while in college. His mother was a department chair at one of the country's historically black college and universities (HBCUs). Consequently, his earlier music and socio-political views exhibited overt pro-black sentiments. The Hollywood Bowl presentation of "Pinocchio Story" should not be interpreted solely as a manifesto on the music industry's control of artists and creatives. It was an emancipatory manifesto on the double consciousness of Mr. Kanye Omari West. In classic Ye fashion, Kanye interrupted his own performance to remind his majority-white audience that he was still a black man in a racist country:

> You gotta do it like this and move your other leg like this. Don't get nobody pissed. Hey nigger don't do this. Because if you miss one step, we gonna treat you like this. We gonna talk shit about you like this. We gonna beat you up like this. We gonna say that people don't like you. We gonna try to make the world hate you. Don't never say what everybody else is thinking. Nigger. Nigger. Nigger don't miss. They told me better stand still Emmett Till. Better stand still Emmett Till.[18]

Kanye has made freedom and empowerment recurring themes in his music and messaging his entire career. John Legend (John Stephens) sang the gospel song "I'll Fly Away" as an interlude to "Spaceships" on Kanye's debut album. "I'll Fly Away" is a common anthem at black jazz funerals in New Orleans, Louisiana. It symbolizes the deceased leaving the hardships of life for a better place in heaven that is free from pain, struggle, poverty, racism, and inequality. "Spaceships" finds a teenage Kanye, feeling exploited by his white employers at Gap, yearning to fly away and be free on his spaceship. This was his version of the P-Funk Mothership, popularized by George Clinton and his Parliament-Funkadelic collective in the 1970s, transporting blacks to their deliverance.[19] "Famous," a duet with Rihanna (Robyn Fenty) on *The Life of Pablo,* sampled an excerpt from Nina Simone's 1968 song "Do What You Gotta Do" about a woman's unhappy lover who desires freedom.[20]

And then there is *Kids See Ghosts,* his 2018 collaborative album with Kid Cudi (Scott Mescudi), which includes the song "Freeeee (Ghost Town, Pt. 2)." The distinguished voice of black nationalist Marcus Garvey is heard in the song's introduction encouraging a live audience to seek truth and become their own masters. Marcus Garvey migrated to the U.S. from Jamaica in 1916 and established an American branch of his Universal Negro Improvement Association (UNIA) in Harlem, New York. The UNIA promoted black entrepreneurship, ownership, political empowerment, and recolonization of Africa. If black men and women could not be free in America, they could return to the motherland on Garvey's Black Star Line.[21]

Kanye continues his messaging on freedom and empowerment with his Sunday Services. He began hosting weekly worship experiences accompanied by a live band and a youthful black gospel choir in 2019. Before the broader public witnessed Sunday Service, clips from the rehearsals streamed on his wife's Instagram Stories and later YouTube. In one clip Kanye testified about his personal empowerment as a freethinker who is uncontrolled by popular opinion and others' expectations. A noticeable aspect of the rehearsals was the room's ambiance, lit in monochromatic shades of red, blue, purple, or pink. Kanye's use of lighting is a nod to James Turrell's light therapy.[22] He explained to Letterman that the lighting helped block out external distractions and negative thoughts that subliminally influence the mind.[23]

Freedom is paramount to the African American experience. Greg Carr, the chair of Afro-American Studies at Howard University, says America translates as irony. "If you're black in America, everything is ironic because it [doesn't] mean the same thing to you."[24] The U.S. Constitution was not intended for black people. Consequently, we had a Three-Fifths Compromise and an Electoral College to benefit slaveholding states. Blacks fought and bled in the Revolutionary War and Civil War for their freedom. Blacks sought education as well as financial independence and enfranchisement during the Reconstruction (1865–1877). More than six million blacks migrated from the South after Reconstruction in search of opportunity and freedom.

Black artists in the 20th century craved the freedom to craft artwork and stories that accurately reflected their culture. Spencer Williams, a star of the television sitcom *The Amos 'n' Andy Show* (1951–1953), quarreled with the show's white creators, who expected him to speak in an exaggerated manner that they believed reflected black vernacular.[25] Robert Townsend satirized this in a sketch called "Black Acting School" in his 1987 comedic film *Hollywood Shuffle*. This craving for artistic freedom was an impetus for the Harlem Renaissance (1920s–1930s) and the Black Arts Movement (1965–1975). Hip-hop, which emerged two years before the latter movement ended, was birthed by a new generation of blacks demanding money, power, and respect.

Kanye West's reference to Emmett Till at the Hollywood Bowl connotes a deeper analysis of these central themes in his messaging. Till was a 14-year-old black boy from Kanye's hometown of Chicago. In 1955 Till's mother, Mamie, sent him to the Mississippi Delta to spend part of the summer with his great uncle, Mose Wright. Till, being unfamiliar with the Deep South's social mores, allegedly whistled at Carolyn Bryant in a small grocery store. However, his cousin said Till had a habit of whistling through his teeth when speaking due to a stutter. Bryant, a 21-year-old white woman, accused him of grabbing her by the waist and speaking in a sexually explicit tone. Her husband, Roy, and his half-brother J.W. Milam abducted Till from his great uncle's house at 2:00 a.m. The men knocked out all but two of his teeth and shot him in the head. Till's mother said there was a hole near his right ear, and she could see daylight on the other side. A broken fan from a cotton gin, weighing 70 pounds, was attached to his mutilated body, presumably to prevent it from surfacing as it floated in the waters of the Tallahatchie River. An all-white jury found Till's assailants innocent after an hour-long deliberation. The decision could have been made sooner, but the jury stopped to take a soda pop break. A year later, the men admitted to committing the murder in an interview with *Look* magazine. In 2008 Carolyn Bryant revealed to historian Timothy Tyson that she fabricated the entire story.[26]

Mamie Till chose to have an open casket funeral and leave the body on display for five days so the world could witness the abominable reach of unrestrained racial hatred. Fifty thousand people went to the Roberts Temple Church of God to view the body. Chicago businessman John Johnson published a photo of Till in the casket on his *Jet* magazine cover. Till's homicide was classified as a lynching, a dominant form of vigilante justice used to terrorize and control black bodies in the South from the end of Reconstruction through the 1960s.[27] Rather than silence blacks, Till's lynching had the opposite effect. It emboldened them to strike what historian Erik Gellman calls a "death blow to Jim Crow" and white supremacy.[28] National organizations, grassroots movements, and celebrities took up the mantle of civil rights and black power over the next two decades. With "Pinocchio Story," Kanye appeared to position himself in the role of the slain teenager who inspired a revolution.

I'm Just Saying How I Feel Man

"George Bush doesn't care about black people!" This statement thrust Kanye West into the global spotlight and birthed the ongoing debate: Is Kanye West a race man or a self-aggrandizing provocateur? On August 29, 2005, Hurricane Katrina struck the Gulf Coast. The Category 5 storm breached poorly constructed levees resulting in catastrophic flooding that displaced more than one million residents—mostly lower-class blacks—in Louisiana, Mississippi, and Alabama. Thousands of individuals who were fortunate enough to safely flee their homes found shelter in the Louisiana Superdome. However, the Superdome's walls were not firm enough to prevent Katrina from turning the safe haven into a cesspool for disease, decay, and death. Civil rights activists and journalists questioned the media's coverage of the storm's black victims, referred to as refugees and looters, and the delayed response of President George W. Bush and Mike Brown, director of the Federal Emergency Management Agency (FEMA), in providing aid.

Kanye was invited to participate in the NBC News telethon "A Concert for Hurricane Relief." The live broadcast, airing on NBC, MSNBC, and CNBC on September 5, 2005, included notable cameos of celebrities Leonardo DiCaprio, Harry Connick, Jr., and Aaron Neville. Rather than have Kanye perform songs from his forthcoming album, *Late Registration,* he was asked to read a prepared statement from a teleprompter. In hindsight, it is unrealistic to assume that Kanye would stay on script when speaking before a live audience. He and comedic actor Mike Myers, better known as Dr. Evilllll from the *Austin Powers* film trilogy, were scheduled to take turns reading the statement. The usually cocksure Mr. West stood to Myers' right looking as visibly nervous as a schoolboy asked to speak in front of the class. When his time came, Kanye veered drastically away from the script and uttered the words that made him legendary:

> I hate the way they portray us in the media. You see a black family, it says, "They're looting." You see a white family, it says, "They're looking for food." And, you know, it's been five days [waiting for federal help] because most of the people are black … and those are my people down there…. I mean, the Red Cross is doing everything they can. We already realize a lot of people that could help are at war right now, fighting another war—and they've given them permission to go down and shoot us! … George Bush doesn't care about black people![29]

Kanye's prosecutorial lament alluded to rumors that federal agents were shooting down black "looters" stealing food and supplies from abandoned stores. It also excoriated the government for being more concerned with defeating terrorists in Afghanistan and Iraq than helping poor blacks in New Orleans. Mike Myers gave Kanye a look of shock and awe before pitifully stumbling over his words to end the segment. When Kanye was interviewed in Spike Lee's 2006 documentary *When the Levees Broke,* he revealed that NBC's prepared statement did not feel heartfelt. The George Bush statement spurred a plethora of reactions. John McWhorter, a black conservative intellectual, dismissed the outburst as self-serving rage. Wendell Pierce, a well-known actor and Katrina survivor, lauded Kanye for his courage to speak out. Civil rights activist the Rev. Al Sharpton called it a breath of fresh air that someone in hip-hop was saying something constructive and standing up for *his* people.[30] Just imagine if Kanye had never made that statement. We might never have viewed him as a voice for the black community. He may have been just another rapper known for making "G.O.O.D" music.[31]

Sarah J. Jackson devoted a chapter of her book *Black Celebrity, Racial Politics, and the Press* to the media's framing of Kanye's jeremiad. Jackson highlighted a *New York Times* column that said broadcast network producers, in the future, would not hesitate to press the mute button whenever he had a mic.[32] Kanye was scheduled to perform songs from *Late Registration,* released five days before the telethon, at the National Football League's (NFL) kickoff weekend activities. The *Chicago Tribune* reported that he would stick to rapping. "Such discourse reflects a mainstream impulse to silence and reprimand the political dissent of black celebrities that parallels that from over half a century before," wrote Jackson.[33]

Kanye West is not the first black celebrity to use a public stage to reprimand an American president. Eartha Kitt created a firestorm following an appearance at the White House three decades earlier. Kitt was a famous singer, dancer, and actress whose career spanned from the 1940s through the 2000s. She is best remembered for her 1953 Christmas song "Santa Baby" and her roles as Catwoman in the *Batman* television series (1966–68) and Lady Eloise in Eddie Murphy's romantic comedy film *Boomerang* (1992). Kitt was a biracial woman born on a cotton plantation in St. Matthews, South Carolina. Her mother was of African and Cherokee descent and her father is suspected to have been a white man who raped her mother. Unlike Kanye West, Kitt's popularity in the black community was low at her moment of full dissidence. In fact, *Ebony* magazine published a 1954 article titled "Why Negroes Do Not Like Eartha Kitt."[34]

On January 18, 1968, Eartha Kitt was a guest at a Women's Doers Luncheon at the White House to address crime and poverty sponsored by Lady Bird Johnson, wife of President Lyndon Johnson. The menu consisted of seafood bisque, chicken, and peppermint ice cream. Kitt was not impressed with the food, the president's brief appearance, or the predominantly white crowd's conversations. She raised her hand to tell the First Lady that juvenile delinquency's real cause was a backlash to the Vietnam War draft.[35] Kitt's damning critique was in line with the rhetoric of the antiwar movement. The Reverend Martin Luther King, Jr., Muhammad Ali, Stokely Carmichael, Angela Davis, and Shirley Chisholm belonged to a growing collective of black objectors to the war.[36] Denouncing American involvement in Vietnam was not universally popular amongst the black masses. King's organization, the Southern Christian Leadership Conference

(SCLC), lost the support of many black leaders and organizations after he broke with the president over the war.

Both the mainstream and the black press viewed Kitt's protest negatively. Sarah Jackson found 72 articles written about the incident in the mainstream press and 29 articles in the black press. Mainstream newspapers used adjectives such as "angry" and "emotional" when describing her. *The Washington Post* front-page headline read "Mrs. Johnson Chides Eartha Kitt: 'Shrill Voice' Jars First Lady" on January 20, 1968.[37] *Newsweek* published a letter sent to the magazine's editor that corrected a story about the 50 women present for the First Lady's luncheon. "Judging from Kitt's behavior, there were 49 ladies present plus Miss Kitt," wrote the author.[38] *The Pittsburgh Courier,* and other members of the black press, used injurious epithets like "sex kitten," "sultry," and "Tigress" to describe her. Sexism was evident here. Some black journalists questioned her commitment to black people and credibility as a spokeswoman, given her biracial heritage and romantic involvement with white men. *The New York Amsterdam News* said her comments were ill timed.[39] In other words, Kitt was not black enough, woman enough, or respectable enough to be the public face for such dissent.

Eartha Kitt was blacklisted for her unpatriotic actions. The FBI and CIA delivered a dossier on Kitt to the white house. Her songs were taken off the radio. She was written off Batman in an episode titled "The Joke's on Catwoman." For the next decade she could only find work in Europe. Kanye West was spared such a punishment. Perhaps gender or his popularity at the time of his protest was a factor. He lost only a few sponsors. *Late Registration* debuted at number one on the *Billboard* 200 chart for albums and sold 860,000 copies in its first week. The album's biggest single, "Gold Digger," was the second longest running number-one single on the *Billboard* Hot 100 chart in 2005. The Grammy Award-winning single was number one in the country for 10 consecutive weeks. In addition to his commercial success, Kanye was compared to other prolific socially conscious rappers.[40] Suddenly his name was on the lips of black scholars and black preachers.

I'm Really Happy for You. I'll Let You Finish, But....

In his memoir *Decision Points* (2010), President George W. Bush called Kanye's accusation that he was a racist the lowest moment of his presidency.[41] Bush reiterated these feelings in a sit-down interview with Matt Lauer on NBC's *Today* in November 2010. Keep in mind that this two-term president was in office during the terrorist attacks on 9/11, two wars in the Middle East, the Great Recession, and Hurricane Katrina. Nevertheless, Kanye

West was keeping him up at night. Vanderbilt University professor Michael Eric Dyson argues in his book *Come Hell or High Water* that Kanye was not calling the president a racist or blaming him as a person. On the contrary, he was condemning the racist political institutions that Bush represented as the head of state.[42]

When Kanye appeared on *Today*, days after the Bush interview, he revealed that the overwhelming praise for criticizing Bush made him very uncomfortable. He did not regret making those unscripted remarks, but it was not his intention to label the president a racist. Kanye expressed empathy for Bush because he, too, had been mislabeled a racist due to another public outburst. The incident of note was the infamous 2009 MTV Video Music Awards (VMAs) at Radio City Music Hall in New York City. Kanye attended the VMAs with his then girlfriend, Amber Rose. The couple grabbed the media's attention from the moment they stepped onto the red carpet. Kanye was in full bad-boy mode dressed in jeans, a black leather sleeveless shirt, black boots, and dark sunglasses. Rose raised more than eyebrows with her skin-tight python catsuit. Perhaps it was the bottle of "Henny" from which Kanye drank all night that infused him with the liquid courage for the outrageous actions he would commit later that evening. As Jamie Foxx (Eric Bishop) once quipped, "Blame it on the a a a a a alcohol."[43]

The moment came with the announcement of the award for Best Female Video. Taylor Swift, a 19-year-old white country music singer, won for her song "You Belong with Me." Swift's video beat out Beyoncé's "Single Ladies (Put a Ring on It)" and came as a shock to many viewers. "Single Ladies" was a two-year global phenomenon. It was the number one song domestically for four consecutive weeks. It was certified quadruple-platinum by the Recording Industry Association of America (RIAA) and won three Grammy Awards, including Song of the Year. Beyoncé's intricate dance moves and hand gestures from the video were copied and spoofed everywhere from *Saturday Night Live* (*SNL*) to *Anderson Cooper 360*. If TikTok had existed at the time it might have been the most viewed video in history.

Taylor Swift came up to the stage to accept her Moonman.[44] As she began speaking, a drunken Kanye stormed the stage, snatched the mic from her, and launched into the diatribe that nearly ruined his career: "Yo Taylor, I'm really happy for you, I'll let you finish, but Beyoncé had one of the best videos of all time. One of the best videos of all time!" He shrugged his shoulders, like Michael Jordan scorching the Portland Trailblazers with a barrage of three-pointers in the 1992 NBA finals, and handed the mic back to Swift, who was frozen like a deer in headlights.[45] She immediately rushed backstage and began crying uncontrollably. Kanye was booed and then discreetly asked to leave the building. When Swift appeared on *The View* the next morning, it was clear that the show's hosts and their majority-female audience were firmly in her corner.[46] Later that night, Kanye sat down with Jay Leno to discuss the incident. He offered a solemn apology, blaming his "douchebag" behavior on his failure to mourn his mother's 2007 death properly.[47]

During Kanye's *Today* interview Matt Lauer suggested that many critics felt that he endorsed Beyoncé over Swift solely because the former was black. Race may not have been his motivating factor, but it was an issue. Immediately after the incident white female pop stars Pink, Katy Perry, and Kelly Clarkson used social media to defend Swift. "Fuck you Kanye. It's like u stepped on a kitten," tweeted Perry. "What happened to you as a child? Did you not get hugged enough?" Clarkson wrote in an open letter.[48] The Kanye West–Taylor Swift firestorm elevated Twitter, only three years old at the time, to international status. Some pop stations temporarily stopped playing his music. There were blacks who sided with Swift over Kanye. His feud with President Barack Obama—possibly the catalyst for his close relationship with Donald Trump— began when Obama called him a "jackass" in an off-the-record comment during a CNBC interview.[49]

The Kanye West-Taylor Swift episode raised the curtains on the racial politics in the music industry. Swift's music can be classified as country pop. Although country music is rooted in the blues music of black artists, in recent decades country has been appropriated by white musicians performing for primarily white audiences. "Patriotic" events, Republican Party-sponsored events, baseball games, and *Sunday* and *Monday Night Football* broadcasts often use country music. Black country singers Kane Brown, Mickey Guyton, and Darius Rucker are anomalies. Many millennials and Generation Zers are unaware of the black influence on the genre. Ray Charles recorded two country albums in 1962: *Modern Sounds in Country and Western Music* and *Modern Sounds in Country and Western Music, Volume 2.*[50] Charley Pride, a black man from Mississippi, recorded 52 songs that reached the top 10 on the *Billboard* Hot Country charts, and 30 number-one hits.

The 2019 controversy surrounding the genre categorization of Lil Nas X's historic hit "Old Town Road" on the *Billboard* charts and the initial disdain from some white country artists is the most recent example of the racial politics of country music.[51] Lil Nas X (Montero Hill), a queer black rapper from Georgia, released the song online in December 2018. After the song rose to the top 20 of the *Billboard* Hot Country charts it was removed because the powers that be said it did not belong in the genre. It took the addition of Billy Ray Cyrus, a white country singer and father of pop star Miley Cyrus, on the song's remix to give it credibility amongst country fans. Prior to Lil Nas X, Beyoncé was shunned by the country music community.

She performed her bluesy country song "Daddy's Lessons" with the Dixie Chicks, a white female country trio, at the 2016 Country Music Awards. Beyoncé, at the time pregnant with twins, was condemned by many white country artists and television viewers not only for trying to cross over into *their* genre but also for her attire, a sheer, floor-length maternity dress. Professor Omise'eke Tinsley, author of *Beyoncé in Formation,* says country's white audience did not consider her to be an appropriate representative.[52]

If Taylor Swift was representative of middle white America and the South, Beyoncé was the opposite. Her performative style was rooted in African diasporic dance, Josephine Baker, Diana Ross, James Brown, Michael Jackson, Prince, "Dirty South" hip-hop, and the bounce music of New Orleans and Houston, Texas. As he did with the Hurricane Katrina telethon, Kanye appeared to be speaking on behalf of black America. "While Taylor Swift is heralded as a musician, songwriter, and artist, black artists have historically been imagined as performers, lacking the same skills and mastery of craft as their white counterparts," wrote scholar David Leonard.[53] Beyoncé's dancing skills displayed in the video are assumed to be innate and require less work. Furthermore, black artists have long watched whites earn awards and millions performing *their* music.[54] Beyoncé lost the Grammy for Album of the Year in 2017 to Adele (Adele Adkins), an English white woman from London who sings soul music.[55]

Let's not ignore the glaring racial optics at the VMAs. You had a drunken 32-year-old black man dressed like he could have been in a motorcycle gang snatching the microphone from a defenseless, 19-year-old blond white woman. The angry black man attacking a white woman is an age-old trope dating back to D.W. Griffith's racist film *The Birth of a Nation* (1915). The Kanye West–Taylor Swift feud resurfaced in 2016 after the release of Kanye's song "Famous." In the opening verse, Kanye suggested that he and Swift should have sex one day because he made her famous. The song was accompanied by a music video inspired by Vincent Desiderio's painting *Sleep*, which features several nude men and women asleep in a large bed. The video depicted a nude wax figure of Swift sleeping beside Kanye and his wife, Kim Kardashian. Most recently Kanye was slated to release his tenth studio album, *Donda*, on July 24, 2020, until Swift dropped a surprise album, *Folklore,* at midnight.

I Know Spike Lee Gon' Kill Me, but Let Me Finish

For most of his career the black community could defend Kanye's commentaries on race. However, he crossed the line with his *TMZ Live* interview on April 30, 2018. While speaking to TMZ founder Harvey Levin and cast member Charles Latibeaudiere, Kanye blurted out the cringe-worthy remark, "You hear about slavery for 400 years. For 400 years? That sounds like a choice."[56] He would later attempt to clarify his statement by referring to "mental slavery" instead of the physical act of bondage in chattel slavery. Nevertheless, the damage was done. Spike Lee, Ava DuVernay, and Karen Hunter, who co-authored his mother's memoir *Raising Kanye*, were among an extensive list of black celebrities to express their dismay.[57] John Legend, a close friend and frequent collaborator, cut ties with him. Nationally syndicated hip-hop radio shows, podcasts, and online series took him to task. HOT 97 radio host Ebro Darden accused Kanye of "trolling" the public. ESPN's *Jalen & Jacoby* dropped an excerpt from his song "Good Life" from the show's opening theme music. Celebrity podcaster Joe Budden (Joseph Budden, II) vowed to cancel Kanye and his music. Even Joe Madison, a distinguished 71-year-old talk radio veteran on SiriusXM Urban View, had something to say: "In the words of Dr. King, there is nothing more dangerous than sincere ignorance and conscientious stupidity."[58]

Black Twitter asked if Kanye had fallen into the sunken place.[59] In Jordan Peele's horror classic *Get Out* (2017), evil white captors, disguised as liberal allies, snatch the bodies and minds of the most talented blacks, for their pleasure and benefit. They befriend their prey and hypnotize them by stirring a cup of tea. The captors leave their black victims void of identity, consciousness, culture, and the ability to perform basic cultural signifiers like giving other blacks "a pound" correctly.[60] The blacks have fallen victim to the sunken place, a terrifying metaphor for mental and psychological oppression. *Get Out's* success at the box office led to a disturbing new trend on social media. It became popular to call out blacks who appeared to have lost touch with the masses, for the sake of mainstream acceptance, pleasing their white counterparts, and financial gain. Gatekeepers immediately relegated these individuals to the dreaded sunken place. Individuals unwilling to reform for their "sunken-ness" risked becoming the latest victims of cancel culture.[61]

Kanye's TMZ appearance was an attempt to explain a photo he took with Lyor Cohen, YouTube's Global Head of Music, and Lucian Grainge, Universal Music Group CEO, while wearing a Make America Great Again (MAGA) hat. The MAGA hat was the official logo of President Trump and his supporters. Many Americans viewed Trump's presidency as a celebration of white supremacy, xenophobia, and Islamophobia. While he was at TMZ Kanye delivered an erratic oral defense of his dissertation on free thought and personal freedom. Kanye stated that people like Candace Owens, the black conservative pundit who accompanied him, are brave because they do not allow themselves to be controlled or brainwashed. Nor do they see themselves as victims of racism.

As the interview continued Kanye walked through the studio speaking to the mostly white employees sitting at their cubicles and standing against the walls. He admitted to becoming addicted to opioids, taking seven pills a day, after having liposuction to prevent the public from calling him fat.[62] Kanye said he ended the addiction once he realized that the prescribed pills were an attempt to control him and stunt his genius. He called Barack Obama's presidency a drug prescribed by the government to appease blacks and white liberals.

Van Lathan, a black cast member and co-host of *TMZ Sports* at the time, disrupted Kanye's rambling nonsense to convey his disgust.

While you are making music and being an artist and living the life that you've earned by being a genius, the rest of us in society deal with these threats to our lives. We deal with the marginalization that has come from the 400 years of slavery that you said for our people was a choice. Frankly I'm disappointed, I'm appalled and brother—I'm unbelievably hurt by the fact that you have morphed into something that's not real…. Bro, you gotta be responsible. Your voice is too big.[63]

Kanye's exchange with Lathan was disturbing for several reasons. First, it became a performance for the majority-white audience in TMZ's studio. These two influential black men found themselves on a metaphorical stage, providing a viral moment for the public to watch, critique, and mock online. Lathan was questioning Kanye's allegiance to black people. Kanye's rebuttal was to victim-blame and shame members of that community. Kanye's unintentional belittlement of American slavery was a horrific slap in the face to most black people. The 1619 Project, the *New York Times Magazine*'s series of essays examining the legacy of slavery, provides an in-depth analysis of that topic. Slavery not only birthed capitalism in the South, but is also to blame for a host of contemporary problems including the racial wealth gap, mass incarceration, police brutality, inequalities in public health and education, voter suppression, the lack of home ownership in the black community, and even traffic congestion in cities like Atlanta.[64] Kanye has since admitted that he was undergoing a manic episode at the time.[65]

While the TMZ incident shocked many fans, this was not the first time Kanye West made blacks cringe and ask themselves to whom he was appealing. Concertgoers attending his 2013 Yeezus tour could purchase T-shirts and other items bearing Confederate logos. A replica Confederate flag hung on the wall of his pop-up store in Los Angeles beneath the words, "I ain't coming down." Kanye claimed that he was reframing the flag's meaning in the same manner as rappers re-appropriating the word *nigger* and rebranding it with a unifying message. He was not the first rapper to attempt this feat. Southern rappers from Lil Jon (Jonathan Smith) to Pastor Troy (Micah Troy) tried this in the 2000s. André 3000 wore a Confederate flag emblem on his belt buckle in Outkast's music video for their hit "Ms. Jackson." Randall Kennedy, a black Harvard University law professor and the author of *Nigger: The Strange Career of a Troublesome Word* (2003), called Kanye's actions another publicity stunt.[66]

The double consciousness places a different responsibility upon the shoulders of black artists. Dave Chappelle turned down $50 million and quit his uber-successful sketch comedy series, *Chappelle's Show*, due to the fear that his sketches were perpetuating negative stereotypes about black people. Rapper Kendrick Lamar (Kendrick Lamar Duckworth) found himself in an awkward situation while performing in Alabama. After a white female fan he brought on stage began reciting the lyrics to his song "M.A.A.D City" without eliminating the N-word, he stopped her.[67] Lamar refused to condone the use of the N-word by his white fans because he understood that many were either unaware of the word's history or used his concert as an excuse to say it without consequence.

Kanye West is an admitted non-reader with little use for historical lessons because he is more concerned with the future. For years he had no issue with his white fans reciting the N-word or selling "merch" with Confederate logos to kids at his shows.[68] He failed to realize the danger in using his fame to condone racism indirectly. Confederate forces from the South fought to maintain a culture and way of life based on slavery. Lost Cause mythology in textbooks, memorial parks, and Hollywood films like *Gone with the Wind* (1939) falsely taught white Southerners to separate the flag from the memory of slavery.[69] However, this flag would be directly associated with the effects of black bondage—Jim Crow, white terror, and voter suppression—throughout the next two centuries. Dylann Roof, the 21-year-old white supremacist responsible for killing nine blacks inside the Emanuel African Methodist Episcopal Church in Charleston, South Carolina, on June 17, 2015, had several pictures posted on his social media pages showing him holding a gun and the Confederate flag.

Jasmine Mans, a black millennial spoken word artist, publicly called out Kanye West in her poem "Footnotes for Kanye," taking him to task for his perceived loss of awareness on black issues:

> Can you hear all the black kids calling your name wondering why the boy who rapped about his momma getting arrested for the sit-ins, didn't sit-in—why he traded in his Nat Turner for Ralph Lauren? Do you know how many kids at the protest had your sneakers on? None of them.[70]

I surveyed 131 respondents over the age of 18 while researching this book. Nearly 56 percent said they did not find Kanye's music empowering for black people. Fifty percent of respondents believed that he idolizes whiteness, and 35.29 percent thought he had a problem with being black while 58.14 percent of respondents think Kanye believes he has transcended race. Kanye released "Ye vs. the People," a duet with Atlanta rapper T.I. (Clifford Harris) in 2018, to defend his affiliation with President Trump. If T.I. spoke from the voice of "the people" (blacks, immigrants, Muslims, women, and anyone who felt oppressed), then for whom was Ye speaking?

Soon as They Like You Make 'Em Unlike You

As previously stated, Kanye West has little concern for making others comfortable. His self-absorption was on full display when he appeared on *SNL*'s Season 44 premiere on September 29, 2018. He wore his infamous MAGA hat for this final performance. The television audience was not able to see the final moments due to time constraints. Luckily, comedian Chris Rock, who was in the audience, recorded the last few moments on his cell phone and posted it on social media. If you listen closely, Rock can be heard saying "oh my God" as Kanye went into a TMZ-like rant about being bullied by the *SNL* staff for wearing his MAGA hat, his love of Trump, and black people being mentally enslaved and exploited by the Democratic Party. The next week Michael Che, a black *SNL* cast member, made a joke that indirectly referenced the black archetype Uncle Tom as Kanye's face flashed on the screen.

Nearly two weeks after the *SNL* debacle Kanye attended a special luncheon with President Trump and a room full of reporters at the White House. Jim Brown, a retired black athlete and movie star turned conservative civil rights activist, accompanied him. As he proudly wore his red MAGA hat, Kanye went on an hour-long profanity-laced rant about a myriad of topics. The luncheon concluded with Kanye hugging Trump and telling the majority-white reporters, "I love this man." Kanye grinned widely from ear to ear as he took photos with the president, his daughter Ivanka Trump, and her husband, Jared Kushner—all adorned in MAGA headgear. Later that day, he visited local Washington, D.C., establishments continuing to sell his newfound conservative ideology and remind anyone willing to listen that the Republican Party freed the slaves.

Two days after his White House visit, Kanye traveled to the East-Central African nation of Uganda. The trip should have been a grand opportunity for Kanye to follow in the footsteps of his hero, boxing legend and humanitarian Muhammad Ali, who embarked upon an African tour in 1964 after winning the boxing heavyweight title. Ali visited Ghana, the first sub-Saharan African country to gain independence from European colonial powers. Ali, dressed in Kente cloth, walked humbly amongst the people.[71] Sadly, Kanye's excursion would have made the champ roll in his grave. He announced that he was visiting the continent to find inspiration for a forthcoming album titled *Yandhi*. The trip was organized by Snapchat star YesJulz (Julieanna Goddard), a white woman who once tweeted a photo of a T-shirt with the N-word written on it and the caption, "So … am I allowed to wear this shirt at the festival tomorrow or nah?"

Kanye and Kim met with Ugandan President Yoweri Museveni, a political leader criticized for his abusive treatment of the opposition and implementation of a law that made homosexuality punishable by life imprisonment. Kanye shared his plans with Museveni of transforming Uganda's Murchison Falls National Park into an African version of Disney World and Jurassic Park. He told Museveni that he could attract tourists to the country by making it a real-life Wakanda, the fictional African nation in Marvel's *Black Panther*.[72]

After the meeting, he and Kim flew the president's private helicopter to Masulita Children's Village. They distributed free pairs of his $220 cream white Yeezy 350 V2 Adidas sneakers and Beats by Dre headphones worth $180. If the couple donated books, school supplies, food, or pledged to use their money to launch an arts program or business opportunities for the people, this was absent from the headlines. The trip looked like an attempt to put African kids in his sneakers and promote Western capitalism in a country that had been oppressed by British colonizers from 1894 to 1962. Seun Kuti, son of the late Nigerian Afrobeat pioneer Fela Kuti, blasted Kanye on social media for having the audacity to tell reporters, while on his trip, that Fela's spirit was flowing through his veins.[73]

How did Kanye West end up in this predicament, where blacks at home and abroad were turning their backs on him, while Trump supporters and Fox News Channel personalities such as Greg Gutfeld, routinely guilty of showing racial bias, were celebrating him? Fox's Tucker Carlson dedicated a monologue to praise of Kanye for calling out "self-righteous" white liberals who told black people which Democrat to vote for and black progressives who determined what it meant to be "woke."[74] When did Carlson, who emphatically stated on live television that former NFL quarterback Michael Vick, who served a 23-month prison sentence for his involvement in illegal dogfighting, should have been executed, become so concerned for black lives? "Kanye West wants freedom—white freedom," wrote Ta-Nehisi Coates in *The Atlantic*.[75] Had being a credit to his race and middle-class black respectability politics become too much of a burden for Mr. West?[76] When Kanye rapped about missing the "Old Kanye" on *The Life of Pablo* was he speaking on behalf of fans or admitting that he was unhappy with the way fame changed him? In 2019 noted hip-hop radio personality Big Boy (Kurt Alexander) asked Kanye if he was still the voice for black America. Although Kanye responded "yes," there are many blacks who would beg to differ. The people say he is mired in the sunken place. Kanye West says he is freeeee!!

Two

"We Major"

"Remind me of when they tried to have Ali enlisted. If I ever wasn't the greatest, nigga, I must have missed it." *Kanye West*[1]

With his debut album, *The College Dropout* (2004), the producer Kanye West became better known for his rhymes than his beats. The triple-platinum album sold more than 3.4 million copies domestically and produced two top 10 singles on the *Billboard* Hot 100 chart: "All Falls Down" and "Slow Jamz," which peaked at number one. *The College Dropout* received the Grammy for Best Rap Album and Best Rap Song, "Jesus Walks." *Time* placed Kanye on the cover of its August 29, 2005, issue, calling him "the smartest man in pop music." Heading into his sophomore album, Kanye reached out to Jon Brion, the soundtrack composer for the film *Eternal Sunshine of the Spotless Mind* (2004), to help create what music critics call his first masterpiece. With Brion, a white man from New Jersey, Kanye was looking to create a new sound that would push hip-hop beyond the limitations placed upon "urban" black music. Brion brought an elaborate orchestral sound that had never appeared on a rap album. This new odd couple spent a year recording music at a staggering cost of $2 million in studio time and sample clearances. Kanye was inspired to add orchestral sounds after hearing the British Trip hop band Portishead's *Roseland NYC Live* (1998) album.

Late Registration not only advanced Kanye's production skills but also manifested his growth as a lyricist. He spent time in poetry houses and spoken word sessions to find inspiration for his rhymes. He went on HBO's *Def Poetry Jam* (2002–2007) to test out lyrics from a song he was working on called "Gold Digger." This was one of three appearances he made on that series. With songs like "Diamonds from Sierra Leone," he delved into domestic and global social issues impacting Africans and the descendants of the African diaspora much further on this 21-track project than he had on *The College Dropout*. The album's eighth track, "Crack Music,"

42

is among his most socially conscious records. Despite his anti–Bush comments on NBC's Hurricane Katrina telethon just days before its release date, *Late Registration* debuted at number one on *Billboard* Hot 200, sold more than three million copies, won the Grammy for Best Rap Album, and earned a Grammy nomination for Album of the Year.[2] At the time Lauryn Hill and Outkast were the only rappers to receive a Grammy nomination for Album of the Year. "Gold Digger" became the second longest running number-one song on the *Billboard* Hot 100 in 2005. The Grammy-winning single topped the charts for 10 weeks. *Late Registration*'s sales were boosted by the sold-out Glow in the Dark world tour featuring a dazzling light show and special guests Rihanna, Lupe Fiasco, and N.E.R.D. "This was pure comic-book adventure…. Glow in the Dark raises the bar for arena tours as no show has since U2's 1992 Zoo TV breakthrough. It's that innovative and galvanizing," wrote Ann Powers in the *Los Angeles Times*.[3]

Kanye turned to white musicians such as Bob Dylan, Johnny Cash, The Killers, and Coldplay to inspire the sound for his next album, *Graduation*. His goal this time around was to make songs that could play in large stadiums that typically only hosted white rock bands like U2 and the Rolling Stones, two groups he toured with in 2005–2006. *Graduation* was a watershed moment for Kanye West, hip-hop, and pop music. The media played up the fact that *Graduation* was to be released on September 11, 2007, the sixth anniversary of the 9/11 terrorist attack and the same day as 50 Cent's *Curtis*. At the time, 50 Cent (Curtis Jackson) was the reigning heavyweight champion of the rap industry. His first two albums, *Get Rich or Die Tryin'* (2003) and *The Massacre* (2005), sold more than 20 million copies worldwide. He had a biopic and a signature sneaker with Reebok.

50 Cent made violent, hyper-macho, hypersexual gangsta rap the dominant sound in pop music during the early 2000s. He pledged to retire if Kanye outsold him during the first week. *Graduation* not only won that battle, but it made Kanye's sound the new standard in hip-hop.[4] His victory was significant because gangsta rap and what 50 Cent perpetuated had been a point of contention for many older blacks since the early 1990s. Civil rights activists like C. Delores Tucker and the Reverend Calvin Butts, III had been demonizing rappers for shouting "thug life" and rhyming about selling drugs. Tucker saw the music, which was primarily consumed by suburban teenage white males, as lyrical pornography further damaging the image and psyche of black America.[5] Kanye's sound, on his earliest albums, was a godsend for individuals sickened by artists like 50 Cent.

Kanye West pushed musical boundaries even further with his fourth studio album, *808s & Heartbreak*. He stunned fans by departing from his trademark use of black soul music samples and incorporating a 1980s synth-pop and electronic sound. The opening track, "Say You

Will," mimicked the sound of English rock star Phil Collins's smash 1980 hit "In the Air Tonight." Kanye abandoned rapping for singing through an Auto-Tune vocal processor.[6] In her short video for *Vox, Kanye Deconstructed: The human voice as the ultimate instrument*, Estelle Caswell praises Kanye's use of technology to manipulate his voice and the vocals of his collaborators to create the sounds of instruments. He used synthesizers to create the sound of a choir singing on his song "Say You Will." Seven years later Kanye re-recorded the song with Caroline Shaw, a classical composer and the youngest person to win a Pulitzer Prize in music. Shaw sang a cappella in place of the synthesizers used on the song's original version.

With *808s & Heartbreak*, an album inspired by the tragic death of his mother, Dr. Donda West, and the end of his 18-month engagement to fiancée Alexis Phifer, Kanye created a new lane for rappers to emote openly about self-doubt, love, heartbreak, spirituality, and vulnerability.[7] André 3000 initially did this on Outkast's *Speakerboxxx/Love Below* (2003). Yet Kanye's success paved the way for newer artists who were breaking the mold of marginalized black masculinity. This group includes Kanye's *808s* collaborator Kid Cudi, Chance the Rapper, Childish Gambino, Big Sean, Tyler, the Creator, Travis Scott, and most notably Drake, the world's most successful rapper since 2011. Drake sampled "Say You Will" for his first commercially successful mixtape, *So Far Gone* (2009). Without *808s*, we do not have Kid Cudi's *The Man on the Moon* (2009), Drake's *Take Care* (2011) or Travis Scott's *Astroworld* (2018).

Riding the wave of success from *808s*, Kanye was preparing to go on the Fame Kills tour with Lady Gaga (Stefani Germanotta) when the Taylor Swift incident at the 2009 VMAs derailed his career. Kanye stepped away from music and followed the advice of his friend Mos Def (Yasiin Bey) to self-exile himself. He spent the next year in Japan and Rome. While in Rome, his focus shifted from music to fashion. Kanye, who had always been fascinated with clothes, used to sit in his fourth-grade class drawing pictures of his favorite Air Jordan sneakers. "Being fresh is more important than having money. The entire time I grew up, I only wanted money so I could be fresh," he stated in the 2015 documentary *Fresh Dressed.*

Kanye and his friend Virgil Abloh, who became the creative director of his DONDA brand a year later, took a $500 per month internship with the Italian luxury brand Fendi. During his exile, Kanye also collaborated with the French luxury brand Louis Vuitton on a men's sneaker. This collaboration culminated in Kanye traveling to Paris Fashion Week with Abloh, Don C (Crawley), and Fonzworth Bentley (Derek Watkins). While in Paris, the group posed for a photo that was later parodied on the animated series *South Park* for the group's flamboyant attire and swagger. Despite the ridicule, Kanye believes that photo was the stimulus for elite European fashion houses like Givenchy making urban "street wear" a major priority since the 2010s. He was soon hired by Nike to collaborate on two sneaker projects: the Air Yeezy (2009) and the Air Yeezy II (2012 and 2014). He eventually launched his own fashion line and began holding runway shows at Paris and New York Fashion Week. Kanye was in talks with French billionaire Bernard Arnault, the CEO of LVMH Moët Hennessy Louis Vuitton SE, about becoming the first black artistic director of Louis Vuitton's menswear collection. However, in 2018, Arnault selected Virgil Abloh instead.

Kanye ended his exile abroad and moved into Avex Studios in Honolulu, Hawaii, to begin crafting his $3 million comeback album, *My Beautiful Dark Twisted Fantasy*. He paid careful attention to every detail of the project. This meant hours spent penning the first verse for the lead single, "Power," and having Kid Cudi, CyHi the Prynce, and Pusha T assist in writing his lyrics. This was the first time Kanye wrote down the raps for his songs and it really showed. Iconic hip-hop producers No I.D., Q-Tip, Swizz Beatz, Pete Rock, and RZA helped with the beats. According to RZA (Robert Diggs), they would be in the studio from 4 p.m. until 4 a.m. creating new music. Justin Vernon, the lead singer of the indie folk band Bon Iver, also contributed to the project. *Pitchfork* magazine described Kanye's collaborative process as a "creative CEO" method of album-making. "It was really on some Quincy Jones shit, man. We could easily be working on one song, thinking we're in a mode, and he'll hear a sound from someone and immediately turn his whole attention to that sound," said Def Jam Recordings Executive Vice President Noah Callahan-Bever.[8] Kanye was at his best on the song "All of the Lights," which blended the voices of 14 of the world's most prominent singers—including a pregnant Alicia Keys, Drake, Fergie, The-Dream, and John Legend—into one chorus. Elton John provided a piano interlude. The song took nearly two years to complete.

Kanye and his crew recorded so much music in Hawaii that they released a total of 14 free songs online through a weekly mixtape series called GOOD Fridays leading up to the album's pre–Thanksgiving release in 2010. Music critics called *Fantasy* his "maximalist perfect album." It had eight fewer songs than the 76-minute *College Dropout* album but ran nearly 70 minutes. The standout track "Runaway" lasts more than nine minutes due to a lengthy post-chorus reprise that included a solo piano countermelody and his voice distorted to sound like a guitar. *Fantasy* is Kanye's best-reviewed project, scoring 94 out of 100 on Metacritic. *Urb* magazine compared it to the seminal works of Miles Davis. *The Washington Post* named it the best and defining album of 2010. *Time, Billboard, Rolling Stone, Spin, Pitchfork*, and *The Village Voice* also rated it as the year's best album. Despite such accolades and capturing the Grammy for Best Rap Album, surprisingly it failed to be nominated for Album of the Year.

My Beautiful Dark Twisted Fantasy is Kanye's most political and militant album. Songs like "Gorgeous" articulated his belief that white America only accepted him in the beginning because he appeared to be the safe "docile" suburban rapper making happy music. Kanye never wanted to make this album. He told the *New York Times* the album was one long backhanded apology for the Taylor Swift incident. Kanye admitted that most of the album's songs appearing to be about failed romances were metaphors for his fractured relationship with society. Thus, we find him on "Runaway" toasting to the douche bags and assholes like himself. If *Fantasy* was Mr. West's endeavor to prove he was worthy of (white) America's forgiveness by making a nearly flawless magnum opus, his next album, *Yeezus*, was one big "Fuck you" to everyone. This becomes immediately evident when the album opens with the jarring "On Sight" rather than the fan favorite "Blood on the Leaves," which was originally the first track. Ironically, there is an interlude in the former song in which the Holy Name of Mary Choral Choir sings "He will give us what we need. It may not be what we want."

At this point in his career, fashion was becoming more important than the music. He was engaged in a bitter feud with Mark Parker, the CEO of Nike, over ownership of his sneaker the Air Yeezy, which was the most sensational shoe on the market. Kanye demanded to own his intellectual property and receive royalties for his work, but Nike refused to agree to these demands. As a result, he left the company and signed a deal with Adidas in 2013 that gave him full creative and financial control of his product. Kanye saw himself as the fashion industry's Malcolm X, the militant Nation of Islam spokesman, unflinching in his castigation of a white controlled apparatus and determined to secure power by any means necessary. The album's third track, "I Am a God," was a direct result of the marginalization he felt from the fashion industry. According to a 2013 interview with *W Magazine*, Kanye was informed by a major fashion designer at Paris Fashion Week that he could attend his exclusive runway show only if he didn't attend anyone else's show. Feeling offended by the gesture, Kanye went into to the studio to vent. If he was god, how dare anyone tell him where he can and cannot go! "Exclusivity is the new euphemism for nigger," Kanye told Apple Music 1 host Alexander "Zane" Lowe.

Yeezus was extremely polarizing. Several fans in the black community despised this new direction in Kanye's sound. Although *Yeezus* delved into racial issues and heavily sampled or interpolated Jamaican dancehall artists, it was Kanye's most Eurocentric-sounding album. It was mostly void of traditional hip-hop beats. His trademark soul samples were absent until the final track, "Bound 2," which sampled "Bound" by Ponderosa Twins Plus One, a 1970s soul quintet from Cleveland. European techno and electronic music producers Daft Punk, Gesaffelstein, Brodinski, Hudson Mohawke,

Mike Dean, and Arca supplied the sound. Rick Rubin, an older white man who co-founded Def Jam Records, served as the album's executive producer. Mainstream critics loved *Yeezus*. *The Washington Post* ranked it number two on their top 10 album list for the year. It was number one on *Time*'s year-ending list, earning Grammy nominations for Best Rap Album and Best Rap Song for "New Slaves." In 2019 *Complex* ranked it as Kanye's fourth best album ahead of *The College Dropout* and *Late Registration*.

For diehard Kanye fans and music nerds, I strongly suggest listening to the *Watching the Thrones* podcast or seasons two and eight of the Spotify podcast series *Dissect*. *Watching the Throne* analyzes every song Kanye has recorded. Cole Cuchna, *Dissect*'s narrator, breaks down the most minute details from every lyric, beat, and sample on *My Beautiful Twisted Fantasy* and *Yeezus* with the precision of a scientist. According to Cuchna, *Yeezus* is the tale of a fallen hero who once desired to be a God-fearing revolutionary for good, succumbing to the temptations of fame, ego, liquor, and unrestrained promiscuity. He positions Kanye's Yeezus narrative within Professor Joseph Campbell's 12 stages of the hero's journey. It takes the arrival of Yeezus's new love interest, Kim Kardashian, on the final track, "Bound 2," to restore the hero to his proper placement on God's path for his life.

All of Kanye's musical achievements, fashion endeavors, controversies, and ranting and raving about his excellence did not go unnoticed by millennials, universities, and the tastemakers of pop culture. In 2013 he was invited to deliver a guest lecture to the students at the Harvard Graduate School of Design. His wife, Kim, and Virgil Abloh participated in the lecture.[9] Kanye's stature reached even loftier heights in 2015, starting in January when he received the Visionary Award at the Black Entertainment Television (BET) Honors in Washington, D.C. On March 2, 2015, Kanye addressed the students at the Oxford Guild Society. This is Oxford's, the United Kingdom's, and Europe's oldest professional society, dating back to 1897. More than 5,000 students sought tickets to hear him speak at Oxford University's Museum of Natural History. His visit, considered the university's most anticipated in decades, was announced just 16 hours prior to the event for the sake of crowd control.

Time named Kanye West one of the "100 Most Influential People" in April 2015. Elon Musk, the founder of SpaceX, Tesla Motors, and the world's second richest person, penned the magazine's profile on Mr. West. Musk credited Kanye as the person who inspired him. A month later, Kanye was the keynote speaker for the spring commencement of the School of the Art Institute of Chicago (SAIC). During the commencement he received an honorary doctorate in fine arts. Kanye, attired in his regal cap and gown, told the crowd, "People say you should not be sorry for your opinions." Kanye was awarded his degree by Dr. Walter E. Massey, the school's chancellor and the former president of Morehouse College. Massey exuded pride as he bestowed this prestigious honor upon "Dr. West."

And then came 2016! Kim was robbed at gunpoint in Paris that October. She was bound and gagged in her hotel room with duct tape. At the time she was wearing only a bathrobe and feared she would be raped before her murder. Not long after that dreadful event, Kanye began "ranting" on stage during the Saint Pablo Tour for his seventh studio album, *The Life of Pablo*, that he had never voted, but if he did, Donald Trump would have been his choice for president instead of Hillary Clinton. He was hospitalized over the Thanksgiving holiday. Rumors began circulating that he was mentally ill, but his handlers blamed exhaustion and stress from Kim's assault. When Kanye resurfaced into public view in December, his hair was dyed blond. Days later he was spotted at Trump Tower in Manhattan for a meeting with President-Elect Trump.[10] He granted Charlamagne tha God (Lenard McKelvey), co-host of *The Breakfast Club* radio morning show, his first public interview after his hospitalization in the spring of 2018. Charlamagne, who is just as outspoken as Kanye, questioned how he could support a president that the majority of blacks found to be a representative of white supremacy. "Racism isn't a deal-breaker for me. If it was, I wouldn't live in America," Kanye replied. "That's some rich nigga shit," said Charlamagne. "Oh no, in this gated community [of Calabasas] I still deal with racism," said Kanye.[11]

Throughout their nearly two-hour conversation, he spoke candidly about Presidents Obama and Trump. A multitude of hip-hop artists graced the White House over Obama's tenure. But Kanye never received the seat at the table he was seeking from the nation's first black president. Not surprisingly, he was disappointed in Obama's refusal to work with or invite him to the White House, especially since he had campaigned for him in 2008. Kanye criticized Obama for not doing more to curb the violence harming blacks in Chicago. In his eyes, Obama was not free to lead effectively and radically because of his quest for perfection as a trailblazer.[12] Perhaps it would have been a stain on the first black president's image, Kanye suggested, to be associated with a "crazy motherfucker" like him who might say anything. But in Trump, he found a kindred spirit who embraced imperfection and narcissism.

Kanye West can preach freethinking and shout out to the world "Can't nobody hold me down" like a shiny suit-wearing Puffy Daddy and Ma$e because of the sacrifices made by those before him. The experiences of the 20th-century black celebrity varied based upon profession, gender, upbringing, and era. The chosen few who achieved mainstream success often paid a dear price. Black celebrities, in the early decades of the century, still faced many of the same indignities that all blacks dealt with. They could perform on stage, for an all-white audience, but as was the case with Dr. Don Shirley, they could not use the bathroom. During the civil rights and black power era of the 1960s and 1970s, many black celebrities used their platforms to uplift the race, while others remained silent for fear of losing white fans and their earnings. As the century ended, a small number of black celebrities were among the most powerful men and women in the entertainment industry. Freed from the pressure to speak out on racial issues as their previous counterparts had, many of these entertainers opted for the Booker T. Washington model of accommodation. This chapter looks at prominent 20th-century celebrities who paved the way for Kanye West and their struggles with being black in America.

So Appalled

CNN host Don Lemon does not mince words. This was certainly evident when he compared Kanye's 2018 White House luncheon with President Donald Trump to a modern-day minstrel show. Minstrelsy was the earliest form of popular entertainment in America. White performers, attempting to portray black characters, darkened their faces with burnt cork, dressed in tattered clothing, spoke in broken English, and sang Negro spirituals. All of this amounted to a less than flattering effort to mimic blackness through grotesque forms of cultural appropriation and racial cross-dressing.[13] Al Jolson's performance of "Mammy" in *The Jazz Singer* (1927) is the most familiar example. Although minstrelsy ended in the early 20th century, blackface has not gone out of style. Robert Downey, Jr., earned an Oscar nomination in 2008 for his blackface performance in *Tropic Thunder*. Students at University of California Los Angeles (UCLA) came under fire after a 2015 party sponsored by the Sigma Pi Epsilon fraternity and Alpha Phi sorority held a "Kanye Western" blackface party.[14] White students blackened up to imitate Kanye and other rappers.

The nation's first black entertainer to achieve crossover success was a blackface minstrel performer named Bert Williams, who migrated from the Bahamas in 1884 when he was 10 years old. Williams, whose father was one-eighth black and whose mother was one-fourth, was light enough to pass for white. In 1903, he and George Walker, his show-business partner, produced and starred in Broadway's first all-black musical, *Dahomey*, about two black detectives trying to locate a missing treasure in Africa. The duo nicknamed themselves "Two Real Coons," which was the equivalent of Ice Cube and Dr. Dre subversively dubbing themselves N.W.A (Niggas With Attitudes) nearly a century later.

The legacy of Bert Williams is extremely complicated. He became one of the highest paid singers of his era. Admirers highlight the intellectual approach he brought to his craft and say that he portrayed his black characters with dignity and humanity. They were not the one-dimensional impersonations done by white performers. Williams dedicated his time to perfecting the dialect and music of Southern blacks. Nevertheless, he chose to appear on stage with dark paint on his face, bright red lips, tattered garments, and white gloves. He spoke with an exaggerated Southern accent. Off stage he spoke the King's English, in his West Indian accent, and wore tailored three-piece suits.[15] Was he satirizing minstrelsy or gaining riches by affirming racist tropes?

Booker T. Washington wrote glowing remarks of Williams's performances. Washington admired his talent and the fact that he never complained about racism. W.E.B. Du Bois called Williams "a great Negro, a great man." Charles W. Anderson, a respected black politician in New York, praised Williams as a credit to the race for opening doors to future black entertainers. Bert Williams's defenders argue that the black paint provided him a level of comfort and protection when he stood before racist audiences. By applying the burnt cork to his skin, Williams embodied the sentiments of Paul Laurence Dunbar's 1913 poem "We Wear the Mask." Harvard professor Henry Louis Gates, Jr., calls Williams a genius who used blackface to spread pro-black messages and challenge stereotypes. But others like Sylvester Russell, a theater critic, did not find anything laudable about what Williams was doing on stage. Russell accused Williams of lacking any racial pride.[16] Don Lemon's critique of Kanye's White House visit expressed similar sentiments. If Kanye had any racial pride, he would not be out there embarrassing us in front of all those white people, right?

Bert Williams suffered from chronic depression, insomnia, and alcoholism in his final years. "The funniest man I ever saw—and the saddest man I ever knew" is how vaudeville actor W.C. Fields described him.[17] As fate would have it, Williams collapsed while performing on stage in Detroit on February 27, 1922. The audience thought it was a part of his routine, but he was taken back to New York, where he died five days later at the age of 46.

His untimely death came just as "New Negroes" were redefining themselves through the art of the Harlem Renaissance. Despite the success of the Renaissance writers and artists, Hollywood overwhelmingly forced black entertainers to maintain the demeaning status quo.

Two of the most famous black entertainers of the 1920s and 1930s were Stepin Fetchit and Hattie McDaniel. In both cases their celebrity came with a consequential price. Stepin Fetchit, born Lincoln Theodore Monroe Andrew Perry, was Hollywood's first black superstar, appearing in an astounding 26 films between 1929 and 1935. Thanks to Fox Pictures, Fetchit became the first black entertainer to sign a movie deal. Cooning was very profitable for Fetchit and other comedic black actors of his era like Mantan Moreland and Willie Best (nicknamed Sleep 'n' Eat). Fox marketed his films by playing on his extravagant lifestyle. According to Fox's marketing department, Fetchit owned six houses tended to by his 16 Chinese servants. He wore $2,000 cashmere suits made in India. He owned 12 cars, including a champagne-pink Cadillac showing his name in neon lights.[18]

Historian Donald Bogle defines the coon as a buffoonish character meant for white people's comic relief. Coons would laugh when there was nothing funny, scratch when they did not itch, and bulge out their eyes to exaggerate their facial expressions. "Look at the Coon" is a funny song played on Kevin Hart's *Straight from the Hart* podcast to mock modern-day blacks guilty of cooning. Theologian Howard Thurman wrote perceptively about the "entertaining buffoon" dating back to slavery.[19] Fetchit perfected the slow "lazy man shuffle" and the "dim-witted, tongue-tied stammer" that white blackface minstrels introduced in previous decades.[20] His characters struggled to pronounce words with more than one syllable, a trait that grossly belied his formal education. "It's really hard to go in front of all these white people and make them laugh by pandering to these racist stereotypes and then have to go home and look at yourself in the mirror," says Professor Todd Boyd.[21]

The term *coon* has been frequently used to describe Kanye West in recent years. When Kanye sat down with Big Boy for a 2019 interview, he revealed his frustration with being labeled a coon for wearing his MAGA hat.

Stepin Fetchit co-starred with Hattie McDaniel in the 1934 film *Judge Priest*. McDaniel was Hollywood's most accomplished female black celebrity before World War II. McDaniel is best known as Mammy in the 1939 adaptation of Margaret Mitchell's Civil War–era novel *Gone with the Wind*. Mammy was the faithful servant of the film's protagonist Scarlett O'Hara (Vivien Leigh). Mammy and *Gone with the Wind* were symbolic of the Lost Cause mythology, which depicted slavery as a benign, paternalistic system.

McDaniel was the first black American to win an Academy Award (Oscar) for Best Supporting Actress. She was not allowed to sit with her cast members from *Gone with the Wind* at the ceremony because the venue did not allow blacks on its premises. The film's producer David Selznick had to pull some strings so that she could enter the building and sit by herself at a table against the wall.[22]

McDaniel, the 13th child of a Wichita, Kansas, Baptist minister, was aware of the racist veil that existed in Hollywood. A heavy, dark-skinned woman, she perfected the mammy (black maid) archetype. Her mammies were sassy, overtly religious, and asexual. McDaniel declared that she would rather play maids in films than be a maid off the screen. McDaniel believed that she was playing her roles with dignity and defying white stereotypes of black womanhood. "I sincerely hope I shall always be a credit to my race and to the motion picture industry," said McDaniel in her Oscar acceptance speech. McDaniel continued to play servant roles right up until her death from breast cancer at 59 in 1952. She played a maid 74 times in her acting career.

Niggas in Paris

It was November 3, 2011; the streets of Washington, D.C., were abuzz with anticipation of the biggest concert of the year. Kanye West and Jay-Z were coming to town that night to promote their new collaborative album, *Watch the Throne*. Earlier that day I spoke at Andrew Rankin Memorial Chapel on the campus of Howard University. I had participated in a panel on hip-hop and religion with Michael Eric Dyson and VaNatta Ford, a doctoral candidate at Howard. Dyson, Jay-Z's future biographer, was kind enough to give Ms. Ford and me floor seat tickets for the concert. Kanye was in his prime, just coming off the success of *My Beautiful Dark Twisted Fantasy* (2010).

The concert, which started almost 90 minutes late, reached its climax when hip-hop's new dynamic duo performed their album's top hit, "Niggas in Paris." The song was performed three consecutive times that night. Each time the song reached its crescendo the 20,000 fans in the sold-out Verizon Center grew more exuberant.[23]

"Niggas in Paris," edited for radio play as "In Paris," was inspired by Kanye's travels through Paris, France, to gain ideas for his new fashion label. The song's title can be interpreted in multiple ways. While the bigots presumed that men who resemble Kanye and Jay-Z could be nothing more than thugs and niggers, look at them now, rubbing shoulders with the one percent at home and overseas. Black excellence and financial freedom are underlying themes of *Watch the Throne*.

An alternative interpretation of the song's message is that no matter how accomplished they become, Kanye and Jay-Z will always be niggers in the eyes of white supremacists.[24] It is also notable that they chose Paris as the geographic location for this song. Paris was one of the few places where black entertainers could find solace from racism in the early and mid–20th century. The writer James Baldwin arrived in Paris at the age of 24, with only $40 and a dream to succeed in a country that was void of American racism. Baldwin's 1956 novel *Giovanni's Room*, a love story about two gay men, was set in 1950s Paris. He spent the latter part of his life in France, settling in Saint-Paul-de-Vence in the south of France in 1970. During his time in France Baldwin enjoyed the company of fellow black celebrities Harry Belafonte, Sidney Poitier, Ray Charles, Nina Simone, and Miles Davis.

Miles Davis had a love affair with Paris. At age 22, Davis traveled to France for the 1949 Paris Jazz Festival after World War II. In his autobiography Davis said of Paris, "Paris was where I understood that all white people were not the same; that some weren't prejudiced."[25] Davis fell in love with Juliette Gréco, a white singer and actress he met in Paris. In his book he reflected on the freedom he experienced walking hand in hand with Greco through the city's streets, listening to music in clubs, and drinking in the cafes.[26] Sadly, when he returned to America, he was so disheartened by the racism—as a victim of police brutality—that he picked up a self-destructive heroin addiction.

During the 20th century no black celebrity was as beloved in Paris as Josephine Baker. Her story shines a light on the extent to which racism stunted the professional and psychological growth of black entertainers, leaving them with little choice but to migrate overseas. Baker, born Freda Josephine McDonald, grew up poor in St. Louis. She was a teenager when race riots left 250 blacks dead and 6,000 blacks vagrant in East St. Louis.[27] Baker started out performing on vaudeville's Chitlin' Circuit until relocating to New York City in 1921. Baker arrived in the Big Apple at the start of the Harlem Renaissance. Her first significant role in New York came in *Shuffle Along*, Broadway's first black play. At this time, black performers not only had to blacken up but also lighten up. Venues like the Cotton Club in Harlem often excluded darker black performers who did not pass the Brown Paper Bag Test. In *Shuffle Along*, Baker lightened her skin.

In 1925 Baker sailed to Paris to appear in the country's first all-black revue. On *The Groucho Marx Show* she described herself as "the girl who left St. Louis to come to Europe to find freedom." Paris provided her with celebrity and acclaim unlike anything she ever experienced in America. In Paris there were no "black hotels." A black woman could go almost anywhere without feeling uncomfortable. Baker's Paris performances were sexually provocative. Unlike Hattie McDaniel, Josephine Baker was a sex symbol. She appeared nude in *La Revue Nègre*. As her fame spread, she became a symbol of sexual liberation, dating both white men and women. In a banana skirt, Baker's gyrating and uninhibited expression of her sexuality made her the black woman about whom most white males in France fantasized. Two years after moving to Paris, she was the highest-paid female entertainer worldwide. Baker had weekly columns in French newspapers and high fashion magazines. French society white women wanted to wear their hair like "Josephine." Baker reveled in her celebrity, but realized that while her blackness was appreciated abroad, she was still forced to adapt and respond to her white Parisian audience's expectations.[28]

Although Josephine Baker's career took her far away from St. Louis and Harlem, she never considered herself disconnected from her American blackness. The black press back in the states covered her international feats. When she returned in 1935, she found that conditions had worsened since her departure. Baker was only allowed to book a hotel on Park Avenue on the condition that she would enter and leave through the servants' entrance. She was even spat on by a white woman while exiting a hotel. Baker was the first black woman to star in the Ziegfeld Follies on Broadway but could not use the theater's microphones. Neither was Baker's sexuality embraced domestically as it was abroad. The U.S. banned one of her foreign films that featured a romance with a white actor. Langston Hughes wrote a poem in which he talked about looking for a house in the world where white shadows do not fall. This poem is such a poignant assessment of black performers who find themselves continually having to navigate within the confines of a society dominated by white bodies.

Baker returned to Paris shortly afterward, knowing that she could never return home to achieve similar success. When World War II erupted, she identified herself as a French citizen. Baker became involved in a French resistance movement and worked as a French spy following Germany's 1940 invasion of France. She used her sheet music to smuggle confidential plans on the position of Nazi forces. Baker returned to America in 1963 to participate in the historic March on Washington. She addressed the crowd, one of only two women to speak at the march, wearing her French military uniform. Baker called her time at the march one of the proudest moments in her life. She finally achieved success in America later in life, headlining four sellout shows at Carnegie Hall in 1974. Her final stage appearance took place in Paris in April 1975. Without Josephine Baker, Paris may not have been as welcoming to Kanye West decades later.

Hell of a Life

Unlike Josephine Baker, Lena Horne and Dorothy Dandridge did not have to relocate to Paris, but they were not strangers to the double burden of race. Lena Horne began singing at 16 in the Cotton Club to help her parents raise money during the Great Depression. She and the other black musicians performed for all-white audiences, yet they were not allowed to use the club's restrooms. She viewed her job at the Cotton Club as a form of indentured servitude, claiming that she had a lifetime contract. Horne left the Cotton Club and began working at Café Society, the first nightclub outside of Harlem to welcome interracial audiences. She befriended Paul Robeson, the famed black athlete turned actor and activist, while singing at Café Society.[29] Robeson taught her about the struggles of black people. He said her identity as a "negro" would be the basis for her entire existence. Horne always felt like she could not trust anyone or be her true self. "I was two Lenas. The one I showed the world and the one inside of me."[30]

Walter White, the NAACP's executive secretary from 1929 to 1955, engaged Horne as their weapon to fight Jim Crow in Hollywood. She admitted that White selected her primarily for her looks. Horne was the first black actress to sign a long-term (seven-year) contract in Hollywood. Her contract stated that she would not perform menial roles such as maids or prostitutes.[31] John Johnson, the founder of *Ebony* magazine, also used Horne as a symbol. She appeared on the cover of *Ebony* three times. Her elevated status bothered some black women who believed her light-skinned complexion made her more acceptable to white audiences.[32] Horne married a white composer named Lennie Hayton in 1947. The wedding was held in Paris because interracial marriage was illegal in California. Horne admitted that she married Hayton because she knew that a white man could get her into places that a black man could not.

Lena Horne had always felt guilty about the acceptance she received in the "white world." Consequently, she became very active in the civil rights protests of the sixties. She began performing on behalf of the NAACP, the Student Nonviolent Coordinating Committee (SNCC), and the National Council of Negro Women (NCNW). She befriended civil rights leaders Martin Luther King, Jr., and Medgar Evers. Horne was among the last people to see Evers before his assassination. His death put her at a crossroads. She had to decide if she would live in the "white world" or the "black world." Horne separated from her husband for a brief period. She was among a collective of black celebrities, including James Baldwin, Lorraine Hansberry, and Harry Belafonte, that met with U.S. Attorney General Robert Kennedy in May 1963 to discuss solutions to America's race problem. Horne fought to have Rosa Parks recognized at the March on Washington. In her twilight years she found her true identity. "I am a black woman. I am free. I no longer have to be a credit, a symbol, a first, an imitation of a white woman, I am me," she said in an interview.[33]

Dorothy Dandridge's career overlapped with Horne's. She received her career-defining role in the musical film *Carmen Jones* (1954), co-starring Harry Belafonte, Pearl Bailey, and Diahann Carroll.[34] *Carmen Jones* earned her the distinction of being the first black woman to grace the cover of *Life* magazine and receive an Oscar nomination for Best Actress. She competed against acting legends Judy Garland, Grace Kelly, and Audrey Hepburn for the 1955 Oscar, which ultimately went to Kelly. Four years later Dandridge received a Golden Globe nomination for her role in the cinematic adaptation of *Porgy and Bess* (1959). The black community did not heap as much praise on her for *Porgy and Bess* as white audiences. Many blacks called her a sellout and disapproved of the film's perpetuation of older stereotypes.

Dandridge's crossover appeal put her on national television shows and earned her performances at exclusive white galas in Los Angeles and Paris. Dandridge successfully demanded a room when she headlined at the Last Frontier, a segregated hotel in Las Vegas. However, when she attempted to use the swimming pool, hotel management discovered an immediate need to drain it for repairs. While in Vegas she began dating Rat Pack actor Peter Lawford. Extenuating circumstances doomed the relationship from the start. Dandridge had several unfulfilling relationships with powerful white men such as Otto Preminger, the Austro-Hungarian director of *Carmen Jones,* who could not freely be with her in public. Her inability to love whom she wanted because of her race led her to abuse alcohol and pills. By the age of 41, Dandridge was living in a rented apartment and self-medicating with drugs and alcohol to cope with her self-hatred. On September 8, 1965, her manager found her lying naked and unresponsive. Dorothy Dandridge died from a fatal overdose of Imipramine, an antidepressant.[35]

Cops Shot the Kid, I Still Hear Him Scream

In 2018 Kanye West executive produced *Nasir*, the 12th studio album from New York rapper Nas (Nasir Jones). Although most critics panned that album, one of its few standout tracks was "Cops Shot the Kid." The song began with a snippet from Richard Pryor's "Cops/The Line-Up," featured on his 1971 comedy album *Craps (After Hours)*. Pryor's track satirized racial profiling and police brutality. Richard Pryor's rise to fame provides a compelling example of the black celebrity's struggle to find his or her voice in a white world.

Born to a pimp and a prostitute, Pryor grew up in an Illinois brothel located three hours from Chicago. Comedy was his ticket out of the ghetto. Early into his career, Richard Pryor chose to model himself after Bill Cosby. He started out doing what culture critic Cecil Brown calls "white bread humor." This style of comedy was void of profanity and controversial topics like race, class, or politics. Pryor, much like Cosby, did his best to be non-confrontational to gain popularity in the mainstream. His non-offensive, physical style of humor earned him multiple appearances on *The Merv Griffin Show* (1962–1963) and invitations to appear at segregated clubs.

In September 1967, Richard Pryor had an epiphany while performing at the Aladdin Hotel in Las Vegas. He looked at the audience and saw a sea of mostly white faces viewing him, he thought, as a buffoon there to amuse them. Suddenly, Pryor's feelings of embarrassment changed to rage. He was so angry that he walked off stage in the wrong direction, but he refused to exit from the correct side. Professor Todd Boyd calls this moment a "coming to consciousness" for the comic. He was walking away from something that was working and provided him celebrity and adulation in white America. Dozens of nightclubs banned Pryor due to the Aladdin incident. Unable to work in Vegas, he relocated to Berkeley, California, for a time. He found himself in the epicenter of the counterculture. The teachings of the free speech movement, the anti-Vietnam War movement, the Black Arts Movement, and the Black Panther Party transformed him into arguably comedy's most radical figure in the 1970s.[36]

Pryor emerged from his exile with a fearless new attitude. He dropped the wannabe Bill Cosby act for an explicit and blunt form of storytelling that drove audiences to tackle uncomfortable issues of race and class. Dick Gregory and Jackie "Moms" Mabley were the only mainstream black comics delivering unabashed monologues at the time. Gregory did not only tackle race on stage. He aided Medgar Evers and Martin King, was arrested for protesting Jim Crow in Mississippi, went on a hunger strike to protest the Vietnam War, and penned an autobiography titled *Nigger*. He was even monitored by the FBI. Richard Pryor never went that far. Nevertheless, Mel Watkins, author of *On the Real Side: A History of African American Comedy*, credits Pryor with introducing a raw, underground brand of black humor performed by comics like Redd Foxx (John Sanford) to mainstream audiences in the late 1960s.[37] In her 2008 book *Laughing Fit to Kill: Black Humor in the Fictions of Slavery*, Glenda Carpio unpacks Pryor's use of satire to force white listeners to not only recognize modern-day examples of racism but reflect upon slavery's legacy. On his 1983 stand-up concert *Here and Now,* Pryor joked about the substantial number of bi-racial people he encountered while touring in New Orleans being the byproduct of all the black women raped by their white slave masters.[38]

Despite his newfound militancy, Pryor still struggled with the double consciousness. "The more successful he is in the white world, the more resentful he becomes, the more afraid that he is not black enough," said film director Paul Schraeder. Writer William Brashler described him as a man torn between being black and a desire to be the biggest star in a white-oriented, white-run industry. Pryor died from multiple sclerosis in 2005; however, the next two generations of black comics continued his legacy. Eddie Murphy took the baton by becoming the highest-paid black comedian in the 1980s and 1990s.

Eddie Murphy made his film debut at the age of 21 in *48 Hours* (1982).[39] The film's creators wanted Murphy's character to be named Willie Biggs. Murphy thought that name sounded like something contrived by a group of culturally insensitive Hollywood executives. He fought to have his character renamed Reggie Hammond after a guy he grew up with in New York City named Terrence Hammond. Chris Rock says that decision manifests how Eddie Murphy was rewriting the rules of the game on his own terms. Murphy, who always appeared to be in control while in majority-white settings, revolutionized the comedic portrayal of black masculinity in Hollywood. The best example of this can be found in *48 Hours*. His character walks into an all-white redneck bar, removes a cowboy hat from the racist bartender, places it on his head, and announces to everyone in the bar, "There's a new sheriff in town, and his name is Reggie Hammond."

Eddie Murphy became the standard for a younger generation of black comics in the 1990s and 2000s. Murphy's decision to model himself after Richard Pryor rather than Bill Cosby is very telling. While the mainstream and middle-class black audiences adored Cosby, his humor did not resonate with all blacks. Cosby was the epitome of post-civil rights black excellence. In 1965, he became the first black man to be cast in a lead role on a primetime television series. He earned Emmy Awards for Outstanding Lead Actor in 1966, 1967, and 1968 for portraying a Cold War–era spy working undercover with a white intelligence agent on NBC's *I Spy* (1965–1968). Cosby is best known for his career-defining role as Dr. Heathcliff "Cliff" Huxtable on *The Cosby Show* (1984–1992). Dr. Huxtable was an obstetrician, fond of colorful sweaters, and married to the beautiful Clair (Phylicia Rashad), an attorney and partner at a law firm. The Huxtables lived in a brownstone in an upper-middle-class Brooklyn neighborhood with their five children: Sondra, Denise, Theo, Vanessa, and Rudy.

The Huxtables were unlike any black family ever seen on television up to that point. Although *The Cosby Show* made subtle references to black culture and history, *Boston Globe* columnist Renée Graham says that the Huxtables did not have to overemphasize their blackness as past fictional sitcom families had. Their mere existence in primetime was enough of a powerful statement. When Dr. Huxtable recited the words "I am an American, and this is my American family" during an acceptance speech as the physician of the year to a room of mostly whites in black-tie attire, that resonated with mainstream audiences. *The Cosby Show* was number one in the Nielsen ratings for five straight seasons, from 1985 through 1989. At its peak, 30,502 million homes watched the show. Cosby used his success to finance black films such as Spike Lee's *Malcolm X* (1992) and to make charitable donations to HBCUs.

In recent years Bill Cosby's reputation has been sullied by his three-year incarceration for rape and sexual assault. Most of his accusers were white women. America's favorite TV dad is now a disturbing punch line on *SNL* and late-night talk shows. Cosby's popularity had already been waning in some black circles since his infamous "Pound Cake" speech, delivered at the NAACP's celebration of the 50th anniversary of the *Brown v. Board of Education* decision. He was accused of blaming poor blacks for their predicament while ignoring the generational effects of systemic racism. While some suggested that Cosby's fame caused him to lose touch with the black masses, Michael Eric Dyson depicted Cosby in his 2006 book *Is Bill Cosby Right?* as an individual who accommodated the white gaze his entire career.

Kanye West was an adolescent at the time of *The Cosby Show*'s reign on primetime. He has made multiple references to the show and its spin-off series, *A Different World* (1987–1993), throughout his discography. One of his most signatures songs, "Can't Tell Me Nothing," referenced Hillman College, Dr. Huxtable's fictional alma mater. Kanye has steadfastly remained in his childhood idol's corner despite the growing backlash. He created a Twitter storm on February 9, 2016, by posting the message: "BILL COSBY INNOCENT !!!!!!!!" Kanye was booed for defending Cosby during his 2019 appearance on David Letterman's Netflix series. On June 20, 2020, during a suspected manic episode, Kanye tweeted that NBC had Cosby incarcerated. Perhaps he was alluding to conspiracy theories that NBC's white executives disapproved of the comedian's attempts to buy the network from General Electric (GE) in 1992.[40] The thought was that no black man would be allowed to become that powerful; hence, a covert campaign to put him in his place ensued. While such conspiracies are not credible, Kanye West is not alone in his defense of the comic legend. Many blacks still watch re-runs of *The Cosby Show* and found his 10-year prison sentence to be excessive and racially motivated.

O.J. Simpson! Amazing!

Kanye recorded his second live album for *VH1 Storytellers* in February 2009. Standing on stage with his mullet haircut and wearing a gray suit, red button-up shirt, and dark sunglasses, he performed a medley of songs from *808s & Heartbreak* and a few past hits. During his nearly eight-and-a-half-minute rendition of his song "Amazing," he began speaking to his interracial audience and calling out the names of the people he considered amazing. The crowd cheered as he called out Michael Jackson and U.S. Olympian Michael Phelps. Next, he called out O.J. Simpson. After no one cheered, he asked the crowd, "Is he not?" The camera panned the room to show a few whites and Latinos clapping their hands in agreement. "What he did, was he not amazing?" Although Simpson's football career was stellar, many assumed Kanye was referring to Simpson's acquittal for the double homicide of his white ex-wife, Nicole, and her male companion, Ron Goldman, in 1995.[41]

At the time Simpson's acquittal was seen in the black community as a long-overdue victory for decades of unjust judicial decisions. The Reverend Cecil Murray, the former senior pastor of First African Methodist Episcopal Church in Los Angeles and the resident chair of Christian Ethics at the University of Southern California, compared the acquittal to Jackie Robinson breaking baseball's color barrier. This was proof that black people—or least those with money and celebrity—could receive a fair trial. Kanye quoted Harvey Dent's line from the DC Comics film *The Dark Knight* (2008) about dying as a hero or living long enough to become the villain. One can infer that he saw O.J. Simpson as an American hero who eventually became the mainstream media's villain. Kanye told the audience that he found himself in a similar predicament. He was the black kid from Chicago who became an American superhero until the media made him the bad guy.

Kanye's decision to compare himself to Simpson might have been self-aggrandizing for shock value. But I believe it deserves some discussion given Simpson's momentous rise and horrific downfall. ESPN's Academy Award-winning documentary *O.J.: Made in America* (2016) paints a picture of Orenthal James "O.J." Simpson as a fallen hero. His tragic Horatio Alger story was based on the myth of transcending race to gain white approval. As a Heisman Trophy-winning running back at the University of Southern California, he was the most famous collegiate athlete in the nation. O.J. Simpson signed a four-year rookie contract for $400,000, which was unheard of in 1969. He was living a very comfortable existence, but he wanted to live an exceptional life. Simpson's counterrevolutionary attitude made him a godsend for white sports fans and white businesses looking for a black celebrity to pitch their products. In the mid–1970s he became America's first great black pitchman in memorable commercials for Chevrolet and Hertz. The white directors went out of their way to remove any hint of blackness, aside from his skin, in these commercials. They taught him to speak like a white man. "For us, O.J. was colorless. None of the people that we associated with looked at him as a black man," says Frank Olson, who recruited O.J. for his famous 1978 Hertz commercial.[42]

Joe Bell, a close friend of Simpson since childhood, believes his buddy was "seduced" by the chance to live like a wealthy white man. After Simpson divorced Marguerite Whitley, his first wife and a black woman, he married Nicole, a younger white woman. He moved into the upscale Brentwood neighborhood where he was one of only three black residents. As Simpson's popularity grew, he surrounded himself with only upper-class white men and beautiful white women. He gained membership in elite country clubs that had no other black members. Frank Olson reflected on how excited the bigots at his country club were to see Simpson show up with Sidney Poitier for a round of golf. Simpson proudly flew an American flag on his property all year to demonstrate his patriotism. I would argue that Simpson allowed his white fans and cronies to feel good about themselves and believe that the past sins of racism were forgiven. If Simpson could be that successful, then the black underclass was not the result of racism.

Carl E. Douglas, an attorney for Simpson's defense, tells an amusing story about their efforts to make Simpson appear black for the majority-black jury in his criminal trial. The defense went into his Brentwood estate and replaced the pictures of white people hanging on the wall with black images and African artwork. A framed lithograph of Norman Rockwell's 1964 painting *The Problem We All Live With,* depicting six-year-old Ruby Bridges escorted by federal marshals as she integrated William Frantz Elementary School in New Orleans, was hung over his fireplace. "If the jury had been Mexican, we would have hired a mariachi band," joked Douglas.[43] Once white America ostracized him, Simpson resorted to the violent black buck archetype. He was paroled in 2017 after serving nine years of a 33-year prison sentence for armed robbery and kidnapping.

O.J. Simpson's collegiate years intersected with the Black Power movement. Harry Edwards, an adjunct professor at San Jose State University, invited him to participate in a boycott of the 1968 Summer Olympics. But Simpson was unwilling to take any risk that might hurt his future financial earnings and marketability to white fans and consumers. He told *New York Times* reporter Robert Lipsyte: "I'm not black; I'm O.J." Simpson, unlike UCLA basketball star Lew Alcindor (now Kareem Abdul-Jabbar), did not want to be a part of the boycott or anything like the Cleveland Summit. On June 4, 1967, the summit in Cleveland, Ohio, included some of the most outspoken black athletes of the day: Bill Russell, Jim Brown, Lew Alcindor, and Bobby Mitchell. They were there to support Muhammad Ali's conscientious objection to serving in the Vietnam War. Ali, formerly Cassius Clay, was never uncomfortable letting everyone know that he was a proud black man. After winning boxing's heavyweight title and abandoning his "slave name," Ali became the public mouthpiece for the Nation of Islam, the controversial organization of black Muslims in America. The former disciple of Malcolm X toured West Africa, where adoring fans mobbed him. Later he delivered speeches on black power at Howard University.

Kanye's mother, Donda, compared his swagger and fearlessness to that of Ali. In 2006 Kanye recreated Ali's famous pose from *Esquire* magazine's

1968 issue for a *Rolling Stone* cover story titled "The Passion of Kanye West." The *Esquire* cover depicted the persecution Ali was facing for his act of full dissidence. A year later, Ali performed the song "We Came in Chains" in the 1969 Broadway play *Buck White*. The song captured his feeling of connection to the enslaved Africans brought to American soil in chains. At the time of the Broadway show, Muhammad Ali was in his third year of exile from professional boxing and faced a potential five-year imprisonment. Ali would tell reporters who questioned his patriotism: "They never called me 'nigger,' they never lynched me, they didn't put dogs on me, they didn't rob me of my nationality."[44]

Joe Louis, the second black man to win the heavyweight belt in boxing, served as a goodwill ambassador during World War II. But Ali was not interested in following Louis's lead. He patterned his showmanship and fighting demeanor in the ring after the welterweight champion Sugar Ray Robinson; however, his muse was Jack Johnson, the first black heavyweight champion. At a time when whites ran everything, Jack Johnson took orders from no one. While the black masses struggled to make ends meet, Jack Johnson was wealthier than most whites. When black men were expected to kowtow to white men, Johnson reveled in beating them to a bloody pulp inside the ring. And at a time when black men could be lynched for merely flirting with a white woman, Johnson slept with whomever he pleased. Jack Johnson, like Ali and Kanye West, refused to be controlled. He was freeee. "Just remember, whatever you write about me, that I was a man," he told a reporter not long before his death.[45]

Jack Johnson, a six-foot, muscular, dark-skinned man with a bald head, refused to be defined by white onlookers. The Galveston, Texas, native was born to two former slaves on March 31, 1878, a year after Reconstruction ended. He began his amateur boxing career competing in battles royal. These illegal fights involved dozens of blindfolded black combatants punching each other until the last man was left standing. White fans threw money in the ring at the fight's conclusion. Johnson's success in these events attracted a professional trainer who began preparing him for professional prizefights. At the turn of the 20th century, boxing was one of the three dominant American sports, next to baseball and horse racing. Since people viewed the heavyweight champion as the "Emperor of Masculinity," blacks could not compete for the title.

Johnson's first significant bout against a white fighter came on May 16, 1902, against Jack Jeffries, the younger brother of the reigning heavyweight champion Jim Jeffries. Johnson knocked him out and then helped carry him back to his corner as Jim Jeffries sat ringside. "You are next," Johnson told him. But the champ drew the color line, pledging to retire once there were no more worthy white opponents. In the meantime, Johnson continued to knock out all the top black competition and lesser white opponents. He typically took it easier on black fighters. But he showed no mercy to the white ones, knocking out one man 20 times in the same fight. Johnson struck one white opponent so hard that an imprint of the man's teeth appeared on his boxing gloves. As Johnson continued to win, the mainstream press became infatuated with his persona, nicknaming him "the Sport" for his larger-than-life demeanor.[46] The press wrote stories about his luxury automobiles, finely tailored suits and top hats, diamond stickpins, and shiny shoes. Johnson, who wore gold caps on his front teeth, had expensive jewelry in his mouth decades before Kanye and other rappers.

Jack Johnson used his earnings to purchase a home in a white neighborhood. When his white manager suggested that he was getting too uppity, Johnson fired him. His cockiness put him at odds with Booker T. Washington, the founder of the Tuskegee Institute, who argued that the best way for blacks to improve their condition was to accept racial separation. "In all things purely social we can be as separate as the fingers, yet one as the hand in all things essential to mutual progress," he told an audience full of cheering white men and weeping white women at the Atlanta Exposition on September 18, 1895.[47] Washington's message of accommodation did not resonate with Jack Johnson and a younger generation of blacks calling themselves "New Negroes."

After Jim Jeffries retired in 1905, Noah Brusso, a Canadian fighter who went by the name Tommy Burns, became the new heavyweight champ two years later. Burns agreed to a fight Johnson in Sydney, Australia, on December 26, 1908. The smug Johnson blew kisses to the predominantly white crowd as they hurled racist remarks at him. Burns taunted Johnson in the fight's early rounds. "Fight like a white man," he yelled out. But Burns proved to be no match for his indomitable black challenger. Whenever Burns appeared to be falling to his knees, Johnson held him up to prolong the beating. "Stop the fight, stop the fight," the audience cried out. Before Johnson knocked him out, police officers rushed into the ring and told camera crews to stop recording.

In 1909 Johnson, now the heavyweight champion, migrated to the South Side of Chicago, ironically the future home to Kanye West. While in Chicago he began frequenting the Everleigh Club, an opulent bordello with white prostitutes who serviced only white patrons. Johnson slept with nine of the club's employees in less than three months. The owner fired the women for sleeping with a black man. One of the women, 23-year-old Belle Schreiber, was the daughter of a police officer. Schreiber and another white prostitute named Hattie McClay began dating and traveling publicly with Johnson. His love for white women ultimately led many "respectable" blacks to turn against him and the federal government to throw him in prison.

A series of "Great White Hope" fighters unsuccessfully tried to dethrone Johnson and restore the white race to its pinnacle of racial hegemony. After two years Jeffries decided to come out of retirement for a bout with the champ. When Johnson prepared for his title defense against Jeffries, some black preachers placed considerable significance on what it meant for black people worldwide. Booker T. Washington, despite his disapproval of Johnson's lifestyle, allowed his students at Tuskegee to track how the fight progressed round by round. Black Pullman porters and cooks bet their wages on a Johnson victory. Extra security was hired to surround the stadium in case someone tried to assassinate him in the ring. The fight, billed as "the battle of the century," was held on July 4, 1910, in Reno, Nevada. This was going to be a celebration of somebody's independence.

Johnson dropped Jeffries to the mat repeatedly in the 15th round. Some whites, among the 20,000 in attendance, could be heard saying, "Don't let the nigger knock him out! Don't let the nigger knock him out!" Jeffries' corner threw in the towel just before that could happen. The next day the *Los Angeles Times* published an article warning "Negroes" not to puff out their chests too much or think they were special just because their skin was the same hue as Johnson's. Riots broke out across the nation between whites feeling sore about the loss and blacks happy about the win. On a Houston streetcar, an enraged white person slit a black man's throat because he had cheered for Jack Johnson. In Manhattan a white crowd set a black tenement on fire, then tried to block the doors and windows so that no one could get out. Not until the 1968 assassination of the Reverend Martin Luther King, Jr., would there be this level of nationwide racial violence.

Despite his celebrity, Johnson was not favored by much of the black middle class. He was not affiliated with the NAACP, the black church, or any black fraternal organizations. *The New York Age,* a black-owned newspaper, warned that his lack of modesty could bring down the whole race. Jack Johnson did not fight to uplift the race. Jack Johnson fought to uplift Jack Johnson. On the surface, he did not appear to be burdened by the double consciousness. Nevertheless, race defined his existence more than his class. His infatuation with white women and desire to live in a white neighborhood made some question if these were defiant acts or if he secretly craved the privileges of white manhood. He was exiled for a time in Europe as a fugitive for violating miscegenation laws. Johnson, who received multiple death threats throughout his tenure as the champ, led a difficult life. His wife, Etta, tormented by Johnson's womanizing and abuse and being treated like an outcast by fellow whites, took her life with a revolver.[48] Johnson suffered from alcoholism, had a mental breakdown, and contemplated suicide. He died on June 10, 1946, at 68, in Raleigh, North Carolina. After being denied service in a diner, Johnson hopped in his sports car and began speeding down U.S. Highway 1. He lost control of the vehicle and was killed by the crash.

When Joe Louis became the second black heavyweight champion in 1937, his handlers went out of their way to make him as docile as possible to avoid any comparison to his predecessor. Louis never smiled when he defeated white opponents. He stayed away from white women in public, though not in private despite being a married man. He always presented a pristine, respectable image.[49] His obedience did not win him white allies. Heading into his historic rematch with German fighter Max Schmeling in 1938, Lewis F. Atchison, a *Washington Post* columnist, described Louis as "a lethargic, chicken-eating colored boy."[50] Henry McLemore, a columnist covering the fight for United Press, referred to Louis as "a jungle man, competing primitive as any savage."[51] And these horrific words appeared in articles that ultimately praised the fighter. Upon winning the heavyweight title, Muhammad Ali was asked if he would be a champion like Joe Louis. Ali's response was an emphatic "no." He flagrantly questioned his opponents' blackness if they were less outspoken—notably Floyd Patterson and Joe Frazier—labeling them "Uncle Toms."[52]

On November 1, 1975, Muhammad Ali spoke to *Playboy* magazine about his views on being black, rich, and famous.

> I was driving down the street and I saw a black man wrapped in an old coat standing on a corner with his wife and a little boy, waiting for a bus—and there I am in my Rolls-Royce. This little boy had holes in shoes…. I started crying. Sure, I know I got it made while the masses of black people are catching hell, but as long as they ain't free, *I* ain't free.[53]

Kanye West grew up admiring Muhammad Ali. Besides posing as Ali for *Rolling Stone*, he compared himself to the champ in his 2010 song "Gorgeous." *Billboard* magazine published an article in 2016 titled "Why Kanye West Is the Hip-Hop Muhammad Ali." In the article RJ Smith wrote, "Nobody has taken on the mantle of being outspoken as self-consciously as West does today or seemed perhaps as eager to be martyred for it." Smith, the author of *The One: The Life of James Brown*, mistakenly saw Kanye's bravado as an apt comparison to Ali. While Ali was outspoken, he was not self-serving like Kanye. We must remember that Kanye had multiple black role models to choose from while growing up. Yes, he admired Ali, but he also admired O.J. Simpson. The latter's achievements were a preview of what was to come in the 1980s and 1990s as a new generation of black celebrities transcended race. Simpson, free from the struggles of previous generations, made it okay for future black celebrities to favor accommodation over agitation for the social equality of the masses. Simpson, Dandridge, and others planted the seeds for Kanye West and his peers to sprout up in the new millennium.

Three

"Be Like Mike"

"Michael Jackson leather and a glove but didn't give me a curl." *Kanye West*[1]

Kanye West was born on June 8, 1977, in Douglasville, Georgia. He came of age in Chicago, Illinois, during the 1980s and 1990s when black celebrity was entering a different stratosphere. Local Chicago figures Michael Jordan and Oprah Winfrey were two of the most famous and adored people globally. Earvin "Magic" Johnson signed the most lucrative contract in professional sports. Eddie Murphy's success in Hollywood paved the way for Denzel Washington and Will Smith to rule the box office. Bill Cosby, "America's dad," had the number-one show on television. Prince (Prince Rogers Nelson) had everyone partying like it's 1999. The Reverend Jesse Jackson made two viable attempts to win the Democratic Party's nomination for the U.S. presidency. But no one's star shined brighter than Michael Joseph Jackson.

Like most young black males of his generation, Kanye West grew up idolizing basketball superstar Michael Jordan, but he really wanted to be like Mike. "I would not be Kanye West if it weren't for Michael Jackson," Kanye told DJ Zane Lowe in an interview for BBC Radio 1.[2] He tailored his musical career and persona after Jackson. From the very start, his goal was to become the Michael Jackson of hip-hop. "I knew when I wrote the line 'light-skinned friend look like Michael Jackson' [from the song "Slow Jamz"] I was going to be a big star," he told *The New York Times* in 2013.[3]

Michael Jackson broke barriers for black musicians and entertainers, selling 750 million albums worldwide and amassing over $1 billion. His success in the 1980s opened the doors of MTV, a 24-hour music television cable network, to other black artists. As his popularity grew, he gradually appeared to move further and further away from the black community. He partnered with conservative U.S. presidents. His skin complexion went from dark to ghostly white, and all his public romantic relationships were with white women. His three children lacked visible black physical features.

The black community's allegiance to Jackson was tested to the highest degree during his fall from grace in the 1990s and 2000s. Despite the criticism, Jackson consistently proclaimed that he was proud to be black. He said it emphatically in interviews. The lyrics of his songs touched on socio-political issues to which most black people could relate. His music videos dripped with pro-blackness and delved into themes of race, identity, civil rights, and the African diaspora. As a result, many blacks remained loyal fans even as the quality of his albums declined and multiple rumors surfaced of criminal activity. Ultimately, Jackson paid a fatal price to become arguably the most influential celebrity of all time. His detractors repeatedly questioned his blackness and sanity until his tragic death. This chapter probes the similarities between Kanye West and his idol. What lessons can we learn from Jackson's story that can be applied when evaluating Mr. West?

Feeling Like Mike at His Baddest

Kanye was at home in Los Angeles on June 25, 2009, when his security guard broke the stunning news of Michael Jackson's passing. Jackson's physician, Dr. Conrad Murray, found the 50-year-old musician unconscious in his bedroom. Jackson was rushed to the Ronald Reagan UCLA Medical Center, ironically the same hospital to which Kanye was taken after he suffered his mental breakdown in 2016. Jackson was pronounced dead as the result of acute propofol and benzodiazepine intoxication. Although Jackson had been suffering addiction to prescription pills for years, Dr. Murray gave him propofol and anti-anxiety benzodiazepines, lorazepam, and midazolam, to help him sleep. Murray was tried and convicted of involuntary manslaughter.[4]

Kanye met Jackson years earlier at the home of Lyor Cohen. While most people would have been intimidated in Jackson's presence, Kanye opted to play his music for him. Jackson listened to a recording of "Good Life," the Grammy Award-winning third single from *Graduation*, which sampled Jackson's 1982 hit "P.Y.T. (Pretty Young Thing)." Jackson was so impressed by the sound of Kanye singing on "Good Life" that he encouraged him to sing more in the future.[5] Jackson's compliment was the impetus for Kanye's decision to abandon rapping and sing through an Auto-Tune vocal processor for the entirety of his next album, *808s & Heartbreak*.[6]

Kanye's fascination with Jackson is well documented. He sampled The Jackson 5's number-one hit "I Want You Back" (1969) when he produced Jay-Z's "Izzo (H.O.V.A.)," and he sampled uncredited vocals from Jackson for "Girls, Girls, Girls (Part 2)," another track on Jay-Z's *The Blueprint*. Kanye referenced Jackson on his first two singles as a solo artist, "Through the Wire" and "Slow Jamz." Jackson's name was spoken again on numerous future songs, including the two-time Grammy Award-winning "All of the Lights," his global number-one hit "Gold Digger," and his cameos on Keri Hilson's "Knock You Down" and Estelle's international chart-topper "American Boy." Although Kanye never recorded an original song with his idol, he produced a remix of "Billie Jean" a year before Jackson's death for *Thriller's* 25th-anniversary edition.

"Stadium status," shouts Kanye at the start of "Big Brother," the final selection on *Graduation*. Kanye's goal when composing *Graduation* was to make an album full of anthemic songs that could be performed at large outdoor stadiums. This was another nod to Michael Jackson, who was the first black artist to have an album successful enough to have his concerts at large outdoor stadiums for sporting events. Questlove (Ahmir Thompson) calls Jackson's *Bad* (1987) pop music's first stadium album. "Every song, I can hear it being thought of in his head as 'this is what I want to be when I perform it in front of 80,000 people,'" says Questlove. Jackson's concerts were spectacles of supreme artistic talent. Kanye followed this model for creating elaborate live shows with his sold-out tours: Glow in the Dark (2008), Watch the Throne (2011–2012), Yeezus (2013–2014), and Saint Pablo (2016). His 2011 Coachella concert, featuring 27 hit songs, ballerinas, Greek iconography, and accompaniment by Bon Iver's Justin Vernon, has been called the greatest live hip-hop performance. Kanye's 2015 Brit Awards performance of "All Day" had frenemy Taylor Swift dancing in the audience as if she was catching the Holy Ghost.

Kanye reflected on Jackson's influence on him in a 2020 interview with Pharrell Williams for *i-D* magazine.

> Michael Jackson was doing covert, super gangsta stuff. He kissed Elvis Presley's daughter on MTV. Black culture used to be … we used to be fronting all night, but Michael was doing stuff that was different [from] what we were programmed to understand as being what we should do. He bought the Beatles' back catalogue. That was Mike Jackson, right there.[7]

Michael Jackson was the first pop artist to turn his music videos into mini-films, working with notable directors: Martin Scorsese, John Landis, Spike Lee, and John Singleton. Kanye adopted this blueprint in the way he uses visual promotions for his music. He premiered three versions of his "Jesus Walks" music video at the 2004 Tribeca Film Festival in Manhattan.[8] Spike Jonze, best known for his Oscar nominated films *Being John Malkovich* (1999) and *Her* (2013), directed a promotional short film for *808s & Heartbreak* called "We Were Once a Fairytale." In the film Kanye played a caricature of himself drowning in excessive alcohol consumption and sex to mask his depression. *Cruel Summer* (2012), a compilation album featuring artists from his record label, G.O.O.D. Music, and several special guests, was the byproduct of Kanye's obsession with filmmaking. *Cruel Summer* began as a short film about a young car thief named Rafi desperately trying to marry a blind Arabian princess by convincing her father of his worth. The narrative centered around Arabian folktales. Kanye co-directed it with French filmmaker Alexandre Moors in Qatar. He used his personal finances to have Rem Koolhaas's agency build a pyramid on a beach to show the film at the Cannes Film Festival in France.[9]

"Runaway," a 34-minute film used to promote *My Beautiful Dark Twisted Fantasy* (2010), was inspired by Stanley Kubrick's final film, *Eyes Wide Shut* (1999). An illuminated, colossal bust of Michael Jackson in a parade surrounded by a marching band and mob of followers that resembled Ku Klux Klansmen appeared in "Runaway." In an interview for MTV News, Kanye told Sway Calloway that he used Jackson's likeness to make a statement on cult mentality. According to Kanye, Jackson's influence on the world was almost Christ-like. People worshipped him as though he was a deity.

Kanye's promotional rollout for his 2019 album *Jesus Is King* included the exclusive release of a 38-minute documentary, *Jesus Is King*, in IMAX theaters. The documentary, filmed in James Turrell's large-scale artwork the Roden Crater, was inspired by another Stanley Kubrick film, *2001: A Space Odyssey* (1968).[10] In June 2020 Kanye released the single "Wash Us in the Blood," which was accompanied by a music video directed by Arthur Jafa, the cinematographer for Julie Dash's groundbreaking film, *Daughters of the Dust* (1991).

Michael Jackson was a fashion maverick and trendsetter who boldly bent models of gender and black masculinity by rejecting stereotypical hyper-macho behavior associated with black men. Whether it was the red leather jackets in "Beat It" and "Thriller," the "Smooth Criminal" suit, his sequin socks and gloves, high-water pants, or the right wrist brace. Likewise, Kanye challenged the dominant hyper-masculine posturing of other rappers in the early 2000s. Before 2003 the standard dress code for many rappers was an oversized white T-shirt, jersey, baggy jeans, Timbs, and a fitted baseball cap or do-rag.[11] He came on the scene wearing pink Ralph Lauren polo shirts, blazers, and Gucci loafers. Kanye dared to wear a Celine women's blouse for his 2011 Coachella concert. When I saw him perform at the Watch the Throne Tour, he sported a black leather kilt designed by the French luxury fashion house Givenchy over his black super skinny jeans the entire concert.

From Motown to Off the Wall

Born on August 29, 1958, Michael Jackson was the eighth of Joseph and Catherine Jackson's 10 children. The family lived in a two-bedroom house in a poor black neighborhood in Gary, Indiana, located just 30 miles from Kanye's hometown, Chicago. In 1967 Gary made history by electing Richard Hatcher to be one of the nation's only two black mayors. Five years later Gary hosted the National Black Political Convention, a three-day meeting dedicated to forging a new black agenda for America. Eight thousand black political, labor, and civil rights leaders descended upon the city. Although Jackson was much too young to understand the magnitude of this moment it did not elude him. He and his brothers posed for a photo with Mayor Hatcher, raising their fists in the air to give the Black Power salute.

The Jacksons were not civil rights activists, but they were creating their own brand of black power.[12] After Joseph Jackson's blues band, the Falcons, failed to receive a record deal, he dedicated his life to honing his children's musical talents. He formed the group The Jackson Brothers with his sons Jackie, Tito, and Jermaine. After his youngest sons, Marlon and Michael, were added, the group was renamed The Jackson 5. They signed their first record deal with Gary's Steeltown Records in 1968, releasing their debut single "Big Boy." The following year the brothers signed a new deal with Motown. Berry Gordy's Motown, a recording company in Detroit, Michigan, was the epicenter of black music in the 1960s. Gordy carefully crafted younger black artists from the ghetto and the church who could make music that would be nonthreatening, not too funky, and easily acceptable to white audiences in the U.S. and abroad.[13] Motown was the sound of "young" America, not "black" America. They were creating beloved international anthems, not race music.[14]

The Jackson 5's first four singles, "I Want You Back," "ABC," "The Love You Saved," and "I'll Be There," all reached number one on the *Billboard* Hot 100 between 1969 and 1970. The group caught the world's attention after a national televised appearance on *The Ed Sullivan Show* (1948–1971) on December 14, 1969. Soon the group was everywhere, appearing in coloring books and the cover of teen idol magazines. ABC aired *The Jackson 5*, a Saturday morning cartoon produced by Motown, from September 1971 to October 1972.[15] The Jackson 5 were the closest thing little black boys growing up in the seventies like Lee Daniels, creator of Fox's *Empire*, had to *The Mickey Mouse Club*. "It's the same nerve the Beatles touched many years ago, only this time it's a group of black teenagers fronted by an eleven-year-old soul brother," commented a white reporter.

As Michael Jackson matured into manhood, he was unable to fight the urge to begin a solo career. Jackson released four solo albums between

1972 and 1975. The albums achieved moderate success. In 1978 he was cast as the Scarecrow in *The Wiz*, Sidney Lumet's cinematic adaptation of the 1974 Broadway Tony Award-winning play.[16] During his time on the set for *The Wiz*, Jackson befriended Quincy Jones, an accomplished black jazz arranger and conductor, hired to score the film's soundtrack. Jones produced Jackson's epic trilogy of history-making albums: *Off the Wall* (1979), *Thriller* (1982), and *Bad* (1987). It should be noted that Kanye West has his own definitive trilogy of albums—*The College Dropout, Late Registration, and Graduation*—that marked the height of his popularity. Jackson's *Off the Wall*, released on August 10, 1979, peaked at number three on the *Billboard* 200 album chart and became the third best-selling album of 1980. Much of the album's success was due to its consecutive number-one singles on the *Billboard* Hot 100: "Don't Stop 'Til You Get Enough" and "Rock with You." *Off the Wall* also included the emotional ballad "She's Out of My Life," satirized in Eddie Murphy's 1983 stand-up comedy special *Delirious*, and the jazzy "I Can't Help It," co-written by Stevie Wonder and Susaye Greene of The Supremes. The album's sixth track, "Girlfriend," was the first of three duets Jackson recorded with Beatles co-lead vocalist and bassist Paul McCartney. Not surprisingly, Kanye recorded three songs—"Only One," "All Day," and "FourFiveSeconds"—with McCartney four decades later.

Off the Wall was rooted in black culture and the African diaspora. Jason King, a director of Global Studies and founding faculty member of The Clive Davis Institute of Recorded Music at New York University, provided commentary on Spike Lee's 2016 documentary *Michael Jackson's Journey from Motown to Off the Wall*. "Michael's reference is certainly R&B, soul, and funk, but I also hear Africa," said King. "And you have to remember The Jackson 5 toured Africa in the seventies."[17] Barry Michael Cooper, the screenwriter for *New Jack City* (1991), gave *Off the Wall* one of its highest compliments, describing it as "soul music's epoch of magic realism. It is transformative and takes you somewhere else."[18]

Off the Wall sold more than six million copies in its first year. To date, it has sold more than 20 million copies worldwide and been certified 9× platinum. At the time, Jackson told reporters that he did not want to make black music. He wanted to make human music that would have a global reach. Unfortunately, the white voters for the major awards and the white radio station programmers did not share his vision. The 22nd Grammy Awards, held on February 27, 1980, in Los Angeles, changed the direction of Jackson's career, secured the worldwide acceptance of black music, and laid the roots for Kanye West. As he sat in front of his television at home, Jackson watched each major award go to one white artist after another that night. *Off the Wall* had been relegated to the "black music" subgenre in the Grammy's initial nominations announcements. Jackson's only award that night was a Grammy for Best R&B Vocal Performance, Male.[19] At that moment he pledged to make his next album so good that it would break all racial barriers.

Jackson was not upset with being considered a black artist. He was a student of black music who studied the great performers such as Jackie Wilson, James Brown, The Nicholas Brothers, Sammy Davis, Jr., Diana Ross, and the amateur teenage dancers on *Soul Train*. Jackson, however, did not limit himself to emulating black entertainers. He admired Fred Astaire and mimicked his dancing and fashion. Astaire inspired Jackson's trademark black loafers and white sequin socks. His 1988 music video for the single "Smooth Criminal" was a tribute to Astaire's film *The Band Wagon* (1953). Jackson's goal was to transcend race and have his music universally recognized. His next album, *Thriller*, released on November 30, 1982, was a nine-song, 42-minute magnum opus of R&B, pop, funk, post-disco, and rock music. *Thriller* broke every record imaginable. By 1984 it had sold more than 66 million copies. It was the first album to go 30× platinum, and it was the bestselling album of all time until the 2018 release of the Eagles' greatest hits album. *Thriller* won a record eight Grammy awards in 1984, thereby achieving the most wins ever for a single album and the most wins by a sole artist. It garnered the Album of the Year, Record of the Year, Producer of the Year, and seven top 10 singles on the *Billboard* Hot 100. With this album, Michael Jackson seized the crown as the greatest entertainer and most recognized celebrity on Earth!

Thriller was the musical equivalent of King's magnificent "I Have a Dream" speech. "His music, sonically and lyrically, does not overtly recall the civil rights struggle or the Black Nationalism movement, but their presence is there in less intuitive ways," writes Sara Tenenbaum.[20] Jackson integrated American popular music by becoming the first artist in *Billboard* history to have the number-one album and single ("Billie Jean") on the R&B (black) and pop (white) charts simultaneously. Until then, it was unfathomable for R&B and pop to mix. Jay-Z once rapped about how he did not cross over; on the contrary, he brought the suburbs to the hood.[21] Michael Jackson never stopped making black music, even though he became the King of Pop. Case in point: In the closing of *Thriller's* opening track, "Wanna Be Startin' Something," Jackson chants "Mama-se, Mama-sa, Ma-macoo-sa" for the final minute and 15 seconds. The chant came from Cameroonian saxophonist Manu Dibango's "Soul Masooka," a popular dance track in Central and West Africa in 1973. As Jason King suggested with *Off the Wall*, Jackson seamlessly incorporated African rhythms that he heard while touring the continent with his brothers. This performance was one of many occasions in which Jackson incorporated the African diaspora's music into his catalog.

Historian Paul Gilroy views music as a channel through which black identity—rooted in Africa—spreads across the globe. Kanye West infused African drums and rhythms into his songs "Love Lockdown" and "Amazing." The Afrofuturistic music video for the former featured African tribal dancers playing West African djembe drums.[22] According to Chris Kjorness, a professor of world music, "Love Lockdown" has a polyrhythm found in Ghanaian culture. Kjorness notes that the song applies Agbekor, a style of dance found in the southern part of the Volta Region of Ghana. Agbekor originated as a war dance for going into battle. "Love is seen as a battle to some people, and the kind of love that [Kanye] mentioned was one in which he had to fight," says Roberta Collier.[23] Kanye's repetitive hook, "Keep your love lockdown," is adapted from the repetitive war slogans found in Agbekor songs. In 2018 Kanye visited Uganda to find inspiration for his unreleased *Yandhi* album. The sounds of the continent can also be heard in the introduction to his Sunday Service Choir's live rendition of Fred Hammond's gospel anthem "This Is the Day."

Even when listeners thought Michael Jackson was crossing over, he was still performing music heavily rooted in black culture. "Beat It," *Thriller*'s third single, was number one on the *Billboard* Hot 100 and won two American Music Awards, as well as Grammys for Best Male Rock Vocal Performance and Record of the Year. A significant factor in its success was Eddie Van Halen's unforgettable guitar solo. He was the lead guitarist in one of the most successful hard rock bands in the early 1980s. Van Halen's feature helped "Beat It" to cross over onto rock stations. Jackson recorded another rock record, "Dirty Diana," with Billy Idol's guitarist Steve Stevens for his next album *Bad* (1987). He was not appropriating rock music; on the contrary, he was following in the tradition of black musicians who invented the genre in the 1950s. Rock 'n' roll originated from the blues; however, like country music, it has come to be primarily associated with white artists and audiences.

"Beat It" received another boost from the frequent play of its music video. It was the first video from a black artist to receive airplay on NBC's *Friday Night Videos.* MTV World premiered "Beat It" in primetime on March 31, 1983. Jackson's previous number-one single, "Billie Jean," had integrated MTV's video playlist three weeks earlier. MTV's refusal to promote "black music" and "black artists" before *Thriller* was an egregious characteristic of the music industry at the time. During the Jim Crow era, the music of black artists was categorized as "race" records. Albums and singles made by black artists that crossed over onto pop radio often displayed whites or physical objects on their covers. For example, the Marvelettes' vinyl single, "Please Mr. Postman," featured a mailbox rather than the singers.

By the 1960s and 1970s, the civil rights movement and the success of Motown integrated radio station playlists. Disco music's oversaturation on mainstream stations and the black and Latino queer artists and fans associated with that genre contributed to the re-segregation of radio playlists. On July 12, 1979, Steve Dahl, a white disc jockey, held Disco Demolition Night (or "Disco Sucks") at Chicago's Comiskey Park before a White Sox baseball game. Fifty thousand whites came to the park to watch Dahl demolish the disco records they brought to receive discounted admission to the game. A mini riot erupted as fans stormed the field, marring the event and exposing the underlying homophobia and racism. Album Oriented Radio (AOR) was created in response to the brief disco takeover to allow radio disc jockeys to format their playlists to only feature rock music. Consequently, white rock artists dominated pop music, the *Billboard* charts, and mainstream radio in the early 1980s.[24]

MTV debuted on August 1, 1981. Within three years the station's subscribers increased from 2.5 million to 25.4 million. Robert Pittman, the network's CEO and co-founder, adopted the AOR format. Pittman and Les Garland, MTV vice president of programming, surveyed suburban middle-class whites between the ages of 12 and 34 to determine what type of videos to put in rotation. Pittman and Garland argued that the respondents preferred rock music. Since most black artists were not considered "rock" artists, they were excluded from the station's rotation.[25] *Thriller's* first single, "The Girl is Mine," featuring Paul McCartney, received airplay exclusively on black radio stations. "Billie Jean" topped the "black" music charts in just three weeks. By week four the song reached the *Billboard* Hot 100 top 10 list. It was the number-one song in the country by March 1983 thanks to frequent play on black and AOR stations. The inclusion of Eddie Van Halen on "Beat It" forced white disc jockeys to place the song in their rotation. Jackson's videos opened MTV's doors to Whitney Houston, Prince, Run-DMC, Public Enemy, and other acclaimed black artists of the decade. *Yo! MTV Raps* would not have existed without *Thriller.* In 1991 MTV renamed its annual vanguard award the Michael Jackson Video Vanguard Award. Kanye received that honor in 2015. He announced his 2020 presidential election bid during his acceptance speech.

MTV premiered "Thriller," the final single from the album, on December 2, 1983. The 13-minute short film would be archived at The Library of Congress and inducted into the National Film Registry in 2009. "Thriller" takes place in the 1950s. Sara Tenenbaum places great significance on the opening scenes in which Jackson takes his girlfriend, played by model Ola Ray, to the movies. Tenenbaum highlights the fact that Jackson wore a letterman's jacket typically worn by white male high school varsity athletes. "This image contradicts what we know of African American experience in the 1950s, especially the experience of black teenagers who were never allowed into this kind of archetypal adolescence in popular culture or real life. As the star of 'Thriller,' Jackson was able to recast blackness itself as normatively American and his audience, his fans, took in those images without recognizing them as problematic."[26]

Thriller introduced America and the rest of the world to Michaelmania. Jackson became a heartthrob for teenage girls of all races and a symbol of Cold War–era American exceptionalism. According to a survey taken by Voice of America, Jackson was the most favored American musician amongst Soviet Bloc residents. He was the first American artist to have his music and videos played in Communist China in the 1980s. On June 15, 2019, a local Jackson fan club in Zhengzhou, China, unveiled a 1.8-meter bronze statue of him to commemorate the 10th anniversary of his death. Jackson's international resonance was arguably more extensive than his domestic influence. He befriended South African president Nelson Mandela during his multiple visits to that country. In 1993 he performed two concerts in Sao Paulo, Brazil, and took children and adults from the city's most impoverished areas to an amusement park. His 1993 Super Bowl XXVII halftime concert concluded with a soul-stirring performance of his ballad "Heal the World." He scheduled a tour of 50 concerts in London before his death. When he passed, images of mourners in Germany, Australia, Japan, South Africa, India, Canada, and the Middle East flooded the internet. One billion people around the globe watched his live memorial service.

The federal government recognized Jackson's sway over the public. President Ronald Reagan and his wife, Nancy, presented him with the Presidential Humanitarian Award on May 14, 1984. Reagan honored his support of anti-drug and anti-alcohol abuse charities. The event also marked the launch of Jackson's drunk driving campaign that used his song "Beat It" as its official anthem. Jackson returned to the White House on April 8, 1990, to be honored by Reagan's successor and former vice president George H.W. Bush. President Bush recognized his continued charitable work and lauded him as the "Artist of the Decade." When Bill Clinton won the presidency in 1992 Jackson performed at his inaugural gala.

In 1983 Jackson and his brothers planned the Victory Tour to promote their new collaborative album *Victory* (1984) and serve as the unofficial *Thriller* tour. Drama ensued with the announcement of the tour in November 1983. The Jackson family hired the now-infamous boxing promoter, Don King, to manage the tour. King expected to sell concert tickets for $30, which was more than most working-class blacks could afford, and he planned to hold the concerts in large stadiums located in predominantly white areas. King proposed to give (poor black) fans the option to win tickets through a poorly planned lottery system. The tour's promotion was the first stain on Jackson's public image. He immediately distanced himself from King and his family and hired his own advisers to oversee his role in the tour. At a national press conference, Jackson denounced the ticketing process in front of 100 reporters. He could not reduce the cost, but he promised to donate tickets to impoverished fans in each city where he performed. He also pledged to donate a portion of all the tour's proceeds to the United Negro College Fund.[27]

Who's Bad?

In 2012 Spike Lee honored the 25th anniversary of *Bad* (1987), Michael Jackson's follow-up to *Thriller*, with his documentary *Bad 25*. *Bad* was the first album to have five consecutive number-one singles on the pop charts—with "I Just Can't Stop Loving You," "Bad," "The Way You Make Me Feel," "Man in the Mirror," and "Dirty Diana." The *Bad* tour, running from September 1987 through January 1989, reached 15 countries and earned $125 million.[28] Lee's film explored the making of that monumental album. Among the various interviewees was Kanye West, dressed in a black leather jacket resembling the one worn by Jackson on the album cover and in the music video for the lead single, "Bad." *Bad* was a very significant chapter in Jackson's career. Some blacks were beginning to accuse him of making music devoid of social consciousness. Although his lyrics may not have screamed "Say it loud, I'm black and I'm proud," the album's promotional music videos painted a different picture. Martin Scorsese, director of the classic films *Raging Bull* (1980) and *Goodfellas* (1990), was hired to direct the extended music video for "Bad."[29] According to Richard Price, the scriptwriter, Jackson's goal was to deploy this project "to show the brothas he was down."[30] Ironically, as Price joked, he hired two white men of Italian and Jewish descent, respectively, to help achieve that.

An article in *New York* magazine about Edmund Perry, a 17-year-old black teenager from Harlem shot to death by a plainclothes police officer on June 12, 1985, inspired Jackson's video. Perry, a graduate from a college-prep high school in New England scheduled to begin attending Stanford University, was accused of attempting to mug the officer. His shooting was ruled a justifiable homicide.[31] In "Bad," Jackson played a high school student named Darryl modeled after Perry. The early scenes, shot in black and white, captured Darryl leaving behind his white friends at the prep school and taking the subway back home. Upon his return to Harlem, he is greeted by his childhood friend Mini Max (played by Wesley Snipes in his acting debut). Max, a local gang leader, questioned Darryl's manhood and blackness. "Are you bad? Or is that what they teach you at that little sissy school, how to forget who your friends are? You either down or you ain't down."[32] Darryl is pressured into mugging an older white man in a subway station, but he warned the man to run to safety seconds before Max's crew arrived.

Greg Tate, a former journalist for *The Village Voice,* described the internal conflict that both Edmund Perry and the fictional Darryl experienced as a metaphor for the feelings blacks experience when they are welcomed into upper-class white environments. Assimilation into the mainstream requires some individuals to distance themselves from their previous ties. Kanye blamed his disastrous 2018 TMZ interview on being detached from the people in his original inner circle, like Don C and Rhymefest. Black Twitter blamed that interview on his new life with the Kardashians and his detachment from black America.

"Bad" was the first time that Michael Jackson dealt with the double consciousness in his music. The video transitioned from this social commentary into a dance battle between Jackson's and Max's crew in the subway station resembling a scene out of *West Side Story* (1961). Jackson brought in several black street dancers to give the choreography a grittier vibe akin to the hip-hop street dance that was becoming popular.[33] The video concluded with a 30-second breakdown that had Jackson delivering a call-and-response routine with his dancers in the tradition of a charismatic black preacher.

Music journalist Danyel Smith says "Bad's" final moment reaffirmed Jackson's blackness for all the doubters who believed he had *souled* out. It reminded everyone that he was rooted in the black church and the soul music of James Brown. The video for *Bad's* fourth single, "Man in the Mirror," used a montage of clips from the Civil Rights Movement, such as children in Birmingham, Alabama, being hosed down by Bull Connor's racist police; Martin Luther King, Jr., speaking; and the KKK. It also included clips of malnourished children in Africa, Nelson Mandela, and post–Apartheid South Africa.[34] "Liberian Girl," *Bad's* ninth and final single, was remarkably progressive for 1989. At the time, no black artist was writing pop songs about African women's beauty for mainstream audiences.[35] And then there was "Scream," a 1995 duet with sister Janet Jackson which addressed racial and social injustice. Kanye references "Scream" and borrows its angry sound for his single "Black Skinhead."

Teddy Riley replaced Quincy Jones as the executive producer for Jackson's next album, *Dangerous* (1991). Riley is best known as the godfather of new jack swing, a popular genre of black music in the late 1980s and early 1990s that fused hip-hop, R&B, and pop using a Roland TR-808 Rhythm Composer. Kanye relied heavily on this device to make *808s & Heartbreak.* My favorite song on *Dangerous* is "Remember the Time." It is the perfect song to get people on the dancefloor. John Singleton, fresh off his Academy Award-nominated directorial debut film *Boyz n the Hood* (1991), directed a nine-minute video for the song. The video was set in ancient Egypt with Jackson as a hooded wizard attempting to steal the heart of the pharaoh's queen. Eddie Murphy and Somali supermodel Iman were cast as the pharaoh and queen. The video incorporated an elaborate Egyptian-style dance routine, choreographed by a young black woman named Fatima Robinson who later directed videos for Aaliyah and Mary J. Blige. The album's next video, "In the Closet," cast Naomi Campbell, a black supermodel from London of Chinese-Jamaican ancestry, as Jackson's love interest. Once again, he was intentionally demonstrating his connection to the African diaspora.

The music video for the album's most popular single, "Black or White," highlighted double consciousness for a second time.[36] The 11-minute video can be divided into three sections. The first section began with Jackson's music blaring from the speakers of a little white boy in the suburbs played by Jackson's pal and *Home Alone* (1990) star Macaulay Culkin. The boy's father, played by *Cheers'* George Wendt, nearly lost his voice trying to yell over the music. To spite his father, the son increased the volume until the music shattered the windows in the house and propelled his father from his seat into the sky.

The second section began with the father landing in an African jungle to find Jackson dancing with a group of African warriors with their faces painted. The scene shifted to display Jackson dancing with other performers representing different racial and ethnic groups. Jackson ends up on a street corner in an urban neighborhood with Culkin's character, two members from the youth hip-hop group Another Bad Creation, and three other kids all wearing hip-hop attire. Culkin, dressed in dark sunglasses, a backwards snapback fitted cap, baggy red hoodie, and a gaudy gold chain with a large dollar sign, lip-synced the lyrics to a rap by L.T.B. (Bill Bottrell) that concluded with the line "I am not gonna spend life being a color."[37] The scene then shifted to Jackson standing inside the Statue of Liberty's torch singing, "It don't matter if you're black or white"—a polarizing line meant to convey Jackson's vision of a color-blind society that wound up being used to question his connection to the black community. The next 48 seconds was one long exercise in racial transcendence. An Asian man morphed into African American supermodel Tyra Banks, who then morphed into a white woman with red hair. She then morphed into an African man with long dreadlocks. If these scenes represented utopia for some looking to escape the social construct of racial designations, the video's final part gave viewers an unpleasant dose of reality.

Elizabeth Chin, the author of "Michael Jackson's Panther Dance: Double Consciousness and the Uncanny Business of Performing While Black," refers to the final four minutes as the "panther dance." Jackson morphs into a black panther as he leaves the set upon which the video was being filmed. The panther roams into a dark alley and morphs back into Jackson. The black panther is a loaded image for both black and white America. In the summer of 1965, Black Power activist Stokely Carmichael helped launch the Lowndes County Freedom Organization, an independent political party, to register disenfranchised black voters in Lowndes County, Alabama. The party used the image of a black panther as their logo. In 1966 Huey P. Newton and Bobby Seale formed the Black Panther Party for Self-Defense in Oakland, California. The party's name was inspired by the Lowndes political party logo. The Panthers intentionally recruited the "brothas and sistas from the block" instead of the more "respectable" middle-class, church-going folk in the non-violent civil rights organizations. Police brutality was an epidemic in Oakland's black community. The Panthers took advantage of California's liberal gun laws to carry concealed weapons in public to "police the police."

The Black Panthers' official newspaper popularized images of black women with large Afro hairstyles, wearing dark sunglasses, dressed in leather jackets and pants, and carrying guns. Eldridge Cleaver, the party's minister of information, called for violence as a means to an end. While younger, more militant blacks saw the Panthers as heroes, many older conservative black civil rights leaders viewed them with condescension. The FBI and local police departments, California Governor Ronald Reagan, conservative whites, and the mainstream press pictured the Panthers as anti-white, domestic terrorists.[38] For millennials, the black panther brings to mind the Marvel Comics blockbuster film *Black Panther* (2018) and its slogan, "Wakanda Forever." While some white millennials and Generation Zers may see Black Panther as a cool superhero within the Avengers universe, the character symbolizes power, excellence, beauty, self-determination, womanism, "the culture," and pride in the African diaspora for many of their black counterparts.

Television networks did not know what to make of Michael Jackson's violent and sexually explicit panther dance. He danced in the alley, suggestively rubbing his chest while repeatedly grabbing his crotch, and yelling angrily. He jumped onto the roof of parked cars, zipped up his pants, smashed the windows with a crowbar, ripped out a car's steering wheel, and used it to break a window. The singer threw a trash can against a wall causing a sign from a hotel to fall to the ground. Electric sparks flared up behind him like homemade fireworks going off on July 4. Jackson, ripping his shirt open as he screamed out in uncontrollable rage, appeared to be channeling an intergenerational protest that could have been expressed in Marvin Gaye's "Inner City Blues (Make Me Wanna Holler)" or Tupac's "Holler

If Ya Hear Me." The video concluded with Jackson morphing back into the panther.

"Black or White" premiered on MTV, BET, VH1, and Fox on November 14, 1991, eight months after a video camera captured four white LAPD officers beating Rodney King, an unarmed black motorist, nearly to death. Jackson's panther dance was a prelude to the fury of the Los Angeles uprisings a year later. Networks initially banned the video's ending. When they began re-airing the full version, they edited in racial epithets, spray-painted on the walls and the cars, in an attempt to blame these visual images for inciting Jackson's violence. But in doing this they sanitized his anger, ignoring systemic racism as the monstrous root cause.

Chin compares Jackson's panther dance to Katherine Dunham's dream sequence in the film *Stormy Weather* (1943). Dunham, nicknamed the "queen mother of black dance," was renowned for introducing black dance to Europe, Latin America, and the U.S. in the 1940s and 1950s. Dunham devoted her life to "the people" and rejected the trappings of mainstream success. In *Stormy Weather*, the lead character, Selina (Lena Horne), envisioned an unknown black woman (Dunham) standing on a rainy street corner. Dunham's character danced off into the stormy clouds onto a stage with other black dancers. Once Selina's daydream ended, she was left standing on a stage singing the song "Stormy Weather" for a white audience. Chin says, "Dunham's dream is that black artists might be freed from the requirement of being explicitly black in ways demanded by onlooking white audiences. However, within the confines of *Stormy Weather*, it is a dream that is emphatically unable to move from the screen to the real world." According to Chin, Jackson recreates this feeling of rebellion by black artists with his panther dance, which was ultimately unacceptable to the white gaze.[39]

Daytona

Bad's second single was a tender ballad with Siedah Garrett titled "I Just Can't Stop Loving You." Originally that duet was supposed to be sung with Whitney Houston, the closest thing to Jackson's female counterpart. Houston experienced many of the same highs and lows that he faced throughout her career. She was born on August 9, 1963, three weeks before Martin Luther King, Jr., delivered his "I Have a Dream" speech at the March on Washington. I mention this because her music served as a conduit for interracial bridge building. Houston was three years old when four days of uprisings left 26 people dead in her hometown of Newark, New Jersey. The city's black residents were fed up with rampant racial profiling, police brutality, redlining, failing schools, unemployment, and housing discrimination. Music was her ticket out of the city's ghetto. Her mother, Cissy, was a member of the Drinkard Singers; leader of the Sweet Inspirations, who sang background for Aretha Franklin and Elvis Presley; and the minister of music at the local New Hope Baptist Church. Her maternal first cousin was Dionne Warwick, an award-winning R&B singer. At the age of 15, Houston provided background vocals for Chaka Khan, the same artist whom Kanye sampled two decades later for his debut single, "Through the Wire."

Whitney Houston's debut album, *Whitney Houston* (1985), was an instant smash going diamond (13× platinum). She scored seven consecutive number-one hits on the *Billboard* Hot 100 between *Whitney Houston* and her sophomore album, *Whitney* (1987). The press dubbed her "The Black Princess" and "The Prom Queen of Soul." Reporters marveled at her pristine image and family background. It was unknown for years that her parents had divorced when she was a teenager because they pretended to be a happily married couple. John and Cissy Houston discovered that for their daughter to be successful, she had to learn the ways of the dominant white culture, speak their language, and wear their clothes. "You must have double consciousness," says the Reverend Dr. Calvin Butts III, the senior pastor of Harlem's historic Abyssinian Baptist Church. "This causes you to ask yourself, 'Am I an extension of that or is that an extension of me?'"[40]

The 2018 biopic *Whitney* included home video footage of a conversation between Houston and her mother about two rival female pop stars of the late 1980s: Paula Abdul and Michael Jackson's younger sister, Janet. Abdul, best known today for her work on the early seasons of Fox's *American Idol* (2002–present), had one of the most triumphant debuts in history with *Forever Your Girl* (1988). The album went 7× platinum and produced four number ones on the *Billboard* Hot 100. Although Abdul is Syrian-Jewish, some, including Houston, mistakenly thought she was black or bi-racial due to her complexion. Houston disparaged Abdul for her lack of singing ability and perpetuating a false public image. "I will not sell out. Don't sell out, kid," she says to her mother in an exaggerated high-pitched voice.[41]

As Houston's fame grew, there was a sizable population in black America that believed she had sold out. During an interview, a white reporter asked how she felt about the emerging criticism from black fans who accused her of losing her identity as her sound became increasingly pop. "What do they want me to do? How do I sing more black?" she asked. "What am I doing that is making me sound white?"[42] Houston cried during a televised interview on *The Arsenio Hall Show* (1989–1994) as she addressed the controversy. Marilyn McCoo, the lead female vocalist in the popular late 1960s group The 5th Dimension, made similar comments because her group was also accused of sounding white. In his essay "Why Is Everyone Always Stealing Black Music?" Wesley Morris discusses the gentrification of black music. In the essay Delvyn Case, a musician and professor at Wheaton College in Massachusetts, explains to Morris the differences between music catered towards black listeners and white listeners. Case emphasized the use of improvisation—music no one "composed"—by black artists and musicians, a skill learned on slave plantations and perfected through decades of struggle.

> Improvisation is one of the most crucial elements in what we think of as black music. Without improvisation, a listener is seduced into the composition of the song itself and not the distorting or deviating elements that noise creates. Particular to black American music is the architecture to create a means by which singers and musicians can be completely free, free in the only way that would have been possible on a plantation: through art, through music—music no one "composed" (because enslaved people were denied literacy), music born of feeling, of play, of exhaustion, of hope. What you're hearing in black music is a miracle of sound, an experience that can really happen only once.[43]

Whitney Houston was booed by the predominantly black audience at the 1989 Soul Train Awards because she failed to master that strategy. The Rev. Al Sharpton urged the black community to boycott "Whitey" Houston. The Fox comedy series *In Living Color* (1990–1994) had a sketch in their first season called "Rhythmless Nation" in which Kim Wayans mocked Houston by dancing offbeat to the tune of Janet Jackson's "Rhythm Nation."[44] More recently, similar accusations of "pandering to a white gaze" have been hurled at Grammy-winning pop artist Lizzo (Melissa Viviane Jefferson), who has been called a "plus-sized magical negro" playing the flute for white consumers.[45]

The taunts from Sharpton and others reminded Houston of bullying she experienced during her childhood for being perceived as less black due to her lighter complexion and private school education. Members of her inner circle viewed her tumultuous marriage to R&B bad boy Bobby Brown as an appalling attempt to prove her doubters wrong. The black community came back to Houston's corner in the 1990s. Her role in *Waiting to Exhale* (1995), the cinematic adaptation of a Terry McMillan novel, resonated with black women across America. Houston's character in *The Preacher's Wife* (1996), alongside Denzel Washington, reminded the black community of her gospel roots. Her rendition of Richard Smallwood's gospel anthem "I Love the Lord" with the Georgia Mass Choir in the film is still a favorite in black churches 26 years later.

Houston's ascendance to American sweetheart and international icon began with her heart-stirring performance of "The Star-Spangled Banner" at Super Bowl XXV on January 27, 1991, in Tampa, Florida. The game was played ten days after the U.S. entered the Persian Gulf War. A global audience of 750 million viewers watched her sing the national anthem during the pre-game show. Houston, standing on stage wearing Nikes, a white tracksuit and white headband, did not look like a glamorous superstar. She looked like an everywoman, who could mix easily amongst the masses, standing there with her arms stretched wide and head flung back looking upwards to heaven. And, at that moment, as the beads of sweat slowly dripped down her face, the fans in the stands waved their American flags, the servicemen stood at attention, and the military planes flew over the field, Houston metamorphosed into an embodiment of rousing American patriotism. Here you had a 27-year-old black woman from the hood singing the national anthem to a sea of white people—waving American flags and wiping away tears—in a stadium in the South. Houston probably would have been prohibited from using the restroom in that stadium 30 years earlier.

Houston's Super Bowl performance was rooted in the black church. Marvin Gaye delivered the first soulful rendition of the national anthem at the 1983 NBA All-Star Game. Rickey Minor, the composer and producer of Houston's anthem, tried to recapture that same feeling for her performance. He gave her one beat extra for each measure from 3/4-time to 4/4-time to allow her sufficient time to draw out the notes and make the anthem sound more soulful and like a gospel song. As Houston sang, she placed more emphasis on the word "freedom." For white audiences, this could have meant freedom from Iraqi President Saddam Hussein and other foreign enemies threatening the New World Order.[46] But for black audiences, this meant emancipation, equality, and empowerment.

Houston's popularity reached another stratosphere thanks to her role in the 1992 film *The Bodyguard*. Houston played bestselling pop diva Rachel Marron and the eventual love interest of her white bodyguard Frank Farmer, played by Kevin Costner. At the film's conclusion she gets off a plane and runs into his arms to passionately kiss him. Interracial love scenes were still taboo. The kiss demonstrated Houston's crossover appeal and ability to transcend race. *The Bodyguard* was the second highest-grossing film worldwide in 1992. The film earned $411 million on a modest $25 million budget. It was accompanied by a record-breaking soundtrack that sold more than a million copies in its first week, won the Grammy for Album of the Year, and was eventually certified 18× platinum. *The Bodyguard,* the bestselling soundtrack in music history, was bolstered by Houston's cover of Dolly Parton's 1973 country song "I Will Always Love You." Houston's version remained atop the *Billboard* Hot 100 for 14 weeks, becoming the sixth bestselling single of all time. The song topped the charts in Australia, Belgium, Canada, France, Germany, Greece, Italy, Japan, Portugal, Spain, Zimbabwe, and 12 other countries.

In 1999, Whitney Houston signed the biggest recording deal in history. Nevertheless, all the riches in the world could not shield her against personal demons. Houston's two older brothers were guilty of introducing her to cocaine and other drugs at age 16. Rumors that she had a drug habit were confirmed when she performed at a televised tribute to Michael Jackson. Her frail appearance created a firestorm in the tabloids. A humiliating televised interview with Diane Sawyer, in which she admitted to using powder cocaine but not crack cocaine because "crack is whack," knocked America's black princess off her throne.[47] She became a punchline on *Saturday Night Live*. Fox's animated sitcom *American Dad* (2005–present) depicted her as a "crack whore" down on her knees, chasing after a crack vial like a dog running after a treat.

With funds depleted and fearing homelessness, Whitney Houston staged a comeback tour to get back on her feet financially. By now drugs had ravaged her vocal cords. Fans walked out during shows as she struggled to barely hit the notes she had mastered for decades. One concertgoer told the press that Houston's voice was so terrible that it could not entertain a dead rat. Abyssinian Baptist Church drew 2,000 black people for a weeknight service to pray for her wellbeing. "When one Whitney Houston emerges black America clings to that star. It's about more than music," said Abyssinian's Reverend Butts. At the age of 48, Houston was found dead the night before the 2012 Grammy Awards ceremony in Los Angeles. Toxicology results revealed multiple prescription drugs and marijuana in her system. The day after her passing, Nicholas Powers wrote the following in his article on her life:

> We loved her for being America's Sweetheart and making the black voice the beating pulse of our language. And in that desperate, perverse way of Black America, we loved her fall. It was as if her marriage to New Edition bad boy Bobby Brown showed that she didn't really climb out of our reach…. But Ghetto Whitney had grown powerful, and no amount of forgiveness or salvation could stop her. She drank away Pop Whitney's voice, spent her money, canceled her shows, and did not stop until she died. Whitney died so young because she straddled Black America's Double Consciousness. We see the image others have of us and the one we have of ourselves, and when they move too far apart, we fall and fall and fall. And no amount of singing can fill the void.[48]

It felt like the entire black community poured into Newark's New Hope Baptist Church for her four-hour funeral. Kanye West offered his tribute to Houston on the song "New God Flow," featuring Pusha T from his *Cruel Summer* album, released seven months after her death. But Kanye upset Houston's closest friends and family members by paying $85,000 to use a photo of her drug-strewn bathroom from the night she drowned in a hotel bathtub as the cover art for Pusha T's 2018 album *Daytona*. Kanye, the album's executive producer, switched the cover art just hours before it began streaming online. Was the decision purely a publicity stunt, or was there an underlying message about the toll fame can have on black celebrities? Years before her death Houston told Oprah Winfrey the drug abuse arose from the pressures of the fame that came after *The Bodyguard*. In *Bad 25*, Kanye revealed that his favorite music video from *Bad* was "Leave Me Alone." Michael Jackson recorded that single in response to the increasingly hostile scrutiny he was under from the tabloids depicting him as a mentally disturbed freak.

MJ Gone, Our Nigga Dead

Michael Jackson's upbringing and connection to the black community makes his demise even more confounding. How could someone who resonated with blackness in his videos and performances desire to turn himself into a white man? When Ta-Nehisi Coates published his damning 2018 article in *The Atlantic* titled "I'm Not Black, I'm Kanye: Kanye West Wants Freedom—White Freedom," he compared Kanye's fall from grace with that of Jackson. Coates provided the following reflection:

> He had always been dying—dying to be white. That was what my mother said, that you could see the dying all over his face, the decaying, the thinning, that he was disappearing into something white, desiccating into something white, erasing himself, so that we would forget that he had once been Africa beautiful and Africa brown, and we would forget his pharaoh's nose, forget his vast eyes, his dazzling smile, and Michael Jackson was but the extreme of what felt in those post-disco years to be a trend.[49]

As a child, I noticed the change in Jackson's appearance when I looked at his album covers. He went from looking black on *Thriller* to bi-racial or Latino on *Bad*. When he debuted the video for "Black or White," my friends joked that he was confused about what color he wanted to be. His hue was so pale in later videos such as "They Don't Care About Us," "You Are Not Alone," and "Childhood" that he looked ghostly. Jackson's changing complexion was a frequent topic on HBO's *Def Comedy Jam*. His shoulder-length straightened hair, thin nose, high cheekbones, and thin lips had comedians calling him a wannabe white woman. In 1993, the 34-year-old Jackson granted Oprah Winfrey a world exclusive 90-minute interview at his 2,700-acre Neverland Valley Ranch in Santa Ynez Valley, California.[50] This was Jackson's first televised interview in 14 years.[51] He denied rumors that he wanted a white child to play him in a Pepsi commercial. "I am a black American. I am proud to be a black American. I am proud of my race. I am proud of who I am," he emphatically told Winfrey.[52]

Jackson told Winfrey he grew up hating his appearance. He washed his face in the dark and avoided looking at himself in the mirror because he had such bad acne as a teenager. His altered facial features spoke of his miserably contorted self-image. The impulse of Jackson's father to berate him as a child for the size of his nose and acne is reminiscent of a scripture verse: "He hath no form nor comeliness, and when we shall see him, there is no beauty that we should desire him."[53] Why were Jackson's children wearing masks in public? Was it to shield his wounded, frail psyche from subliminal messaging that his own children, because of their preferred appearance, were due affirmation and entitlements denied him in childhood? What of himself did he squander lodging in the sunken place as he reached for and held fast to the pinnacle of achievement and dazzling global acclaim? It should be noted that in 2021 Kanye began appeared in public wearing face coverings and a white prosthetic mask. Was this an ode to Jackson, publicity stunt, or something deeper?

Jackson denied bleaching his skin tone and blamed the skin disease vitiligo for his new appearance. Although vitiligo is now destigmatized thanks to the success of Canadian model Winnie Harlow, that was not the case 20–30 years ago.[54] Skin bleaching is a public health problem in West African countries. During a trip to Ghana in 2015, I observed several billboards advertising bleaching cream with the faces of light-skinned black American celebrities such as Chris Brown. Retired Dominican baseball player Sammy Sosa and American rapper Lil' Kim (Kimberly Jones) have been ridiculed for skin bleaching. Kim has also altered her face with plastic surgery. Toni Morrison addressed the vexing self-alienating illusion of inferiority with which some dark-skinned blacks, who yearned to look white, struggled in her first novel, *The Bluest Eye*.[55] For decades it was also common for extremely light-skinned blacks to pass for white at times for safety, at times for advancement. As historian Allyson Hobbs points out in her book *Chosen Exile* (2016), these blacks often experienced loneliness and rejection from fellow blacks and even family members. The 1959 film *Imitation of Life* painted a compelling portrait of Sarah Jane, "a tragic mulatto," longing so desperately to be white that she rejected her own mother.[56]

Jackson denied skin bleaching and told Winfrey vitiligo was hereditary on his father's side of the family. He admitted to getting plastic surgery for his nose but denied altering his eyes and cheekbones. Despite Jackson's proclamations, many blacks struggled to accept his explanation for his drastic change in appearance. Was he struggling with the obsession with whiteness that Frantz Fanon probed in *Black Skin, White Masks*? Although his leading ladies in videos were often black, his public romantic relationships were primarily with white females. Jackson socialized with the teenage actresses Tatum O'Neal and *The Brady Bunch*'s Maureen McCormick during his youth. During the *Thriller* award season, Brooke Shields escorted Jackson to the American Music Awards and Grammy Awards ceremonies. Shields, an actress and former Calvin Klein model of English, German, Scotch-Irish, Italian, and Welsh descent, was viewed as the standard of American beauty. The optics of Jackson, a self-described "ugly kid," having this famous white model on his arm cannot be understated.

Jackson married Lisa Marie Presley, the daughter of Elvis and Priscilla Presley, in 1994. Once again, he was romantically pairing himself with a renowned white woman. In this case, the daughter of mainstream America's "King of Rock 'n' Roll." Their marriage lasted just two years. Many in the press thought it was a publicity stunt to distract the world from recent child molestation accusations against him. His second marriage came in 1997 to his dermatology nurse Debbie Rowe, another white woman. Their marriage lasted two years and produced two children: Michael Jr., and Paris. His third child, Prince Michael II (nicknamed Blanket), was conceived by artificial insemination in 2002. Jackson told British reporter Martin Bashir that Blanket's mother was black, even though the child, like his others, appeared white. It is also interesting that Jackson recorded "I Just Can't Stop Loving You" with Siedah Garrett, a black woman, but performed the song live with Sheryl Crow, then an unknown backup singer, during the Bad World Tour.

We may never know if Michael Jackson was more attracted to white women than black women or if there were not many black women in his inner circle. Nor will we know if his handlers thought it would be better for him to date Brooke Shields and Lisa Marie Presley rather than a black celebrity. He briefly dated Stephanie Mills, a black R&B singer who played Dorothy in the Broadway version of *The Wiz*. Jackson and Mills dated while he was filming *The Wiz*. To Jackson's credit, he never disconnected from the black community as O.J. Simpson had done. Consequently, when he turned to the black community for support while facing sexual molestation allegations in 1993 and 2002, it did not look disingenuous. Jackson hired civil rights lawyer Johnnie Cochran to defend him against the first set of allegations. Two years later, Cochran gained notoriety for successfully defending Simpson in his criminal trial.

Michael Jackson made headline news for defiantly dancing atop the roof of a car after pleading not guilty and then coming to court late and wearing pajamas another day. He was in the news again for hiring the Nation of Islam (NOI) to provide his security during the 2002 trial. The NOI came to prominence in the black community in the late 1950s with the ascendency of Malcolm X. The NOI's notoriety surged again in the mid–1990s under the leadership of Louis Farrakhan. The Southern Poverty Law Center has labeled the NOI a black supremacist hate group for anti–Semitic and anti–white statements. Jackson eventually cut ties with the group due to the controversy. In 2015 Kanye began speaking publicly of his relationship with Farrakhan and referenced him in two songs on *The Life of Pablo*.

A new firestorm of sexual molestation accusations made by two white men, Wade Robson and James Safechuck, in the 2019 HBO documentary *Leaving Neverland* further tarnished Michael Jackson's reputation.[57] MTV has discussed the possibility of removing his name from their Vanguard Award. With the rumors about his appearance, mental sanity, and inappropriate interest in young boys looming since the late 1980s, mainstream media has judged Jackson severely for years. Tabloids mocked him and called him "Wacko Jacko." His effeminate appearance and soft voice ignited curiosity about his sexuality. In 1985 James Baldwin addressed the backlash against Jackson that was beginning to fester after *Thriller*'s success. "The Michael Jackson cacophony is fascinating in that it is not about Jackson at all. I hope he has the good sense to know it and the good fortune to snatch his life out of the jaws of a carnivorous success. He will not swiftly be forgiven for turning so many tables," wrote Baldwin.[58] Jason King suggests that some of this backlash against Jackson resulted from his purchase of the Beatles' song catalog for $47.5 million. The King of Pop was making power moves deemed inappropriate for a black man in 1985, regardless of his celebrity.[59]

They want to find me not breathin' like they found Mike

While large segments of the black community never canceled Michael Jackson, his support waned over the years.[60] "Another kid? Another kid? I thought it was Groundhog's Day. We love Michael so much we let the first kid slide," Chris Rock joked in his 2004 HBO standup special *Never Scared*. Katt Williams lampooned Jackson much more harshly on *The Pimp Chronicles* (2006), emphatically declaring that "Michael forgot he was a nigga. It was us supporting him when he had that big ass, greasy ass, bell pepper nose. We kept giving him chances. Michael spent his whole life trying to look like a white woman, and then as soon as he gets in trouble, he wants to be surrounded by Muslims."[61]

Michael Jackson's momentous rise and alarming fall provide a cautionary tale for Kanye West about the enormous price that comes with celebrity for a black man or woman. In his June 2020 interview with Pharrell

Williams, Kanye defended Jackson and compared himself to his idol. "We should have something that says we can't allow any company to tear down our heroes." he told Williams. "I'm like every time the media isn't happy with me it's like, they're gonna Wacko Jacko me. Which in some ways, they've tried to do."[62] Kanye's 2010 single "Power" addressed the pressures of fame that drive many celebrities to an early death. Is Kanye destined to fill that void in the culture left by Michael Jackson's absence or succumb to the pitfalls that accompanied Jackson's racial transcendence? None of these questions mattered back in 1987, when Kanye was a 10-year-old kid on the South Side of Chicago, dressed in his leather and glove, dreaming to Be Like Mike!

PART II

Everything I Am

Becoming Kanye

FOUR

"Family Business"

"I'm reminded of the first time my children ever got an opportunity to be in snow. They were very fearful in terms of the steps that they would take. And what I did was, I walked in front of them. And I said to them, instead of creating your own footprints, walk in the footprints that I've already made." *Ray West*[1]

Kanye West's familial upbringing has heavily influenced the evolution of his image and worldview. His biological family instilled in him a strong sense of blackness and black pride. When he proclaimed to the world that "George Bush doesn't care about black people," it was rooted in something more profound than ego or "clout chasing."[2] Therefore, when Kanye loudly trumpeted his love for President Donald Trump and his thoughts on slavery, many blacks pointed to the loss of those family values instilled in him from childhood. Hip-hop legend Snoop Dogg (Calvin Broadus, Jr.) blamed the absence of strong, black women in Kanye's life for his recent behavior:

Let's just keep it 100. I got aunties that'll pull up with those big ole church hats on, 'nigga what's happening? What you on, Nephew. You bullshitting. We taught you way better than that….' Maybe the women that are around him should look into getting help from women stronger than them.[3]

Although Snoop did not directly call out Kanye's then wife, Kim Kardashian, or her mom and sisters, one can read in between the lines. Others have supported these accusations that Kanye's "struggles" resulted from his assimilation into a world that was overwhelmingly wealthy and white after his mother passed. Kanye even accused his wife's family of trapping him in the sunken place during a bizarre Twitter rant in 2020 as he appeared to be undergoing a manic episode. This chapter analyzes the role that Kanye West's biological family and marriage have played in developing his self-identity.

I Don't Care 'Bout (All the Diamond Rings)

Kanye premiered the music video for "Follow God," the first single from his ninth studio album, *Jesus Is King*, on November 8, 2019. As the video began an unfamiliar voice could he heard reciting a parable about his young children using his footprints to guide them through the snow. The parable alluded to the Christian poem "Footprints in the Sand," which describes a person following God's footprints to walk across the beach. The surprise narrator was Kanye's father, Ray West. Ray's parable served dual purposes, identifying the song's theme, "follow God," and representing his private relationship with his son. Throughout the video, Kanye and Ray drove over snow-covered terrain, "doing donuts" in multiple off-road vehicles on Kanye's recently purchased land in Cody, Wyoming.[4] The video concluded with the following text written across a bright blue screen:

> My dad came to visit me at one of our ranches in Cody, Wyoming. He talked about his love for fishing, and how he would like to come here in the summers. It took me 42 years to realize that my dad was my best friend. He asked me, "How many acres is this?" I told him 4000. He replied in these three words: "A black man?"[5]

Kanye's statement about land ownership alludes not only to his success, but to the sacrifices by those before him who made such inconceivable accomplishments possible. Contrary to popular opinion, the Kanye West origin story did not commence in the Windy City. It started decades earlier in Oklahoma with his maternal grandparents, Mr. Portwood Williams, Sr., and Mrs. Lucille Williams.[6] Portwood, affectionately called "Buddy," grew up in an America that paled in comparison to the one his grandson knows. As a boy he picked cotton and shined the shoes of white men who spat on him. In return for his labor he received a measly dime to take home to his parents. As Portwood matured his employers still routinely referred to him as "boy," a step up from "nigger," which they also called him. His daily commute to work involved passing by a sign that read: "NO NIGGERS AND DOGS AFTER SUNDOWN."[7]

Lucille, affectionately called "Chick," worked various jobs as a domestic servant, hairdresser, and a keypunch operator at Tinker Air Force Base, where femininity did not shield her from the bigotry Portwood encountered. The white matriarch required her, as a domestic, to enter the house through the back door and wear a uniform whenever she was on duty. Professor Elizabeth Clark-Lewis states in her study on black domestic workers, *Living In, Living Out*, that the uniform was a way of disempowering black domestics and relegating them to second-class status.[8] Lucille's mother had worked for the Robinsons, a white family, for 48 years. The Robinsons were benevolent and even paid off her mother's mortgage. Lucille, who was very strong-willed, struggled to hold her tongue whenever she felt disrespected. Not surprisingly, her days as a domestic laborer were short-lived. Lucille passed down her assertiveness and defiant demeanor to her daughter and grandson.[9] If she took her children shopping, Lucille made them drink from the "White Only" water fountains and use the "White Only" toilets.

Portwood and Lucille built their lives in Oklahoma, a state that holds a unique place within the African American experience. The beloved Rodgers and Hammerstein 1943 musical *Oklahoma!* depicted the territory as a land for white settlers and cowboys during westward expansion. However, the musical's mythical image of manifest destiny ignored the racial dynamics that existed. The first black settlers were slaves of the Cherokee, Creek, Chickasaw, Choctaw, and Seminole Indians who traveled to Oklahoma during the Trail of Tears (1830–1850). After the Civil War those slaves were freed and given a portion (160 acres each) of the Indians' land. Segregation came to Oklahoma in 1890 when schools were separated by race. The railway system was segregated in 1907. Black suffrage was banned three years later. Oklahoma adopted a residential segregation law in 1916. As the federal courts contributed to Jim Crow's slow demise in the sixties, Oklahoma maintained de jure segregation until 1967.[10]

The threat of racism did not deter other blacks from migrating to the territory. A movement began called Boosterism led by Edward McCabe, a former auditor for the state of Kansas, to encourage free black southerners to venture westward and claim this "Dreamland" as a new black state. Blacks in Tulsa, Oklahoma's Greenwood District built an empire that included 30 restaurants, 45 groceries, meat markets, and dental offices. The dollar would stay in Greenwood for nearly four years before moving outside that community. Greenwood's prosperity led Booker T. Washington to give it the nickname Black Wall Street. The presence of all these black "bosses" was a thorn in the side of jealous whites.[11] On May 31, 1921, Dick Rowland, a 19-year-old black man, accidentally bumped into Sarah Page, a 17-year-old white girl, in an elevator. Rowland tripped and attempted to break his fall by grabbing onto Page, the elevator operator. She screamed, causing a nearby store clerk to summon the police. *The Tulsa Tribune*, a local newspaper, falsely reported that Rowland sexually assaulted Page, inciting mobs of angry white men on the streets of Greenwood. Rather than subdue the terror, police officers deputized mob members and distributed guns.

The Tulsa race riot was not about the elevator incident. It was an attempt to put these self-empowered black property owners back in their place. The destruction went block by block. Anyone who resisted was either shot or arrested. More than 1,000 black homes and businesses were looted and burned to the ground. By June 1, death-dealing rage of the self-obsessed mob had reduced Black Wall Street to a smoldering ruin resembling a war zone.[12] The Tulsa massacre, depicted in the HBO series *Watchmen* (2019) and *Lovecraft Country* (2020), was the largest single incident of racial violence in American history. Officially, 36 citizens died during the riot, including 26 blacks and 10 whites. However, some reports claim that as many as 300 people lost their lives. Only two victims received proper burials. Six thousand blacks, displaced from their homes, spent eight days confined at the city's fairgrounds and convention center.[13]

Kanye's mother, Dr. Donda West, was born less than two hours away from Tulsa in Oklahoma City on July 12, 1949. She was the fourth child of Portwood and Lucille, who nicknamed her "Big Girl." Donda attended Culbertson and Dunbar Elementary Schools, F.D. Moon Junior High, and graduated from Douglass High School.[14] The Civil Rights Movement shaped her childhood and teenage years. Although Oklahoma City does not appear in many civil rights narratives, the NAACP opened an office there in 1913. The NAACP's Legal Defense Fund used the state as the testing ground for two of its earliest U.S. Supreme Court battles: *Sipuel v. Board of Regents of the University of Oklahoma* (1948) and *McLaurin v. Oklahoma State Regents* (1950). In the former case, the court ruled to admit a black woman named Ada Lois Sipuel to the University of Oklahoma School of Law. In *McLaurin v. Oklahoma State Regents*, the court ruled unanimously (9–0) in favor of the admittance of George W. McLaurin, a black doctoral student, to the University of Oklahoma Graduate School of Education. These cases paved the way for *Brown v. the Board of Education* (1954).

These judicial victories in higher education invigorated the city's black residents to demand their freedom. They formed the Citizens Committee, which partnered with the NAACP, YMCA, YWCA, and the Oklahoma City Council of Churches. Historian Jeanne Theoharis reminds us in *A More Beautiful and Terrible History* (2019) that the Civil Rights Movement would not have achieved as much without youth activists.[15] The NAACP Youth Council, under the leadership of Mrs. Clara Luper, became very instrumental in the fight to desegregate Oklahoma City's public accommodations in 1957. Luper, a local teacher at Dunjee High School, used her classroom to recruit students, teach them black history, and train them in civil disobedience.[16] On August 19, 1958, the Youth Council staged the city's first mass sit-in demonstrations at Green's Variety Store and Katz Drug Store. The protestors ranged in age from six to 17. More demonstrations occurred later that week, resulting in the immediate integration of the lunch counters at both establishments. The Kress Variety Store removed their stools from the lunch counter, forcing all patrons to stand as they ate their food. The John

A. Brown Department Store resisted change by hiring white teenagers to sit at the counters and only give up their seats for white patrons.

In addition to targeting lunch counters, the Youth Council tried to integrate local churches that were unwilling to welcome them with open arms. The pastor at Kelham Avenue Baptist Church rudely told them, "God doesn't want the races to mix" and then cited Biblical passages to support his vindictive ignorance.[17] Despite white resistance, the students escaped the violence experienced by their counterparts in Birmingham, Selma, and other parts of the nation. There were isolated events such as Clara Luper receiving a bomb threat and incendiary phone calls. On another occasion, a white youth attacked one of the demonstrators. But for the most part violence was minimal. One reason for this restraint and civility was the ongoing communication between adult leaders on both sides of the color line. Furthermore, the Oklahoma City Police Department was not complicit in the resistance. The NAACP suspended the sit-ins for a year to focus on negotiating with the white restaurateurs. After this strategy failed, the demonstrations resumed.

Mrs. Luper called for a citywide boycott in 1960. Blacks, comprising eight percent of the city's population, had the power to enact change with their wallets. The boycott attracted the attention of Martin Luther King, Jr., who visited the city to speak at the Calvary Baptist Church. In the wake of the boycott, only a small number of businesses refused to integrate. Kanye rapped about his mother's involvement in the demonstrations on the 2004 song "Never Let Me Down." Donda reflected on her time working with the Youth Council in her memoir *Raising Kanye: Life Lessons from the Mother of a Hip-Hop Superstar* (2007).

> When I was six, I was arrested for a sit-in at a segregated restaurant in Oklahoma City. I remember crying, my little legs dangling over the seat of that big chair at the police station. I wasn't crying because I'd been arrested, though. I was crying because I wanted to ride to jail in the paddy wagon just like my older brother and the older kids…. We sat in a hamburger place called Split-T Restaurant and violated an injunction forbidding us to do so. So they took us to jail. Within two years, almost every restaurant was integrated because of our efforts.[18]

Kanye has emphatically proclaimed that his mother's rebellious spirit to uplift her people flows through his veins, and with that in his blood, he was born to be different.[19] Donda acknowledged the differences between her struggles and those of Kanye's generation. However, she drew parallels between her activism and her son's decision to highlight the incompetence of President George W. Bush and the Federal Emergency Management Agency (FEMA) following Hurricane Katrina. The sight of hundreds of black bodies stretched out on cots at the New Orleans Superdome—and the federal government's apparent disregard—reminded her of the disrespect she was fighting against as a child. Perhaps it was conversations with her that motivated Kanye to blurt "George Bush doesn't care about black people" on national television. Perhaps it was something in Kanye's consciousness as a black man, the son of an activist, and the grandson of Portwood and Lucille Williams that kept nudging him when common sense and a good publicist would have advised him to "shut up and rap."

Kanye's telethon outburst was one of his mother's proudest moments. "We must teach our children to speak their minds and speak the truth," she said. Donda visited New Orleans with Kanye days after Katrina ravaged the city. Kanye planned to speak to 2,000 people receiving shelter at the Houston Astrodome, but the Red Cross advised him against doing this. Kanye and his mother ended up speaking at two churches in Houston. He also partnered with the local chapter of the Urban League, a national civil rights organization, to conduct interviews and help displaced families. His foundation provided 15 families with yearlong residence in a furnished home.

Kanye was a guest on *The Oprah Winfrey Show* in 2005. Winfrey told the audience that she thought he was self-absorbed and extremely arrogant when they initially met backstage at the NAACP Image Awards. In Kanye's mind, he was behaving like his mother's son and following in the footsteps of his idol Muhammad Ali. Nobody could tell Donda's son that he was not the greatest. "I am disrespecting the blessings that God has given me not to scream out loud and testify every single day," he told Winfrey.[20] Donda loved Ali's confidence and swagger. She was in college when he was at the forefront of the Black Power and anti–Vietnam War movements. Her mother, Lucille, rooted for Ali inside the boxing ring; she could, however, do without his excessive braggadocio. Lucille thought he was arrogant and full of himself, but Donda loved it, making it no surprise that she would raise her son to embody that same swagger. In a 2005 episode of VH1's defunct docuseries *Driven*, Donda remarked that Kanye's teachers noted his healthy dose of extreme self-confidence from the time he was in elementary school. His 2007 song "The Glory" is one long boastful salute to himself. Not even the Holy Spirit could contain Kanye's bravado during his 2019 visit to the Lakewood Church in Houston, Texas, as he informed Pastor Joel Osteen that he was the "greatest artist that God has ever created."[21]

Black folks loved Muhammad Ali because he made them feel "pretty" and powerful enough to "shake up the world." That affirmation was necessary at a time when blacks were made to feel inferior and ugly if they lacked European physical features. Sports historians Randy Roberts and Johnny Smith compared Ali to the prolific writer James Baldwin. "I did not intend to allow the white people of this country to tell me who I was, and limit me that way," wrote Baldwin.[22] In Ali, black Americans saw a black man who was unwilling to lower his head, speak softly, or kowtow to the white gaze. His defiant refusal to serve in "the white man's" war in Vietnam only magnified his adoration in the black community and the eyes of Donda West.

Kanye's Ali-like swag was not only evident when he spoke on Hurricane Katrina; it was apparent four years later when he spoke on behalf of the LGBTQ community.[23] In 2009 he chastised his fellow rappers for their homophobic lyrics and using derogatory phrases like "that's gay" and "no homo." Kanye, who had his masculinity questioned because of his interest in fashion, was among the earliest rappers to record music with Frank Ocean, hip-hop's first openly bisexual artist. "In the black community, when I was growing up, being gay was something to be ashamed of," said Donda.[24] Homophobia was rampant within the Civil Rights Movement and the black church when she was an adolescent. Little had changed by the time Kanye came around. The first hit rap song on the radio, Sugarhill Gang's "Rapper's Delight" (1979), used the epithet "fairy" to put down a man.

Homophobic lyrics were common in gangsta rap albums. Even socially conscious artists contributed to this diatribe in the music. Mos Def and Talib Kweli (Talib Kweli Greene), appearing in a 2006 PBS film *Hip Hop: Beyond Beats and Rhymes*, declined discussing the possibility of befriending a homosexual. Muslim rapper Lord Jamar, a member of the 1990s rap duo Brand Nubian, released a diss song "Lift Up Your Skirt" specially aimed at Kanye and accusing him of polluting hip-hop with "questionable" fashion choices and homosexual tendencies. Kanye's willingness to contradict popular opinions within the black community, the black church, and hip-hop regarding LGBTQ rights exemplified the spirit of Ali.

Donda always publicly defended her son's actions. In her memoir, she addressed his constant use of the N-word in his music. She wrote that the N-word was the equivalent of a curse word when she was a child. It was a chilling epithet that her family associated with slavery, Jim Crow, and lynching. It was a term that conjured up images of that infamous *Jet* photo of Emmett Till's mutilated body in a casket. When Donda became the English department chair at Chicago State University, Chicago's lone HBCU, she addressed the Illinois state legislature about the term's detrimental effects on blacks' psychological health.[25] Her stance softened after Kanye became a world-famous rapper. She defended Kanye by referencing conscious rappers like Common (Lonnie Lynn, Jr.), who used that word artistically in their rhymes.

"What bothers me is not the word 'nigger,' but the joblessness, the poor housing, the inferior schooling, and the low salaries for all who white racists might label 'nigger.' I don't believe the kids in [Dr. Kenneth] Clark's doll test [in the 1950s] or the ones who took the test again in 2007 did not suffer self-hatred because they were called nigger on a regular basis," she stated.[26] Donda credited rappers with disempowering the offensive racial slur and reframing it on their terms. If she were still alive, I wonder if she would have used this same argument to defend Kanye's use of the Confederate flag or the MAGA hat. Would she object to his saying racism is no longer a problem, his support of President Trump, or the fact that he has never voted when so many blacks of her generation were jailed, lost employment, and died for registering to vote?

You Want Me to Give You a Testimony About My Life

After Donda completed her undergraduate studies at Virginia Union University, she enrolled in a master's program at Atlanta University. While in graduate school she began working at Spelman College, the nation's oldest private historically black liberal arts college for women, as an assistant to the head of public relations. Perhaps it was not coincidental that she met Kanye's father, Ray West, at this time. Ray, who owned a photography business, was an independent contractor hired to take photos for Spelman's brochures. He eventually became one of the first black photojournalists at *The Atlanta Journal-Constitution*. Ray West has remained a hidden figure throughout much of his son's time in the spotlight. Kanye has mentioned him in multiple songs, but his face has not been seen much in public. Ray has become more visible publicly since surviving prostate cancer in 2018. He celebrated recovery by eating bugs with Kanye and posting an image on Instagram with the caption "No more fear." Ray appeared in his son's music videos for "Follow God" and "Closed on Sunday" a year later.

Kanye's paternal grandparents, James (Pop-Pop) and Fannie (Mom-Mom), met and gave birth to his father in Tucson, Arizona. James served 23 years in the military, which meant that the family was always on the move. His career took the family from Tucson to Salina, Kansas; Delmar, Delaware; Altus, Oklahoma; Roswell, New Mexico; and Seville, Spain. The Wests faced the same discrimination that the Williams family dealt with in Oklahoma. They could not lodge at motels in many cities. James drove miles to find a store that would allow him to purchase water and other essential items for the family.

"Ray sounded *absolutely* white," Donda said of her first encounter with Ray over the telephone. "He lived a different experience than most black kids. He even lived overseas for a while. He never had a black teacher until he went to college. And he never really lived what one might call a black experience."[27] Her comments raise several questions about how blackness is defined and how this might apply to Kanye. First, there is the issue of "speaking white." In 1996 the Oakland, California, school board approved African American Vernacular English (AAVE), better known as Ebonics. Ebonics had grammar and pronunciations that differed from what schools had traditionally recognized as "proper" or "standard" English. Blacks who spoke "proper" or used more complex vocabulary were said to be "talking white." The negative consequence of this mentality was an oppositional culture that viewed using "standard" English as selling out.[28]

"Talking white" is associated with code-switching, which occurs when people from marginalized groups adjust their language, behavior, or appearance to make the dominant group feel more comfortable in professional and social situations. A person with an accent, be it from a Southern state or foreign country, may try to mask it for the sake of fitting in. Although code-switching is not limited to race, it impacts many blacks from a young age. Many black parents and guardians teach their children how to present themselves when in majority-white professional settings. When I taught at the University of Maryland Eastern Shore, the career counselor advised the students to avoid speaking "urban" and cut off their dreadlocks if potential white employers were interviewing them. A similar scenario played out in the first season of HBO's *Insecure* (2016–present). Molly (Yvonne Oriji), the lone black attorney at a prestigious law firm, unsuccessfully attempted to counsel a younger black summer associate at the firm named Rasheeda who failed to play the code-switching game. Rasheeda was eventually fired for being her authentic self at work.

In the 2018 film *The Hate U Give*, the protagonist Starr (Amandla Stenberg) talks of being Starr #2 when at school with her rich white classmates. Starr's childhood black friends from the hood clown her for "talking white" and listening to pop music. Former First Lady Michelle Obama reflects on similar experiences in her memoir, *Becoming*. As a child, growing up on the South Side of Chicago she mastered the art of code-switching. Her cousin ridiculed her when she forgot to stop "talking white" around them. Mrs. Obama compared her experience with that of her husband, Barack, as he vied to become the nation's first black president.

> America would bring to Barack that same question my cousin was unconsciously putting to me that day on the stoop: Are you what you appear to be? Do I trust you or not?[29]

Kanye West has mastered the art of code-switching. Fans on Twitter questioned his cadence when giving his acceptance speech for the Michael Jackson Video Vanguard Award at the 2015 VMAs. Arienne Thompson, in an article for *USA Today*, noted that Kanye speaks differently in certain settings. When he was interviewed on his mother-in-law Kris Jenner's daytime talk show, *Kris*, before a majority-white audience, his voice sounded different.[30] "It wasn't about race; it's about class," said Kanye in an interview with *The JV Show*. "Even when you are invited to certain dinner parties ... are they inviting you to be a part of what you're doing? Or to laugh at your (gold) teeth and ask you a million questions?"[31] As Kanye spoke to students at Howard University during the 2019 homecoming weekend, he talked about blacks having to adopt a language and speech pattern that was not their native tongue to fit in white society. Code-switching subconsciously teaches blacks that their natural being is not good enough. It ghettoizes blackness and equates it with that "ugly" darker doll in Kenneth and Mamie Clark's famous experiment, with whom no black children wanted to play.[32]

What did Donda mean by suggesting that Kanye's father did not live a traditional black experience? Does that imply that individuals who live a cosmopolitan existence apart from the black community are less black? Is some form of struggle and inequality a necessary characteristic of a genuine black experience? One of my students told me she had a harder time fitting in around blacks because she grew up around whites and attended majority-white schools in the suburbs. She found herself code-switching around other blacks to meet their approval. Another student shared a similar experience. Her mother's high-paying job allowed her to attend private schools where she was in the minority. Accordingly, she felt the need to demonstrate her blackness by dressing a certain way or speaking Ebonics around her black peers. This scenario was a dominant subject in the 2006 film *ATL*. Lauren London's character Erin was a rich private-school kid who masqueraded as a sassy girl from the hood named New New.

Kanye compares himself to the late basketball legend Kobe Bryant. The two mavericks paired up a for Nike's hilarious "Kobe System" commercials in 2012. Bryant's blackness was questioned throughout his playing career. As the son of Joe "Jellybean" Bryant, a retired NBA and overseas basketball player, he enjoyed a privileged lifestyle. Bryant became fluent in Italian, Spanish, and English at a young age. After his family moved from Italy to the United States, he attended Lower Merion High School, a majority-white school outside Philadelphia, Pennsylvania. Basketball was the tool he used to prove that he was just as cool as the black kids from less fortunate backgrounds whom he competed against on the court.

Kobe Bryant's draft class in 1996 was headlined by Allen Iverson (A.I.), who appeared to be his polar opposite. Iverson survived poverty in Hampton, Virginia, and four months in prison for his involvement in a bowling alley brawl as a high school junior. Despite his two-year stay at the elite Georgetown University, he spoke with a cadence bereft of code-switching. Iverson was the first professional athlete to normalize wearing cornrows, gaudy platinum jewelry, and multiple tattoos. He became an icon for the hip-hop generation and the quintessential symbol for the anti-establishment.[33] Sway Calloway described him as Tupac (Shakur) in basketball shorts.

When Iverson's less talented Philadelphia 76ers faced the defending world champion Los Angeles Lakers in the 2001 NBA Finals the differences between him and Bryant were highlighted. He was the player for whom most young blacks, who were not Lakers fans, were rooting. Although Iverson was never politically active, his refusal to conform to mainstream standards and respectability politics earned him the respect of black youth. Iverson was the bridge between Michael Jordan's generation of black athletes who were racial accommodationists and today's activist athletes. By contrast, Bryant's attempts to be *perfect* and his refusal to address social issues early in his career cost him support.[34] He was booed by fans when he was named the Most Valuable Player of the 2002 All-Star game in Philadelphia, his adopted hometown. Ten years later when Bryant did not join the masses in their condemnation of George Zimmerman for killing Trayvon Martin, Jim Brown insinuated that Bryant was out of touch because he was not a product of the black experience. Brown added, "If I had to invite people to the [black athlete] summit all over there'd be some athletes I wouldn't call. He'd be one of them."[35]

Did Kanye's father grow up feeling alienated because his upbringing did not mirror that of other blacks? According to Donda, Ray underwent a cultural awakening as a student at the predominantly white University of Delaware. The mild-mannered young man who "spoke white" transformed into one of the most militant figures on campus and was even elected to serve as the Black Student Government president. He also joined a chapter of the Black Panther Party. It is unclear what prompted this radical transformation. Maybe it was the sign of the times. Some blacks were trading in their suits and Western attire for dashikis. They replaced permed hairstyles with natural hairstyles. Was Ray initially caught up in the sprit of the times or had this always been a part of his psyche?

Ray and Donda spent their first date at the Piccadilly Cafeteria in the Greenbriar Mall. A far cry from the five-star restaurants that Kanye and Kim would frequent. Donda tossed three pennies into a fountain and wished that Ray would become her husband someday. Three months later, on January 1, 1973, they were married in Oklahoma City. Their wedding invitations displayed a photograph of them with large Afro hairstyles. The ceremony was held at her family's church, with the reception downstairs in the church's basement. Afterward they went to her parents' home to eat fried chicken, grits, biscuits, and gravy.

The cover art for *The Life of Pablo* (2016) has two images against an orange backdrop and the title written repeatedly in black font. The first is a picture of Kanye's parents and their families at the wedding. The picture displays beautiful black people, attired in their Sunday best, standing in front of a modest church. Beneath their image is Sheniz Halil, a white British model, wearing only sunglasses and a bikini thong. She stands with her backside to the camera. Kanye chose Halil because of her physical resemblance to Kim Kardashian.[36] The album cover art presented an interesting juxtaposition of Kanye's past and present life in 2016. You had the black family and the black church that raised him alongside this model who represented a version of white beauty, admired in the mainstream, that appropriated black women's bodies. The model also represented a prize and the forbidden fruit that the average black man was not supposed to taste.

After their marriage, the Wests purchased a small townhouse and later a four-bedroom, two-story home in Atlanta. Ray taught photography and media production at Clark College; Donda taught English and speech at Morris Brown College. After a year of marriage, she moved to Alabama to complete her doctorate at Auburn University. Ray moved to Alabama a year later to teach medical illustration at the Tuskegee Institute. He used the opportunity to complete his master's degree in audiovisual studies and media. During their time in Auburn, the Wests separated twice. After Ray finished school and Donda reached the dissertation phase of her graduate program, they moved back to Atlanta.

Kanye blemished his father's reputation during his rally in Charleston, South Carolina, to get his name added to the ballot for the 2020 presidential election. He broke down in tears as he told the crowd Ray wanted to abort him upon learning that Donda was pregnant. Kanye credits his mother with refusing to go through with the medical procedure. He was born in Douglasville, Georgia, on June 8, 1977, after many grueling hours of natural childbirth, forcing his mother to have a C-section.[37] Kanye is an African name that means "the only one." Initially, Ray was mainly responsible for Kanye because Donda was working and attending school. Kanye was only 11 months old when his parents separated and two years old when they divorced.

Around the time that Donda gained custody of Kanye, she received faculty job offers from Roosevelt University and Chicago State University. She accepted a position at Chicago State and relocated when Kanye was three.[38] For kindergarten, she enrolled him into Vanderpoel Magnet School, which was known for the arts. Donda intentionally chose not to send him to a school in nearby Lincoln Park because she did not want Kanye being the only student of color in the school. It was vital for her to instill a sense of black culture and history in Kanye from a young age. She always wore natural hairstyles. They traveled to Washington, D.C., to trace the route of the 1963 March on Washington. She took him to her home in Oklahoma City at least twice a year. When her parents celebrated their 65th wedding anniversary, everyone wore African attire.[39]

Although Donda raised Kanye for much of his formative years, Ray maintained a presence in his life. Kanye spent every spring break and summer vacation with his dad.[40] Kanye reflected on these times in his 2007 song "Champion." As I think about those summers that he spent with his dad, it conjures up images of young Tre Styles and his dad, Furious, giving him lessons on manhood and the black experience in *Boyz n the Hood* (1991). Given Ray's unique upbringing, those conversations undoubtedly had a profound influence on molding the person that Kanye would become. Unlike many of his hip-hop peers, Kanye did not have to look to the hustlers, thugs, ball players, and rappers to emulate a cartoonish model of black masculinity.

Ray was raised in the church, and he conveyed Christian values to his son. Kanye told the 40,000 attendees at Lakewood Church in Houston, Texas, that his dad had him in church three times a week. He would miss basketball practice and playing video games on weeknights to attend the weekly Bible study. Donda was not as religious as Ray, but she too was raised in the church. "As a kid, I went to church every Sunday except for when I had chickenpox," she said.[41] Consequently, she raised Kanye in the church. They attended Christ Universal Temple in Chicago every Sunday morning. The church, founded by the late Reverend Johnnie Colemon in 1956, grew from 35 members to a megachurch with more than 20,000 members. The Reverend Colemon, a black woman from Mississippi, has been called the "First Lady of the New Thought Christian community."[42] Metaphysical New Thought originated in the United States during the 19th century. According to historian Carol V.R. George, this marginal homegrown alternative to traditional religious thinking and piety would eventually influence the rise and proliferation of the self-help movement and the distancing of popular American spirituality from creedal religion.[43]

New Thought can be broadly characterized by its recommended psychologized biblical principles and prescriptions for cultivating mental gatekeeping habits to stave off negative thought-forces' power to enthrall in vicious circles. Self-affirmation intrepidly overcoming self-loathing and its attraction of negative mental, spiritual, and relational reinforcements is the Creator's plan for happiness, health, and prosperity. Simply stated, if you can believe it you can achieve it. The Rev. Dr. Norman Vincent Peale, pastor of Marble Collegiate Church in New York City, famously epitomized New Thought as a mainstream religious option in his best-seller, *The Power of Positive Thinking* (1952).[44] The Reverend Colemon was beloved for her ability to simplify religion and make it relatable. This orientation is what attracted Donda to her congregation. "I liked the church because the minister, Johnnie Colemon, preached prosperity.... I wanted Kanye to be steeped in that kind of exposure to God."[45]

The gospel music of the black church was a significant part of Kanye's childhood soundtrack. His maternal aunt Shirlie was a choir director at multiple churches. It should not have come as a surprise that Kanye's first Grammy Award for Best Rap Song came for "Jesus Walks." Early in his career, Kanye tried to practice what he preached. He was the opening act for Usher's The Truth Tour in 2004. He arrived two hours late and missed his entire set during one of the tour stops. Rather than travel on the tour bus, Kanye stayed behind to perform at a youth revival in which his father was participating. Three hundred youth at the revival joined the church that night. Kanye ended up taking a taxi to the concert, which was 200 miles away, and was able to perform as part of Usher's set.

That Ain't No Takashi Murakami Bear

Donda spent a year teaching English as part of an exchange program at Nanjing University in the People's Republic of China. She took Kanye with her. He was one of only three children who traveled on the trip. The other children were younger boys from France and Mexico, respectively. Diego, a Mexican child, served as the Wests' translator for the first few months. Kanye, who was 10 years old, was placed in the first grade due to his inability to speak Mandarin. He was the only foreign-born child in his class and the lone black student in the school. His Chinese classmates would rub his skin to see if the black would come off and yell out "breakdance, breakdance" when he came around. "He was no doubt a novelty and the first black kid they'd seen in person," said Donda.[46] Kanye's interactions with his classmates are reminiscent of the opening pages of Frantz Fanon's *Black Skin, White Mask*. Fanon tells a story about a white girl on a train whose reaction to seeing a black passenger is, "Look mama, a negro." At that moment, the black passenger remembers his "otherness."[47]

Donda disliked the children viewing Kanye through their narrow lens of American popular culture. Breakdancing movies about black and Latinx youth in New York City were very popular in the 1980s. But it did not bother Kanye, perhaps because he was too young to understand. Even now, he says the kids were not racist; rather, they behaved that way because his presence was their first encounter with blackness. The kids may have viewed him as the exotic "other," but their intent was not malicious and mean-spirited. They did not see him as inferior—something to be demeaned or exploited—thus, Kanye did not believe that his race impeded him overseas. His time in China made Kanye see himself as more than a black male from Chicago. He was a global citizen who happened to be a very proud African American.

Kanye West embodies what Duke University professor Mark Anthony Neal described as a hip-hop cosmopolitan. Kasper Rørsted, CEO of Adidas, told Bloomberg TV, "Kanye is not an American brand; Kanye is a global brand, and Yeezy is a global brand."[48] Kanye's appreciation for foreign cultures is evident in his music, fashion, and artwork.[49] The French electronic music duo Daft Punk produced the chorus to his international hit "Stronger," which was based upon German philosopher Friedrich Nietzsche's assertion that what does not kill us makes us stronger. "Stronger's" music video paid homage to the Japanese animated film *Akira* (1988). After the fallout from the Taylor Swift incident, Kanye self-exiled himself in Japan and Rome for nearly a year. While in Rome, he interned with the Italian luxury fashion house Fendi.

Takashi Murakami, a Japanese contemporary artist from Tokyo, designed the cover artwork for two of Kanye West's albums: *Graduation* (2007) and *Kids See Ghosts* (2018). Murakami will direct a new CGI animated series, *Kids See Ghosts*, with Kanye and Kid Cudi voicing the lead characters. Belgian artist Peter De Potter designed the cover artwork for *The Life of Pablo*. Vanessa Beecroft, an Italian contemporary performance artist, has designed and assisted Kanye on numerous projects, including his Yeezy season fashion shows, the short film "Runaway," the 2013 Yeezus Tour, and his 2019 Christian themed operas *Nebuchadnezzar* and *Mary*.[50] Kanye's wardrobe for The Yeezus Tour consisted of a crystal-embroidered veil designed by French luxury fashion house Maison Margiela. The *Yeezus* album was heavily influenced by European electronic music. Jamaican dancehall stars Beenie Man, Capleton, Popcaan, and Assassin also inspired the sound of *Yeezus*. Kanye and Kim wed at Forte di Belvedere in Florence, Italy, and had their oldest daughter, North, baptized at the Cathedral of St. James in Jerusalem.

The Roses

Kanye West was seven years old when he performed a cover of Stevie Wonder's "I Just Called to Say I Love You" at a local talent show. He wore his hair in beaded braids and put on Wonder's trademark dark sunshades to get in character. Upon returning to Chicago from his year abroad, he and three friends formed a group called the Quatro Posse. The fifth-grade dance crew won their school's talent show with a rousing performance of Chicago Steppin.[51] Three years later Kanye penned his first rap, "Green Eggs and

Ham." He saved $500 to purchase his first keyboard and later added turntables, mixers, and a drum machine to his collection. By the time he turned 15, he abandoned spending summers in Atlanta with his dad to remain in Chicago to focus on his music.

Donda helped to nurture Kanye's musical aspirations by introducing him to Ernest Dion Wilson, an older record producer and house music DJ in Chicago who went by the moniker No I.D.[52] Donda worked with No I.D.'s mother at Chicago State. He began mentoring Kanye and teaching him how to make beats. Kanye sold his first professional beat for $8,800 to a local rapper named Grav, who included eight songs he produced on his debut album, *Down to Earth* (1996). Although Kanye was a better producer, his ultimate goal was to rap.[53] He formed a group called The Go Getters with Really Doe (Warren Trotter) and GLC (Leonard Harris), two Chicago teens.[54] The trio organized a boycott to have people picket the local radio station 107.5 WGCI-FM until they played their song "Oh Oh." The song was a modest local hit.

Donda did not foresee her son's love for music interfering with his college education when she introduced him to No I.D. Kanye attended Chicago's American Academy of Art on a scholarship before transferring to Chicago State. However, his stint at his mother's university was short-lived. He dropped out to pursue a music career full-time after receiving $5,000 to produce a track on Jermaine Dupri's album *Jermaine Dupri Presents Life in 1472: The Original Soundtrack* (1998).[55] Quitting college was a crushing blow to his mother. "I had the black, middle-class ethic that said you must go to school, do very well, and get at least one degree and probably more," she said.[56] Donda allowed him to live at home for a year before he found his own apartment. Kanye took odd jobs as a busboy at a Bob Evans restaurant, which lasted one day, and various telemarketing positions to supplement his income.

He flew out to New York City with No I.D. for a meeting with Michael Mauldin to discuss signing a production deal with Columbia Records. In typical Kanye fashion, he was unable to hold his tongue during the meeting. He boasted that he would become a better producer than Jermaine Dupri, not realizing that Dupri, the CEO of So So Def Recordings, was Mauldin's son. Kanye pulled up to the meeting in a limousine and departed in a taxi without a production deal. He returned to Chicago and buried himself in the studio. He did not hang out, shower, or cut his hair. Kanye began producing beats that he would send to bigger-name producers who received the credit for his work. Frustrated with a lack of progress, he moved to Newark, New Jersey, to be closer to New York City. Kanye details his struggles to get a deal and Donda driving him to IKEA to find furniture for his new apartment on his 2004 song "Last Call." The risky move paid off when

Gee Roberson and Kyambo "Hip-Hop" Joshua, the heads of artists and rep-ertoire (A&R) at Roc-A-Fella Records, signed Kanye to their production and management company. They used his beats for Beanie Sigel's debut single "The Truth" (2000) and Jay-Z's "This Can't Be Life" (2000). Kanye was also given the opportunity to produce five tracks for Jay-Z's *The Blueprint*.

Although *The Blueprint* made Kanye one of hip-hop's most sought-out producers, he still desired to be a rapper. He was invited to perform his early music on tours with Talib Kweli and Dead Prez, a rap duo from New York known for their militant, pro-black music. Kanye began visiting record labels in search of a recording deal. He went into the offices of major record label executives such as Antonio "L.A." Reid, jumped on top of their tables, and rapped unreleased songs from his demo tape. One of the songs he performed was "Jesus Walks." Reid and the other executives were unimpressed. Some executives even laughed at him once he left their offices. Kanye was undeterred by their rejection. He befriended Joe "3H" Weinberger, a young white A&R representative at Capitol Records. 3H was the only person at a label fighting hard to sign Kanye. After the potential deal with Capitol fell through, Damon "Dame" Dash, the co-founder of Roc-A-Fella Records, signed him. Dash admitted that if Kanye's raps were bad, he would at least have the license to use his beats for the label's other artists.[57] With Dash's blessing Kanye began working on his debut album, aptly titled *The College Dropout*.

On October 23, 2002, Donda received a devastating phone call at five in the morning. Kanye had fallen asleep while driving his rented Lexus on his way from the studio to his residence at the W Hotel. He crashed head-on into another vehicle. His jaw was shattered in three places and wired shut for six weeks. Doctors said he could have died if he had been hit in the nose. The other driver suffered two broken legs. The accident led Kanye to renew his faith in God. He abandoned his attempts to be a gangsta rapper and began writing more socially conscious lyrics. The accident was also the impetus for "Through the Wire," his first single to receive national airplay on the radio. He rapped the entire song with his jaw still wired shut, causing him to slur his speech.

Kanye continued to produce hits for other artists as he finished making *The College Dropout*. There was Ludacris's "Stand Up," and Alicia Keys's riveting R&B ballad "You Don't Know My Name," which reached number one and three on the *Billboard* Hot 100, respectively. Kanye executive produced Common's most successful album, *Be* (2005), before dropping his own sophomore album, *Late Registration*. In the spring of 2018, Kanye served as the executive producer for five new albums released over five consecutive weekends: his eighth solo project, *Ye*; Pusha T's *Daytona*; Nas's

Nasir; Teyana Taylor's *K.T.S.E.*; and *Kids See Ghosts*, a collaborative album he recorded with Kid Cudi.

Donda played an integral role in the early portion of his rap career, resigning from her position at Chicago State to become his full-time manager. Kanye brought her on stage at the 2005 Grammy Awards ceremony to perform with a choir he used for "Jesus Walks." During his appearance on *The Oprah Winfrey Show* Kanye world premiered "Hey Mama," a song written in the year 2000 that ended up on *Late Registration*. He finished the performance by bringing his parents and Winfrey on stage and giving each a big hug. *The College Dropout* concluded with "Family Business," an ode to his relatives. Family has been a significant theme in almost every Kanye West album. The underlying theme of *The Life of Pablo* was his inner struggle to balance marriage and fatherhood with the debauchery of being the world's biggest pop star. "Roses," a remake of Bill Withers's "Rosie" (1977) featured on *Late Registration,* was based upon his family's ordeal when his maternal grandmother, Lucille, was deathly ill in 2004. She had been hospitalized several times since undergoing 12 hours of surgery in 1986. Kanye and his family members flew to Oklahoma to be at her side. "From California to New York, Texas to Illinois, Maryland to Delaware, Alabama to Arizona, Michigan to New Jersey, the flowers came. And we formed one big bouquet," said Donda.[58] Kanye, his mom, granddad, cousins, and Aunts Shirlie, Beverly, Klaye, and Jean—the Auntie team—became Lucille's living bouquet of get-well roses.

The roses would be called upon again to boost Kanye's spirits on November 10, 2007, the day his mother transitioned to her eternal reward. Donda underwent elective liposuction and a mammoplasty procedure. The surgery was performed by Dr. Jan Adams, a celebrity doctor who hosted a plastic surgery show on the Discovery Health Channel and was a repeat guest on *The Oprah Winfrey Show*. At the time of the surgery, Adams's license was in danger of being suspended due to multiple alcohol-related arrests and malpractice accusations. Donda left the clinic after the five-and-a-half-hour surgery heavily bandaged. Dr. Adams prescribed her Vicodin to ease the pain. She chose to return home to be cared for by a nurse and two caregivers rather than go to another facility for post-operative care. The next morning, Donda experienced a sore throat and tightening in her chest. Early that evening, she collapsed to the floor. Dr. Donda West was pronounced dead at age 58 when she reached the hospital emergency room.[59]

Kanye's mother was his best friend. "I have family, but I was with my mother 80 percent of the time," he told *The New York Times*.[60] Kanye blamed himself for her death and suffered depression. Music became his coping mechanism and his bouquet of roses. Three days before Thanksgiving in

2008, he released *808s & Heartbreak*. The album at times felt like one long sorrowful lament on the loss of his mother. "Goodbye, my friend, I won't ever love again," Kanye sang accompanied by an Auto-Tune vocal processor.[61] At this same time, Kanye's life began spiraling out of control and his behavior started becoming more erratic. His engagement to girlfriend Alexis Phifer was called off. The following year he stormed the stage at the MTV Video Music Awards ceremony, drunk off Hennessy, to interrupt Taylor Swift's acceptance speech. Four years later Kanye celebrated the birth of his first child, North, with girlfriend Kim Kardashian. A year later, the couple married in Florence, Italy. The next chapter in the Kanye West saga had begun, and it was vastly different from anything in his past.

KUWTK

Dr. Donda West would have celebrated her 71st birthday on July 12, 2020. Kanye honored the occasion with the world premiere of "Donda," a new song and music video featuring her reciting lyrics from KRS-One's 1993 protest anthem "Sound of Da Police" over gospel music. The next week Kanye announced that his 10th studio would be titled *Donda: With Child*. As Kanye was promoting this forthcoming album, which failed to release, he announced his candidacy for the 2020 U.S. presidential election. A day after his first campaign rally, in which he told the audience that his father wanted to abort him, Kanye went on a reckless Twitter rant disparaging his wife and her family. He accused Kim of cheating on him and attempting to have him hospitalized for mental issues. He called his mother-in-law "Kris Jong-un," a reference to the North Korean dictator, Kim Jong-un. Kanye also compared himself to the protagonist in the film *Get Out,* who discovers that he has been mentally enslaved in the sunken place by his white girlfriend's family. Kanye's tweets were surprising to most people outside of his inner circle who assumed that he was content within his new family unit.

On Thanksgiving 2019, the music video for "Closed on Sunday," the second single on *Jesus Is King,* world premiered. In the opening scene Kanye and Kim are sleeping on a rock formation near his Wyoming ranch with their four kids: North (six), Saint (four), Chicago (one), and Psalm (six months). A fleet of all-terrain vehicles arrives on the ranch carrying Kim's mother, her sister Kourtney, and Kourtney's children. The video ends with a group photo of Kanye's dad, members of his biological family, his Sunday Service Choir, and his wife's relatives. "Closed on Sunday" captured the duality of Kanye's life since becoming a member of the Kardashian-Jenner family in 2014. Many Generation Zers only know the Kardashians as Kanye's family unit. The Kardashians, a blended family that includes the

Jenners, are an American-made brand that celebrates the tenets of mainstream culture and capitalism that have not always been welcoming to people who resemble Kanye's biological relatives.

The Kardashians' celebrity results from an innovative matriarch, a steamy sex tape, and a successful cable network reality television series. Kris Jenner (born Kristen Houghton), known to her fans as "momager" in chief for overseeing her daughters' careers, was not born with a silver spoon in her mouth. The San Diego, California, native worked as an American Airlines flight attendant with only a high school diploma in 1976. She married Robert Kardashian, an Armenian-American lawyer and successful entrepreneur with multiple businesses, in 1978. O.J. Simpson, Kardashian's college buddy from the University of Southern California, was the best man at their wedding. In 1995 Kardashian joined the notorious "Dream Team" that defended Simpson in his criminal trial for the murder of his estranged wife and her male friend.[62] Kardashian read Simpson's suicide letter on live television after the police announced that he was a fugitive. Kardashian escorted Simpson back home to celebrate once he was acquitted.

Kris and Robert Kardashian had four children: Kourtney, Kim, Khloe, and Robert, Jr. The couple divorced in 1991. Kris married Bruce Jenner, the 1976 Olympic gold medalist in the decathlon, later that same year.[63] She and Bruce gave birth to two daughters, Kendall and Kylie.[64] After Kim's sex tape with R&B star Ray J (William Ray Norwood, Jr.) made her a household name, the family parlayed that buzz into a new reality show on the E! cable network. *Keeping Up with the Kardashians (KUWTK*, 2007–2021) presented the family as "a modern Brady Bunch with a twist."[65] The series premiere revolved around Kim's upcoming appearance on *The Tyra Banks Show* (2005–2010) to give her first televised interview since her sex tape. Meanwhile, the family was planning a party to celebrate Kris and Bruce's 16th wedding anniversary. During the episode Kris and daughter Kourtney get drunk from tasting the alcohol to be served at the party. Kim's younger sisters Kendall and Kylie, both under 13 at the time, were busy making martinis for their party guests and playing on a stripper pole purchased as an anniversary gift.

Critiques of the Kardashian clan range from disgust with their self-absorbed behavior to adoration of their unconventional version of the American Dream.[66] The Kardashians do not come from old money. If they were characters in F. Scott Fitzgerald's timeless classic *The Great Gatsby* (1925), they would be residents in West Egg.[67] They are the *nouveau riche.* Their wealth began with Robert Kardashian, who left the family a $100 million estate when he died from esophageal cancer in 2003. Kris's second marriage to Bruce Jenner (now transgender celebrity Caitlyn Jenner) increased the family's net worth. *KUWTK* opened the doors to numerous business ventures that have turned the family into an empire. According to *Forbes*, Kim's net worth reached $1 billion in 2021. Her fortune comes from various ventures including her KKW beauty line and Skims, her reality series, endorsements, and investments. She has over 68 million Twitter followers and over 200 million Instagram followers. Her siblings have done quite well for themselves too. Kendall Jenner was the world's highest-paid model in 2017 and 2018. Kylie Jenner was listed as the youngest self-made billionaire in American history.[68]

Kanye's life with Kim was extravagant enough to make Robin Leach blush.[69] He rented out Oracle Park, home of the San Francisco Giants, for $250,000 to propose. He paid a 50-piece orchestra $5,000 per hour, $20,000 for a fireworks display, and $20,000 for private jets to transport each of Kim's family members for the occasion. Beyoncé's famous phrase "put a ring on it" should have been playing from the ballpark's sound system as he placed an $8 million 15-carat ring on her finger. Earlier, he spent $600,000 on Kim's maternity wardrobe when she became pregnant with their first child, North. Over the course of her pregnancy Kim spent $25,000 a week on her prenatal massages, mani-pedis, and yoga.[70] Her delivery took place in a private wing of Cedars-Sinai Medical Center that cost $4,000 a day, with catered meals, a room full of white flowers, a photographer for $1,000 a day, and a separate wing for Kanye to rest. When North was born, she had $25,000 in baby clothes and a $40,000 baby room at Kris's estate. Kanye hired four security guards—former Israeli army agents for $1 million a year—to protect Kim and their newborn child.

When the Kardashians took a family vacation on the Greek island of Mykonos, they resided in an $80,000-a-week villa and chartered a $200,000-a-week yacht. Lauren Greenfield's documentary film *Generation Wealth* (2018) asks the question, "How rich is too rich?" Greenfield blames the "Kardashian effect" for turning the American Dream into a nightmare based on self-indulgence, celebrity, and narcissism. The Kardashians have been called out of touch with reality due to their extravagant lifestyle. Kim's daily shopping sprees can pay for a student's four-year college education. One example would be her $100,000 shopping spree at Hermès in Paris. She owns more than 50 Hermès Birkin bags, which sell for $10,000 a bag. And then there is the money she spends on her physical appearance. Besides spending over one million dollars on plastic surgery, Kim has her infamous $11,000 platelet-rich fibrin matrix "vampire facelifts." Blood is drawn from her arm and spun in a centrifuge to separate the platelets, which are then injected back under her facial skin to remove wrinkles.

The 16th season premiere of *KUWTK* focused on Kanye taking Kim and North to his childhood home in Chicago to see where he grew up. A poignant moment occurred when they met with Rhymefest (Che Smith),

Kanye's estranged best friend. Rhymefest expressed concern that his longtime buddy had lost his way. "Kanye is from a village, and the village was feeling like our dear brother turn his back on the village," he told Kim. Rhymefest's assessment of his "dear brother" harkened back to Snoop's suggestion that Kanye had forgotten who he was and from where he came. Was this state of amnesia caused by celebrity, wealth, newfound friends, or the Kardashian effect?

This incident with Rhymefest is reminiscent of a scene from the ESPN docuseries *O.J.: Made in America*. Simpson's childhood buddy Joe Bell reflects on a time when they were hanging out at Robert Kardashian's home in the exclusive Brentwood neighborhood of Los Angeles. Bell told Simpson that the only reason those white people cared about him was because of his celebrity. However, the oblivious Simpson eagerly and fully embraced this new environment and all the trappings that came along with it. Kanye West's life had evolved tremendously from those summer vacations with his grandparents in Oklahoma and his dad in Atlanta to $300,000 trips to Greek Islands with the Kardashians. Could Mr. West still be the angry black man so many people fell in love with on *The College Dropout* and *Late Registration* condemning racism all the time if he was living in this luxurious bubble of white privilege?

FIVE

"Kardashian-West"

"They will accept your money, Dre, but they will never accept your black ass. I don't give a damn how many white women you marry." *Lucious Lyon*[1]

Kanye West and Kim Kardashian tied the knot at the Forte di Belvedere in Florence, Italy, on May 24, 2014. The elegant couple graced the cover of *Vogue* magazine a month before the wedding with the caption "#WORLDSMOSTTALKEDABOUTCOUPLE." The Annie Leibovitz cover shot displayed Kanye with his arms wrapped tenderly around his betrothed's waist. Kim looked stunning in a gray strapless Lanvin bridal gown, designed by Alber Elbaz's French fashion house. Her $8-million, 15-carat engagement ring perfectly complemented her gown. Why was this cover the most scrutinized and disfavored in the magazine's 120-plus year history?

When Kanye received the Visionary Award at the Black Entertainment Television (BET) Honors ceremony in January 2015, he addressed a room full of black luminaries, including former U.S. Attorney General Eric Holder. He spoke of the prejudice that he and Kim experienced as an interracial couple.

This chapter explores the racial politics behind Kanye's marriage to Kim Kardashian by analyzing their relationship within the historical context of black celebrities who have dated and married outside of their race. Many of these figures dealt with racism in the mainstream. It was also hard for them to find support within the black community. They were accused of dating and marrying non-black partners to facilitate assimilation. Consequently, their children often had the challenge of choosing to identify more with one race or the other. Will this be an unfair burden placed upon Kanye's eldest daughter North, already a star at eight years old, and her younger siblings?

Bound (Uh-Huh, Honey)

Kim and Kanye, or Kimye as they were affectionately nicknamed, began dating in April of 2012. They met years earlier on the set of a music video for Brandy's (Brandy Norwood) 2004 single "Talk About Our Love," which featured Kanye. At the time Kim was dating Brandy's younger brother, Ray J (William Ray Norwood, Jr.); however, she was far from being a celebrity. Her minor claim to fame came from being the daughter of O.J. Simpson's defense attorney and the stylist of socialite Paris Hilton.[2] Kanye was smitten with Kim from the moment they met, but their romance would have to wait for almost a decade. Kanye's first serious love was Alexis Phifer, a black fashion designer he began dating sporadically in 2002 and was engaged to for a brief period. There is a picture of the couple with Kim at a party in 2007, a year after Kanye proposed to Phifer. Kanye's mother was especially fond of Phifer; however, the engagement ended while Kanye was mourning her sudden passing. Their break-up was well documented on *808s & Heartbreak*'s tracks "Heartless," "Robocop," and "Welcome to Heartbreak."

Kanye discovered his next love, Amber Rose (Amber Levonchuck), while watching the music video for Ludacris's and Chris Brown's "What Them Girls Like." Rose, a former stripper from Philadelphia of Irish, Italian, Scottish, and Cape Verdean descent, was one of the video's lead models. Rose is a fair-skinned woman known for her curvaceous figure and dyed blonde buzz-cut hairstyle. She was cast in an unreleased music video for "Robocop." In April 2009, she appeared nude with her face down in Kanye's lap for a Louis Vuitton ad. Rose accompanied Kanye to the VMAs when he infamously snatched the mic from Taylor Swift. After their relationship ended, Kanye took subliminal shots at Rose on his songs "Blame Game" and "Hell of a Life" and his video for "Famous." Rose told *Star* magazine that Kim Kardashian was the "homewrecker" responsible for the relationship's demise, accusing her of texting Kanye sexually suggestive pictures while they were dating. Kanye's first verse to his 2010 song "Lost in the World" was derived from a love letter he had written to Kim.

By the time Kanye and Kim became a public item, they were both global icons. Kanye already had seven number-one albums, multiple awards, and signature sneakers with Nike and Louis Vuitton. Kim had five fragrances, the highest-rated American reality television series, and a popular spin-off. Her previous marriage to NBA player Kris Humphries was a tabloid sensation. Their 2011 wedding was covered in a two-part prime-time television special on *E!* Kim filed for divorce after 72 days of marriage, citing irreconcilable differences. Kanye finally had his opening. After her embarrassing divorce, which affirmed the media's belief that the wedding was little more than a publicity stunt, Kim was in a dark place. Kanye invited her to attend his upcoming fashion show in Paris to lift her spirits and secure the first date.[3]

Kimye was a godsend for social media sites and paparazzi thirsty for headlines. Simultaneously, they have been a lightning rod for controversy since the 2013 world premiere of the "Bound 2" music video on *The Ellen DeGeneres Show* (2003–2022). In the video a topless Kim straddles Kanye on a motorcycle as he rides through Utah's Monument Valley. The media had a field day panning "Bound 2." "Geez, haven't Utah's red rocks suffered enough?" said a reporter for *The Salt Lake Tribune*.[4] As of July 17, 2021, the video had been viewed over 85 million times and had 706,000 likes and 491,000 dislikes. While participating in the 2014 Cannes Lions International Festival of Creativity panel Kanye suggested that the backlash stemmed from something more profound than its tacky visual presentation meant to satirize "white trash" T-shirts.

> You have to be able to take the lashes of people not understanding. It took two years of people not understanding an interracial relationship like that…. I always say that if *Vogue* had come out before the "Bound" video, then everyone would have been like, "Oh, it's OK," and that's the endorsement.[5]

King Kong Ain't Got Shit on Me!

Vogue, the Conde Nast monthly publication founded in 1892 and now with 23 international editions, is the gold standard for high-end women's fashion and lifestyle. Kanye's suggestion that it took the endorsement of *Vogue*'s editor-in-chief Anna Wintour, a 71-year-old white English woman, to make his romance with Kim Kardashian acceptable, says a lot about interracial relationships in America. Wintour's decision to place them on the cover of an upper-crust periodical with mostly white subscribers was admittedly one of the hardest in her career and met with incredible vitriol.[6]

The Kimye cover had a lot of people feeling some type of way. Days after the announcement for the special issue, most of the 700 comments posted online were negative. A reader on *The Guardian*'s website called it "disgusting" and the "epitome of VULGARITY." Sarah Michelle Gellar, best known for her role in the teen series *Buffy the Vampire Slayer* (1997–2003), tweeted: "Well…. I guess I'm canceling my *Vogue* subscription. Who is with me???"[7] Ben Henry, a writer for *Buzzfeed,* explained the backlash as a class issue. The Kardashian-West unit was not taken seriously by the fashion elite. Kanye was viewed as rapper and a designer of urban streetwear. Kim was a reality star with a sex tape. In a 2019 tweet, she admitted to crying when she returned home from her first Met Gala with Kanye because she felt insecure and unwelcome at the $30,000-per-ticket annual fundraiser for the Metropolitan Museum of Art's Costume Institute in New York City. Although class may have been one variable in the *Vogue* controversy, race was the 6,000-pound elephant in the room. Kim told NBC *Late Night* host Seth Meyers that it was an honor to be the first interracial couple on the cover. The photo makes a stunning statement given the magazine's century-long existence; however, *Vogue* has never been an exemplar of progress. Liberals criticized the magazine for having white models in blackface as recently as its March 2014 issue. It took *Vogue* 125 years to have a black photographer shoot its cover art.[8] Supermodel Beverly Johnson became the first black woman featured on the cover in August 1974. Several black women have been cover models over the past 40 years. Only two black men share that distinction: LeBron James and Kanye West. James, then a 23-year-old emerging superstar on the Cleveland Cavaliers basketball team, was placed on the cover with Brazilian supermodel Gisele Bündchen, wife of NFL quarterback Tom Brady, in April 2008. What should have been a celebratory occasion was ruined by an offensive image rooted in racist tropes and pejoratives.

James dribbled a basketball in his right hand and had his left hand wrapped around Bündchen's waist. His mouth hung wide open in a menacing manner. The Annie Leibovitz cover was inspired by a 1917 U.S. Army recruiting poster during World War I. The poster depicted a giant black ape, with its mouth open in an exaggerated terrifying way, holding a club in his right hand and a white damsel in distress in his left arm. The poster's caption read, "Destroy this mad brute. Enlist. U.S. Army." The wild beast symbolized the evil German army blamed for the war. With her dress falling off to show her breasts, the defenseless blond white woman represented American innocence ravaged by war and a vile enemy.

The *Vogue* cover also resembled a promotional poster for the 1976 remake of *King Kong*, the famous tale of the exotic beast that kidnaps a white woman and is shot down while climbing the Empire State Building in New York. *Vanity Fair* described *King Kong* as an anti-colonial allegory about "a king and free soul in his own world, taken in shackles across the ocean, and forced to put on a show for the amusement of debauched white people."[9] The ape is among the oldest symbols used to demean people of African descent. When NBA Hall-of-Famer Patrick Ewing was a student-athlete at Georgetown University in the 1980s, opposing white fans at Villanova University and other rival schools would waive banana peels at him. Kanye, in his 2013 single "Black Skinhead," references *King Kong* to describe his relationship with Kim.

King Kong was initially released in theaters in 1933 during a lynching epidemic throughout the South. According to the Tuskegee Institute, 4,730 people, mostly black, were lynched from 1882 to 1951. Victims were tortured, burned alive, dragged behind vehicles, dismembered, and hung from trees with rope. Through the research of Ida B. Wells, a black investigative reporter and co-founder of the National Association for the Advancement of Colored People (NAACP), it was discovered that many of these victims were black men falsely accused of raping white women.[10] A myth has persisted since slavery that black men have this insatiable fetish for white female skin.[11] In Hollywood's first full-length motion picture, D.W. Griffith's *The Birth of a Nation* (1915), the Ku Klux Klan (KKK) assembles after a white woman jumps from a cliff to her death to avoid being the prey of a ravenous black rapist. In 1931, nine black males, ages 13–20, in Scottsboro, Alabama, were falsely accused of raping two white women on a train. Their harsh punishment foreshadowed a similar predicament facing the Central Park Five 60 years later.

Sexual intimacy with white women was the only thing that could defeat Jack Johnson, professional boxing's first black heavyweight champion. Johnson's success in knocking out countless white men in the ring was an affront to white supremacists. It was well known that Johnson openly dated and engaged in interstate travel with white prostitutes. The U.S. Congress passed the Mann Act, also known as the White-Slave Traffic Act, in 1910 to ban the transport of white women across state lines for sex. Johnson was found guilty of violating the new law and became an international fugitive to avoid arrest.[12] The backlash from the 2014 *Vogue* cover appears quite different when placing these past events in context. To be sure, social class was an issue, and some persons disliked the couple's self-absorbed antics. But it is hard to ignore this country's historical disdain of interracial relationships, especially those involving black men and white women. Kanye alludes to this in his 2010 song "Hell of a Life," when he mentions a white porn star's value dropping if she has sex on camera with "a black guy."

You Getting Blackmailed for That White Girl

Kanye West's *My Beautiful Dark Twisted Fantasy* celebrated its 10th anniversary on November 20, 2020. Most people forget the album's controversial cover. George Condo drew a cartoon of a naked black man, supposedly Kanye, being straddled by a nude, armless white woman with wings and a tail. She was supposed to represent the phoenix from Greek folklore. When the album was released the image was pixelated. Interracial romance is one of America's oldest taboos. After the Civil War, all but nine of the 50 states enacted anti-miscegenation laws banning the races from mixing. A

1958 Gallup poll reported that 94 percent of whites disapproved of interracial marriage. Mildred and Richard Loving became victims of this prejudice on July 11, 1958, when a county sheriff entered their home, forced them out of their bed, and placed them under arrest. Mildred Loving, a woman of black and Cherokee Indian descent, and Richard Loving, a white man, were found guilty of violating Virginia's Racial Integrity Act of 1924. They were given an ultimatum: spend a year in prison or leave Virginia for 25 years. The Lovings chose to relocate to Washington, D.C., where interracial marriage was legal.

Five years later, they returned to Virginia and were arrested for traveling together. After their release, Mrs. Loving wrote a letter to U.S. Attorney General Robert Kennedy asking for his assistance. Kennedy referred her to the American Civil Liberties Union (ACLU), who assigned the case to two young white lawyers. After multiple defeats at the state level, their lawyers appealed the case to the U.S. Supreme Court, arguing that Virginia's law violated the Equal Protection Clause of the 14th Amendment. On June 12, 1967, the court ruled unanimously in favor of the Lovings, officially legalizing interracial marriage nationwide.[13] Six months after the court's decision, Hollywood released the groundbreaking film *Guess Who's Coming to Dinner.* Sidney Poitier played a widowed, 37-year-old assistant director for tropical medicine with the World Health Organization engaged to a 23-year-old white woman he met 10 days earlier.[14] The young, idealistic couple visits the future bride's "liberal" parents to receive their blessing. Poitier's character in the film was flawless and completely passive in the presence of his fiancée's parents. He refrained from all forms of sensual contact with his fiancée. Hollywood still was not ready to show the public a genuine relationship between a black man and a white woman. Southern states refused to carry the film in their theaters.

Two years later the Western film *100 Rifles*, starring Jim Brown and Raquel Welch, shattered taboos. Brown, a recently retired black football player with the Cleveland Browns, had sex with Welch, his white co-star, in the film. A promotional poster for the film displayed Welch's arms wrapped around his robust, bare chest. The film's producers said the film was shot in Spain to save money. However, it was very unlikely that such a film could be made in America in 1969. Jim Brown was among a bevy of macho black male actors who took Hollywood by storm during the blaxploitation cinema era from 1971 to 1976. Many of these low-budget films made by white directors and screenwriters exploited negative aspects of the black experience for profit. A common feature in this cinematic genre was sexual relationships between black men and white women. Scenes with black men having sex with beautiful white women were supposed to be revolutionary and a way to stick it to "the man," but there were unforeseen consequences.

In Quentin Tarantino's *Jackie Brown* (1997), an homage to the blaxploitation-era queen Pam Grier, the film's antagonist, Ordell Robbie (Samuel L. Jackson), is asked by his partner in crime, Louis (Robert De Niro), why he puts up with his lazy lover, Melanie (Bridget Fonda). Robbie replies with a grin on his face that while she might be nagging and her beauty was fading with age, she was still white. By the turn of the 21st century, debates in the black community raged over the preference for "exotic" models in hip-hop music videos. These women tended to be very fair-skinned black women, bi-racial, Latina, Asian, or white with thicker body types traditionally associated with black women. Kanye's most quotable song lyric involves a black man leaving his girl for white woman once he makes it. There was Kanye's "30 white bitches" line from the hook for "So Appalled," a song about the ridiculousness of the celebrity rapper's lifestyle. Kanye enraged Black Twitter when a model casting call for his Yeezy Season 4 collection fashion show requested that only biracial and multiracial women apply.

Celebrities were among the earliest blacks to date and marry outside of their race. Miles Davis dated Juliette Gréco, a white singer and actress he met in Paris in 1949. Quincy Jones married three white women between 1957 and 1990. Sidney Poitier could personally relate to his character from *Guess Who's Coming to Dinner*. After 15 years of marriage to a black woman, he married a white Canadian actress.[15] Sammy Davis, Jr., married May Britt, a Swedish actress, in 1960. Years earlier, he dated another white actress, Kim Novak. *Confidential* magazine ran a story on their relationship, which did not sit well with Harry Cohn, the president of Columbia Pictures. Cohn ordered Davis to stop dating Novak immediately if he wanted to continue working in Hollywood. To appease his white bosses, Davis paid a black woman named Loray White $10,000 to participate in a big public wedding. He divorced her a year later and married Britt. Michele Simms-Burton, a retired professor, sees this as Davis's way of showing the world he was a free man who could marry whomever he pleased.

Harry Belafonte rivaled Sammy Davis, Jr., and Sidney Poitier for the title of Hollywood's black leading man during the civil rights era. The Jamaican-American calypso singer and actor married Julie Robinson, a white dancer, three years before Davis broke the color barrier. Belafonte had previously been married to Marguerite Byrd, a middle-class black teacher, for nine years. *The Amsterdam News* cover read, "BELAFONTE WEDS WHITE DANCER." The black-owned newspaper published a series of articles that asked questions being raised in black households, barbershops, salons, and churches. "Many Negroes are wondering why a man who has waved the flag of justice for his race should turn from a Negro wife to a white wife," wrote Betty Granger.[16]

Belafonte responded to the criticism in the article "Why I Married Julie," which he published in *Ebony*. The nation's most popular black-owned periodical included an accompanying story that asked if interracial marriage was detrimental to black progress. Six years later Malcolm X called out Belafonte, Lena Horne, Eartha Kitt, and Pearl Bailey for their white partners. Malcolm identified intermarriage as a manifestation of self-hatred ingrained in the black psyche.[17] "It may even be seen as a manifestation of what Du Bois had described as the black man's 'double consciousness' in American society," wrote Mark Hayward in "Harry Belafonte, Race, and the Politics of Success."[18]

Belafonte was always active in the Civil Rights Movement. He spoke at the 1963 March on Washington and sang at a rally during the final march of the 1965 Selma campaign. When he filled in for Johnny Carson as the host of *The Tonight Show* (1954–present) in 1968, he used the opportunity to interview the Rev. Martin Luther King, Jr., and Robert Kennedy. Both men were assassinated later that year. Belafonte, a close friend of King, speaks fondly of King's admiration for his marriage to Robinson. Belafonte believes that King never condemned their marriage because his first love was Betty Moitz, a white woman he met while he was a student at Crozer Theological Seminary. David Garrow details their time together in his book *Bearing the Cross* (1986).[19] By the fall of 1949, King and Moitz felt comfortable enough to sit together on public benches on campus and go on dates at the local restaurants in Chester, Pennsylvania. Despite his love for Moitz, King's doting father, a respected preacher in Atlanta, would not condone his son's dating a white woman. Furthermore, most of the blacks in the Southern churches in which King might be preaching after seminary would object to having a white first lady.

The popular belief is that wealthy black men date white women, sometimes called "Beckys," and other non-black women to boost their status. These men are not supposed to be as socially conscious as their counterparts who remain loyal to only dating their beautiful, black queens. If Eldrick "Tiger" Woods showed up to the Masters with a black woman on his arm the internet might crash.[20] Since Woods has never stood for black causes or identified as a black man, few black people are surprised by his preference for white women. But the problem with this logic is that it can be refuted with evidence of proud black males who have dated or married outside their race. Senator Cory Booker, Dave Chappelle, Jeezy, Johnnie Cochran, Donald Glover, Omari Hardwick, Julius "Dr. J" Erving, Michael B. Jordan, Eddie Murphy, Prince, Richard Pryor, Jalen Rose, Russell Simmons, Touré Neblett, William Darrell "Bubba" Wallace, Jr., Jay Williams, Jesse Williams, and Kanye West are some notable examples.

Kareem Abdul-Jabbar and Bill Russell are two of the most respected black athlete-activists in history. Jabbar, who described himself as "black rage personified" used to be escorted by FBI agents due to assassination threats. Jabbar supported Harry Edwards's plan to boycott the 1968 Summer Olympics when he was a student at UCLA. He participated in the 1967 Cleveland Summit along with activist-athletes Muhammad Ali, Jim Brown, Bobby Mitchell, and Bill Russell. Jabbar was the NBA's best player in the 1970s, winning the Most Valuable Player award five times and leading the Los Angeles Lakers to five world championships during the 1980s. On the court nobody could touch him. Off the court nobody could talk to him. He was aloof with the white journalists trying to cover him. His conversion to Islam and his brand of intellectualism, which embraced black pride, made many whites uncomfortable. Ironically, the mother of Jabbar's son, Amir, is a white woman named Cheryl Pistono Jenkins whom he dated for seven years.

Bill Russell's dating history is even more interesting. In 1961, Russell organized a boycott of a pre-season game in Lexington, Kentucky, with his black teammates and their black opponents on the St. Louis Hawks. The boycott came after they were denied service in a local coffee shop. The Boston Celtics center participated in the 1963 March on Washington and visited Mississippi after the assassination of NAACP leader Medgar Evers. Russell, who refused to befriend local white fans, once referred to Boston as a "flea market of racism" after vandals broke into his home and defecated on his bed.[21] Oddly enough, after divorcing Rose Swisher, his first wife of 17 years, he married two white women between 1977 and 1996. His second wife was Dorothy Anstett, the 1968 Miss USA pageant winner. Was this Russell's way of subconsciously spiting in the face of those racists who thought they could control him?

Footnotes for Kanye

Jasmine Mans caught the nation's attention with her scathing poem "Footnotes for Kanye" which went viral in 2016. Mans's poem was one of the first viral critiques of Kanye's evolution from a vocal mouthpiece for black activism to what he has become today. His relationship with Kim was at the center of the young poet's critique.

> You look hungry. Like that girl don't make you no fried chicken or macaroni & cheese. Like she don't feel you on the inside…. Do you regret the Marilyn Monroe in your decision? And wish that you could've taken Billie Holiday as your bride…. Even though you traded in your spaceship to buy back your forty acres and a mule. Purchased the plantation and master's daughters, too….[22]

Is Mans's critique an example of black nationalism or bitterness because another *good* black man was taken by a white woman? Her words reflect Queen Latifah playing the angry black waitress in Spike Lee's 1991 film *Jungle Fever* who refuses to provide quality service to an interracial couple. Her words mirror neo-soul great Jill Scott's 2010 essay in *Essence* magazine describing the pain she feels when seeing accomplished "brothers" with white women.[23] Her words reflect the backlash that Black Twitter had for NBA star Kyrie Irving's 2016 post–NBA championship yacht party with mostly bikini-clad "Beckys." Some might dismiss Mans's critique with Ice-T's (Tracey Marrow) classic line from *Chappelle's Show*, "hate, hate, hate, hate, hate."

In defense of Ms. Mans, I think her disappointment in Kanye West had more to do with his failure to uphold the values he espoused at the start of his career when he compared himself to Gil Scott-Heron. Furthermore, the poem expressed her specific disdain for Kim Kardashian, not all white women. Kim and her sisters are magnets for black women's vitriol for three reasons: (1) their affinity for dating and having children with prominent black men; (2) their repeated examples of cultural appropriation to grow their personal brands and financial empire;[24] and (3) the way they benefit from misogynoir, which describes praise given white women for appropriating the same attributes and behavior for which black women are rebuked.[25]

Kim's first marriage was to Damon Thomas when she was 19. She revealed in an episode of *Keeping Up with the Kardashians* that she was high on ecstasy when they eloped. Thomas, a black songwriter and music producer, had success working with R&B producer Kenneth "Babyface" Edmonds in the late 1990s. Thomas was also a member of the Underdogs, an R&B and pop production duo that worked with Justin Timberlake and Jordin Sparks. When the couple divorced in 2003, Kim cited physical and emotional abuse as a reason for their failed union. Before the divorce was officially finalized, she began dating Ray J. Kim says that she was high on ecstasy again when she and Ray J made a private sex tape that was leaked to the public in 2007 without her knowledge. The infamous tape helped to make her television's most famous reality star and a household name.

After Ray J, Kim dated black celebrities Nick Cannon, Reggie Bush, and The Game (Jayceon Taylor). She was at Bush's side on television as he gave victorious post-game interviews following the New Orleans Saints win in Super Bowl XLIV. She married Kris Humphries in 2011. The former NBA player has a black father and white mother. The same was true of Miles Austin, a former starting wide receiver for the Dallas Cowboys, whom she dated in 2010. Kim's younger sisters have followed her lead in choosing partners and the fathers of their children. Devin Booker, Lamar

Odom, Ben Simmons, Tristin Thompson, and Tyga have all been linked to one of the sisters. Her mother, Kris Jenner, has been dating Corey Gamble, a black man 25 years her junior who previously worked for Kanye's former manager, Scott "Scooter" Braun, since 2014.

The Kardashian-Jenner history of interracial romance has long been a source of the media's fascination and mockery. Comedian George Lopez questioned Kim and Khloe's passion for "black guys" during an appearance on *Lopez Tonight*. The sisters broke out in laughter as the live audience erupted in applause. But not everyone is laughing. Ezinne Ukoha published the article "How the Kardashians Keep Getting Away with Villainizing Black Men" for the online platform *Medium*. Ukoha chastised the Kardashians for what she saw as a fetish for black men and a penchant for "villainizing" their former lovers as serial cheaters.[26]

Ukoha's argument that the Kardashians and Jenners have an infatuation with black men has uncomfortable undertones dating back to slavery. Nineteenth-century Southern white women, oppressed by the chains of patriarchy and the cult of domesticity, were believed to have repressed sexual desires about the black male help. Historians have uncovered stories detailing fully developed adolescent male slaves wearing only shirts too short to provide them a small modicum of dignity while serving tea to their plantation mistresses and female visitors. According to historian Elizabeth Fox-Genovese, slave-holding white women (plantation mistresses), like their husbands, engaged in pre- and extra-marital sex with slaves.[27] Some of these relationships were consensual, and others were coerced. Colonel Richard J. Hinton, an abolitionist commander in the Civil War, told the story of a former slave telling him about his master's wife ordering him to sleep with her once her husband died.[28] The rape of male slaves did occur on a small scale.[29] Some elite white women applied early methods of contraception and abortion to prevent or disrupt pregnancies with enslaved men. Others accused their secret black lovers of rape if they were accidentally impregnated.

In *White Over Black* (1968), historian Winthrop Jordan described the attempts by slave masters to paint black men as sexually deviant and licentious due to what masters perceived as abnormally oversized genitalia.[30] The white woman's curiosity about the black male's large penis is believed to be what attracted her to him.[31] This became a popular myth in black folklore and satire. The 1970 film *Watermelon Man* exaggerated this myth for an underlying storyline. Comedian Godfrey Cambridge played Jeff Gerber, a white bigot who wakes up one morning as a black man. The first thing his wife does after his transformation is look under his towel to see if the myth was true. Days later an attractive European secretary at Gerber's job sleeps with him so she can experience being with "a negro."

During the *Lopez Tonight* interview, George Lopez discussed having past black guests take DNA tests to determine how black they were. Kim asked Lopez if she could take the test too. "You have some black [in you too] with that booty," Lopez sarcastically replied. In 2013 CNN correspondent Dr. Anthony Youn cited Kim as the "poster child for a large and shapely backside." A year later, the *Vogue* article "Started from the Bottom: Experts Weigh in on the Cultural Obsession with Butts" referenced Kim. *Vogue*'s Kristin Tice Studeman declared this era to be "the dawn of the butt," led by Kardashian. Helen Mirren, a 70-year-old English actress, credited her for being an advocate of body positivity by making it acceptable and beautiful for women to have big butts and thick thighs.[32]

Kim's "big ole butt" was on full display in her 2014 photo spread for *Paper* magazine. The pictures "broke the internet," receiving more than five million views in less than 24 hours.[33] All the fuss was over a nude image of her, taken by French photographer Jean-Paul Goude, exposing her oiled-up bottom. The magazine included another popular image of Kim recreating Goude's famous 1976 photograph, "Carolina Beaumont, New York" (commonly referred to as "Champagne Incident"). In that picture Kim held an opened champagne bottle that sprayed the liquid into a glass propped up on her butt. "And they say I didn't have a talent … try balancing a champagne glass on your ass LOL #BreakTheInternet#PaperMagazine," she tweeted.[34]

The model used for the original version of "Champagne Incident" was a naked, dark-skinned black woman with a very thin figure and large backside. Her photo appeared in Goude's 1982 book *Jungle Fever*. Goude, the art director for *Esquire*, has been accused of eroticizing black women's bodies with pictures such as that and others that he shot of Jamaican entertainer Grace Jones, with whom he has a son. Some black feminists compared Kim's *Paper* spread to Saartjie Baartman, a Khoisan woman from South Africa with large breasts and buttocks, who was forced to pose nude in 19th-century freak show exhibits for white spectators. Baartman traveled throughout Europe performing under the name the Hottentot Venus. According to A. Lynn Bolles, an anthropologist and Women's Studies professor at the University of Maryland, Baartman was treated like an animal. After her death white scientists dissected her body parts.

Kierna Mayo, the vice president of digital content for *Ebony*, appeared on MSNBC's *Melissa Harris-Perry* in 2014 to discuss the racial politics associated with Kim Kardashian. Mayo noted how Kim had monetized her surgically altered figure, which resembles that of a black woman, in ways that actual black women historically have not. She compared mainstream media's appreciation for Kim's *Paper* spread with its condemnation of Trinidadian-American rapper Nicki Minaj (Onika Maraj-Petty) for wearing a G-string thong on the cover of her 2014 single "Anaconda."[35] Likewise,

Patrice Brown, a black fourth-grade teacher in Atlanta, nicknamed Teacherbae on the internet, was reprimanded for wearing fitted dresses over thick hips for which Kim would be celebrated.

When Kim is not being judged for her body, she is raising eyebrows for her hair. In March 2020, she posted pictures on Instagram wearing waist-length Fulani braids with white beads. The hairstyle originated from black women in West Africa, but it was popularized in America in the 1970s by a white model named Bo Derek. Kim claims that she wore the braids to match her daughter, North, who was performing at the Yeezy Season 8 fashion show in Paris. Black women took to social media accusing her of "blackfishing" (or "niggerfishing"), a derogatory term used to describe white females who manipulate their physical appearance to look black in their Instagram pictures. "YOU ARE NOT BLACK," tweeted @MisaJaymes. "I can't stand Kim K and her damn braids, like bitch when are y'all gonna stop appropriating our culture," tweeted @KvuittonD. "I wish I could be a Kardashian so I could be black," said R&B singer K. Michelle (Kimberly Michelle Pate).

Matthew Rozsa, a writer for *The Daily Dot,* suggests that people's problem with Kim Kardashian has more to do with their insecurities about race and identity than her behavior. "The core of the problem is that her ethnic background doesn't fully sync with her image. Although Armenians were legally considered white in this country as of 1909, Kardashian's physical attributes make it easy for her to be juxtaposed with stereotypes about African Americans," says Rozsa.[36] "Similarly, her determination to self-identify with black culture further blurs the lines of her racial perception."[37] Kim does not see any harm with her behavior. She is white because society has categorized her as white because of her family's European descent. Rozsa points out that Armenians, like Irish and Italian immigrants, were not always considered white enough by American standards. What does that mean for Kim, who acts as if such racial categorization does not apply to her? Rozsa believes race is Kim's problem because it is everyone else's problem. However, I would argue that race is her problem because she benefits from a privilege that is unavailable to the black women she imitates. Kimberle Crenshaw, who defined the theory of intersectionality in her 1991 article "Mapping the Margins," says that black women are double burdened and oppressed by race and gender. Thus, their marginalization is vastly different from their more privileged white female counterparts like Kim who can wear braids and fake butts like fashion accessories without consequence.[38]

Lauren Michele Jackson, professor of African American Studies at Northwestern University, takes Kim Kardashian to task in her book *White Negroes: When Cornrows Were in Vogue ... and Other Thoughts on Cultural Appropriation* (2019). Kim and others like her become contemporary versions of the white negro that essayist Norman Mailer wrote about in 1957.[39] Jackson says her popularity lies in her ability to ping pong between racial significations and borrow from others' cultural aesthetics as she pleases.[40] *Marie Claire* magazine documented five Kardashian-Jenner enterprises that are guilty of stealing from black culture. Examples include Kylie Jenner's blue hair extensions for her brand Kylie Hair Kouture by Bellami Hair, which were inspired by Heather Sanders, the black owner of Sorella Boutique. According to *Marie Claire*, Kylie failed to acknowledge Sanders when the brand was released. Multiple black women tweeted their displeasure with Kylie's inclusion in Cardi B (Belcalis Almánzar) and Megan Thee Stallion's (Megan Pete) "WAP" music video, which was supposed to celebrate black women's sexuality. Kendall Jenner was berated for making a Pepsi commercial that belittled more serious Black Lives Matter protest rallies. Kendall casually walks up to an armed guardsman and hands him a Pepsi soda. This offended many blacks on social media, who posted images of Leshia Evans, a harmless young black nurse, accosted by multiple police wearing riot gear at a protest rally in Baton Rouge, Louisiana.[41]

Kanye's mother died before he began dating Kim. She loved his previous girlfriend, Alexis Phifer, which is one reason that he proposed to her. What would Dr. West think of her daughter-in-law? Would she be bothered by her hips and hair? Kanye did not appear to have any problem with his wife's appropriation of the black female aesthetic. Perhaps, in his mind, he had the best of both worlds. A "white" woman with coveted physical features of black women, minus what Frances Beal calls the double burden of racism and sexism.[42]

Yeezy Taught Me: Raising North

Kanye and Kim welcomed their first child, North, on June 15, 2013. Two and a half years later Kim gave birth to their son Saint. Doctors advised her against having any more children because she suffered from a physical condition called placenta accreta. This condition causes the placenta to attach too deeply to the mother's uterine wall. As a result, the Wests used surrogates for the birth of their second daughter, Chicago, and their youngest son, Psalm. A 2019 Christmas photo featured the entire family. All the kids, who look like they could be models in a Baby Gap ad, have a light-caramel complexion and straight or curly hair. The West children are celebrities by default. Only time will tell if they opt to remain out of the public's attention and live in anonymity as they mature. All the children appeared in the "Closed on Sunday" music video, but North stole the show by screaming out the song's final line in high-pitched voice, "CHICK-FIL-AAAAAA."

Thus far, North appears to love the spotlight and will follow in her parents' footsteps. She routinely came on stage with Kanye during his Sunday Services. She would stand beside him during his keyboard solo performance. She gave her debut performance at his Yeezy Collection Season 8 runway presentation at the 2020 Paris Fashion Week. North, decked out in a neutral matching pant set and a bright fuchsia padded gilet, rhymed as the models ripped the runway. All that "hot fire" she was spitting quickly went viral thanks to Kim posting it on her Instagram Stories. North popped up again at end of her dad's music video "Wash Us in the Blood."

Despite her age, North has already become a lightning rod for controversy. Veronica Wells, a writer for *MadameNoire*, published an article titled "Let's Be Real, Kim Kardashian West is Teaching the Next Generation to Steal from Black Women Too." Wells not so subtly charged the six-year-old with pulling a Melania Trump.[43] Her rap's beat and cadence had been borrowed from a song called "What I Do?" by ZaZa, a five-year-old black female rapper. What complicates matters is the fact that North, unlike her mother, is black based upon societal standards.

Kim was interviewed by BET about her plans for raising a biracial child before North was born. She told the interviewer that her goal was to raise her daughter not to see color.[44] Kim's Pollyannaish and problematic attitude did not last very long; four years later, she and North posed for the cover of *Interview* magazine's September issue.[45] This was to be North's first magazine cover and interview. In the cover story Kim stated that she was teaching North about race and emphasized how strong Kanye's biological relatives' presence was in their daughter's life.[46] Kim also spoke of North's fascination with her curly hair, a signifier of racial identity for mixed race children. The third episode of the ABC sitcom *Mixed-ish* (2019–2021) tackled this issue in a storyline involving the show's biracial protagonist. Rainbow, a light-skinned girl with curly hair, faced a dilemma when the time came to take school pictures. She asked her aunt to take her to the beauty parlor to straighten her hair to "look pretty" for picture day. Rainbow's mom was furious with her. Black Twitter was just as outraged when Kim straightened North's naturally curly hair for her sixth birthday.

How one wears his or her hair is a complex subject in the black community. "Good and Bad Hair," the famous musical number in Spike Lee's film *School Daze* (1988), manifested an internal struggle experienced by blacks. Motown's female artists in the early 1960s wore permed wigs or straightened hairstyles to conform to white beauty standards. In the late 1960s, the "black is beautiful" mantra of the Black Power movement made natural hairstyles acceptable, trendy, and a badge of honor for black women and girls. Since the 2000s, straightened hair weaves and wigs have rivaled natural hairstyles for dominance. The passage of the CROWN Act (SB 188) brought black hair politics to the public's consciousness after several blacks were either punished or criminalized for wearing their hair naturally.[47] Consequently, North and her siblings may be unfairly scrutinized in both the mainstream and black public spaces for their hairstyles.

Choosing the "right" hairstyle is just one of many issues Kanye's kids may face while growing up. *Psychology Today* stated that there are advantages that come with being biracial. Comedians Keegan-Michael Key and Jordan Peele, both of whom have a black father and a white mother, were able to attract a larger audience to their Emmy-winning Comedy Central series *Key & Peele* (2012–2015) because they were relatable to multiple demographics. But as Sarah Gaither, a social psychologist at Duke University, points out, being biracial in America is no easy journey. Society expects the children of mixed marriages to choose one race over the other.[48] In her 2010 bestseller *The Girl Who Fell from the Sky*, Heidi Durrow, the daughter of a Danish mother and African American father, said she identified as black because that is what the rules of society dictated.[49] Historically the one-drop rule has required anyone in America with a drop of black blood to be classified as black. The most famous example of this rule is Homer Plessy, who could pass for white but had one-eighth African heritage. Plessy was removed from the whites-only first-class section on a New Orleans streetcar in 1892, leading to the U.S. Supreme Court's *Plessy v. Ferguson* (1896) decision that legalized segregation. Tennessee was the first state to add this one-drop rule to its laws in 1910.[50] Virginia's Racial Integrity Act (1924) required all individuals of mixed race to classified as "colored" on their birth certificate.

The U.S. Census did not begin recognizing biracial and mixed individuals until the year 2000. The Pew Research Center estimates that 20 percent of Americans will be either biracial or mixed by 2050.[51] Tiger Woods offended many blacks in 1997 by telling Oprah Winfrey, days after he became the first black man to win golf's prestigious Masters Tournament, he was Cablinasian and not African American.[52] Woods rejected his father Earl's vision for him to be a vanguard for racial progress and the expectations of the black masses who initially viewed him as an ally. He rejected the expectations placed upon him in his first Nike commercial to be golf's great black hope. "I was troubled by it," sports activists Harry Edwards recalled, "not so much because [Woods] seemed to be disassociating himself from African American roots, but given the inevitability of trials and tribulations ahead, he undercut his support base."[53] This was certainly true after Woods' 2009 sex scandal. Billy Payne, chairman of the Masters at Augusta National, publicly shamed Woods a day before the 2010 tournament. Payne's scolding was magnified given Augusta's hypocrisy in failing to admit its first black golfer until 1990.

Howard Bryant reminds readers in *Full Dissidence* (2020) that when Woods was arrested in 2017 for driving with five different drugs in his system, his police report read "black" male.[54] Bryant expressed similar frustration with biracial tennis player Madison Keys, considered the heir apparent to Venus and Serena Williams, for her refusal to publicly embrace her blackness. Keys, like Woods, in Bryant's mind, was intentionally choosing not to identify as black to relieve herself of that historical burden of being a problem for some in white America.[55]

Racial identity is the underlying theme of Barack Obama's 1995 memoir, *Dreams from My Father*. The 44th president's father was a black man from Kenya, and his mother was a white woman, of European ancestry, from Kansas. To master the performance of black masculinity, a teenage Obama growing up in Hawaii routinely played basketball with older black males. He watched old Richard Pryor comedy routines and blaxploitation films to adopt his swagger and black cool.[56] When Obama ran for office in 2008, some older blacks doubted his ability to advocate for the black community due to his upbringing. Kamala Harris (CA), the first female vice president, has never shied away from reminding anyone who questioned her blackness that she came of age as a student at Howard University. She participated in anti–Apartheid demonstrations and pledged Alpha Kappa Alpha (AKA) sorority. Harris, who is married to a white man, is the daughter of a black man of Jamaican descent and an Asian mother of Indian descent.[57]

The struggles of Obama and Harris with their racial identity paled in comparison to that of pop singer Mariah Carey and Academy Award-winner Halle Berry. Mariah Carey is the daughter of an Irish mother and a black and Afro-Venezuelan father. She first gained fame in the early 1990s as a wholesome pop star who appealed to white fans. The strategy served her well financially. Only Whitney Houston rivaled her on the *Billboard* charts. As a child, she dreamed of being darker to fit in with the black kids and not get mistaken for a white girl. Carey did not publicly share these feelings until her 2018 song "8th Grade." Halle Berry went from being Eddie Murphy's co-star in *Boomerang* (1992) to one of Hollywood's highest paid actresses in the 2000s. She was ranked number one on *People's* 2003 "Most Beautiful People in the World" list. Berry revealed, in an interview with *People* 14 years later, that she was bullied by the white students at her majority-white elementary school. The white kids and some blacks called her an Oreo, a reference to the popular chocolate sandwich cookies that have a sweet white cream filling. Berry considers herself a black woman and identifies her daughter, Nahla, as black even though the child's father is white.[58]

Being biracial will not shield any of the West's children from the pervasive racist absurdity that whiteness is the quintessential embodiment of the entire species.[59] In *The Birth of a Nation*, mixed individuals were called "half-breeds" and described as the most dangerous people because they possessed the white man's intellect and the "Negro's" savagery. President Obama dealt with a constant barrage of direct and indirect racist attacks during his White House tenure. Rival politicians such as Newt Gingrich trumpeted racially coded characterizations like "the food stamp president" to disparage his image. Internet trolls were far less subtle, comparing Obama to a monkey. Donald Trump questioned the American citizenship of both Obama and Kamala Harris.

New York Yankees shortstop Derek Jeter was Major League Baseball's premier star in the late 1990s and early 2000s. He was an MVP on and off the field. Jeter, the son of a black father and Irish American mother, generally dated beautiful white models and actresses. He is currently married to Hannah Davis, a white model from the U.S. Virgin Islands. The couple has two children. During his playing days, the FBI and the New York City Police Department's hate crimes unit had to investigate death threats. Jeter was warned to stop dating white women or risk being shot and set on fire. Racism precipitated the breach that drove Prince Harry and his biracial wife, Meghan Markle, out of the British royal family. Members of the British press referred to their son, Archie, as a chimp and wrote articles describing Markle as "(almost) straight outta Compton" and having "exotic" DNA. Markle and her husband revealed to Oprah Winfrey in a bombshell 2021 interview that individuals close to the family raised concerns about how dark Archie's skin might when she was pregnant. Other stories insisted that her black mother lived in a gang-infested ghetto.[60]

When Kim was a girl her late father, Robert Kardashian, predicted that she would have a "beautiful black child" one day and life would be very difficult.[61] North's first encounter with racism came as an infant during an international trip. After a white woman in Vienna, Austria, approached Kim in blackface mimicking Kanye, another white woman on her return flight to Los Angeles shouted out, "She's with a black guy, and that baby is black! And you need to shut that black baby up!"[62] How North and her siblings learn to deal with racism and relate to other black people depends on Kim and Kanye's nurturing. Episode five of the Kenya Barris Netflix series *#blackAF* revolved around this very issue. A fictional biracial mother, Joya Barris, was concerned with her children's lack of cultural awareness because they did not refer to themselves as black and lacked rhythm on the dance floor. When Joya was a teenager, dancing was what always saved her when others doubted her cultural authenticity. Never mind the fact that she mouthed the words to the songs as she danced to stay on beat.

Rashida Jones, the actress playing the role of Joya Barris, has spent her entire life handling questions about her racial identity. Rashida Jones is the 44-year-old daughter of music producer Quincy Jones and Peggy Lipton, a white Jewish-American actress who became famous for her role on *The Mod Squad* (1968–1973). She is the younger sister of Kidada Jones, the best friend of the late R&B star Aaliyah and Tupac Shakur's girlfriend at the time of his death. While Kidada has a darker complexion and curly hair like her father, Rashida has green eyes, straight hair, and a complexion light enough to pass for white. Rashida lived with her mother and saw Kidada and her father only on weekends. In a 2005 interview with *Glamour* magazine, Kidada said her sister passed for white when she attended primarily white secondary schools and Harvard University.[63]

Rashida's racial ambiguity made her a young star in Hollywood during the 2000s.[64] She had a small role as Karen Scarfolli, a sexually promiscuous bully on Judd Apatow's teen comedy-drama *Freaks and Geeks* (1999–2000). She was one of the few non-white actors on the show, which introduced future stars James Franco and Seth Rogen. Rashida's racial identity was an ongoing joke related to her character Karen Filippelli on the NBC sitcom *The Office*. Karen's white co-workers secretly debated if she was black, Italian, Filipina, or biracial. Michael Scott (Steve Carell), the company's regional manager at her branch, mistakenly identified her as an attractive Filipina. In her white male co-workers' eyes, there was something more exotic and appealing about her as a Filipina than a black woman.[65]

Rashida's first major film role came in the 2009 comedy *I Love You, Man*, where she was cast as Zooey Rice, the fiancée of the lead character Peter Klaven (Paul Rudd). Despite being the film's only prominent non-white character, Zooey's racial background and familial ties were never explored. Then came a career-defining role as Ann Perkins on the sitcom *Parks and Recreation* (2009–2015). Ann was primarily coded as a white woman in a majority white environment. However, there were moments such as Season 4, Episode 4, "Win, Lose, or Draw," in which her white colleagues used her racial ambiguity as proof that they were post-racial.[66] Rashida played more racially ambiguous characters in the films *The Social Network* (2009) and *Tag* (2018). In her defense, Dwayne "The Rock" Johnson has made a career of playing racially ambiguous roles in the *Fast & Furious* series, *Jumanji*, and other films without receiving criticism.[67]

A surprisingly large number of blacks were unaware that Rashida was Quincy Jones's daughter until she directed and appeared in his Netflix documentary *Quincy* (2018). When she was cast in *#blackAF*, a collective on social media talked incessantly about her finally embracing her blackness on camera. "Rasheeda Jones is BLACK?????" tweeted @Reinelaetia.[68] The new Netflix series was attacked on Black Twitter and by black journalists for its portrayal of black authenticity and casting her as the mother. Kenya

Barris, who also created the sitcoms *Black-ish* and *Mixed-ish*, defended his selection of her during an interview on T.I.'s podcast *expediTIously*. Joya's character is based on his wife, Dr. Raina "Rainbow" Barris, who is biracial. *#blackAF* intentionally spoofs Joya's attempts to overcompensate for her mixed heritage. Whether this comes at the expense of Rainbow Barris or Rashida Jones is unknown.[69]

Even though North and her siblings will not have the option of passing for white like Rashida Jones, will they overtly identify as black? In interviews Kim has said that she is pursuing a law degree because, as the mother of *black* children she wants to do something to fight racial inequality in the judicial system. Will Kim and Kanye feel the need to have "the talk" with their children? "The talk" is a rite of passage for black children when their parents impart the rules for surviving police encounters and knowing their legal rights. In 2018, Kanye told TMZ's Harvey Levin and Charles Latibeaudiere that he was disturbed by North's teacher telling her she was black. In Kanye's opinion, North was being stripped of her right to choose how she would identify herself. "What does it mean to be black in America if a white person defines your blackness from childhood?" he asked.[70]

How Kanye's children self-identify could have a lot to do with his relationship with Kim. During his 2020 presidential campaign rally in South Carolina, Kanye revealed that Kim considered having an abortion before North was born. The following day Kanye posted several tweets disparaging Kim and her family. On February 19, 2021, multiple news outlets reported that Kim had filed for divorce and was seeking joint custody of the children.[71] Despite Kanye's admission to infidelity, flings with models Irina Shayk and Vinetria, and Kim dating Pete Davidson, Kanye is still fighting to save the marriage.

Six

"Homecoming"

"Kanye is from a village and the village was feeling like our
dear brother turned his back on the village." *Rhymefest*[1]

I have never been an avid fan of *Keeping Up with the Kardashians*
(KUWTK), but I was mildly excited to tune in for the 16th season premiere.
Flavor Flav (William Drayton, Jr.) famously said "don't believe the hype,"
but I was falling for it. Perhaps I was suckered in by all the talk of a big fight
between Kim and Kanye's ex–BFF Rhymefest.[2] The premiere began with
Kim and North traveling to Chicago to visit Kanye, who was there working
on his upcoming album, *Yandhi*. When he was not busy in the studio, Kanye
helped with the efforts to reopen the Regal. The Avalon Regal Theater is Chicago's version of Harlem's Apollo. Billie Holiday, Louis Armstrong, John
Coltrane, B.B. King, Isaac Hayes, and The Jackson 5 were among the notable acts to grace the Regal, which opened in 1927 and had served as a performance venue, a movie theater and a church and meeting place at different
times before closing in 1985. The Regal was reopened in 1987 and given land-
mark status in 1992. When Kanye was a 17-year-old aspiring rapper, he performed at the theater as an opening act for a concert co-headlined by Tupac
and Biggie. After its 2003 closure and subsequent troubles, the Regal was
foreclosed in 2011. In 2018 Kanye put one million dollars into the renovation,
his involvement signifying that he had not turned his back on his hometown
and black Chicagoans had not lost their beloved superhero. Or did it? This
chapter explores Kanye West's relationship with Chicago and its influence
on his music, self-identity, and worldview as a black man.

Windy

Kanye West owes a portion of his success to Rhymefest, whom he met
in Chicago when he was a 16-year-old producer trying to get his career off
the ground. Rhymefest co-wrote "Jesus Walks," "New Slaves," and other

songs on Kanye's first six albums. Kanye and Rhymefest began Donda's House, a charity in Chicago named in honor of his late mother, to teach at-risk local youth to write and record music. Rhymefest purchased Kanye's childhood home in 2016 to serve as "a community arts incubator for Donda's House." It was shocking when Rhymefest tweeted in 2016 that he was no longer working with his friend. "My brother needs help in the form of counseling."[3] Two years later it was announced that Donda's House was struggling to stay afloat due to a loss of donors following Kanye's endorsement of President Donald Trump. Rhymefest added fuel to the fire by tweeting Kanye's musical nemesis, Drake: "When G.O.O.D. Music sends the money they owe you, will you please help us build Kanye's mother's house for the youth of Chicago. I spoke to Kanye about it. His response was, 'fuck the youth of Chicago.'"[4]

Although Kanye was willing to forgive his old friend, Kim was adamantly opposed to meeting with him. She and Rhymefest had sparred verbally via Twitter months earlier.[5] Kim saw Rhymefest as a disloyal associate publicizing his personal gripes with her husband. Rhymefest tried to explain that, from his perspective, Kanye had lost sight of *the village* that raised him. That village is one that Kim Kardashian entered as an outsider. This village refers to Kanye's biological kin, who had to overcome decades of horrific segregation. The village refers to the black teachers and preachers who shaped young Kanye's intellectual and spiritual growth. Most importantly, the village refers to Chicago, a mecca of black life since the turn of the 20th century.

Kanye first addressed the rumors that he had turned his back on Chicago on "Homecoming," the final single from his 2007 *Graduation* album. "Homecoming," which was a new version of an older song called "Home (Windy)" that was recorded for his 2001 demo tape, used metaphors to characterize Chicago as a long-lost love with whom he was reuniting. The song's concept was derived from "I Used to Love H.E.R.," a 1994 composition by fellow Chicago emcee Common, which depicted hip-hop as his long-lost childhood love.[6] Throughout the song Kanye expressed remorse for leaving his love behind to pursue his dreams in other cities and around the globe. He acknowledged those he inspired in Chicago to make music and his refusal to forget his love no matter how far he strayed. The song's infectious hook promised listeners that he was "coming home again."

Harold "Hype" Williams, the definitive hip-hop video director of the 1990s and early 2000s, directed the song's music video. Hype's mini film was a black-and-white montage of Kanye West walking through the city. His travels take him from the beautiful tourist sections along the Magnificent Mile to the impoverished neighborhoods of Chicago's South Side. The video highlights various Chicago landmarks such as the famous 1,450-foot

Willis (Sears) Tower and the DuSable Museum of African American History. The DuSable, formally called the Ebony Museum of Negro History and Art, was established in 1961 to celebrate black history and culture. The DuSable's inclusion, along with several cameos from Common, connoted Kanye's connection to the city's black experience.

"Homecoming" highlighted Kanye's proximity to, and distance from, Chicago's working-class blacks. He walked through the South Side streets wearing a designer keffiyeh scarf, an Arab headdress worn in the Middle East that became a popular hip-hop fashion accessory. The remainder of his two outfits included a fitted patchwork shirt, a fitted denim jacket, a fitted outdoor vest, a preppy sweater, and slim-fitting khaki pants. Kanye's preppy, New York Fashion Week-ready attire stuck out as he moved amongst the working-class black men wearing oversized coats, baggy jeans, baseball caps, and hoodies. Rather than have a local black vocalist accompany him, Chris Martin provided the song's chorus. Martin is the lead vocalist of the English rock band Coldplay. In one sense, Kanye has left Chicago and gone off into the larger world to find himself and build an empire. Despite his new cosmopolitan lifestyle, he still wanted to come back home at the end of the day. Likewise, he still wants to feel welcome in the black community despite his interracial marriage, conservative politics, and largely white fan base.

I Guess That's Why I'm Here, and I Can't Come Back Home

Nearly four months after Kanye's disastrous 2018 TMZ interview he returned to Chicago to provide multiple two-hour radio interviews to explain himself. The first interview was on August 29 with Kyle Santillian, Kendra G., and Leon Rogers for *The WGCI Morning Show*. This was the same radio station that a teenage Kanye and his group The Go Getters picketed trying to get their music played. Kyle began the interview by stating that black Chicagoans questioned Kanye's loyalty because other local artists like Chance the Rapper (Chancelor Bennett) and Vic Mensa (Victor Mensah) were working tirelessly to elevate local youth. Chance had led a social media campaign to halt escalating gun violence for 42 hours over the 2014 Memorial Day weekend, and he donated a million dollars to Chicago's public schools. Vic Mensa released the song "16 Shots" in response to the fatal shooting of 17-year-old Laquan McDonald by Jason Van Dyke, a local white police officer. Mensa also inserted himself into efforts to curb gang violence. Although Kanye was still making conscious rap, he appeared to be more concerned with European luxury fashion brands and the pop charts.

Midway through the interview, the conversation shifted to Kanye's support of Trump. He preached that black people must be able to openly express different opinions without condemnation. "If we have a mono-lithic thought, we are easily controlled and could possibly be easily elim-inated.... I know black people that voted for Trump that were scared to say that they did out loud. That's some *Nineteen Eighty-Four* mind control shit."[7] *Nineteen Eighty-Four* refers to George Orwell's 1949 novel about liv-ing in a repressive, totalitarian state modeled after Stalinist Russia. Once again, Kanye spoke about freedom, not just free thought, but freedom for blacks to do as they pleased. While he understood why his *brothers* and *sis-ters* celebrated Obama's presidency, Kanye was unsatisfied with the amount of progress made over his eight years in the White House.[8] He refused to support Hillary Clinton just because most blacks had voted for Dem-ocrats since the 1960s. Kyle challenged him by referencing his past lyrics about his mother's involvement in the Oklahoma City sit-in movement. Given her sacrifices, Kyle wondered how he could proudly stand in Trump's corner.

Kanye credited Donald Trump with airing out America's dirty laun-dry—racism, sexism, classism, Islamophobia, and nativism—for the world to witness. He described Trump's presidency as black America's *Get Out* moment. In Kanye's opinion, blacks had been lulled to sleep during Obama's eight years in office. One can take issue with that statement. Obama's pres-idency pulled back the cover on just how racist the nation still was despite his historic election wins. I can point to a plethora of examples, beginning with South Carolina's U.S. Representative Joe Wilson calling Obama a liar in the middle of his 2009 address to the joint session of Congress, the birth of the Tea Party movement, and the false arrest of Harvard professor Henry Louis Gates, Jr., in July 2009. There was the 2013 acquittal of George Zim-merman for the murder of Trayvon Martin; numerous police slayings of unarmed black bodies that ignited the Black Lives Matter movement; and the 2015 Charleston church shooting that left nine blacks dead.

Kendra G. asked Kanye if he believed that President Trump cared about black people. The question was a play on his famous post–Hurricane Katrina remarks about President George W. Bush. Kanye paused dramati-cally for 22 seconds before explaining that he thought Trump cared what all people thought of him, but he realized that he would never be the great-est leader in history without the love and support of black people. Kanye explained his TMZ comments by telling Kendra G. that he thought a race of people held captive for 400 years sounded like a choice that was not aligned with the rebellious spirit of Harriet Tubman and Nat Turner. He went on to discuss how black people have been brainwashed by liberalism to view themselves as victims. "You see 100 slave movies, but there is no class on how Magic Johnson became a billionaire. You go to the African American History museum, and they start with the [slave]boats. They don't start with the [Egyptian] pyramids."[9] While I disagree with his belittlement of slavery on TMZ, he makes a valid point regarding how African American history is often presented. Most primary and secondary social studies textbooks devote little attention to the African kingdoms prior to the Atlantic slave trade. I have taught and mentored student teachers at the secondary level. Unless the teacher provides lessons on black entrepreneurs like Annie Malone and Madame C.J. Walker that information is typically excluded from the curriculum.

Kanye took exception to Kendra G.'s use of the phrase "my people" during the conversation. He told her to stop talking about race. He is now only concerned with uplifting the entire human race. Kanye adamantly stood behind this outlook, but he apologized to Chicagoans and the rest of black America for not adequately articulating his reasons for wearing the MAGA hat and making the slavery comments. Kyle thanked Kanye for his unexpected apology and told him many black Chicagoans feared that they had lost him to the Kardashians. That was a very loaded statement given that many blacks blame Kanye's marriage to Kim and her family for his perceived downfall.

Things took a sharp turn during an emotional exchange between Kanye and Kendra G. She began crying, with tears streaming down her face, as she expressed her reasons for being disappointed with his new direction.

> You're in a position that not everyone gets to be in. When you speak, the whole world listens. God has blessed you with this ability that when you speak, change can happen. I respect when you say you're about the human race, but as an African American woman, I see things that my people, black people, go through every single day, so I have to fight and speak for them. When you were apologizing, I felt as though you got it. And I humbly accept your apology.[10]

Are you with us or with them? This is a question that some black nationalists and black Chicagoans may have been asking when they saw Kanye fraternizing with President Trump. In West African societies there are revered storytellers called domas whom the people trust. If the doma betrays the people's trust he must quit his profession. Kanye West's music made him the equivalent of a doma for devoted fans like Kendra G. Thus, his act of donning the MAGA hat and not being fully committed to black causes was the ultimate betrayal. Moved by Kendra G.'s tears, Kanye left his seat to hug and thank her. He stated that being away from the public and the lack of that personal connection caused him to forget just how much weight his voice carried back in Chicago and the rest of black America. As a celebrity, he had lost track of what was most important. He was more concerned with the number of hit songs he had streaming online and how many "likes" he accumulated on social media. Kanye spoke of the lack of real friends in his life, blaming the TMZ incident on the absence of people like Rhymefest and Don C, his close friend from Chicago and former manager, who genuinely had his best interests in mind. Perhaps caught up in the moment, he broke down in tears, covering his face with his hand. Kendra consoled him by reminding him that he was back home with *his* family. Once he composed himself, Kanye elaborated on his need to maintain the support from his village.

> I'm pitted in competitions directly with Drake. I'm in competition directly with Virgil (Abloh) at the same damn time. I literally gotta have the shoes poppin' to the Off-White Nike-Louis Vuitton level. I got to have a record poppin' to the Kiki level. Then my blackness gets challenged. Am I talking black enough? Am I talking white enough? Am I representing enough inside a country that we got brought into, and then I still gotta get the sandals the right size![11]

The quip about the ill-fitting Yeezy slides lightened the mood and brought some much-needed humor to an intense conversation. The interview concluded with Kyle and Leon reminding Kanye that it was not only crucial for him to give back to Chicago, but to be present in the city and work directly with the people. The next day Kanye was interviewed by DJ Pharris at WPWX Power 92.3 FM. Pharris has been a fixture in Chicago radio and the city's house music scene since the late 1980s. He was one of the first Chicago tastemakers to embrace Kanye when he was a teenager being mentored by Chicago producer No I.D. Kanye returned the favor years later by giving Pharris cameos on his songs "Cold" and "I Don't Like (Remix)." Pharris reminded Kanye that his polarizing behavior might not affect his privileged existence, but it severely hurts his supporters back in the village. After reviewing these two interviews I asked myself, why do we expect so much from these entertainers? We want Kanye West to live up to unrealistic expectations set nearly 20 years ago when he made two phenomenal albums and forget that he is a flawed individual who evolves, for better or worse, over time. Weeks later, Kanye was back in Chicago, appearing at an event for local high school students hosted by Chance the Rapper. Kanye announced to everyone's surprise—including his wife and her family—that he was permanently moving back to the Chi.

J-A-Y and Ye so Chi

Kanye had recently purchased 300 acres of land in Calabasas, California, at the time of his Chicago radio interviews. "I am buying America and making it mine. The land of the free," he told the hosts at WGCI.[12] A year later, he bought 4,500 acres of land in Wyoming for $14 million. His 4,500-acre property, renamed West Lake Ranch, has two lakes across it. The ranch is home to 160 cows, 700 sheep, and other livestock. He uses the wool from the sheep for his Yeezy brand clothing. GQ published an April 2020 cover story highlighting the manufacturing and production at the ranch. "They don't teach about buying property. They teach you how to become somebody's property," Kanye told GQ.[13] Kanye's moves and attitude reflect the entrepreneurial spirit of black Chicagoans such as Don Cornelius, the founder and host of the nationally syndicated series Soul Train (1971–2006). Cornelius's series, modeled after Dick Clark's American Bandstand, gave the civil rights movement the weapon of joy to strike back at Jim Crow through the latest dance moves, fashion, and a heavy dose of black pride. Cornelius was the first black man to have such a loft television platform.

Although they were not born in Chicago, Sarah Goode, John H. Johnson, Oprah Winfrey, and Michael Jordan achieved much of their fortunes there. Goode, a former slave born in Toledo, Ohio, migrated to Chicago, where she and her husband, Archibald, ran a custom furniture business. In 1885 she became the first black woman to receive a patent after she invented the foldaway bed.[14] John Johnson's family migrated to Chicago from Arkansas when he was in the eighth grade. After completing his studies at the University of Chicago, Johnson used the $6,000 that he raised and a $500 loan to start his first periodical, Negro Digest, which evolved into Black World. Johnson began publishing Ebony and Jet magazines in 1945 and 1951, respectively. Ebony became the number-one black-owned magazine for the remainder of the century. Jet was the world's top-selling black newsweekly magazine.[15] The publishing empire's success made John Johnson the first black American included on the Forbes 400, a list of the 400 wealthiest Americans.

Oprah Winfrey graced multiple covers of Ebony and Jet, then transcended race unlike any black celebrity before or since her ascendency. She founded Harpo Studios, home to her daily ABC talk series, in Chicago in 1986. With a unique brand of entertainment that was part therapeutic, part spiritual, Winfrey used her series to reach the American public's hearts and minds. At its peak, The Oprah Winfrey Show (1986–2011), which won 47 Daytime Emmy Awards, averaged 42 million viewers a week. White women adopted her as the black sister they wish that they had. Winfrey was the ultimate embodiment of racial uplift, overcoming poverty and teenage pregnancy in rural Mississippi to become the first black female billionaire in North America and the CEO of her own cable television network. She was so beloved that the media was clamoring for her to run for the presidency in 2020.

Michael Jordan was the only Chicagoan more famous than Oprah in the 1990s. Sports journalist Robert "Scoop" Jackson credits Jordan and his Chicago Bulls teams with birthing the "can't tell me nothing" demeanor embodied by Kanye West.[16] Jordan's dazzling moves on the basketball court evoked fits of exuberance among spectators that would make one think they were catching the Holy Ghost at a Pentecostal church revival.[17] At the height of Jordan's playing career, his endorsements included Chevrolet, Coca-Cola, Gatorade, Hanes, McDonald's, Upper Deck, and Wheaties. In 2010 he purchased the Charlotte Hornets basketball franchise from BET founder Robert L. Johnson. Michael Jordan is currently the only black American majority owner in American professional sports. His financial empire, built largely on the sales of his Nike Air Jordan sneakers and team ownership, made him a billionaire in 2015.

Kanye West officially became a billionaire in 2020 due to the mind-numbing sales of his lucrative Yeezy brand sneakers distributed by Adidas.[18] It was quite a feat considering the fact that there were only five other black billionaires in the country and a total of 16 worldwide.[19] Two months later, Kanye announced Yeezy Gap, his new apparel line coming to Gap, one of the largest American retailers in the world with nearly 6,000 stores. Kanye worked there as a teenager and secretly interned there during his self-imposed exile to learn the fashion industry. Gap's shares on the stock market increased by 39 percent because of Kanye's partnership.[20] Entrepreneurship is only one characteristic of the Chi that defines Kanye West. To understand the soul of Mr. West, you must first understand the soul of Chicago. The Windy City was the prime location for black Americans during the Great Migration. The city's black population increased from 44,103 in 1910 to 109,458 within a decade. By 1930 more than 235,000 blacks were Chicago residents. Davarian Baldwin, author of *Chicago's New Negroes* (2007), says a black mass consumer marketplace developed in the city, generating a vibrant intellectual life and planting seeds of political dissent.

The Pittsburg Courier and *The Chicago Defender* were largely responsible for enticing black Southerners to pack their bags and travel north and westward in search of the American Dream.[21] *The Defender* marketed Chicago as a "Mecca for Pleasure" and a "poor man's paradise."[22] According to sociologists St. Clair Drake and Horace Cayton, a trip to the Windy City was a flight to freedom.[23] However, migrants soon discovered that racial violence and discrimination could be just as rampant in the Midwest as in the South. On July 27, 1919, Eugene Williams, a 17-year-old black teenager, chose to test out his freedom by taking a swim in the deadly waters of Chicago's 29th Street beach. The city's de facto color line confined blacks' swimming to 25th Street. As Williams floated in the water, his body was pounded down by a hailstorm of rocks thrown by a group of white hooligans.[24] His death lit the match under longstanding racial tensions that had been simmering each year as more blacks "invaded" the city once dominated by white European immigrants. A riot erupted following a white police officer's arrest of an innocent black male instead of the actual culprits.

The riot dragged on for seven days, resulting in 38 deaths; 23 of the victims were black. More than 1,000 blacks lost their homes. The *Chicago Daily Tribune* blamed the black community for the riot; in actuality, Irish gangs encouraged other white ethnics to attack black neighborhoods and businesses.[25] Of the 25 race riots that tore apart American cities in the "Red Summer" of 1919, following the return of emboldened black World War I veterans, the Chicago riot was arguably the worst.[26] The violence could have been less extensive if the local police department had shown concern for the black residents. *The Crisis*, the NAACP's official magazine, highlighted the lack of arrests in occurrences of white-on-black violence. The 1929 *Illinois Crime Survey* reported that 30 percent of the fatalities in Chicago from police shootings were black victims—a startling number because blacks barely comprised five percent of the population.[27] It is a wonder that such brutality did not transform all law-abiding blacks into Bigger Thomas.[28]

Housing was another problem that burdened the city's black residents. Historian Arnold Hirsch said the municipal government's solution to their Negro problem was creating public housing projects such as the Robert Taylor Homes and Cabrini-Green Homes, which became what he called "the second ghetto."[29] In July 1965, civil rights groups led by Albert Raby, cofounder of the Coordinating Council of Community Organizations, invited the Reverend Martin Luther King, Jr., to assist in their efforts to eliminate housing discrimination. For King and his organization, the Southern Christian Leadership Conference (SCLC), Chicago was a test case to see if nonviolence could work outside of the South.

The SCLC announced plans for the Chicago Freedom movement on January 6, 1966. When King arrived, he and his wife Coretta moved into one of the city's slums that housed poor black families. The Kings and their allies endured a lack of heat and risked being robbed by junkies in search of $20 to get a "fix" as they slept at night. The SCLC's strategy was to send black and white applicants to real estate offices to apply for homes. The whites always received an assortment of houses from which to choose. Black applicants were either turned away or directed to something in the ghetto.[30] The SCLC's efforts in Chicago exposed the blatant racism of the North. The Reverend Andrew Young called Chicago the most segregated city in America, noting that neighborhoods were not solely segregated by race, but also by ethnicity. The Irish had their block. The Polish and Italians had their blocks.

In the documentary *Becoming* (2020), former First Lady Michelle Obama, reflecting on her childhood in Chicago's South Side, described white residents moving out of the neighborhood once her family moved in. The Reverend King experienced the city's racism firsthand when he was struck by a rock while leading a march through a white neighborhood full of protestors draped in Confederate flags.[31] King told his personal assistant Clarence Jones that Chicago's racial intolerance was worse than anything he ever experienced in Alabama or Mississippi.

Kanye West was born on June 8, 1977, in a tiny city located west of Atlanta, Georgia. It would be three years before he moved to Chicago, but the winds of change were already blowing in the city weeks after his birth. The administration of Mayor Richard J. Daley, referred to as the Daley Machine, oversaw municipal politics from 1955 until he died in 1976. On April 19, 1977, Harold Washington, who was vying to become the city's first black mayor, lost to Michael Bilandic in the primary election. Mayor Bilandic's failure to provide for black residents' needs during a historic blizzard in 1979 led to the election of Mayor Jane Byrne. Despite strong black support initially, black voters began to feel neglected by the Byrne administration and turned to Washington as the answer to their prayers. Harold Washington faced off against Richard M. Daley, son of the late Mayor Daley, and the incumbent Mayor Byrne in the 1983 democratic primary. Washington relied on black and Latinx residents to form his base, winning the Democratic Party primary. Seven weeks later he won the general election. Washington's campaign laid a blueprint for future black Chicago politicians Carol Moseley Braun, Jesse Jackson, Sr., and Jr., and Barack Obama to follow. Kanye was only 10 at the time of Washington's untimely death from a heart attack in 1987, but he was old enough to comprehend the magnitude of having a black man leading his hometown.[32]

Touch the Sky

Hundreds of Chicago's new migrants were musicians. Their tunes provided a soundtrack to the daily experiences and struggles of the city's black residents. By the early 1950s, Chicago was a leader in recording, distributing, and broadcasting popular music nationwide. The city was a cradle for jazz, the blues, and gospel music. Muddy Waters (McKinley Morganfield) migrated from Mississippi in 1943. He became the father of modern Chicago blues and laid the blueprint for rock and roll. Thomas Dorsey originated gospel music at Pilgrim Baptist Church on the South Side. Chicago was home to Steppin', a form of swing dancing that started in the 1970s but was popularized nationwide by R. Kelly's 2003 hit, "Step in the Name of Love (Remix)." While each of these musical genres influenced a young Kanye West, it was Chicago's soul music that blessed the world with his signature sound.

Robert Pruter's *Chicago Soul* (1992) and Aaron Cohen's *Move On Up: Chicago Soul Music and Black Cultural Power* (2019) document the history of soul music in the Chi.[33] Soul is a musical genre derived from gospel and rhythm and blues. Historian Peter Guralnick, author of *Sweet Soul Music* (1999), draws parallels between its beginnings and the death of the Reverend Martin Luther King, Jr. "Once it emerged from the underground, it accompanied the Civil Rights Movement almost step by step, its success directly reflecting the giant strides that integration was making, its popularity almost a mirror image of the social changes that were taking place," says Guralnick.[34] Many of the musicians who defined the genre were active in the movement. Aretha Franklin, the daughter of preaching giant the Rev. Clarence LaVaughn (C.L.) Franklin, went on an 11-city tour with King to help the SCLC make payroll. Franklin also hosted the movement's leaders at her home to help them save on the cost of hotel accommodations.[35]

Soul intersected with the rise of the Motown sound. In 1959 Berry Gordy used an $800 loan from his family to launch Motown Records, the first black music empire.[36] Motown's first hit record was Jackie Wilson's "Reet Petite." The song worked because it was non-threatening, not too funky or too bluesy to cross over on white radio stations. Within a year, Motown had the number-two song on the charts with The Miracles' "Shop Around." Gordy scored his first number-one hit on the pop charts in 1961 with the Marvelettes' "Please Mr. Postman." An illustrated picture of a mailbox was used in place of a photograph of the three black teenage Marvelettes to ensure that whites would feel comfortable buying the music. Motown's artists were not the first black singers to achieve crossover success. Fats Domino (Antoine Domino, Jr.) and Little Richard (Richard Penniman) blazed a trail in the mid–1950s with songs such as "Ain't That a Shame," "Blueberry Hill," "Long Tall Sally," and "Tutti Frutti." Little Richard's music was overwhelmingly popular with white teenagers, but still "too black" and not refined enough for some mainstream radio stations. Pat Boone, the second-biggest charting pop artist at the time, behind Elvis Presley, recorded a more *respectable* cover of Little Richard's "Tutti Frutti" in 1956.

Motown's primary objective was to make music that would become America's sound. Since most of Berry Gordy's artists were "ghetto kids from single-parent homes," he hired Maxine Powell to head the Motown Finishing School. Mrs. Powell was an older black woman trained in etiquette.

Mary Wilson of the Supremes says Powell taught Motown's singers how to be elegant and respectable. She taught Diana Ross and the Supremes how to stand correctly on stage and always look pleasant when they sang. "You do not protrude the buttocks. Everything had to be done in a classy way. If they were doing the shake or whatever, we didn't do it in a vulgar way. Class will help you crossover anywhere. It doesn't have to do with being black," said Powell.[37] The male artists were taught movements that would attract the ladies. But if their dance moves looked too "primitive," like something found on the R&B circuit catering to segregated black audiences, the artists were taught to make their moves more sophisticated for the white audiences at the Las Vegas venues and on television. Motown artists Boyz II Men applied this strategy to dominate the pop charts in the 1990s until younger white boy bands copied their style and stole their (white) fans.

Suzanne E. Smith writes in *Dancing in the Street: Motown and the Cultural Politics of Detroit* (2003) that Motown's mainstream success signified black America's advancement.

> Some found in Motown's ability to reach white audiences the hope that interracial understanding was possible. Others considered Motown's music less about bridging racial divides than about advancing race pride. Many of Motown's performers began to feel "twice tried"—wanting to be accepted as entertainers, but also remembering that "they are Negroes." In the midst of these competing forces, the company maintained its agenda of maximizing its music's commercial potential with national and international audiences.[38]

Some blacks found Motown's cabaret presentation too polished and sanitized for a white gaze. Soul music was not polished and pretty. Instead, it was raw and uncut. It was the secular alternative to the sanctified sounds of the black church. Sydney Pollack's grainy 1972 footage of Aretha Franklin's two-night concert at New Temple Missionary Baptist Church in the Watts neighborhood of Southern California, remastered in the 2018 documentary *Saving Grace*, captured the Queen of Soul at her finest belting out tunes with a local choir. The Reverend James Cleveland accompanied Franklin on the piano and wiped away the perspiration pouring down her face like a faucet. The concert captured the unpolished emotions and sounds that were too much for most white audiences to fully comprehend. In Questlove's 2021 documentary *Summer of Soul*, gospel greats like Mahalia Jackson and Mavis Staples share the stage with secular soul singers at the 1969 Harlem Cultural Festival.

Memphis, Tennessee, was the headquarters of Stax Records, where black artists did not need anyone instructing them how to sing, dance, stand, or speak. The white-owned label's roster included Wilson Pickett, Isaac Hayes, Otis Redding, and Sam & Dave. Pickett had listeners feeling his love tumbling down "In the Midnight Hour." Hayes was the architect of the timeless *Shaft* soundtrack (1971). Redding was the label's brightest star until his tragic plane crash. Kanye sampled Redding's 1966 cover of Valerian Rosing's "Try a Little Tenderness" and credited him as a feature on his 2011 Grammy Award-winning single "Otis."[39]

Soul music experienced a renaissance in the form of neo-soul in the mid–1990s. A cadre of artists including Maxwell, D'Angelo, Bilal, Erykah Badu, Jill Scott, India.Arie, and Lauryn Hill fused elements of R&B, funk, jazz, hip-hop, and traditional soul music. This new sound could be heard on some rap albums such as The Roots' *Things Fall Apart* (1999). Kanye West was credited with reintroducing soul in hip-hop during the 2000s. Rather than rely on these Neo-soul artists, he turned back to the classics. He used the music of David Ruffin, Bobby "Blue" Bland, and The Jackson 5 to provide the soul-stirring production on Jay-Z's *The Blueprint*. Duke University professor Mark Anthony Neal discussed Kanye's reliance on soul samples from the 1960s and 1970s in his 2015 essay "Now I Ain't Saying He's a Crate Digger." Neal called Kanye's music "chipmunk soul" due to its high-pitched, cartoonish sound.[40] Kanye could make Lenny Williams's classic "Cause I Love You" (1975) sound like it was sung by the animated children's band Alvin and the Chipmunks.

This distinctive soulful sound permeated Kanye's first three albums. "Spaceships" sampled Marvin Gaye's "Distant Lover" (1974). "School Spirit" sampled Aretha Franklin's "Spirit in the Dark" (1970). "Addictive" sampled a 1994 cover of "My Funny Valentine" by Etta James. "Roses" sampled Bill Withers's "Rosie" (1977). "Devil in a New Dress" sampled Smokey Robinson's "Will You Love Me Tomorrow" (1973). Kanye's first number-one single on the *Billboard* Hot 100 was "Slow Jamz." The song, which featured Chicago emcee Twista (Carl Mitchell) and Jamie Foxx, sampled "A House is Not a Home" by Luther Vandross. "Gold Digger" (2005), his next number-one hit with Jamie Foxx, sampled Ray Charles's "I Got a Woman" (1954), which was a secular version of the gospel song "It Must Be Jesus" by the Southern Tones.[41]

Lauryn Hill and Nina Simone are among Kanye West's muses. He referred to himself as the youth's answer to Hill after she stopped recording new music in the early 2000s. Kanye sampled Hill's "Mystery of Iniquity" (2002) for his 2004 single "All Falls Down" and he sampled her hit "Doo Wop (That Thing)" on his 2021 album *Donda*. At her peak Hill was compared to Nina Simone (Eunice Waymon). As a dark-skinned black woman from North Carolina, who was a classically trained pianist at the Julliard School of Music in New York, Simone experienced the veil of racism early in life. With songs like "Mississippi Goddam" and "To Be Young, Gifted and Black," Nina Simone became one of the most outspoken vocalists of her era. Andy Stroud, her husband and manager, unsuccessfully advised her to abandon "the black shit" if she wanted to be successful. Kanye's sample of Simone's "Strange Fruit" for "Blood on the Leaves" is one of his most sonically daring works.

Nina Simon's "Strange Fruit" was a cover of Billie Holiday's gut-wrenching 1939 protest anthem. In March 1939, a 23-year-old Billie Holiday debuted "Strange Fruit" at West 4th's Café Society in New York City. The song was adapted from a poem written by Abel Meeropol, a Jewish communist teacher from the Bronx. Meeropol's poem was evoked by a photo of two black men, Thomas Shipp and Abram Smith, being lynched in Marion, Indiana, on August 7, 1930. Holiday was targeted by the FBI and Henry Anslinger, the first commissioner of the Federal Bureau of Narcotics, for performing this song. She spent a year in jail for narcotics possession, an excuse to silence her voice. Kanye's choice to use Simone's 1965 cover of that song was a bold statement.

Kanye intentionally aligned himself within the lineage of Chicago's most revered and socially conscious soul artists. In turn, this association led fans to view him as an emcee who was more concerned with uplifting the race and society than glorifying bling, booze, and bitches. The masses first learned of Kanye's lyrical gifts when they heard "Through the Wire," a song he rapped as his mouth was wired shut from a nearly fatal car accident. The song was a remake of Chaka Khan's 1984 single "Through the Fire." Khan, a native of Chicago's South Side, won 10 Grammys and crossed genres of soul, R&B, jazz, funk, and rock. Her 1979 hit "I Feel for You," written and composed by Prince, peaked at number three on the *Billboard* Hot 100. "I Feel for You" transformed Khan into an international star who sold more than 70 million records worldwide. Despite her acclaim, Khan never forgot the village that raised her.

Chaka Khan, christened the "wild child of soul," was born Yvette Marie Stevens on March 23, 1953. She came of age as much of Chicago's black community absorbed the ethos of Black Nationalism. Filled with black pride, a 13-year-old Khan joined Shades of Black, a local African culture band that wore traditional African attire and performed African songs. At this time a Yoruba Babalawo (or priest) gave her the name Chaka Khan, which was taken from the Zulu warrior Shaka Zulu. Khan led protests as the president of the Afro student organization at her high school, befriended activist Fred Hampton, and joined the local chapter of the Black Panther Party. Khan's radical ways caused increasing tension in her strict Catholic home. At 14, she ran away from her mother's home to live with her father and his second wife. Her stepmother was a civil rights activist who encouraged her to speak at local rallies.[42] Three years later, she replaced the lead singer in Rufus, Chicago's hottest soul band. Kanye's "Through the Wire" helped to introduce Chaka Khan, whose star had faded due to cocaine and alcohol abuse, to millennials. When she sang the national anthem at the 2020 NBA All-Star Game held at Chicago's United Center, Kanye sat courtside.

"Touch the Sky," featuring Chicago emcee Lupe Fiasco (Wasalu Muhammad Jaco), is one of my favorite songs on Kanye's sophomore album, *Late Registration*. Its uplifting chorus walks the fine line between the sacred and the secular as Kanye testifies about how extra "fly" his wardrobe is.[43] Curtis Mayfield's "Move on Up" (1971) provided the song's celebratory, gospel-infused vibe.[44] Mayfield was Chicago's definitive male soul artist. When he was 14, Mayfield joined The Impressions, a local soul group known for their gospel sound. The group's songs "Keep on Pushing" (1964), "People Get Ready" (1965), and "We're a Winner" (1968) were the drumbeat to the civil rights and black power protests throughout the country. Despite his critically acclaimed *Super Fly* soundtrack (1972), Mayfield did not achieve the international appeal of Chaka Khan. The lack of crossover hits did not bother him because he was singing for *his* people.

"Touch the Sky" became an intergenerational hit bridging the gap between the civil rights generation and the hip-hop generation. Years later Kanye credited Mayfield as a guest vocalist on "The Joy," a bonus track on the deluxe edition of *Watch the Throne*. Two other Chicago soul legends, Gil Scott-Heron and Sam Cooke were honored on *Late Registration*. The album's seventh track, "My Way Home," performed by Common, sampled Scott-Heron's "Home Is Where the Hatred Is" (1971). Kanye also sampled Scott-Heron's politically charged 1970 poem "Comment No. 1" for "Who Will Survive in America," the closing track on *My Beautiful Dark Twisted Fantasy*. Hip-hop historians have called Scott-Heron's poems, along with those of the Last Poets, the precursors to rap music. Gilbert Scott-Heron, a jazz poet and soul singer, was born in Chicago on April 1, 1949. His sophomore album, *Pieces of a Man* (1971), included the most notable recording of his career: "The Revolution Will Not Be Televised." The selection, the B-side to *Pieces of a Man's* first single, "Home Is Where the Hatred Is," became synonymous with the Black Power and anti-war movements.

The genesis of this recording came during Scott-Heron's time as a student at Lincoln University, an HBCU in Pennsylvania.[45] His concern for social issues grew as he witnessed, from afar, student protests of the Vietnam War at Kent State University (Ohio) and Jackson State University (Mississippi). Both demonstrations resulted in the death of multiple students at the hands of the National Guard and the Mississippi State Highway Patrol, respectively. Friends of his were targeted by the FBI's

COINTELPRO program, which conducted covert surveillance on black activists and anti-war protesters. Scott-Heron's objection to the treatment of the students at Lincoln, Kent State, and elsewhere inspired him to publish a novel titled *The Nigger Factory*. The book dealt with the student body president's efforts at an HBCU that is guilty of benefiting from systems of white privilege. Oddly enough, the student finds himself being targeted and discredited by his black classmates who disapproved of his activism and contrary free thought.

One evening in 1970, Scott-Heron was sitting in his dorm watching television when he began crafting lyrics to a new poem in his notebook. Over the next few weeks, he wrote more words to what eventually became "The Revolution Will Not Be Televised."[46] Scott-Heron's resounding voice is heard reciting the words "Who will survive in America? Who will survive in America? Who will survive in America?" as Kanye sprints through the forest, like a runaway Kunta Kinte in *Roots*, at the end of his 2010 music short film *Runaway*. Those lines, taken from "Comment No. 1," serve as a bookend to arguably the most politically charged album of Kanye's catalog. "I am in the lineage of Gil Scott-Heron, great activist-type artists," he proclaimed in a 2013 *New York Times* story titled "Behind Kanye's Mask."[47]

During his lifetime Sam Cooke would have never been perceived as radical as Gil Scott-Heron; however, nothing could have been further from the truth. Nas referenced Cooke's seminal recording "A Change is Gonna Come" (1963) in the final line of his guest verse on the *Late Registration* track "We Major." When Kanye produced Common's 2005 album *Be*, he used an interpolation of Cooke's "Nothing Can Change This Love" (1962) for its lead single, "The Food." Sam Cooke, born Samuel Cook in 1931, was the grandson of a slave from Mississippi. His father relocated the family to Chicago, where he became a minister in the Church of Christ (Holiness) two years later.

When he was 14, Cooke became the lead singer of The QCs, a local gospel group. In 1950 he replaced the lead singer of another gospel group, The Soul Stirrers. While on tour in Memphis, he and his group members took a group of girls they met to a segregated park. The boys, being from Chicago, were unaccustomed to the Southern city's mores. A police car pulled up and forced them to line up. The white officers did not appreciate Cooke's uppity attitude. "You are not in Chicago. We will hang you down here, and they'll never find your body."[48] This encounter was five years before Emmett Till, another Chicago teenager, was lynched in Mississippi for disobeying local customs. The incident had profound effects on Cooke's psyche.

Sam Cooke realized that he could not achieve the fame and fortune he sought singing in the church. Between 1957 and 1964, he recorded 30 top-40 singles on the pop charts. "You Send Me," "Cupid," and "Twisting the Night Away" were major crossover hits beloved by white teenagers. Cooke left Chicago and moved to Los Angeles, where he enjoyed rubbing shoulders with influential white executives who could open doors for him that were closed to most blacks. His crossover acclaim did not dull his sensibilities as a young black man living in a segregated society. He continued to perform for black audiences in the South and refused to play segregated white venues. Years before King's assassination at the Lorraine Motel in Memphis, Cooke stayed there when he chose to boycott a local venue that barred black patrons. He used code-switching to transmit different messages in his music to mixed audiences. When most whites listened to "Chain Gang" (1960), all they heard was a fun song. But for blacks, the lyrics conjured up images of black convict laborers in chains.

Sam Cooke befriended a young fighter from Louisville, Kentucky, named Cassius Clay who was training to fight Sonny Liston. Clay defeated Liston on February 25, 1964, in Miami, Florida, to become professional boxing's youngest heavyweight champion. As Clay was being honored and interviewed by reporters in the ring, he called for Sam Cooke to join him ringside and introduced him to the press as the world's greatest singer.[49] Later that night, Cooke joined Clay, Jim Brown, and Malcolm X at the Hampton House Motel and Villas to celebrate with the local blacks. A famous photograph was taken that night at the motel. A year later, Clay became known worldwide as Muhammad Ali, the most outspoken member of the Nation of Islam. Cooke and Malcolm X would both fall to assassins' bullets that same year.

At the age of 33, Cooke was fatally shot on December 11, 1964, at the Hacienda Motel in Los Angles. His killer was Bertha Franklin, a black manager at the motel. Franklin claimed that she shot him in self-defense. Earlier that evening Elisa Boyer, an Asian woman at the motel, accused Cooke of attempted rape and kidnapping. Cooke's murder is shrouded in conspiracy. Boyer was arrested for prostitution a year later. Some believe that Cooke's relationship with black militants Muhammad Ali and Malcolm X factored into his death. Before his death, his pristine image drew comparisons to Frank Sinatra. Mark Anthony Neal says white record labels did their best to conceal Cooke's politics for fear of alienating white fans and sponsors. Others believe that Cooke crossed the line, as a black man, by starting his own publishing company and record label in the sixties. He was planting seeds of empowerment and ownership in the minds of black artists who had long been exploited by white record labels. According to Neal and other interviewees in the 2019 Netflix documentary *ReMastered: The Two Killings of Sam Cooke,* this infringement had to be stopped.

The unfulfilled promise of Sam Cooke as a civil rights activist is captured in his posthumously released anthem "A Change Is Gonna Come," which he wrote after his band was denied rooms at a Holiday Inn near Shreveport, Louisiana.[50] Cooke and his group were arrested for disturbing the peace. Although "A Change Is Gonna Come" failed to achieve the adoration of his pop-friendly hits, it is arguably the most important record in his catalog.[51] Chaka Khan, Sam Cooke, Curtis Mayfield, and Gil Scott-Heron all contributed to the making of *The College Dropout* and *Late Registration*. Kanye West will never compare to any of these Chicago luminaries when it comes to activism. Perhaps that is to be expected given the period in which he rose to fame. His precursors paid the dues 50 years ago that allowed him to focus primarily on music, fashion, and crossing over to white America without perpetually feeling obligated to uplift the race.

Hold My Liquor

Kanye West Presents: Good Music—Cruel Summer (2012), a compilation album of new music from artists affiliated with Kanye's record label G.O.O.D. Music, was an ode to two other musical genres native to Chicago: house and drill. "Mercy," the album's lead single, was co-produced by The Twilite Tone (Anthony Christopher Khan). Tone, a famous house music DJ, also co-produced the album tracks "The One" and "I Don't Like (Remix)." House music started as an indirect reaction to the disco sucks movement led by Steve Dahl, a local white radio morning show host who lost his previous job after his station changed its format from rock to disco. Since gay black artists created many disco records, Dahl's anti-disco campaign was both racist and homophobic.

The death of mainstream disco forced Chicago's gay black partygoers underground. The Warehouse was the city's most popular underground nightclub. Frankie Knuckles, a DJ from New York City, was the club's main attraction. Knuckles popularized Chicago's house sound as mixtapes from his parties spread throughout the city. House is a genre of electronic dance music that alters disco by adding deeper basslines and more mechanical beats. House DJs use the Roland TB-303 bass synthesizer, the Korg Poly-61 synthesizer, and the Roland TR-808 drum machine to create their sound.[52] As house music spread throughout the city its target demographic expanded from the original underground crowd to middle-class, heterosexual black teens.

"Fade," the third single from *The Life of Pablo*, is best remembered for its music video, which had G.O.O.D. Music artist Teyana Taylor reenacting

Jennifer Beals's epic dance routine from the cult classic *Flashdance* (1983). Most people outside of Chicago are unaware that "Fade" sampled the house record "Mystery of Love" by Mr. Fingers (Larry Heard), another prominent figure on the scene. Kanye routinely hops on the keyboard towards the end of his Sunday Services to play the house record "Brighter Days" by Cajmere. *Jesus Is Born,* the 2019 debut album from his Sunday Service Choir, includes a gospel rendition of "Follow Me" by the New Jersey house music band Aly-Us. House DJ Pharris makes a cameo on "Cold," *Cruel Summer*'s the second single.

Cruel Summer* concluded with a remix to Chief Keef's "I Don't Like" (2012). Kanye worked with Chief Keef again on "Hold My Liquor" for *Yeezus*. Their working relationship symbolized Kanye's embrace of drill, a version of trap music that originated in Chicago's South Side after 2010. Trap music, founded in Atlanta in the early 2000s, is identified by its sub-divided hi-hats, heavy sub-bass layered kick drums, 808s in half time syncopated rhythms, and synthesizers. The genre's lyrical content centers around the trap, a Southern hip-hop slang term for the dope house where illegal drugs are sold. Before trap went mainstream it was primarily relegated to Southern hip-hop radio stations, strip clubs, and underground mixtapes from Atlanta's DJ Drama (Tyree Simmons).[53] Chicago's drill sound was birthed by poor black teenagers who expressed nihilistic feelings of anger, resistance, and violence. Chicago emcee G Herbo (Herbert Wright III) calls drill "dead music" because of its violent content.

In 2009 underground rapper King Louie recorded a mixtape, *Chiraq Drillinois,* in response to a close friend's death by gun violence. Louie, who is credited with coining Chicago's non-flattering monikers "Chiraq" and "Drillinois," appeared on *Yeezus*'s ninth track "Send It Up." Drill's origin story is a byproduct of the death of black power in Chicago. Beginning in the late 1950s, several street gangs formed in the city. The Almighty Vice Lord Nation (1957), The Black Disciples (1966), Gangster Disciples (1968), and the Almighty Black P. Stone Nation (1959) provided surrogate familial units and protection to poor black males against racist whites. Over time these gangs became violent rivals for turf. Fred Hampton, a 21-year-old youth leader in the NAACP and the chairman of the Illinois chapter of the Black Panther Party, founded the Rainbow Coalition, a peaceful alliance of the city's black and Puerto Rican gangs and southern white leftists. Hampton saw the potential in these gangs to provide outlets for positive change and constructive activism.

Fred Hampton's revolutionary work in Chicago put him in J. Edgar Hoover and the FBI's crosshairs. Hoover hired William O'Neal, as part of the FBI's counterintelligence program, COINTELPRO, to infiltrate the Panthers. O'Neal, a black man arrested twice for impersonating the police and interstate car theft, was promised to have his felony charges dropped by cooperating. He provided the FBI with the floor plan of Hampton's apartment. On the morning of December 4, 1969, the Chicago Police Department in conjunction with the FBI and the Cook County State's Attorney's Office, conducted a raid on Hampton's apartment as he slept in bed with his pregnant girlfriend. Hampton and fellow Panther Mark Clark were shot to death.[54] The murder of Fred Hampton, depicted in the 2021 film *Judas and the Black Messiah,* ended all serious attempts to curb emerging gang violence and left a void in positive, nonviolent leadership on the streets.

Chicago was not spared as the crack cocaine epidemic and the proliferation of illegal guns transformed American cities into overpoliced war zones. In 1984 the FBI and the Chicago Police Department created "Operation REACT," which resulted in the arrests of 417 gang members, including Gangster Disciples founder Larry Hoover, who received six consecutive life sentences. Lil Durk (Durk Banks), a former drill rapper turned singer, was interviewed for the documentary *In the Field.* According to Durk, Hoover's arrest made things worse on the streets because there was no O.G. (original gangster) to mediate the "beefs" between the younger gangbangers.[55] Drill music became one outlet for rival gangs to beef with each other.

Chief Keef (Keith Cozart) was the first drill artist to gain a national spotlight. By 2012 he was the hottest artist on the *Billboard* charts from Chicago, other than Kanye West, due to a trio of hits produced by local producer Young Chop (Tyree Pittman): "I Don't Like" featuring Lil Reese, "Love Sosa," and "3Hunna." Keef caught Kanye's attention after posting a series of YouTube videos while serving 30 days of house arrest in his grandmother's home. The next year he signed a record deal with Interscope worth $6 million. As drill became increasingly profitable, multiple documentaries and specials were released, including ABC *Nightline*'s *Inside Chicago's Gang Wars* (2012); *Chicago Tribune*'s *Chicago under the Gun* (2012); and WorldStarHipHop's *The Field: Violence, Hip-Hop, and Hope in Chicago* (2014). Spike Lee's musical film *Chi-Raq* (2015) satirized the gang culture surrounding drill.[56] The VICELAND docuseries *Noisey* did an eight-part series on drill titled *Chiraq.* Thomas Morton, a preppy white journalist and contributing editor of *Vice* magazine, took viewers on a safari-like experience through Chicago's streets with Keef, Durk, Chop, and other drill artists.

Despite drill's appeal on the pop charts by the early-mid 2010s, the music was still associated with gang violence.[57] Before Chief Keef began rapping, he and his crew, 3Hunna, were members of the Black Disciples. In 2012 a teenage rapper named Lil Jojo (Joseph Coleman), associated with the rival Gangster Disciples, released a song and music video titled "3 HUNNAK (BDK) [Black Disciple Killers]" mocking Chief Keef's "I Don't Like." Jojo and his crew appeared in the video shirtless waving guns in the air. A few months later, Jojo filmed himself and other Gangster Disciples harassing Lil Reese, a local rapper featured on "I Don't Like," on the streets of Black Disciple territory. Hours after the video was uploaded to YouTube, Jojo was murdered in a drive-by shooting in the Englewood neighborhood.[58] Kanye squashed his beef with Drake to co-host a "Free Larry Hoover" benefit concert in Los Angeles on December 9, 2021.

Father Michael Pfleger, the head priest of the majority-black Catholic parish Saint Sabina, and a social activist in Englewood since the 1970s, blamed drill music for escalating the violence in Chicago. In 2019 the city had 2,242 shooting victims and 424 murders by October, an improvement from previous years. President Trump deployed 154 federal agents to Chicago in July 2020 to quell the violence. Chicago had already recorded 414 homicides that year when Trump acted. Was Kanye West exploiting his hometown's gang culture and misguided youth by hopping on the drill wave a decade earlier? Kanye has been speaking out on Chicago's gang problem for years. "We Don't Care," the first song on *The College Dropout* (2004), touched on young black men growing up idolizing hustlers and gangsters. He specifically called attention to Chicago's gang violence on "Everything I Am" (*Graduation*) and "Murder to Excellence" (*Watch the Throne*). He collaborated with Malik Yusef (Malik Yusef El Shabazz Jones), a former gang member of the Almighty Black P. Stone Nation turned spoken word artist and social activist, on multiple albums. Kanye criticized President Obama, a former community organizer in the South Side, for his failure to do more to help Chicago while he was in office. Chicago's gang problem and murder rate were major talking points for Kanye when he met with President Trump at the White House.[59] He encouraged Trump to pardon Larry Hoover, arguing that a rehabilitated Hoover could be used as a positive change agent to curb the violence.[60]

But for all of Kanye's rhetoric, there is little evidence of his work to help the black people in these communities or halt the violence. Kanye is a product of Chicago, but not those environments. He lived a middle-class lifestyle and was fortunate enough to have a mom who was a college professor. He lived in China as a youth, traveled, made beats with No I.D., and briefly attended college with white classmates and other middle-class black students. He had a different upbringing and black experience from Chicago kids like Chief Keef and Lil Durk. Even though Kanye provides a counter to the black males' stereotypical image, his authenticity and identity has also been validated by connecting himself to the city's black underclass. Kanye raps about being from the hood on DJ Khaled's (Khaled Khaled) 2008 single "Go Hard." He did this again by appearing on Jeezy's "Put On" and Common's "The Corner." The video for Jeezy's song is filled with images of poor inner-city blacks hurt by the 2008 recession. While Common's corner is a metaphor for the neighborhood urban dwellers reside in.

I Put On for My City, On On for My City

A year after Kanye pledged to move back to Chicago, the *Chicago Sun-Times* reported on his unfulfilled promise. The paper reported that Kanye had not returned to the Regal since his first visit. There was no involvement in the Sweetest Day Comedy Jam that he promised to support. Yet Kanye was making headlines for purchasing his $14-million ranch in Cody, Wyoming. He was also in the news for building domes, inspired by the fictional structures in Planet Tatooine from the *Star Wars* films, to serve as low-income housing for the homeless in Calabasas. Keep in mind that the median income in Calabasas, home to the Kardashians and Jenners, is $140,929. The racial demographics in Calabasas are 83.9 percent white and 1.6 percent black. The racial demographics in Cody are 95.9 percent white and 0.2 percent black. These statistics bring us back to the points being made by Rhymefest and the morning show hosts at WGCI. Had Kanye forgotten about Chicago and the village that raised him? Was he more concerned with helping himself and pleasing the millions of non-black social media followers that love *KUWTK* and Yeezys? How did Kim's refusal to leave Calabasas and move their family to Chicago influence his actions?

Lori Lightfoot, Chicago's first black female mayor, rejected Kanye's endorsement when she was running for office in 2018. Perhaps that says something about the love lost for Mr. West by some Chicagoans. The city hosted the NBA All-Star weekend in February 2020. Kanye's presence was felt; however, he was not as visible as his peers. On February 15, he had a fleet of armored off-road vehicles, like the ones in his "Closed on Sunday" music video, ride through the city giving out free pairs of his unreleased $250 Yeezy Quantum high-top basketball sneakers. The next day he held a Sunday Service at the Credit Union 1 Arena six hours before the All-Star game. He and Kim sat courtside at the game, on celebrity row. Chicago natives Chaka Khan, Chance the Rapper, Common, and Jennifer Hudson took center stage for the nationally televised pre-game and halftime festivities. ESPN's Bomani Jones called Common's pre-game freestyle the most powerful and emotion-stirring ode to black Chicago that he has ever heard. While it was great to see Kanye West in the building, he appeared detached from Common and the other Chicago performers as he sat there beside Kim wearing his dark sunglasses and new Yeezys.

PART III

The Miseducation
of Kanye West

Politics, Prayer, and Platforms

SEVEN

"Republicans Buy Yeezys Too"

"I'll never let my son have an ego.... I mean, I might even make 'em be Republican, so everybody know he love white people." *Kanye West*[1]

The thought of Kanye West becoming a detested mouthpiece for Donald Trump, the Republican Party, Fox News, and conservatism would have been unfathomable 10 years ago. For some this transition is an indelible stain on his brilliant legacy. Although this evolution was confounding for most of his liberal fans, his song lyrics have included conservative themes since the start of his career. Some critics believe that Kanye's unsuccessful run for president in 2020 to steal votes from the Democrats' eventual winner, Joe Biden, was encouraged by Trump and the Republicans. Others view his politics as a manifestation of a need for white validation. Since 2016 it has become extremely difficult to separate Kanye's music from his political views. This chapter delves into Kanye's politics, which provide a fascinating analysis of conservatism's historical and contemporary archetypes. The ridicule that Kanye faced for his politics is a microcosm of the experiences of other black celebrities and non-famous blacks who publicly espouse political values that are out of sync with the majority in black America.

The Hug

Black America loved Sammy Davis, Jr., until he became a lightning rod for conservative politics. Davis's relationship with Richard Nixon and the Republican Party provides a unique backdrop for understanding the optics of Kanye West's coziness with President Trump. Whites loved Davis's singing and dancing ability and his uncanny knack for impersonating great white celebrities such as Humphrey Bogart. He was one of the few black artists who could successfully cover hits by famous white singers. Davis, who began performing as a child in blackface routines, always wanted to be viewed as an entertainer who transcended race. He converted to Judaism in 1954. Professor Gerald Early says Davis saw himself combating racism and uplifting the entire race through his own transcendence.[2] Davis attended the 1963 March on Washington and publicly endorsed Dr. King. He participated in the 1964 Selma campaign, and raised the equivalent of $5.5 million today for civil rights organizations. The NAACP awarded him the Spingarn Medal, their highest honor, in 1968. Nevertheless, Davis always felt like a member of the black race due to his color, but an outsider within the black community.

In the wake of King's traumatizing assassination, the Reverend Jesse Jackson and entertainment powerbroker Clarence Avant came up with an ambitious idea to honor his memory. The result was Save the Children, a five-day music festival held in Chicago that brought together 30 of the most prominent black artists in 1972 signed to Motown, Stax, and Atlantic Records. The festival's star-studded lineup included The Jackson 5, Marvin Gaye, The Temptations, Isaac Hayes, The Staples Sisters, and Gladys Knight.[3] Sammy Davis, Jr., provided the festival's most memorable moment. At the time he was starring in films with Rat Pack members Frank Sinatra and Dean Martin, and headlining in Las Vegas casinos. He had the number-one song, "The Candy Man," on the *Billboard* Hot 100 chart. But none of that mattered to the black concertgoers who booed him in Chicago that weekend.

Why was Sammy Davis, Jr., booed? The answer lies in the White House. Richard Nixon, the Republican candidate, won the presidency in 1968. Tricky Dick was no Jack Kennedy or even a poor man's version of Lyndon Johnson. Presidents Kennedy and Johnson won the black vote with very liberal policies. Johnson signed the 1964 Civil Rights Act and the 1965 Voting Rights Act into law. He brought the late Kennedy's idea for a War on Poverty to fruition after his assassination. Kennedy and Johnson were allies of Dr. King and the civil rights activists. Most blacks saw Nixon's conservatism and law-and-order rhetoric as a counter to their progress under his two Democratic predecessors. The Congressional Black Caucus boycotted Nixon's 1971 State of the Union Address.

President Nixon attempted to win over black constituents by befriending black celebrities Jim Brown and James Brown. He sent Bob Brown, one of his few black aides, to Beverly Hills to meet with Sammy Davis, Jr., and offer him a position on the President's National Advisory Council on Economic Opportunity. Davis jumped at the opportunity despite the Black Caucus's animosity towards the administration. Davis's motivation to work with Nixon resulted from the Democrats' dismissiveness in the past. When Kennedy defeated Nixon in 1960, he had been endorsed by the Rat Pack. Kennedy asked Frank Sinatra, who was hosting an inaugural ball, to remove Davis from the guest list because he feared alienating southern voters who disapproved of his marriage to a white woman.

Wil Haygood, Author of *In Black and White: The Life of Sammy Davis, Jr.* (2003), describes Davis's demeanor at the council meetings:

> Davis loved sweeping into the White House, pulling open his Gucci briefcase, chatting up Bob Brown and the other black businessmen on the council. Davis walked like his Rat Pack pal Frank Sinatra: both summoned by presidents. When the meetings adjourned, Davis would hobnob with James Brown. Hearty slaps and soul-brother handshakes—the thumb slapping against the palm of the other hand, then the viselike grip. Ha-ha-ha. Nixon's soul brothers.[4]

Davis quickly became Nixon's right-hand (black) man. He was the first black to sleep in Lincoln's bedroom at the White House. Nixon was caught on a secret tape saying that "this was the first time a nig … an American black stayed in the White House."[5] When gospel legend Mahalia Jackson died, Davis attended her funeral on the president's behalf. The White House arranged for a private jet to pick up Davis, who was in Las Vegas, fly him to the service in New Orleans and then fly him back to Vegas in time for his next concert. The White House sent Davis to Vietnam a few weeks later to entertain the troops. He would raise his fist to make the Black Power salute when he performed for the soldiers. This simple gesture signified to the black soldiers in "Nam" that he was still "down" with them and the social causes in which they believed.[6]

Davis was in Vietnam as a goodwill ambassador, but he was also there to make sure the black GIs were not getting addicted to "smack" and other drugs.[7] Often blacks were being dishonorably discharged for their rampant drug use, while their white counterparts were given a slap on their wrists. Many of the black troops distrusted Davis because of his politics and his marriage to a white woman. When Davis returned stateside, Nixon asked him to assist in his reelection campaign. Once again, Davis proudly accepted the offer to "cape" for the president and GOP.[8] Davis attended the Republican Party's national convention that summer in Miami Beach, Florida. After Nixon received his party's nomination, he went to a Republican youth rally where Davis was performing. As the president entered the room, the young Republicans began gleefully chanting "Four more years! Four more years!" With an open shirt baring his bony chest, Davis quickly walked over to Nixon and hugged him. The president awkwardly wrapped his arms around the diminutive entertainer in a warm embrace made for TV.

To use today's phraseology, the photograph of Davis hugging Nixon went viral. The photo did not sit well with much of black America. Eartha Kitt, a black celebrity who caught the ire of Lyndon Johnson years earlier for her anti-war comments at a White House luncheon, was flying on a plane with Davis. Once the plane landed, she gave him a piece of her mind. This confrontation foreshadowed the reception waiting for Davis when he stepped on the stage at the Save the Children music festival. The majority-black crowd in Chicago showered boos down on him. Davis addressed his detractors, "Disagree with my politics, but I will not allow anyone to take away the fact that I am black." He then began singing his hit song "I've Gotta Be Me." By the conclusion of his performance, people were applauding; others were crying. Davis sang with so much conviction, as if his life depended on it. Here was a man saying to the crowd, "I am one of you." As many of the boos turned into cheers, he fought back the tears and held up his fist in the Black Power salute.

Davis continued to pal around with Nixon, giving a one-person performance at the White House on March 3, 1973. He retreated from the Republican Party and registered with the Democrats once the Watergate scandal forced Nixon's resignation.[9] The modern-day equivalent of "the hug" occurred when Kanye West accompanied former Nixon ally Jim Brown to the White House for lunch with Trump on October 11, 2018. What was supposed to be a luncheon between three "friends" turned into one of the strangest spectacles ever at 1600 Pennsylvania Avenue. The lunch happened barely two weeks after Kanye's polarizing appearance on *Saturday Night Live*'s season premiere. Kanye's underwhelming performance of his Lil' Pump duet "I Love It"—in which he dressed up as a giant bottle of Perrier water—was overshadowed by his pro–Trump, anti-liberal diatribe after the closing credits. Media members from across the globe were curious to find out what Mr. West would have to say now. A standing-room-only crowd packed the Oval Office. Reporters standing against the wall and cameramen on their knees snapping photos formed a circle around Kanye and Brown as they sat across from the president. Everyone in the room appeared to be white except Trump's two special guests and a well-dressed black woman and man sitting to Kanye's right side.

The unofficial press conference began with Trump lauding Jim Brown for his past athletic accomplishments. The president then began boasting about his work with Kim Kardashian to pardon Alice Johnson, an older black woman unfairly sentenced to life without parole for cocaine trafficking in 1996. Kanye was especially adamant about former Chicago street gang leader Larry Hoover receiving a similar pardon. Hoover, the founder of the Gangster Disciples, has been incarcerated since 1973 and is serving six life sentences. Kanye told the president that Hoover had been rehabilitated and could be his best asset in curbing the gang violence ravaging Chicago's black neighborhoods. He blamed the violence on welfare programs

sponsored by liberal Democrats and accused the 13th Amendment of sepa-
rating black families.[10]

Kanye told reporters that he was initially attracted to Trump because
Hillary Clinton's message appeared to run counter to his personal feelings:

> I love Hillary. But the campaign "I'm with her" just didn't make me feel, as a
> guy, that didn't get to see my dad all the time—like a guy that could play catch
> with his son. It was something about when I put this hat on; it made me feel like
> Superman. You made a Superman. That was my—that's my favorite superhero.
> And you made a Superman cape.[11]

Kanye's admiration of Trump at this moment seemed quite odd. He spoke as
though Trump was the daddy that he never had. Although Kanye's mother
primarily raised him from the age of three, his father was ever-present
throughout his lifetime. This interaction made me think of paternalistic
relationships between "benevolent" slave masters and their faithful black
servants. Kanye was displaying the same blind loyalty and admiration for
Trump that was shown by the noble house slave Stephen (Samuel L. Jackson) to his master Mr. Candie (Leonardo DiCaprio,) in Quentin Tarantino's
Django Unchained (2012). Perhaps that is too harsh a comparison. Let us
remember that Kanye had recently recovered from his mental breakdown
when he first started referring to Trump's red Make America Great Again
(MAGA) hat as his Superman cape.

During the 24-minute press conference Kanye touched on several
issues including mental illness, innovative ways to improve the curriculum
in American schools, protection of the Second Amendment, empowering
American manufacturers and pharmaceutical companies, and redesigning
the MAGA hat and slogan to make blacks more comfortable with it. He
suggested having Apple design a new iPlane to replace Air Force One so
that Trump could be "fly" as he traveled. Kanye called out black-on-black
crime to highlight the catastrophe of blacks killing each other and the lack
of attention being spent on that by liberals. While most of the reporters
behaved like kids in the cafeteria eager to be in the presence of the cool
kids, there was one who dared challenge Kanye's cheerleading for the
president.

> REPORTER: So you had said, of President Bush, that he doesn't care about
> black people. And you've heard some people say that about this President.
> What do you—how do you respond to that?
> KANYE: I think we need to care about all people. And I believe that when I
> went on NBC, I was very emotional, and I was programmed to think from
> a victimized mentality. A welfare mentality.
>   I think that with blacks and African Americans, we really get caught up
> in the idea of racism over the idea of industry. If people don't have land,

they settle for brands. We want Polo-sporting Obama again. We want a brand more than we want land. We haven't known how it feels to actually have our own land and have ownership of our own blocks.

So we focus more on, is somebody wearing something; is someone disrespecting so I got to shoot them. Or the idea of someone being racist.... One of the moves that I love that liberals try to do—the liberal would try to control a black person through the concept of racism, because they know that we are very proud, emotional people. So when I said, "I like Trump" to someone that's liberal, they'll say, "Oh, but he's racist." You think racism could control me?[12]

By the time Kanye finished speaking, both Trump and Jim Brown were at a loss for words. All Trump could do was promise to help Kanye improve conditions in Chicago. Then the president asked his special guests how they felt to be in the Oval Office—as if to say, "Are you all grateful to be seated in this sacred place?" Both men played along with this pandering and grinned as they expressed their gratitude. Trump told the press that he did not intend for this to have become a big event. It was only planned as a lunch with two people whom he likes and who he believes like him. Trump's comment led Kanye to publicly pledge his love to Trump in a similar fashion as Davis with Nixon. He walked over to Trump and wrapped his arms around him, grinning widely from ear to ear. "I love this guy right here. Let me give this guy a hug," said Kanye. Trump hugged him back without ever bothering to get out of his seat. Afterward, Kanye posed for pictures with Trump and his daughter Ivanka and her husband, Jared Kushner, sporting the new fitted MAGA hats that were designed for the occasion.

Don Lemon issued a damning assessment of Kanye West's 2018 White House luncheon hours after the event ended:

What I saw was a minstrel show today. Him [Kanye] in front of all these people, mostly white people, embarrassing himself and embarrassing Americans, but mostly African Americans, because every one of them is sitting either at home or with their phones, watching this, cringing. Kanye needs help, this has nothing to do with being liberal or conservative.... This was an embarrassment. Kanye's mother is rolling over in her grave.[13]

Y'All Do Know Martin Luther King Was Republican

Don Lemon's harsh critique of Kanye's White House visit undoubtedly expressed many black Americans' feeling watching highlights on the evening news. Why was the man who proclaimed "George Bush doesn't care about black people" caping for Trump? Had he made a Faustian bargain for a taste of power?[14] How Ye? CyHi da Prynce (Cydel Charles Young), a song-writer and an artist on the G.O.O.D Music label, came to Kanye's defense on Twitter. "Y'all do know Martin Luther King was Republican," he tweet-ed.[15] While it is a well-known fact that King's niece Alveda is an Evangeli-cal supporter of Trump, people have debated her uncle's political affiliation for decades.

Clayborne Carson, the editor of King's autobiography and the found-ing director of The Martin Luther King, Jr., Research and Education Insti-tute at Stanford University, never provided a definitive answer to this question. Carson says King voted Democratic; however, he may have been a registered Republican. Most blacks were Republican until the late 1950s. The Democratic party in Georgia and Alabama, the states where King spent much of his adult years, was "staunchly segregationist."[16] When I was a young boy spending summers in Sumter, South Carolina, with my grand-parents, I never understood why my adult cousin Charles enjoyed listening to *The Rush Limbaugh Show* (1988–2021). I was too young to understand politics, but I knew I did not like the flavor of Kool-Aid that Limbaugh was serving.[17] Charles was a Republican and so were his parents, my grandaunt Mildred and her husband Edward. My grandfather Arthur would often poke fun at Uncle Ed for being a Republican, reminding him that Lincoln was no longer in the White House. In her book *Raising Kanye* Donda West described her older sister, Kanye's Aunt Shirley, as a "militant Republican."[18]

Once upon a time, "not so long ago, when people wore pajamas and lived life slow," the Republican Party was the party of black America.[19] Polit-ical party affiliation has always been fluid. Abraham Lincoln, the Republi-can candidate in the 1860 presidential election, had been calling for an end to the expansion of slavery in the new western territories since his 1858 debates with Democrat Stephen Douglas for the U.S. Senate seat in Illinois. Lincoln's main objective was free soil, which meant that non-landowning white laborers migrating to the West would not have to compete with black slaves for work. Southerners misinterpreted this and assumed that he was hell-bent on disrupting their precious way of life. Lincoln won the presi-dency with only 40 percent of the popular vote, and no Electoral College votes in the South. Seven southern states seceded from the Union before his inauguration to form the Confederate States of America.[20] The Confed-eracy had its own president, Jefferson Davis, and government.

Two years into the Civil War, President Lincoln issued the Emancipa-tion Proclamation ending slavery in the rebelling states. The 13th Amend-ment, spearheaded by Lincoln and a majority-Republican Congress, marked an end to slavery nationwide. After Lincoln's assassination, the Radical Republicans, led by Pennsylvania Congressman Thaddeus Stevens, rewarded black men with citizenship and voting rights. These Republicans oversaw the creation of the Freedmen's Bureau, which provided shelter to destitute freedmen and poor whites, opened primary schools and colleges to educate black Southerners, and built hospitals.[21] The Republican Party's commitment to the freedmen gained them black voters and the support of abolitionist Frederick Douglass, the most influential African American in the mid–19th century. This commitment did not mean that all Republicans favored black equality. Before his death Lincoln evolved from advocating colonization of freed blacks abroad to equality in the Union. At the end of the 19th century some Republicans attempting to reclaim their party and appeal to white southern voters formed the Lily-white movement.

While 65 black delegates participated in the national Republican convention in 1912, the Democratic convention was void of any black representation until 1936. The Republicans' kung fu grip on the black vote began to loosen during the Hoover administration and Great Depression. President Herbert Hoover's support for the lily-white faction cost the party some black votes. His failure to improve the economy and provide relief resulted in the election of his Democratic challenger Franklin Roosevelt in 1932. President Roosevelt was not a strong advocate for civil rights. His fear of alienating racist white southerners and losing southern Democratic support for his New Deal in Congress prevented him from supporting an anti-lynching bill or desegregating the military. It was his wife, Eleanor, who was the black community's genuine ally. She agitated to have Marian Anderson perform at the Lincoln Memorial and the White House after being prohibited from singing at Constitution Hall because she was black. Mrs. Roosevelt was also responsible for the Tuskegee Airmen fighting in World War II.[22] Her activism contributed to a small exodus of blacks to the Democratic Party in the 1940s.

On October 19, 1960, Martin Luther King, Jr., was arrested and sentenced to six months of hard labor for his involvement in an Atlanta sit-in. His wife Coretta, who was pregnant with their third child Dexter, was contacted by the Democratic presidential nominee John F. Kennedy offering his assistance. King was released from jail after Kennedy spoke to the governor on Mrs. King's behalf. Five days later, King publicly expressed his gratitude to the young Massachusetts senator. King's endorsement was enough to encourage black preachers across the country to urge their congregations to vote for Jack on November 8. With Kennedy in office, blacks believed they finally had a seat at the table.

Kennedy's successor Lyndon Johnson maintained the black vote with the passage of the 1964 Civil Rights Act, the 1965 Voting Rights Act, the war on poverty, and affirmative action. His utterance of the phrase "We shall overcome" before a full session of Congress brought tears to the eyes of black listeners. Howard University invited him to be their 1965 commencement speaker. Johnson's legislation alienated the racist wing of Southern segregationists in the Democratic Party, known as Dixiecrats. Nevertheless, the presence of the Dixiecrats was not enough to halt blacks' great migration to the party in the sixties. Nor was President Johnson's Law Enforcement Assistance Act, which may have planted the seeds of 21st-century mass incarceration by empowering the federal government to militarize local police departments, enough to make black voters rethink their exodus.[23]

The Republican Party did not make much of an effort to maintain their once faithful constituency. Conservative presidential candidates Barry Goldwater and Richard Nixon went out of their way with dog-whistle politics to attract white Southerners who opposed civil rights. Goldwater's and Nixon's overemphasis on law and order, which disproportionately disadvantaged blacks and Latinos, did little to help. By the 1980s and 1990s, the War on Drugs, Reaganomics, the rise of conservative talk radio, and Roger Ailes's right-wing empire at Fox News unintentionally secured the Democrats over 90 percent of the black vote.[24]

Blacks who remained loyal to the Grand Old Party (GOP) risked being called sellouts.[25] Sammy Davis, Jr., was not the only black celebrity to have his blackness questioned for endorsing Nixon. When James Brown got behind the president, he felt the need to tell reporters, "I'm not selling out, I'm selling in." WHUR, Howard University's radio station, continued to play his music, but condemned his politics. When Brown held a concert in Baltimore, 50 protesters picketed the event. Brown's 2,500 fans could hardly fill up the 13,000-seat arena. James Brown favored Nixon's economic policies, not his stance on social issues.[26] Economic policies were also the basis for Jim Brown's admiration for Nixon. Brown, a retired NFL star and actor who broke interracial taboos by making love to a white woman in a film, was viewed as a hero for Black Power activists. Blacks cheered him when he debated Georgia's racist governor Lester Maddox on *The Dick Cavett Show* in 1970 over Muhammad Ali's refusal to serve in the Vietnam War.[27] Yet Jim Brown disapproved of King's nonviolent methods and supported Nixon's pledge to build up the black community's economic base. Brown's endorsement of Nixon foreshadowed his love for Trump.[28] He told former Fox Sports Radio host JT The Brick (John Tournour) he was willing to risk being vilified to stand in Trump's corner.[29]

According to the National Black Survey, 1972–1974, 43 percent of black voters and 50 percent of black non-voters identified as liberals. By the early 1980s, black Republicans like Jim Brown were becoming an endangered species. A month after Ronald Reagan won the presidency, *Saturday Night Live* aired a short sketch titled "In Search of the Negro Republican." A 19-year-old Eddie Murphy made his television debut in this sketch about a white zoologist who attended a Manhattan cocktail party in search of the elusive black conservative. The zoologist initially mistook a dignified black man dressed in a dark suit for his prize, but it turned out that the man owned a funeral home. He suspected another man in the room based upon his diction, attire, taste in music, and financial interests. The zoologist sedated this gentleman to study him once he awoke.[30]

During the 1984 national political conventions, 17.7 percent of the Democratic delegates (697 delegates) were black, compared to only 3.1 percent, or 69 black participants, among the Republicans.[31] The black Republican had gone from being the norm to an anomaly. Gina McNelley completed her dissertation, "Black Republicans' Beliefs and its Effects on their Identity and Relationships," in 1998. From her research, McNelley discovered that most black Republicans and conservatives were stigmatized as being "anti-black," "race traitors," "sellouts," "Uncle Toms," and "Oreos."[32] According to McNelley, black Republicans were seen as morally tainted and socially rejected.[33]

For years U.S. Supreme Court Justice Clarence Thomas has been an outcast in black circles due to his conservatism. Unlike Colin Powell, a well-liked and respected (moderate) black Republican, Thomas would not receive an invitation to most black cookouts and family reunions. Thomas vented his frustration with being ostracized in a 1987 address to the Heritage Foundation, a conservative think tank based in Washington, D.C. His speech, subsequently published in *Policy Review*, was titled "No Room at the Inn: The Loneliness of the Black Conservative." Thomas expressed feelings of alienation in the presence of black liberals, white liberals, the liberal media, and even some white conservatives. "One person asked rhetorically, 'why do we need blacks thinking like whites?'" said Thomas.[34]

What the Hell Do You Have to Lose?

It was hard out here for a black Republican who supported Donald Trump. Lee Adams, host of the popular docuseries *Minority Reports* for the VICE television network, found this out in 2019. Adams dedicated the third episode of the show's second season to the increase in black millennial Trump supporters. The episode began with his trip to the inaugural Young Black Leadership Summit in Washington, D.C. The summit, a four-day conference for black conservatives and Trump supporters, was organized by Candace Owens (more on her later). Adams's mouth dropped to the floor as he witnessed a room full of black millennials chanting "USA, USA, USA" as their beloved hero entered the room.

"Look where you are standing. In the White House, not bad," Trump said once the cheering ceased. He reminded the group that the Democrats never did anything for them.

One young man in the audience shouted out, "No more plantation!"

Trump replied, "I can live with that. I was never a fan." He told the crowd the Democrats ruined the black community by creating massive unemployment and mass incarceration. He reminded them that when he ran for office, he asked blacks to trust him with their vote by asking them: "What the hell do you have to lose?"

The crowd said the same with him in unison and then broke out into the "USA, USA, USA" chant again. The next scene captured the conference attendees at an outdoor rally on Capitol Hill chanting, "We are free! We are free!" One passionate young man grabbed a bullhorn and told the crowd, "The only reason black men are out here stomping on flags and burning them is because the Democrats never taught them to love that fucking flag!"

Donald Trump won more black votes than Mitt Romney or John McCain in 2008 and 2012. Nonetheless, black Trump supporters faced far more scrutiny than most black Republicans and conservatives. Jason Johnson, a professor at Morgan State University and MSNBC contributor, called the young people at the summit lost, disturbed, and self-loathing. The Reverend Al Sharpton characterized them as a bunch of props in MAGA hats. When Kanye West was on David Letterman's Netflix series, *My Next Guest Needs No Introduction*, he accused liberals of bullying conservatives. Shekinah Geist, a budding conservative social media influencer interviewed by Lee Adams for *Minority Reports*, spoke about how cyberbullying affected her. A white family in Greeley, Colorado, raised Geist after her teenage mother gave her up for adoption. She lost the few black friends that she did have once she began supporting Trump publicly. Students at her college attacked her on social media and accused her family of brainwashing her. Eventually, Geist dropped out of school because of excessive bullying.

Antonia Okafor, another social media influencer and ardent Second Amendment activist, was featured on *Minority Reports*. At the time, she was being honored at Iowa congressman Steve King's annual pheasant hunt, a GOP tradition. Past honorees included Ted Cruz and Donald Trump, Jr. The 31-year-old daughter of Nigerian immigrants was born and reared in a predominantly white area in Carrollton, Texas. She voted for Barack Obama twice but was disappointed by his inability to fulfill campaign promises of hope and change to her liking. Although her mom is an immigrant, she was willing to ignore Trump calling African nations "shithole" countries. Okafor does not view Republican-led voter suppression tactics in states like North Carolina and Georgia as harmful to minorities. She believes tactics such as requiring ID cards, labeled suppressive, are necessary to protect voters from exploitation by the Democratic Party. Okafor's support for Trump cost her familial relationships. Her sister severed ties and labeled her a race traitor.

In 2019 Lee Adams moderated a debate on VICE between black millennial liberals and conservative Trump supporters. During the discussion, the conservatives shared personal stories of verbal abuse and ostracism. Beveline, a black woman from the South serving probation for grand larceny and money laundering, attributed her love for Trump to his Christian values and economic empowerment policies. Her support for the president resulted in an assortment of racist and sexually explicit epithets hurled at her by black men on social media. Family members shunned her as someone wanting to be white. Christopher Wright, another debater, said he did not experience real prejudice until he revealed that he was a Republican and a Trump supporter. Wright had both liberal blacks and whites calling him an Uncle Tom and unfriending him on Facebook. Rob Smith, a veteran in the U.S. military who voted for Obama twice before placing his faith in Trump, said many treated him worse when he came out as a conservative than when he came out of the closet years earlier. Other gays called him a "house nigger" on Facebook and Twitter.

Before Kanye West, retired NBA Hall of Famer Dennis Rodman was President Trump's most famous black friend. Rodman, known for his outrageous antics dating back to the 1990s, faced little scrutiny. Some credit Rodman for Trump's successful diplomatic summit with North Korean dictator Kim Jong-un. When Trump was elected, he staged a series of meetings with black celebrities at Trump Tower in Manhattan. Jim Brown and recently retired NFL star Ray Lewis were among the earliest visitors. Their visit did not cause much fuss due to Brown's affiliation with the Republican Party and Lewis's conservative views on issues like black NFL players kneeling for the national anthem. However, entertainers Steve Harvey, Chrisette Michele, and Ice Cube were not as fortunate.

Monique Judge published an article on Harvey's meeting for *The Root*, an African American oriented online magazine, in which she voiced her disdain for the popular *Family Feud* (1976–present) host for "skinnin' and grinnin'" at Trump Tower. According to Harvey, President Obama's transition team asked him to meet with Trump and Dr. Ben Carson, a black conservative who ran for president in 2016. Carson was appointed to be the Secretary of Housing and Urban Development in 2017; therefore, Harvey intended to discuss solutions to the problems affecting the black poor in cities like Chicago and Detroit. Months later, Harvey admitted that he should have listened to his wife's advice and skipped the meeting. He told *The Hollywood Reporter* that other blacks called him a "coon" and an "Uncle Tom." Throughout her article, Judge showed little pity for Harvey, referring to him as "negro" and making fun of the veneers in his mouth.[35] Harvey's star was big enough to rebound from this debacle.

Ice Cube (O'Shea Jackson) became a lightning rod for controversy when his "Contract for Black America," a plan to end financial inequality in the black community, drew the public's attention a month before Election Day 2020. Cube, best known for his rap career in the 1980s and 1990s, his films, and his Big3 league for retired NBA players, entered a new lane by going into politics. This "contract" was not new idea. Black nationalists introduced a black agenda in 1973. Talk show host Tavis Smiley promoted his contract for black America after President Obama was inaugurated in 2009. The Trump administration used some of Cube's ideas to help model their "Platinum Plan." Rumors quickly spread that Cube was supporting Trump's reelection. Feeling the pressure from the black community, Cube appeared on CNN's *Cuomo Prime Time* and HOT 97's *Ebro in the Morning* to explain himself. Although he admitted to only voting Democrat in past elections, Cube did not object to working with Trump's administration if they were willing to support his plan. Historian Peniel Joseph published a critical piece in *The Philadelphia Inquirer* calling Ice Cube's political logic "dangerous." It should be noted that Cube never formally endorsed Trump's reelection as fellow rappers Lil Wayne and 50 Cent had done.

Chrisette Michele suffered the worst fallout for her association with the Trump administration. She won the Grammy for Best Urban/Alternative Performance for her debut album in 2007. Michele built up a substantial following in the R&B and jazz communities over the next decade. First Lady Michelle Obama attended one of her concerts in 2014 and invited her to perform at an official state dinner in 2016. When she accepted an invitation and $75,000 to give a five-minute performance at one of Trump's inaugural balls, Michele saw it as an opportunity to bridge the gap between Trump supporters and detractors. Pastor John Gray, an associate pastor at Joel Osteen's Lakewood Church, preached a sermonette at Oprah Winfrey's *Super Soul Sessions* titled "The Bridge," in which he stressed the need for Americans to reach across the aisle and look past their differences. If this was the message that Michele intended to convey, it landed on deaf ears. Neither her colorful skirt with African motifs nor the accompaniment of gospel singer Travis Greene was enough to prevent her black card from being revoked.[36]

Chrisette Michele issued a public apology on *The Breakfast Club* on November 2, 2017. She revealed to Charlamagne and his co-hosts Angela Yee and DJ Envy that she suffered a miscarriage due to the criticism and the death threats she received for singing at the Trump inauguration. She was dropped from her record label, Motown, and started her own independent label, Rich Hipster, to distribute her music. *The Washington Post* wrote a profile on Michele in 2019. At the time she was headlining a concert at the Keswick Theater in Philadelphia. The last time she performed at the 1,500-seat venue it was nearly filled, but now it was half empty.

Despite the backlash that accompanied supporting Trump, there were celebrities, other than Kanye West, who proudly accepted being labeled "sellouts." Jason Whitlock, the former host of Fox Sports 1's daily series *Speak for Yourself*, went on Fox News's *Tucker Carlson Tonight* in May 2018 to applaud Kanye for tweeting in support of Trump and admonishing black voters for being tools of the Democrats. Whitlock criticized writer Ta-Nehisi Coates for acting as the "overseer of black thought." He addressed 250 MAGA-hatted Trump supporters at the Young Black Leadership Summit two months later. He told his young listeners to "disconnect from this social media garbage; disconnect from these celebrity athletes who don't really care nothing about you." He was referring to NBA players LeBron James, Kevin Durant, and Stephen Curry, who were critical of the president and outspoken on several issues related to race in America.[37] Whitlock thought it was disingenuous for them to complain about racism given their seven-figure salaries and endorsement deals.

Azealia Banks, a moderately successful rapper/singer in the early 2010s, has been described as an internet troll for her controversial tweets on race, colorism, and politics. For critics who accused her of voting for a racist, she tweeted that she was a racist too, and "racism/racialism" was sewn into the nation's fabric. She and Rihanna engaged in a war of words in 2017 over Trump's travel ban to keep Syrian refugees from entering America in search of asylum. "As far as Rihanna (who isn't a citizen, and can't vote) and all the rest of the celebrities who are using their influence to stir the public, you really REALLY need to shut up and sit down," tweeted Banks.[38] Some members of the media have excused her comments and reckless behavior on social media as a symptom of mental illness. The disturbing pattern with Ms. Banks and Kanye West's behavior is that it paints blacks who supported Trump and his Republican cronies as mentally disturbed individuals.

It All Falls Down

Bill Cosby was canceled by many blacks, years before his 2018 rape conviction. Cosby's cancelation had nothing to do with Trump but resulted from comments he made that espoused far-right conservative talking points. In his infamous "Pound Cake" speech, delivered at the NAACP's celebration of the 50th anniversary of the *Brown v. Board of Education* decision, Cosby blamed the black underclass for their plight by failing to live up to the promises of the Civil Rights Movement.[39] He took young black single mothers to task for giving their children "ghetto" names that would give white teachers and employers an excuse to stigmatize them. He accused them of buying their children expensive sneakers rather than books and school supplies. Cosby chastised them for allowing their children to speak Ebonics instead of standard English. All these shortcomings contributed to the growth of a generation that valued a piece of pound cake more than a human life.[40]

Cosby's speech received mixed reviews. There were many blacks who praised him for using his platform to address uncomfortable issues within the community. But for others he sounded out of touch and came across as victim shaming. Michael Eric Dyson refuted Cosby's claims in his 2006 book *Is Bill Cosby Right?: Or Has the Black Middle Class Lost Its Mind?* (2006). Dyson gave multiple examples that painted the comedian as a person who benefited from black folk even as he worked to detach himself from their problems for decades. He cited Cosby's failure to tackle racial injustice in his stand-up routines and on *The Cosby Show*. Dyson compared Cosby's speech to a 2004 Kanye West song "All Falls Down," which he praised for airing out the black community's dirty laundry from a place of love that did not condemn or ignore the role of systemic racism.[41]

Upon my review of Kanye's discography, I discovered that many of his early songs manifested undertones of the conservative rhetoric for which he is reprimanded today. Right after he praises his mother for being arrested in the Oklahoma City sit-in as a child, he calls out "niggas" for being at the dealership buying cars they could not afford instead of at the ballot box.[42] An underlying theme of his song "All of the Lights" was the dysfunction that bred broken families and pathologies in the "Ghetto University" of black America. Kanye proclaimed that money was the source of happiness and freedom on "Good Life," "School Spirit," and "Can't Tell Me Nothing." He first insinuated that Planned Parenthood, which he sees as liberal ploy, was a form of black genocide in "The Joy" back in 2010. On "New Day" Kanye rapped that his unborn son might have an easier life than himself if he was more accommodating and voted Republican.

In the 2012 single "Clique," Kanye joked that while white people invest their money, blacks "buy 80 gold chains and go ig'nant."[43] While "All Falls Down" was praised for Kanye's ability to admit his insecurities—"I'm so self-conscious"—that song depicted blacks as basing their self-worth on material items and expensive college degrees in an attempt to buy back their 40 acres.[44] One of the song's best lines was directed to young black mothers who named their daughters after the luxury cars they dreamt of owning. I do not find a lot of difference between Kanye's early rhetoric and that of Chris Rock, who has been known to call out black people. Rock's most famous joke might be "Niggas vs. Black People" from his 1996 HBO special *Bring the Pain*. It was a much more profane version of the "Pound Cake" speech and "All Falls Down." The joke was so polarizing that Rock told *60 Minutes* in 2005 that he never performed it again.

The star of the music video for "All Falls Down," was a beautiful young black woman on her way to airport to catch a flight. The woman—attired in designer sunglasses covering half her face, a Juicy Couture-esque baby-blue tube dress, high heels, and Louis Vuitton tote handbag—was Kanye's fictional girlfriend. As she stepped out of her taxi the baggage handlers came to get her six to 10 pieces of expensive Louis Vuitton luggage. This stunning woman, epitomizing materialistic extravagance, was played by Stacey Dash. In the mid–1990s, Dash became a Hollywood starlet when she was cast as Dionne Davenport in the film and television series *Clueless*. Her character Dionne could be described as a Beverly Hills "valley girl" in the same vein as Will Smith's pretentious cousin Hillary Banks (Karyn Parsons) on *The Fresh Prince of Bel-Air* (1990–1996).

Stacey Dash, the cousin of Roc-A-Fella co-founder Damon Dash, became a harsh critic of the Democratic Party after being disappointed by Obama's presidency. She was hired as a contributor for Fox News in 2014 and immediately ruffled feathers by demonizing President Obama, calling for the cancellation of BET, and demanding an end to Black History Month. Dash claimed that if black people are Americans, they do not need a special month to acknowledge their history and culture. "These insidious things only keep us segregated and invoke false narratives," she wrote in a blog. Dash was a keynote speaker at the pro–Trump Young Black Leadership Summit. She told the audience that she was "blacked" into voting for Obama and the Democrats. Now she is a "free" thinker who supports the Republican Party's conservative ideas for economic advancement, which can be likened to the survival skills she learned growing up in the hood. Dash issued a public apology in March 2021 for supporting Trump and the comments she made while working at Fox.

The leadership summit was organized by Candace Owens. Her profile was boosted when Kanye West tweeted his love for her ideas. She was at his side when made his "slavery is choice" remark at TMZ. Candace Owens rose to the forefront of the conservative movement for black millennials between 2017 and 2019. Her YouTube videos grabbed the attention of Charlie Kirk, who appointed her to be the director of urban engagement for his nonprofit organization Turning Point USA (TPUSA). Owens gained further popularity appearing on Fox News and InfoWars, a website founded by Alex Jones and accused of intentionally spreading far-right conspiracy theories. Brenton Tarrant, a 28-year-old white supremacist who livestreamed himself killing 51 and injuring 49 worshippers at a mosque in New Zealand, called Candace Owens his hero.[45]

The 32-year-old Owens, who identifies as a Trump supporter, not a Republican, has become public enemy number one for liberal white millennials and throughout parts of black America for her views. She has incorrectly argued that the National Rifle Association (NRA) began as a civil rights organization to defend blacks from the KKK. She regularly comes across as an internet "troll" acting like Tomi Lahren, a white millennial conservative provocateur, in blackface.[46] She labeled George Floyd a symbol of a broken culture in black America today and Colin Kaepernick a "half-black" man profiting from victimhood. She accused Cardi B of disgracing American values and corrupting the youth with her racy 2021 Grammy Awards performance of "WAP" with Megan Thee Stallion.[47] Dave Chappelle called her "the most articulate idiot I've ever seen in my fucking life."[48]

At the 2019 Conservative Political Action Conference (CPAC), Owens remarked that racism was over because she had never been a slave. An ironic statement given the fact that her family was paid $37,500 by the Board of Education when she was a student at Stamford High School in Connecticut. Owens told authorities white students called her "dirty" and threatened to burn her parents' home, tar and feather her, and eventually kill her. The traumatizing indignities drove her to stay at home from school for six weeks.[49] Kanye severed ties with Owens after she used his name to tout clothing merchandise for her "Blexit" campaign without his permission. "Blexit," a play on Brexit, calls for blacks to leave the Democratic Party's plantation.[50] Owens debuted a new late night television talk show, *Candace*, in March 2021.

The Art of the Deal

I do not think most sensible, open-minded black people have an issue with blacks who vote Republican or have conservative views. It is unproductive to call black Republicans "sellouts." Likewise, it is insulting and ignorant to refer to black Democrats as mentally enslaved individuals residing on a plantation. The elephant in the room for four years was Donald Trump and what his movement represented. This ethnic nationalism would have been unthinkable 20 years ago when most Americans still loved The Donald. Russell Simmons, hip-hop's first mogul, appearing in the fifth episode of the Netflix docuseries *Dirty Money,* spoke of the fondness that younger blacks in the hip-hop generation once had for the 45th president. Trump appeared on an episode of *The Fresh Prince of Bel-Air.* Nelly (Cornell Haynes) gave him a shout-out in his smash hit "Country Grammar." Jay-Z did the same in "What More Can I Say." Rappers admired what

Trump represented: power, riches, the American Dream, and an unwavering determination to accomplish anything.

In his book chapter "Putting Donald Trump in Historical Perspective," Doug McAdam explains how Trump connected himself to the racial politics of past Republican presidential candidates when he decided to run for office for the second time in 2016. Trump had initially run for office as an independent in 2000 on a platform for universal health care and called Oprah Winfrey his ideal running mate. After his failed campaign, he began hosting NBC's *The Apprentice* (2004–2015). He teased the idea of running as a Republican in 2012 but chose to stick to reality television. Many believe that it was a public spat with President Obama over his legitimacy as a U.S. citizen, prompting Obama to roast him at the 2011 White House Correspondents' Dinner, that motivated Trump's 2016 campaign.

When Trump reemerged in politics, he was a different character using a very familiar playbook. Richard Nixon and Alabama Governor George Wallace split the vote in the South in the 1968 presidential election. Wallace won the Deep South by running on a segregationist platform. In their book *Chain Reaction* (1991), Thomas and Mary Edsall explain how Nixon applied Wallace's strategy to grow his base and reshape the GOP as the party of the law-abiding, silent (mostly white) majority.[51] Nixon's adviser Kevin Phillips portrayed liberals and Democrats as being in favor of a big government that taxes the many for the benefit of the few. McAdam believes "the few" was coded language denoting blacks and other undeserving minorities. Nixon called for more law and order, which was also seen as coded language to halt militant black power groups with guns and race uprisings.

As Ronald Reagan ran against Gerald Ford in the 1976 Republican primary election, he began sharing a story of a black woman on welfare with 80 names, 30 addresses, 12 social security cards, Medicaid, food stamps, a Cadillac, and $150,000 in tax-free cash income.[52] Chicago resident Linda Taylor became the face of this new "Welfare Queen" mythology that Republican politicians would continue to use over the next three decades.[53] Reagan lost that election but won over Nixon's silent majority to become president from 1981 to 1989. His vice president, George H.W. Bush, was losing to the Democratic challenger, Michael Dukakis, in the 1988 general election. With the help of Republican Party strategist Harvey LeRoy (Lee) Atwater, Bush rebounded to win once he began running television ads titled "Weekend Pass."

The ad focused on Dukakis allowing first-degree murderers to have weekend passes from prison. One of the recipients of the passes was a black man named Willie Horton serving a life sentence. According to the commercial Horton kidnapped a young white couple, stabbed the man, and raped his girlfriend multiple times. Two terrifying pictures of Horton, appearing in the ad, were used as dog whistles to attract voters who harbored implicit biases towards blacks. Robin Means Coleman, author of *Horror Noire: Blacks in Horror Films from the 1890s to Present* (2011), says Horton became a living version of the boogeyman for white people. Although Atwater denied playing the race card to win the election an audio recording exists of him explaining his Southern Strategy, off-the-record, during a 1981 interview. Replace the N-word with "forced busing," "states' rights," and "lower taxes," said Atwater.[54]

Barack Obama's election in 2008 was the impetus for the rise of the Tea Party, which took over the GOP in the early 2010s. The Tea Party's popularity coincided with the rise of identity politics and the birther movement onto which Trump latched his designer belt. He became a hero for a group of whites, opposed to Obama's policies and his skin color, who used the argument that he was not a U.S. citizen to call for his impeachment after a few months in office. In 2012 Republican presidential candidate Newt Gingrich called Obama the "Food Stamp President." Mitt Romney, the Republican Party's 2012 nominee, called Obama supporters the "47 percent" who saw themselves as victims and were dependent upon "big government" aid.

Trump's strategist Steve Bannon ramped up these tactics to help him achieve an unprecedented victory in the Electoral College against Hillary Clinton in the 2016 presidential election.[55] Trump was also advised by Roger Ailes, who made it his mission at Fox News to ruin Bill Clinton's and Barack Obama's presidencies with negative stories.[56] On the campaign trail Trump, speaking at sold-out rallies that resembled rock festivals, characterized Mexican immigrants as criminals, drug dealers, and rapists stealing jobs and threatening the safety of hard-working Americans.[57] He villainized Black Lives Matter activists and called the athletes who supported their protests "sons of bitches." He encouraged his crowd to beat up black protestors at one of his rallies and take them out on hospital stretchers. At an event in Orlando, Florida, his crowd chanted, "USA! USA! USA!" as two protestors—one black and the other Latino—were tackled by Trump supporters.[58] Such actions won Trump the endorsement of noted white supremacists and neo-Nazis Richard Spencer and David Duke.[59]

For many blacks, Trump's "I think there is blame on both sides" comment after Heather Heyer, a white protestor, was killed at an alt-right 2017 Unite the Right rally in Charlottesville, Virginia, signified a refusal to condemn white nationalism.[60] He repeated this behavior three years later when he refused to condemn Kyle Rittenhouse, a 17-year-old white male who killed two Black Lives Matter protestors and wounded another in Kenosha, Wisconsin.[61] Trump said the boy was trying to defend himself. And he did it again by chanting "stand back and stand by," the motto of an anti-immigrant group called The Proud Boys, when he was asked to condemn white supremacists during the first 2020 presidential debate. The red MAGA hat that Trump and his supports proudly wore symbolized hate and prejudice in the eyes of many non–Trump supporters.

While Trump was president there were numerous stories about his public spats with black female members of the media, from White House correspondent April Ryan to former ESPN sports journalist Jemele Hill.[62] The president attacked the four freshman congresswomen of color, known as the Squad, and suggested deporting one of the women back to Africa.[63] He called Muriel Bowser, mayor of Washington, D.C., incompetent after she opposed his use of the National Guard to police Black Lives Matter protestors in June 2020.[64] None of this bothered Kanye West, who sat down with *WSJ Magazine* for an interview in 2020. "I'm a black guy with a red [MAGA] hat, can you imagine? … This is your place, Ye, you're black, so you're a Democrat," he said.[65] He spoke about classism being a more significant issue than racism today.[66] In the May 2020 cover story for *GQ* magazine, Kanye admitted that he would be casting his very first ballot in a presidential election for Donald Trump later that fall.[67] But he changed his tune two months later.

At 8:38 p.m. on the July 4 holiday, Kanye tweeted his 29.5 million followers his intention to run for president. Elon Musk and Kim Kardashian tweeted their support. Was this a poorly planned publicity stunt to promote his new Yeezy Foam Runner sneakers or his forthcoming album? Kanye named Michelle Tidball, a self-described "biblical life coach" from Wyoming, as his potential running mate. Days later *Forbes* published excerpts from a rambling, four-hour interview in which he explained his reasons for running. Kanye announced that he was running as an independent under a new banner, the Birthday Party, and officially severing ties with Trump.[68] "I am taking the red hat off, with this interview," he proclaimed. Kanye admitted to having COVID-19 earlier in the year, viewing Planned Parenthood as an attempt by white supremacists to destroy the black family, and developing an economic plan modeled after the fictional African country Wakanda in Marvel's *Black Panther.* Fellow celebrities called this move "self-serving" and detrimental to black voters. Chance the Rapper was among the few celebrities who pledged his support to Kanye over Democratic nominee Joe Biden. Revered radio host Joe Madison had a strong warning: "Chance and Kanye, we don't have time to fuck around with this election. Grow up!"[69]

Fox News reported that Kanye had ended his campaign on July 15 after missing too many deadlines to be placed on ballots and receiving a mere two percent of the vote in a presidential poll conducted by Redfield & Wilton Strategies. However, conflicting reports the next day said he paid $35,000 to run and filed documents with the Federal Election Commission. The Oklahoma State Election Board announced later that evening that he had qualified for their General Election ballot.[70] Three days later he traveled to Charleston, South Carolina, to hold his first official campaign rally. The state's deadline to file signatures for independent candidates was the next day. Kanye desperately needed to get on the ballot in South Carolina and the remaining five states with deadlines in August to have any chance of winning.[71]

The Charleston rally was a horrific disaster that revealed Kanye's lack of a political platform and the severity of his mental illness. Kanye stood before the crowd wearing a bulletproof vest with the numbers "2020" shaved into his hair. He mocked Harriet Tubman, accusing her of freeing slaves to go work for more white people. He spoke about preserving Second Amendment rights, which was stunning given Chicago's problem with gun violence. Kanye cried uncontrollably over his father's and his wife's thoughts to abort him and his unborn daughter North, respectively. A disgusted black woman in the audience could be overhead telling her companion(s), "Yo, we leavin' right now."

Was the Charleston rally performance art, or a shocking cry for help? Kanye's family told reporters that he was undergoing another manic episode resulting from his refusal to take his prescribed medication for months. Skeptics questioned if mental illness would be the excuse to gain the public's sympathy. Despite his poor performance at the rally, questions about his mental health, and a series of disturbing tweets 24 hours later that jeopardized his marriage, Kanye continued his efforts to get on the ballot for November's election, filing petitions to appear on the presidential ticket in 10 states. Two of those states, Illinois and New Jersey, questioned the validity of most signatures on his petitions. By early September his name was added to the ballots in Arkansas, Colorado, Idaho, Iowa, Kentucky, Minnesota, Mississippi, Oklahoma, Louisiana, Tennessee, Utah, and Vermont. In October he qualified to be a write-in candidate on Maryland's ballot. Although he still lacked a realistic chance of winning the 270 Electoral College votes needed to win,[72] he was listed on California's ballot as a write-in vice presidential candidate for the American Independent Party.

According to the Federal Election Commission Kanye spent nearly $6.8 million of his own money on the campaign. He received less than $12,000 in outside donations.[73] On August 3, 2020, New York magazine and The New York Times reported that two prominent figures with ties to Trump or the Republican Party, Chuck Wilton and Gregg Keller, were associated with his campaign.[74] Lane Ruhland, a lawyer representing the Trump campaign in a lawsuit against a Wisconsin television network for airing commercials critical of the president's response to COVID-19, delivered ballot signatures on behalf of Kanye to election officials in Wisconsin.[75] Kanye confirmed in a second interview with Forbes on August 6 that he was running to siphon votes from Joe Biden. It was also reported that Kanye was having daily chats with Jared Kushner, the president's son-in-law and a senior White House advisor.[76] Kushner denied having daily chats with Kanye but confirmed meeting with him in Colorado to discuss policy.[77]

A POLITICO/Morning Consult poll on August 12 showed six percent of Kanye's support came from Generation Z voters. Latinx voters made up four percent of his support, but only two percent of registered black voters were in his corner.[78] Although he presented some valid points about blacks not blindly supporting one political party, it was overshadowed by his haphazard campaign and the fact that the Trump administration repeatedly proved that it was not endorsing an agenda beneficial to most blacks. The president's selling point for Kanye and other blacks was financial empowerment. Still, it negligently ignored the institutional factors that created this generational need for economic empowerment. Trump's failure to show empathy to the black victims of police brutality, his condemnation of Black Lives Matter supporters, and the outright disrespect that he showed upon U.S. Representative John Lewis's death in July 2020 were other glaring examples. Kanye West conceded after only receiving 0.5 percent (60,000) of the vote. Joe Biden won the election, despite Trump's efforts to claim voter fraud. Kamala Harris became the nation's first female and first black vice president. Shortly after conceding Kanye pledged to run again in the 2024 presidential election.

Eight

"Closed on Sunday"

"This a mission, not a show. This is my eternal soul." *Kanye West*[1]

With hands raised to the sky, hearts and minds stayed on Jesus, and melodic voices uplifted in one accord, a mass choir of more than 100 black millennials and Generation Zers led college students on The Yard at Howard University in an early Saturday morning praise and worship experience with Kanye West in the role of worship leader. The Howard Sunday Service on October 12, 2019, during homecoming weekend, highlighted the paradoxes that have made Kanye one of the most complicated figures in recent memory. His decision to have Sunday Service at an HBCU after the TMZ and Trump controversies, two weeks before releasing his "comeback" album *Jesus Is King*, was strategically astute, given Howard University's stature and history. If *My Dark Twisted Fantasy* was his apology to the mainstream for the 2009 VMAs, was this gospel rap album partially an apology to black America? In the past two years religious faith has influenced Kanye's music, politics, marriage, and even the names of his sneakers.[2] His lone presidential campaign ad could have been an advertisement for a religious network. During a 2020 podcast interview with Joe Rogan he admitted that his past arrogance and egotistical behavior was due to insecurities and a disconnection with God.

Kanye pledged in 2019 to only make sacred music for God. Although he has appeared on secular albums with Pop Smoke (Bashar Jackson) and Ty Dolla $ign (Tyrone Griffin, Jr.), he has primarily restrained from using explicit content. While much of his new music has been rooted in the gospel music of the black American church, his messaging often resembles something rooted in a Southern white evangelism that has run counter to black progress. This chapter focuses on Kanye's spiritual evolution, his transition to gospel music, the significance of his Howard University service, and the complex relationship between his newfound faith and conservative politics.

God Is

What's up with Ye? This was a common question among Kanye West fans as his life spiraled out of control between 2016 and 2018. He battled an opioid addiction, suffered a mental breakdown, and was hospitalized for days. His wife, Kim, was robbed at gunpoint for $11 million worth of jewelry while at Paris Fashion Week. Rumors spread across the internet that their marriage was in danger of crumbling. The resale value for Yeezys had plummeted and sneaker vloggers were asking if the Yeezy hype was dead.[3] Critics panned his latest albums, *Ye* and *Kids See Ghosts,* which failed to produce chart-topping singles and lacked the focus of his past work. Albums he executive produced for Nas and Teyana Taylor were not well received. His highest-charting single, "I Love It," with teenage SoundCloud rapper Lil Pump (Gazzy Garcia), was the most misogynistic record of his career. Gunshots were fired at the set of a music video he was filming with Tekashi69 (Daniel Hernandez) and Nicki Minaj on November 8, 2018.

Black Twitter canceled Kanye because of his comments on slavery and his endorsement of President Donald Trump. Hip-hop media personalities Ebro Darden, Joe Budden, Wayno, and Nadeska Alexis were through with him. Former allies, John Legend and T.I., severed ties. Jay-Z and Beyoncé were absent from his corner. West Coast rapper Daz Dillinger threatened to call out the Crips on him. Snoop Dogg questioned the influence of the Kardashian-Jenner women in his life. Kanye's new album, *Yandhi,* was shelved after months of delay. A trip to Uganda turned into another public blunder. Even LeBron James and his business partner, Maverick Carter, were taking jabs at him on their HBO series *The Shop* (2019–present). If there was anyone who needed a personal makeover, it was Mr. West.

The seeds for Kanye West's makeover were planted at nine o'clock one morning in the first week of January 2019. Jason White was at home when he received a phone call from Ray Romulus, a producer for Bruno Mars (Peter Hernandez). "Ye is looking for a choir. Would you be interested? [Kanye needs] 100 people by Friday, and put a band together, too," said Romulus.[4] Immediately, White put out a call for choir members, telling them that they would be providing vocals for an unknown A-list artist. By Friday the earliest foundation of the Sunday Service Choir, initially called The Samples, was formed. When White answered his phone, he had no idea that he would change Kanye's life, his music, and rebrand his image.

Before linking up with the hip-hop mogul, Jason White had made quite a name for himself within the music industry. White served as the segment producer for Cirque du Soleil's Michael Jackson: The Immortal World Tour and worked with Whitney Houston on new music before her untimely death. He also collaborated with Aretha Franklin, Janet Jackson, Dolly Parton, Sean "Diddy" Combs, Kurt Carr, Tramaine Hawkins, and Andraé Crouch. He and his wife, Geneen, formed White Throne Productions, which handles television vocal contracting for the likes of *American Idol*, *X-Factor*, *Dancing with the Stars*, and televised broadcasts of the Grammy Awards and the Academy Awards.

White started singing and playing the piano by ear when he was five years old. One morning he was singing the hymn "At the Cross" in his grandmother's kitchen when she anointed his head with oil and prayed over him. From that day forward, he was aware of God's unique calling to minister to the world with music. By the time he was an adult White was the music director at West Angeles Church of God in Christ (WACOGIC). West Angeles is a Pentecostal megachurch in Los Angeles with more than 22,000 members, including Denzel Washington, Earvin "Magic" Johnson, Stevie Wonder, and Angela Bassett. White left the church in 2016 to play music for his brother's much smaller congregation.

In the beginning Jason White was skeptical about working with Kanye, but his opinion changed after their first rehearsal. Kanye was a Christian, but he wanted to "be saved" and establish a closer relationship with God. "We're not gonna do any profanity; I want you to re-write these songs," Kanye told him.[5] White hired Nikki Grier, a lyricist who had previously worked with secular rappers Dr. Dre (Andre Young) and Busta Rhymes (Trevor Smith, Jr.), to re-write Kanye's songs to be appropriate for Christian-oriented venues. White still did not see this becoming a long-term venture. He was not alone in his suspicion and doubt of Kanye; many of his vocalists shared those reservations.

A reason for the skepticism is that several celebrities have publicly "turned to God" in times of scrutiny. The most egregious example is R. Kelly, who fresh off criminal charges released a gospel album, *U Saved Me* (2004). Tom Joyner, a retired syndicated black radio personality, suggested that Kelly's brief transition to gospel allowed him to connect with the black community's spiritual ethos and garner their support and forgiveness. Before long Kelly was singing about sex again and facing new charges of having sex with minors. Similarly O.J. Simpson began worshipping at black churches in Los Angeles as part of an image makeover after he was acquitted for the double murder and lost his white fan base.

Other musical artists have ventured into sacred music without leaving behind their more explicit secular ways. Harlem's number one Bad Boy Ma$e (Mason Betha) left the industry while he was hot to pursue the ministry. Ma$e became an ordained pastor at El Elyon International Church in Atlanta. In 2014 he stepped down from the church following a brewing controversy surrounding his divorce after 12 years of marriage. Ma$e appeared on *The Angie Martinez Show* three years later. He described himself as a spiritual person, but not a religious being. Furthermore, he denied ever being a pastor. Snoop Dogg dropped a gospel rap album in 2018. The next year he was rapping alongside strippers swinging from poles at the University of Kansas.

The Reverend Melvin Maxwell, the senior pastor of East Friendship Baptist Church in Washington, D.C., has an indirect connection to Kanye West through his daughter Mariah. She belongs to the Sunday Service Choir and played the lead female role in Kanye's Christmas opera *Mary* staged at Lincoln Theater on December 22, 2019.[6] The Reverend Maxwell, who formerly served as youth pastor at the church I attend, shared his thoughts on Kanye's religious conversion:

> I saw two interviews in early 2019 that cued me into the transformative Salvific process Kayne was undergoing. Then a few months later my daughter was hired to sing in his choir. She informed me that they would be working on an album and opera in the near future. I went to assess this for myself and I found him not only sincere in his Christian conversion, but he was walking with a new vision and mission—advancing the Kingdom and Cause of Christ in the earth.[7]

The Reverend Maxwell spoke of his first-hand encounters at the Sunday Service and the impact it had on participants.

> I can say the experience has been breathtaking as it relates to ministering to thousands, even millions of people. Praying and engaging with the audiences in stadiums, prisons, churches, ships, lawns, and other venues around the world.[8]

Kanye West has walked the fine line between the sacred and the secular throughout his entire career. His first Grammy award came for "Jesus Walks." He brazenly graced a 2006 cover of *Rolling Stone*, titled "The Passion of Kanye West," wearing a crown of thorns like Christ. He referenced the line "Jesus Wept" from John 11:35 on "Bound 2." Each concert during his Yeezus tour featured Christian iconography, 12 women on stage—Kanye's 12 apostles—and concluded with an actor portraying Jesus Christ who instructed Kanye to use his talents to show people the light. *The Life of Pablo*, named after Paul the Apostle, was supposed to be his first gospel album. It opened with the audio of an Instagram post featuring Natalie Green, a four-year-old black girl, in the backseat of a car praying, as her relative Samoria Green participated in a call-and-response. Green's prayer led into the first track "Ultralight Beam," which was highlighted by vocals from a ten-piece gospel choir, a cameo by Kanye's protégé Chance the Rapper, and a rousing prayer delivered by gospel legend Kirk Franklin. The album's second track, "Father Stretch My Hands, Pt. 1," sampled an older gospel song. The sixth track, "Lowlights," used a recording of a black woman giving a two-minute testimony about God's grace. By the album's conclusion

Kanye was renouncing lewd parties in LA and searching for God in the nightlife he once enjoyed.

Kanye West has always come across as an individual who has been on a long journey to figure out his relationship with Jesus Christ. Despite his upbringing in the Reverend Johnnie Colemon's Christ Universal Temple in Chicago and his time spent in church while spending summers with his father, he lacked a close relationship with God after achieving celebrity. Kanye told Pastor Joel Osteen that he received a call from God while hospitalized after a mental breakdown, instructing him to start a church in Calabasas. His religious conversion has been closely tied to very public bouts with bipolar disorder. Kanye often credits his faith, not prescribed medication, as his source of healing. During a Sunday Service he told the audience he had gone seven months without using medicine thanks to the power of prayer.

University of Texas professor King Davis studies the history of mental health in the black American community. Davis tells a story of a black pastor in Texas who encouraged his members to bring all their prescription drugs to the front of the church and give them over to the Lord.[9] A large number of black Christians, skeptical of white psychiatric clinicians, believe that prayer is all they need to cure their ailments. Kanye told Joe Rogan that prescribed medication was an attempt to curb his "superhero" genius and block God's blessings. However, Sherrill McMillan, a licensed counselor and an ordained minister, believes that Kanye and other black Christians are unwell because they refuse help or are being misdiagnosed by pastors with no training in mental health.

During Kanye's second month of working with Jason White, he began adding drummers and trumpeters to accompany the choir. The majority of choir and band members were black millennials. All the Sunday Services were free to the public, but the tickets to these sold-out events went for hundreds on the resale market. Kanye spent $50 million of his own money, from Yeezys sales, to finance Sunday Service.[10] The choir's musical selections consisted of church-inspired remakes of Kanye's hits and secular R&B songs such as SWV's "Weak" and Destiny's Child's "Say My Name." Even songs that would seem blasphemous in a religious setting, like Shirley Murdock's "As We Lay" and Ginuwine's "So Anxious," have been reworked into uplifting praise anthems like "As We Pray" and "Souls Anchored." Over time the choir, which Kanye dubbed "the Wu-Tang Clan of Choirs," began adding traditional church hymns and gospel songs to their performances.

Initially, the Sunday Service was reserved for close friends, family members, and special guests of the West family. But that exclusivity came to an end with a grand service on Easter Sunday morning, open to the general public and livestreamed globally on YouTube, at the

Coachella Valley Music and Arts Festival in California. The service had so many memorable moments, including the choir singing atop a mountain, the late rapper DMX (Earl Simmons) giving a soul-stirring prayer, and Kanye breaking down in tears. Kanye says that he gave his life to Christ on that Easter morning and pledged to only make sacred music for Christ.

With Coachella's success came more Sunday Service worship events around the country for the remainder of 2019. Kanye and the Sunday Service Choir provided ministry at Pastor Jamal Bryant's New Birth Missionary Church in Georgia in September. He took his worship experience abroad to Kingston, Jamaica, in October. In November, Sunday Service traveled to Houston, Texas, to give an astonishing two-hour worship experience at Joel Osteen's Lakewood Church. The final Sunday Service of the year was held at the Union Rescue Mission, a homeless shelter on Skid Row in Los Angeles, California. Kanye told the Skid Row audience that Sunday Service saved his life.

Jesus Is King, Kanye's first gospel album void of any explicit content, was released on October 25, 2019, with Jason White and the Sunday Service Choir providing vocals. Adam Tyson, the senior pastor of Placerita Bible Church in California, helped him craft his lyrics. The album, which introduced new songs and sampled gospel classics such as the Reverend James Cleveland's "God Is," debuted at number one on the charts worldwide. "Follow God," the album's first single, was number one on *Billboard*'s Hot Gospel Songs chart for over 24 consecutive weeks. It was a top 10 single in nine other countries. *Jesus Is King* received three nominations at the 2020 Dove Awards for gospel music. "Follow God" won the award for Rap/Hip Hop Recorded Song of the Year. Kanye earned his first Grammy in eight years when *Jesus Is King* was awarded Best Contemporary Christian Music Album.

Femi Olutade, a culture critic on music and religion, provides an intricate breakdown of *Jesus Is King* and its utilization of the scriptures for Spotify's *Dissect*. Olutade frames the album as Kanye's battle against evil and ego. This is Kanye's ultimate moment of humility as he shuns past addictions to become a disciple for Christ. Kanye acknowledges God as his everything, water, and sustaining energy. The Sunday Service choir debuted their own 19-track album, *Jesus Is Born*, on Christmas day 2019. The following Christmas they released *Emmanuel*, a 12-minute EP composed of music inspired by Gregorian chants. Kanye included the choir in a short film, *Jesus Is King*, and two operas for the 2019 Christmas season, *Nebuchadnezzar* and *Mary*.

Use This Gospel

The news of Kanye's appearance at the Howard University homecoming was kept under wraps until the last minute. Whispers began spreading the night before of a potential concert on The Yard that would come hours before a special screening of Kanye's unreleased short film, *Jesus Is King*, at nearby George Washington University's Lisner Auditorium. Only Howard students lucky enough to wake up early that morning or those who had not gone to sleep from the previous night's festivities were able to attend. There were some alumni, staff, members of the media, and DC residents in attendance. Other special guests included Kim Kardashian and their kids; Terrence J, the former host of BET's *106 & Park*; and Howard University president Wayne A.I. Frederick. The choir members, who typically wear coordinated outfits, blended in with the students on The Yard in their jeans, hoodies, and Howard University apparel. The students formed a circle around Kanye and his musical collective. There was a small, elevated stage, but most of the performers stood on the grass with the students. In the backdrop were famous Howard landmarks: The Founders Library, Frederick Douglass Hall, the Armour J. Blackburn University Center, the Mordecai Wyatt Johnson Administration Building, and Andrew Rankin Memorial Chapel.

The weather was exceptionally mild that morning, with beautiful clear skies providing a heavenly atmosphere for the sacred occasion. Jason White offered brief opening remarks and asked the students to make some noise if they love Jesus. The choir then broke out into a seven-minute performance of the gospel anthem "Revelation 19:1."[11] After the choir sang together, White had each section—altos, sopranos, tenors, and baritones—sing their part with only piano and organ accompaniment. White then brought the choir back together with the full band's accompaniment to form a musical euphony that could make nonbelievers want to praise God. As the song reached its climax, the choir members went low to the ground. They swayed back and forth, in a similar fashion to students swag surfing to Southern hip-hop tunes on HBCU campuses nationwide, silently chanting the "Hallelujah" chorus before enthusiastically leaping to the heavens as they sang out with all the might in their voices.[12]

"Hallelujah, Hallelujah, Hallelujah, Hallelujah, Hallelujah, Hallelujah, he is wonderful."

The second track on *Jesus Is King* is titled "Selah," a reference to a Hebrew musical notation, frequently appearing in the Old Testament Psalms, which means "pause" or "reflect." "Selah" samples the Hallelujah chorus from "Revelation 19:1" written in 1984 by Jeffrey LaValley, an older black man and the musical director at New Jerusalem Full Gospel

Church in Flint, Michigan. The Sunday Service Choir followed "Revelation 19:1" with "Perfect Praise (How Excellent)," which appears on *Jesus Is Born* under the title "Excellent." "Perfect Praise" was popularized in the mid–1990s by Dr. Walt Whitman and the Soul Children of Chicago. Whitman formed the choir to save at-risk black youth in Chicago by educating their minds, elevating their spirits, and illuminating their souls. "Perfect Praise" has become a beloved anthem in the black church. It has a way of bringing worshippers to their feet and reminding them that, no matter how difficult their struggles, God's grace and mercy are excellent, and thus there is no need to despair.

As the choir finished singing, White instructed the audience to call out "Father," which provided a perfect transition into the choir's performance of "Father Stretch," the sixth track on *Jesus Is Born*. The song initially appeared on *The Life of Pablo* in the form of the profane, double-platinum single "Father Stretch My Hands, Pt. 1." Both versions sample the 1976 gospel song "Father Stretch My Hands" by Thomas Lee (T.L.) Barrett, Jr., a Pentecostal preacher and musician who founded the Life Center COGIC church in Chicago. The phrase "father stretch my hands" comes from the Bible verse "I stretch forth my hands unto thee," found in the King James version of Psalm 143:6. "Father Stretch," like "Revelation 19:1," began slowly and softly before reaching an exuberant climax that had the choir members and trumpeters dancing ecstatically. For the first time during the service Kanye joined in with the vocalists. "I just want to feel liberated, I, I, I," he sang, with a voice better suited for inside of the shower.

A week after Howard's homecoming, *Rolling Stone* published an article titled "Can Kanye West Save Gospel Choirs?" The piece began with a quote from Donald Lawrence, an acclaimed gospel singer, who attended a listening party for *Jesus Is King* at the Auditorium Theatre in Chicago. Lawrence spoke in awe of the crowd's reaction to "Selah" and the choir's "Hallelujah" hook. He was amazed to see an audience that was 75 percent white go "bananas."[13] Lawrence put faith in Kanye's ability to revitalize the importance of traditional gospel choirs. Smaller praise teams have replaced large choirs in the past two decades because it is cheaper for record labels to fly smaller praise teams around the country and overseas. The music provided by praise teams tends to be more engaging and accessible to the masses. "It's often got more of a rock sound to it; it sounds more like secular music," says Phillip Carter, a black gospel artist and founder of Bring Back the Choir. Donald Lawrence believes that this deemphasis on the traditional gospel choir, coming out of the black American church, to please the mainstream dilutes the message behind the music.

It is not surprising that Kanye is attracted to gospel music, given his penchant for soul music and the fact that most of the soul artists he samples started off singing gospel in black churches.[14] Before going too much further, it is necessary to answer two questions: "What is gospel music?" and "Why is it so closely tied to the black Christian worship experience?" According to Bishop Iona Locke, the work of the gospel and the song of the gospel together express how what we do for God, in service or song, work together. The song becomes our work, our feelings, our message, our hope, and our joy. "Gospel means good news. The message in the music is not our message as much as it is good news," Dr. Locke explains. "Sometimes when we sing, we are singing out of our pain. Gospel turns our pain into celebration, and that's when we get happy in church."[15]

America's black church is intrinsically linked to the African diaspora and slavery. Notable works such as Henry Louis Gates, Jr.'s, *The Black Church* (2021), E. Franklin Frazier's *The Negro Church in America* (1963) and Albert J. Raboteau's *Slave Religion: The "Invisible Institution" in the Antebellum South* (2004) state that the black church is a manifestation of God's love and liberation for the descendants of the Atlantic slave trade.[16] The 2021 PBS documentary *The Black Church* brilliantly displays how the church has always been at the center of the black American experience. Thus, the black church becomes more than a building with four walls. Historically it has been a sustaining force that has kept black Americans grounded in their African and Caribbean/Latin American roots while playing a role in their identity, culture, and politics. The typical black worship experience includes hand clapping and foot stomping. These are elements of the ring shout, which was initially practiced by African slaves in the Caribbean and later the American South. This shout was the cornerstone for understanding the nexus between African religion and emerging black American religion.[17]

Call-and-response is another common feature of the black worship experience. Jazz musician Wynton Marsalis refers to this as co-signing. The tradition of call-and-response developed in sub-Saharan African cultures that used it to encourage audience participation at religious gatherings and special ceremonies. Most of the Africans brought to America could not speak or read their European captors' language. The select few slaves who were literate and able to comprehend the "oppressor's" language learned to read the Bible and became preachers. The black preacher would revise passages from white preachers' sermons for the other slaves. As he spoke the audience was expected to "speak back to him" as a form of confirmation. This was vastly different from European worship style which was more subdued.

The earliest form of black music on Southern plantations was work songs used to make the time go by faster, express anger and frustration, or relay covert messages of rebellion and resistance.[18] With the conversion of slaves to Christianity, work songs evolved into spirituals by the late 18th century. Although it was common for plantation owners to force their slaves to attend church services to hear sermons carefully tailored to justify their bondage, the enslaved men and women created spirituals containing coded messages of hope and visions of escape.[19] A great example of this would be the spiritual "Roll, Jordan, Roll." Jordan represented a river, perhaps the Mississippi or the Ohio River, that those in bondage metaphorically crossed to reach the Promised Land. While the lyrics were biblical, their meanings were very personal to the enslaved participants who recited or heard them. The Reverend Dr. Howard Thurman described spirituals as "an expression of the slaves' determination to *be* in a society that seeks to destroy their personhood."[20] Theologian James Cone said in *The Spirituals and the Blues* (1992), "the essence of antebellum black religion was the emphasis on the *somebodiness* of black slaves."[21]

Thomas Dorsey, the music director at Pilgrim Baptist Church in Chicago, is called the father of gospel music. The Georgia native began writing and recording gospel, a hybrid of Christian praise music, jazz, and the blues, in the mid–1920s. Dorsey composed his most famous anthem, "Precious Lord, Take My Hand," in 1931 as he was grieving the death of his wife Nettie Harper, who died in labor with the couple's stillborn baby.[22] "Precious Lord" became gospel great Mahalia Jackson's trademark song, and a favorite of the Reverend Martin Luther King, Jr. As fate would have it, Jackson sang it at King's funeral. Black churches began incorporating gospel into their worship in the 20th century.

Gospel entered a new phase with the advent of the modern civil rights movement. The collegiate gospel choir movement began in the 1960s and early 1970s. When black students were demanding courses on black history and culture at PWIs and HBCUs, gospel choirs became popular on campuses. Richard Smallwood founded the gospel choir at Howard University in the early 1970s. He penned his hit "I Love the Lord" while studying at Howard. In "Resistance, Rebellion, and Reform: The Collegiate Gospel Choir Movement in the United States," Cheryl Sanders writes that the choir worked in concert with the revolutionary spirit of the times. Black students who were feeling alienated within a societal structure that disregarded them and their cultural identity saw the choir as a way of reclaiming their African roots.[23]

Gospel music was too good to remain confined to churches and HBCUs. Mahalia Jackson, the Reverend C.L. Franklin, the Reverend James Cleveland, Shirley Caesar, and Edwin Hawkins were among the early gospel artists to achieve mainstream success.[24] The 1967 gospel song "Oh Happy Day" became an international hit that crossed over onto non-religious radio stations. Andraé Crouch revolutionized the genre in the 1980s and early 1990s by infusing traditional gospel with contemporary secular music. Crouch, featured on Michael Jackson's "Man in the Mirror," Madonna's "Like a Prayer," and a 1982 episode of *The Jeffersons*, paved the path for younger gospel artists Mary Mary, Hezekiah Walker, Fred Hammond, and Kirk Franklin to dominate the late 1990s pop charts with hits like "Stomp."[25]

Set My People Free, Set My People Free

Kanye returned to the mic to accompany the choir on their gospel remake of Soul II Soul's 1989 house music hit "Back to Life (However Do You Want Me)." "Set my people free, set my people free. Jesus gonna set my people free. 13th Amendment gotta end it; that's on me. Jesus set my people free. Jesus set my people free," he rapped. Kanye's politically charged freestyle coincided with his yearlong demands to repeal the 13th Amendment, which outlawed slavery. Kanye is not alone in his criticism of this amendment. Michelle Alexander, Jelani Cobb, Ava DuVernay, and Bryan Stevenson have all spoken out against a loophole in the amendment that has allowed the penal system to indirectly enslave blacks.

Prison reform was an underlying theme of the homecoming concert. Momolu Stewart and Halim Flowers provided the service's most emotional moment. Stewart grew up in Washington, D.C., during the crack cocaine epidemic that earned "Chocolate City" the infamous title of the nation's murder capital. He was six years old when his father was murdered, and his mother was sent to prison for aiding and abetting in the murder. Stewart was convicted and sentenced to life, at the age of 16, for killing Mark Rosebure. While incarcerated, Stewart met Mark Howard, a professor of Government and Law at Georgetown University. Professor Howard is the founding director of the Prisons and Justice Initiative to fight mass incarceration and the author of *Unusually Cruel: Prisons, Punishment, and the Real American Exceptionalism* (2017). He introduced Stewart to Kim Kardashian, who was filming a documentary for the cable network Oxygen at the D.C. jail called *Kim Kardashian West: The Justice Project*.

Kim has become arguably the most notable celebrity advocate for black women and men who have been wrongly incarcerated. She deserves a great deal of credit for President Trump pardoning Alice Johnson, a black great-grandmother who had served 21 years in prison for cocaine trafficking in Memphis, Tennessee. Johnson was serving a life sentence despite her being a first-time felon.[26] Kim helped to raise attention to the plight of Cyntoia Brown and Rodney Reed. Brown, incarcerated for murdering a white man when she was 16, was released from prison after serving 15 years of a life sentence.[27] Reed, a Texas inmate on death row believed to be wrongfully accused of killing a white woman, had his execution halted.[28] Kim also encouraged President Trump to demand that Harlem rapper A$AP Rocky (Rakim Athelaston Mayers) be released from a Swedish prison and have a pending two-year sentence for assaulting a man in the country dropped. She is currently enrolled in a program called Reading the Law, which is offered in California and three other states. She spends 20 hours per week completing an apprenticeship with attorneys and law professors in preparation to eventually pass the bar exam.

Stewart petitioned the court for an early release under Washington, D.C.'s Incarceration Reduction Amendment Act of 2017, which reduces juvenile offenders' sentences if they have already served at least 15 years. By homecoming weekend, Stewart had been out of prison for four days thanks to the assistance of Kim and Professor Howard. He shared his testimony at the Sunday Service. Upon learning this news, the audience erupted in applause, and the choir began singing Teyana Taylor's "Never Would Have Made It," a remake of Bishop Marvin Sapp's gospel song of the same name. Afterward, Halim Flowers took the microphone to share his emotional testimony. He, too, was a DC native sentenced to life imprisonment at 16. Flowers started a publishing company, published 11 books, and launched a social justice media website called Unchained Media Collective while in prison. He had been free for seven months after serving 22 years. Flowers delivered a powerful poem he wrote, "When They See Us," which asked listeners to reach across political lines and use love to bring justice to all.[29]

As he spoke, Flowers referenced "Crack Music," an older song by Kanye West, which blamed Ronald Reagan and the federal government for dismantling black liberation groups such as the Black Panthers and alluded to claims that the Central Intelligence Agency (CIA) intentionally funneled crack into poor black neighborhoods. Kanye has become a strong advocate for ending mass incarceration, the result of crack cocaine and Reagan's War on Drugs, in recent years. A few weeks after Howard's homecoming, he held Sunday Service at the Harris County Jail in Houston. Cameras inside the jail offered footage of Kanye and the choir rocking back and forth as the inmates—mostly black and Latino men and women—stood on the other side of the room dancing and nodding their heads to the music. Female inmates shed tears. Only heavily armed guards separated the two groups. Several inmates embraced Kanye as he entered the jail. Those unable to touch the hem of his garment yelled out "What up, Yeezy" as he passed by. Later many of the inmates got down on their knees to pray as Jason White extended the right hand of fellowship, asking them to accept Christ as their lord and savior. Before leaving the jail, Kanye and the choir met with correctional officers to discuss ways to curb crime and proper rehabilitation methods for offenders. Shortly before the 2020 Martin Luther King, Jr., holiday weekend, Kanye and Kim partnered with Represent Justice, a non-profit, to buy out theaters in Atlanta, Chicago, Dallas, Miami, Oklahoma City, and Washington, D.C., for people to see the film *Just Mercy* (2019) about a wrongfully accused black man on death row in Alabama.[30]

Kanye's advocacy for prison reform is not surprising given his history of using his albums to speak out on racial and social injustice. *The College Dropout's* opening track, "We Don't Care," was about black youth who grew up admiring the neighborhood drug dealers "drug dealin' just to get by," because they had the money to buy nice things and provide tuition to send their relatives to college. "We Don't Care" pointed to cuts in afterschool programs that kept kids off the streets, the failure of schools to educate students with learning disabilities properly, and the inability of the government to help single black mothers get off welfare.[31] On "Heard 'Em Say," the third single from *Late Registration*, Kanye declared that the judicial system was set up to put black men and women behind bars.

My Beautiful Dark Twisted Fantasy and *Yeezus* explored racial injustice more profoundly than any of his past albums. "Gorgeous," the second track on *Fantasy*, painted a picture of young hustlers getting busted by the police at the airport with 30 rocks [of crack] in their luggage. No one shed tears on their behalf because going to prison was viewed as a predestined rite of passage for these men when they exited their mothers' wombs. Sha-Dawn Battle says Kanye's lyrics in "Gorgeous" applied Frantz Fanon's "epidermal racial schema," which perceives blacks as problems under the white gaze because of their skin color. Kanye rapped that Jerome is more likely to get targeted by the police and receive more jail time than Brandon. The implication is that Brandon is either white or viewed as nonthreatening due to his more privileged social class. Jerome, who denotes a black man from the hood, represents the "super predator" that Hillary Clinton spoke of when promoting her husband's disastrous 1994 crime bill, which ballooned the black prison population.[32]

Once men like "Jerome" are institutionalized, they become "new slaves" in the penal system. On his *Yeezus* track "New Slaves," Kanye spewed venom at wealthy corporations that benefited from the labor supplied by privately owned prisons.[33] He specifically called out the Corrections Corporation of America (CCA), now known as CoreCivic, which manages more than 65 state and federal correctional and detention facilities with revenue in the billions.[34] The private prison system has been called a modern-day version of convict leasing. From Reconstruction through World War II, Southern states enacted laws to imprison black men for unjustifiably long sentences for trivial offenses such as stealing chickens, owing a debt, playing dice, or behaving uppity. Under this system of forced labor, black male and female prisoners were leased by the Southern state, county, and local governments to the coal mining, steel, railroad, and lumber industries for profit. States such as Alabama would lease black convicts to private industries for as little as nine dollars a month. In 1874 the state of Alabama earned $164,000 in revenue from convict leasing.[35]

Kanye debuted his song "New Slaves" for his performance on *SNL*'s Season 39 finale. In his most chilling nationally televised performance Kanye stood on stage, motionless at a standing microphone, with a wicked ice grill on his face for the entire three minutes. The camera cut to a black and white close-up of his face as he angrily rapped about privately owned prisons, the Drug Enforcement Agency (DEA), and blood on the leaves, a direct reference to Billie Holiday's anti-lynching anthem "Strange Fruit." The likelihood of a black person going to prison for drug trafficking tripled between 1985 and 2000 due to bipartisan legislation following the death of college basketball star Len Bias from a cocaine overdose. It became common practice to over-police poor black neighborhoods. Black fathers were removed from households making it the most significant separation of black families since slavery. By 2015, one in every 14 black children had a parent in prison.[36]

A vivid image of this reality is painted in Kanye's music video for "All of the Lights," a song originally titled "Ghetto University" about an ex-convict returning home and attempting to reconnect with his young daughter. The song was also a metaphor for Kanye's feelings of isolation from his music following the VMA debacle. The video began with a black girl, probably no more than seven years old, leaving her apartment alone and walking down the snow-covered streets late at night. As the music began, Kanye appeared rapping atop a police car with the blue and red "flashing lights, lights, lights" of its sirens illuminating the night sky.[37] Tommy Curry wrote the following critique of the song in "You Can't Stand the Nigger I See! Kanye West's Analysis of Anti-Black Death":

> In "All of the Lights," West highlights the symbiosis between the ghettoized existence of blackness, its policed reality, and the desire for unneeded possessions. The "cop lights, flashlights, spotlights" that define the watching/monitoring/criminalizing confinement of black people is dealt with at the psychical level. The deprivation of life and wealth "educates" blacks into a pathology of false expectation, or what West calls the "ghetto university."[38]

I Want Jesus to Walk with Me

The students on The Yard erupted in cheers once the beat dropped for "Jesus Walks." The song's military drill sergeant-like introduction brought everyone to attention for the concert's magnificent grand finale. "Jesus Walks" is one of Kanye West's few songs received well in almost any setting. Its beat is hard enough to rock any secular hip-hop club, while the song's message is strong enough to "bring 'em out" to Jesus. The Reverend Tony Lee, the youth pastor of the Ebenezer African Methodist Episcopal Church in Fort Washington, Maryland, invited Kanye to perform. According to the Reverend Lee, more than 300 young people walked up to the pulpit to give their lives to Christ that day in 2004. Upon its release, "Jesus Walks" was promoted with three different music videos. The most viewed version featured Kanye as a preacher rapping from the pulpit as a black choir sang behind him. The video included images of white police officers accosting black protestors and three broken individuals—a young prostitute, an older alcoholic, and a gang member—searching for God's forgiveness. The opening scene for the video's second version started with a white prison warden instructing black men marching in a chain gang like extras in Eddie Murphy's *Life* (1999). The final scene was of a Ku Klux Klansman chopping wood for a cross burning.

In the third and final video, Kanye is joined by a white man who is portraying Jesus Christ. The pair walks through the "hood" before making their way to a tiny black church where Kanye goes up to the pulpit to testify. In one scene, Kanye walks through a black household with a picture of a white Jesus hanging on the wall. There is an age-old joke in the black community that if you enter the home of someone over the age of 70, you will find framed pictures of Martin Luther King, Jr., and a white Jesus on the wall. John Henrik Clarke, a noted historian and pioneer in Pan African Studies, described praying to a white deity as a detrimental form of brainwashing. Kanye might call this mental slavery; however, the fact that he cast a white Jesus as "his homeboy" in the video and used a white Jesus on his Yeezus Tour years later was either a flagrant contradiction or an attempt to incite dialogue.

"Jesus Walks" debuted a year after the U.S. began the Iraq War and a year before Hurricane Katrina. Kanye begins the song with a call to arms. We are at war with terrorism, racism, and ourselves. Only Jesus can save us! Scholars Angela M. Nelson and Conā Marshall offered valuable critiques on the meaning of "Jesus Walks" for black people in a special issue that I co-edited for *The Journal of Hip Hop Studies*. Nelson described the song as a commentary on black suffering and oppression, and conceptions of God and the devil. She compared Kanye's talk of the devil, as the force trying to break him down, to the black bluesmen and blueswomen who spoke of the devil in similar terms. Nelson said the source of suffering and oppression here that Kanye spoke of was not the devil, but "white supremacy" theodicy and "slave mentality" theodicy.[39] The former posits white suprem-acy as to blame for black suffering. The latter says blacks are responsible for their oppression because they cannot overcome the scars of slavery. This attribution is in line with Kanye's TMZ assertion that 400 years of slav-ery was a choice for some blacks.[40] Nelson's theory plays out in the first two visual versions of "Jesus Walks." The first version, which falls into the "slave mentality" category, appeared to blame the three individuals for their own plight. There is no provocation to consider what social factors may have led those blacks into prostitution, alcoholism, or gang banging; however, the second version acknowledges a racist penal system and white supremacist groups like the Klan as a source of suffering.

Conā Marshall observed that in "Jesus Walks" Kanye asked what role God plays in black suffering. Marshall argued that Kanye equates black individuals living on welfare and food stamps and struggling to make ends meet to living in hell. Black people were at war with racism and their own self-destructive behavior. Thus, he says the black community needed Jesus to alleviate their pain and end their holy war.[41] Kanye made similar claims in "Ultralight Beam." A verse on that latter song asked why God sent "oppression, not blessings." Marshall called attention to the philoso-pher of religion William R. Jones's 1973 book *Is God a White Racist?: A Pre-amble to Black Theology,* which questioned the black liberation theology of James Cone, James Deotis Roberts, and Joseph Washington. Jones pon-dered if black people's devotion to an omnibenevolent God could disman-tle the systemic causes of their oppression.[42] As the narrator of these two songs, Kanye spoke for the black masses who believe that Christ is essential to their daily lives and the source of their deliverance. Kanye reiterated this belief as he addressed the students at Howard:

> He brought me to my knees. I was one of them Muhammad Ali types. Oh, it's about me. Talking about Yeezus. I was in debt. I was in a mental hospital. I was canceled. But the power belongs to God. As we stand here right on The Yard of Howard University. DO THIS LOOK LIKE CANCEL TO YOU?

I Gotta Testify

"Jesus Walks" was the high point of the homecoming Sunday Service. As the song was coming to an end, Kanye began singing the choir's part a cappella and noticeably off-key. He then knelt and began to freestyle a prayer:

> God show my people the way…. The media attacks me constantly like shut up and dribble, damn nigger, shut up. Oh, I ain't supposed to play the N-word, I'm just supposed to keep this frustration inwards. Hey N-words quit acting like a

nerd.... And they want to front on me; meanwhile, my people locked up one in three. Go figure and what they talk about on Instagram and Twitter. That's all distractions while they make subtractions.... We was set up to get locked up. Modern-day slavery.

Kanye stopped freestyling to warn his young listeners about the seductions of a culture that is guilty of glorifying negative images for black youth such as "the trap," sexual promiscuity, excessive materialism, and designer brand worship. Kanye's proclamation, derided as a rant in several media outlets, harkened back to his views on Orwellian mind programming that opposes what he calls free thought. Kanye's views on free-thinking are slightly reminiscent of former Howard University professor Carter G. Woodson's writings in *The Miseducation of the Negro* (1933), which stated that you could control a person once you were able to shape the person's thinking.[43] Kanye told listeners the following:

> I'm in a position that very few black people are. On TV, on the internet, saying exactly what I feel. You tell me somebody else [who is doing that?] You ain't always got to agree with me. But I tell you what, if they throwing slave nets again, how bout we don't all stand in the exact same place? And they call this a rant. Does this sound like a rant to you? Anything to diminish. First, we black in America. Then they say he crazy don't listen to him.... That sounds like control. That sounds like shut up and dribble to me.... Harriett Tubman said she could have freed more if they knew they were slaves.[44]

At face value, Kanye's words sound very disrespectful. Africans were not enslaved because they stood idly by and watched Europeans capture them. Often other Africans from rival tribes working in cahoots with the slave catchers duped them. Africans fought back on land and, in the *Amistad* story, on the ships during the Middle Passage.[45] However, they were often overpowered and unsuccessful in their attempts to free themselves. Kanye has a responsibility to his audience to do more research before speaking publicly, given the magnitude of his voice. With that said, his opinions should not be wholly trivialized or ignored. Kanye's thoughts about young people being brainwashed by self-destructive forces in the culture coincides with admonitions that countless liberal black pastors preach from their pulpits every week.

Kanye's statement to the Howard students about his exceptional status to speak freely was part braggadocious bravado and motivational speak for these young people attending one of the world's leading universities. He was speaking to them from a platform that few black people have been privileged to attain. Kanye explored similar thoughts on *Watch the Throne* (2011), his lofty collaborative album with Jay-Z, and the album's promotional tour (2011–2012). *Watch the Throne* was luxury rap, an ode to both men's travels abroad, and what it meant to them to be rich and black in America.[46] Initially, that album was supposed to be an EP with only five songs. At the time, Kanye was basking in the glow of *My Beautiful Dark Twisted Fantasy* and traveling to Paris to study fashion for his forthcoming apparel line. Jay-Z was transitioning from being rap's leading emcee into one of the world's most influential entrepreneurs. The five-song EP metamorphosed into a 12-track album, which reflected on the lives and worlds they left behind due to their celebrity and wealth.

Watch the Throne was heavily criticized upon its release for its overemphasis on decadence and opulent living. The album was recorded in some of the world's finest hotels and had a shiny gold cover designed by Riccardo Tisci, the famous Italian fashion designer associated with Givenchy and Burberry. However, looking back at the album through a 2022 lens, it sounds more like a lyrical dissertation on the price of black excellence. *Watch the Throne* was supposed to teach listeners that owning European artwork, traveling the world, and using sophisticated vocabulary did not lessen their blackness or indicate that they were acting white. In a 2017 *New York Times* interview Jay-Z acknowledged the fact that joining a private country club and vacationing in Greece does not provide an escape from one's connection to the black masses. On the contrary, such astounding wealth enhances the obligation to do more to see others join that social stratum. Exclusivity becomes inclusivity.

W.E.B. Du Bois, serving as the commencement speaker, told the 1898 graduating class of his alma mater, Fisk University, that they were obligated to use their talents for the betterment of the entire race.[47] *Watch the Throne* cast Kanye and Jay-Z in the role of Du Bois's Talented Tenth for the age of Obama. While the music promoted financial freedom, its intent was not to preach that wealth and the ownership of material objects were the end goals. Kanye and Jay-Z destroyed a $350,000 customized (Mercedes) Maybach 57 in the music video for the album's single "Otis" to demonstrate that these material objects were nothing more than artifacts.[48]

Watch the Throne was released a year before the murder of Trayvon Martin. Some white conservatives called President Obama a racist for stating that if he had a son, he would look like Trayvon. Obama's critics failed to comprehend that the president was acknowledging that neither he nor his children were immune from racial profiling simply because they resided at 1600 Pennsylvania Avenue. As I listened to the rappers offer fatherly advice to their unborn sons on the Nina Simone sampled track "New Day," I thought about Obama's statement. I was reminded of James Baldwin talking to his nephew in *The Fire Next Time* (1963) about the stresses of being a black male. And I was reminded of Ta-Nehisi Coates giving his son similar advice, four decades later, in *Between the World and Me* (2015).

Kanye and Jay-Z juxtaposed their lyrics about their jet-setting lifestyles with other verses accentuating the plight of Chicago's black poor and the 1969 assassination of civil rights martyr Fred Hampton. "The goal is not to be successful and famous … we have a responsibility to push the conversation forward until we're all equal," said Jay-Z.[49] He and Kanye addressed that issue on the album's 10th track, "Murder to Excellence," rapping about the few blacks they come into contact with the higher up they climb the social ladder. Responding to the question of why Will (Smith), Oprah (Winfrey), Barack (Obama), and Michelle (Obama) were the few familiar faces they see at black tie events, Kanye said the system was programmed to exclude blacks from those social networks. The privileged blacks, like himself and Jay-Z, allowed into such circles dealt with members of their race not only questioning their blackness but accusing them of belonging to some corrupt secret society, better known as the Illuminati.

London based artist Esmeralda "Es" Devlin, well known for designing the opening and closing ceremonies at the Summer Olympics in 2012 and 2016, created the stage for the album's promotional tour in the U.S. and overseas. Both men had their own cube-shaped mini-stage, with fireballs shooting from the floor, from which they performed. Devlin's idea for the dual stages was to place these two powerful black men on thrones while making them utterly vulnerable to the audience that was out there judging their every move. An intriguing concept when you consider that at least half of their audience was white. This symbolism holds even more weight today now that they are two of only 17 black billionaires worldwide.

Images of Martin Luther King, Jr., appeared on the jumbotron as Kanye performed his verse to "Made in America." The Throne, a moniker given to this dynamic duo, stood with their backs to the crowd as pictures of Hurricane Katrina's destruction, black church worshippers, and a little white boy dressed in a Ku Klux Klan costume were shown on the screen. Louis Armstrong's 1967 jazz classic "What a Wonderful World" trumpeted from the speakers during this montage, leading into a performance of "No Church in the Wild." As The Throne performed "Who Gon Stop Me," an American flag that they had designed by Givenchy flashed on the screen, symbolizing that they were redefining the American Dream and the nation's most sacred item on their own terms.

False Prophet

As Kanye West made his closing remarks to the Howard students before leaving campus with his family, the prestigious tower of the

Founders Library provided a picturesque backdrop. The irony of this moment cannot be understated. Here was Mr. West, accused of being a sell-out to his race and ignorant of history, preaching to a congregation of attentive students on the historic Yard in front of one of the school's most iconic buildings, and on its most important weekend. Kanye built his career critiquing higher education on his first three albums: *The College Dropout, Late Registration,* and *Graduation.* In her 2014 book chapter "An Examination of Kanye West's Higher Education Trilogy," Heidi Lewis credited him with challenging the notion that an expensive post-secondary education was the only means to financial security for blacks almost a decade before student debt became a talking point of politicians, sociologists, and educators.[50]

This was not Kanye's first time at a Howard homecoming. He performed at Yardfest in 2003, four months before *College Dropout*'s release. While homecoming weekend has become one of the most significant social events in black America, the university is known for much more than hip-hop concerts, Greek step shows, marching band drumlines, and fashion. Proud alumni refer to Howard as "the Mecca" of black higher education. Howard ranked second among all HBCUs in 2020, according to *U.S. News & World Report.* The *Princeton Review* ranked its School of Business number one for students of color. The Howard Law School was ranked in the top 25 nationally by *The National Law Journal.* The Founders Library houses the Moorland-Spingarn Research Center, the second-largest repository for black history after the Schomburg Center for Research in Black Culture in Harlem. Howard is also the founding location for the original chapters of the most prestigious black Greek-letter organizations.

President Mordecai Johnson, the son of former slaves, envisioned Howard to be the nation's "Black Harvard." A telling statement, Johnson was modeling the university after an institution for white elites in the Northeast. Howard made national headlines for hiring Phylicia Rashad, Ta-Nehisi Coates, and Nikole Hannah-Jones in 2021. Today we find many of the nation's top black scholars teaching at predominantly white schools to majority-white student bodies. However, this was not the case for much of the 20th century due to Jim Crow. Howard was able to hire the nation's top black intellectuals, such as Carter G. Woodson, the founder of Negro History Week, and notable alumni like Zora Neale Hurston and Toni Morrison. U.S. Supreme Court Justice Thurgood Marshall, Howard University School of Law's star pupil, was the leading force behind school integration between the 1930s and 1960s. Sean "Diddy" Combs spent two years at Howard, while Nick Cannon completed his bachelor's degree in Criminal Justice and African American Studies at the university on May 9, 2020. The university marching band accompanied Vice President Kamala Harris, a proud alumnus, at her inauguration parade.

Since its founding, the university, located three miles from Capitol Hill, has relied on funding from the federal government to function.[51] This relationship to the federal government, which has typically been controlled by white lawmakers, has been a point of contention for decades. Howard's first 10 presidents were white men until the installation of the Reverend Mordecai Wyatt Johnson in 1926. As black power became a rallying cry, many Howard students became dissatisfied with their university's image of blackness. In October 1966, students and alumni gathered for their annual homecoming celebration. Five women ran for homecoming queen, and among them was junior Robin Gregory. "She had an afro, which was the statement. Robin was not the traditional homecoming queen candidate," says Dr. Paula Giddings (class of 1969).[52] Gregory saw her natural hairstyle as a statement on black beauty and not conforming to mainstream standards. After a two-week campaign, students gathered for the coronation of their new queen. The stage lights were down. The curtains opened. Before the crowd saw Gregory, they saw the lights cast a silhouette of her Afro. People started jumping and screaming. Some were raising their fists. Then a chant began…. Ungawa. Black Power.

The following April, a student group invited Muhammad Ali to speak on campus. Ali's visit came a month after he began his three-year suspension from professional boxing due to his opposition to the Vietnam War. With a copy of Elijah Muhammad's book *A Message to the Blackman* in hand, Ali preached black power as he stood on The Yard. A year later 1,000 Howard students took over the administration building to demand the creation of an African-American Studies major and center, the resignation of university president James Nabrit, a more prominent role in addressing the local black community's concerns, and a public declaration that Howard was a "black" university. Adrienne Manns, one of the leaders of the takeover, had published a column in the school newspaper a year earlier titled "Coon's Corner. Times Change," in which she denounced the administration as a puppet of a white government.

My father was a student at Howard's Divinity School at the time. Earlier that year, he published a column about the student body's growing displeasure. The takeover pitted students against administrators and each other over the question of what defines authentic blackness. Charles Epps, Jr., a 1955 graduate and former dean of Howard's College of Medicine, said in an interview for the PBS docuseries *Eyes on the Prize*, there was no such thing as "black" physics or "black" engineering. In his opinion, the university provided students with a mainstream education to prepare them for the broader world. The wife of esteemed Howard faculty member E. Franklin Frazier was captured on camera during the takeover saying that the students needed to conform to mainstream expectations if they wanted to succeed.

Professor Greg Carr, the chair of the Afro-American Studies Department and the co-host of a weekly YouTube series with radio personality Karen Hunter, tweeted that Kanye needed to stop by his office in Founders Library to read some books and dialogue with him. He cited Carter G. Woodson's *The Miseducation of the Negro* in his tweet and said the following:

> Kanye West is not crazy. He's not misled. He's a very shrewd businessman. What you're not gonna do is come to Howard and not be engaged. It's our responsibility as teachers, as faculty, as intellectuals at a historically black college, to use that [visit] as a moment.[53]

Kanye's performance on The Yard was a short walking distance from Andrew Rankin Memorial Chapel. The university's chapel has hosted many of the nation's leading black pastors and theologians over the last two centuries. Speakers such as Martin Luther King, Jr., Desmond Tutu, Gardner Taylor, Vernon Johns, Jeremiah Wright, Vashti McKenzie, Renita Weems, and H. Beecher Hicks, Jr., have preached from the chapel's pulpit. All these figures are rooted in the social activism of the black church dating back to slavery. According to the Rev. Frederick Douglass Haynes, III, senior pastor of Friendship-West Baptist Church in Dallas, Texas, black leaders like John Lewis and the Rev. C.T. Vivian who grew up in the church used their faith to guide their actions. Although Kanye embraced the music, style of worship, the optics, and some of the black church's rhetoric in 2019, much of his messaging and political activism was out of touch.

As Kanye was running for office in 2020, his political messaging often sounded more in line with Southern white evangelical Christianity. According to a 2016 National Election Pool survey, 46 percent of Trump voters were white evangelicals from the South.[54] Nancy Wadsworth detailed the history of this religious group in an article for *Vox*. "Evangelical history is inseparable from America's tortured racial history," wrote Wadsworth.[55] The Southern Baptist Convention apologized after issuing a 72-page report in 2018 acknowledging that their flagship seminary was primarily financed by Joseph E. Brown, who earned his fortune from black convict lease laborers who worked in coal mines. The black workers were subjected to the same harsh treatment as slaves on plantations. During the Reconstruction era and early 20th century, many faculty members at the seminary advocated legalizing segregation and promoted the Lost Cause mythology.[56]

Televangelist the Rev. Jerry Falwell, the founder of Liberty University in Lynchburg, Virginia, and the Moral Majority, argued that Lyndon Johnson's Great Society programs in the sixties caused the federal government to turn its back on white Americans.[57] Southern evangelicals opened private *Christian* schools to counter school desegregation ordinances.[58] They became loyal supporters of the GOP with Ronald Reagan's 1980 election. Neither Bill Clinton nor Barack Obama was invited to address the group during his term.[59] Large numbers of evangelical pastors have been opposed to Black Lives Matter, opting for an All Lives Matter theology. Is this the spiritual group that Kanye West aligned with and in which his political ideology was rooted? Andrew T. Walker, an evangelical professor at the Southern Baptist Theological Seminary, compared Kanye's potential to be a revolutionary force to that of 19th-century abolitionist William Wilberforce.

As early as 2019 some members of the press were asking if evangelicals were using Kanye and the appeal of gospel music to spread their gospel to the masses. He and the Sunday Service Choir performed for 17,000 young people at the Strength to Stand conference in Tennessee. The annual event is geared towards young evangelicals and the creation of Scott Dawson, a 2018 Republican gubernatorial candidate in Alabama. Kanye's budding friendship with televangelist Joel Osteen and former Liberty University president Jerry Falwell, Jr., further heightened suspicion that he was either being exploited or fully aware of what he was doing.[60] Kanye was invited to speak for nearly 30 minutes during Osteen's morning service and then perform a full concert later that evening. The Sunday Service at Osteen's Lakewood Church, the largest congregation in America, was livestreamed and received more than a million YouTube views. Kanye and Osteen were planning a major event to be held at Yankee Stadium in New York City prior to the global pandemic. Kanye was still scheduled to perform at Lakewood for Easter 2020, but pulled out at the last minute.

And then there was the hit *Jesus Is King* single "Closed on Sunday." Many liberal critics and LGBTQ activists saw the song as a salute to Chick-fil-A. The fast-food restaurant chain, founded in Georgia, has sparked national boycotts over the years due to the actions of its CEO Dan Cathy, a devout evangelist. Cathy has been criticized for his opposition to same-sex marriage and for making financial donations to charities with anti–LGBTQ stances.[61] Kanye, who has a long history of supporting LGBTQ rights, denies the allegations. He compares the anti–LGBTQ charges being hurled at him to the anti-black charges. It should be noted that there are many black Southern evangelicals. While some are conservative, most of these black Christians are Democrats. They voted for Presidents Barack Obama and Joe Biden. In the national exit polls for the 2016 election 57 percent of black voters identified as evangelical or born again.

Black evangelicals in Southern states like Alabama tend to be less motivated by pro-life and anti–LGBTQ rights issues than their white counterparts.[62]

Kanye is not the first black celebrity to have close ties to Southern white evangelicalism. Ethel Waters was a legendary jazz singer, film star, and the first black woman to have her own television show. She became a born-again Christian after singing for the late Billy Graham, the world's most famous evangelist preacher. Waters toured with Graham for his crusades to spread the gospel. Graham was a Democrat who joined the Republican Party after his friend Richard Nixon was elected. However, he was strongly opposed to segregation and began integrating his crusades in the 1950s. Graham was a spiritual advisor to multiple presidents, including Barack Obama. His son Franklin, however, is an evangelical leader who supported President Trump.

Kanye West's spirituality is just as complicated as his politics, celebrity, and importance to black America. Kanye certainly benefits from the huge platforms of these Southern white evangelicals, but I doubt that this is his sole reason for working with them. Most black church leaders with that level of clout are far less welcoming. He has expressed his hurt feelings after being dismissed by megachurch pastor T.D. Jakes. The Reverend Jamal Bryant initially supported Kanye, but quickly rejected him because of his Trump ties. For critics who argue that he is being exploited or selling out, Kanye believes that faith in God trumps all racial and political divisions.

Nine

"Wash Us in the Blood"

"I have achieved celebrity, earned great wealth, reached the
pinnacle of my profession, and yet, I am George Floyd. I am
Ahmaud Arbery. I am Tamir Rice. I am Trayvon Martin. I
am Emmett Till." *Von Miller*[1]

The illustrious jazz songstress Ella Fitzgerald made history by winning a Grammy Award in 1958. As the first black artist to win the prestigious honor it was a proud moment for the entire race. Why? The answer
lies in Du Bois's theory of the double consciousness. Blacks were taught to
measure their worth through the eyes of white America. Thus, musicians
were validated by having their songs played on mainstream radio stations
and chart on *Billboard*.[2] Their recognition at the major award shows, which
white voters judged, was the ultimate validation. In chapter three I discussed
Michael Jackson's dismay when *Off the Wall* was snubbed at the Grammys.
That inspired him to make *Thriller*, history's greatest "pop" album.

Kanye West, who modeled his career after Jackson's, was a victim of
this "need for white validation" for much of his career. He threw temper
tantrums when the major awards shows declined to acknowledge his great-
ness. "I plan to celebrate, scream, and pop champagne every chance I get
because I am at the Grammys, baby," he shouted during his 2005 acceptance speech for Best Rap Album. He has acknowledged that the significance placed upon his 22 Grammys, as opposed to his BET and NAACP
awards, is based on class. However, debates over class often come back to
race. *My Dark Twisted Fantasy* was his apology to the mainstream for his
over-inflated ego and offending Taylor Swift. Perhaps, subconsciously, he
felt the need to be "twice as good" on this album to reclaim their favor. *Yeezus* was a nearly 40-minute response to Kanye's feelings of rejection by the
white executives at Nike and the elite European fashion houses. His frustration resulted in his infamous 2013 "How Sway" rant on *Sway in the Morning*. "I'm in that Michael Jackson position where he couldn't get his video
played on MTV because he was considered urban," he told Sway.[3]

J.A.M. Aiwuyor criticized Kanye in her 2016 article "Kanye's Frantz Fanon Complex" for exhibiting the colonized mindset that the French West Indian philosopher Frantz Fanon spoke of in his book *Wretched of the Earth* (1961). Aiwuyor wrote that Kanye was not seeking to end the racism in the fashion industry that was the source of his oppression. On the contrary, his gripe stemmed from not being allowed a seat at the colonizer's table. He could not be that drum major that the Reverend Martin Luther King, Jr., spoke of at the front of the marching band receiving all the attention.[4] "Kanye has an obsession with getting acceptance, but not the 'colored' kind," wrote Aiwuyor. "With every new rant, we are witnessing a public display of internal conflict consisting of Du Bois's double consciousness."[5]

Until recently black celebrities risked their careers by behaving "too black" or saying anything that might offend the fragile sensibilities of their adoring white fanbase. They were expected to remain silent and display gratitude for whatever they received. Louis Armstrong felt the public's ire in 1957 when he refused to be a Cold War era "Jazz Diplomat" overseas due to President Dwight Eisenhower's poor handling of school desegregation. Many black people loved Kanye West because, like Armstrong, he refused to play this game. *Yeezus* was a watershed moment in his career. The "new Kanye" was born. I would divide his career into three stages thus far. The first phase was characterized by his trilogy of college themed albums. Kanye was on a journey to become the biggest pop star in the world. The second phase represented Kanye's bouts with personal hardships, loss, and the self-destructive behavior that resulted from his newfound stardom and mother's passing. He is currently in the third phase and could be entering a fourth phase post-divorce. While *Yeezus* was a very militant album that exhibited a politically charged black consciousness it came as his focus shifted to fashion, classism, and Kim. It was released just shy of a month before a jury acquitted George Zimmerman for the murder of Trayvon Martin. The verdict led to a series of events over the next three years that would force black celebrities to reexamine their priorities, indicators of success, and the value of their platform. At a time when blacks were expecting the "old Kanye" to be a leading voice, they were often confused and dismayed by this newer version.

This final chapter compares Kanye West with other contemporary black celebrities who have become more political and adopted overtly pro-black stances akin to their counterparts' behavior in the civil rights era. This new phase for the black celebrity began in 2016 and reached a plateau during the protests over the police killings of unarmed blacks in 2020. As the country was facing two pandemics, the coronavirus (COVID-19) and systemic racism, black entertainers were at the forefront of social activism. Why have these celebrities become so outspoken and culturally aware?

Does this prove that they no longer fear mainstream disapproval of their activism or need the validation of white America? The chapter also explores the significance of cancel culture and how it influences Kanye West and his contemporaries to speak out or remain silent.

Lift Up Your Voices

Kanye West came of age during a period accentuating black celebrity's duality at the end of the 20th century. Two prime examples of this were the rise of Michael Jordan and hip-hop's Golden Era. In 1984, Jordan's agent, David Falk, worked out a deal with Nike, a then moderately successful shoe company known for running shoes, to have the 21-year-old basketball star distribute a signature line of sneakers. By hiking the price up to over $100, Air Jordans became status symbols for black youth. However, neither Jordan nor Falk was content with limiting his appeal to black America. After Jordan dazzled worldwide spectators at the 1984 Summer Olympics, Falk believed that he could sell Jordan to the public as an all-American hero. Falk did not want the public to see race when they watched his client play or market sneakers. At the time it was unheard of for a global corporation to have a bald, dark-skinned black man as its face.

Michael Jordan became the model pitchman for selling Americana. He was the face of team USA at the 1992 Summer Olympics in Barcelona, Spain. Jemele Hill called him a chameleon who could represent everything to everybody. He mastered the art of saying everything and nothing at the same time. As Chicago sportswriter Sam Smith described in *The Jordan Rules* (1992), Jordan developed an exquisitely crafted image of perfection.[6] Race became a moot issue for him. David Halberstam, author of *Playing for Keeps: Michael Jordan and the World He Made* (2000), writes:

> As Jordan smiled, race simply fell away. Michael was no longer a black man; he was just someone you wanted to be with, someone you wanted as your friend.... If Michael Jordan was not burdened by race, why should you be burdened by it either?[7]

In 1992, a group of black students at the University of North Carolina Chapel Hill, Jordan's alma mater, demanded that the university build a center for the study of black culture. The proposed center would house a library named in Jordan's honor. The students contacted his mother, Mrs. Deloris Jordan, and gained her blessing. But Jordan declined to lend his support, arguing that any new building projects should be dedicated to the entire student body and not exclusive to one group. Four years later, Harvey Gantt, a black Democrat, challenged Republican incumbent Jesse Helms for his Senate seat. Gantt would have made history as North Carolina's first black U.S. senator. Helms, a staunch segregationists, once staged a filibuster to prevent the extension of the 1965 Voting Rights Act and voted against both the establishment of the King holiday and the creation of a national black history museum. It should have been easy for Jordan to back Gantt's campaign, but he refused to do so, saying in jest, "Republicans buy sneakers, too."[8]

For Jordan, it was safer and more lucrative to take Booker T. Washington's accommodationist approach rather than rocking the boat with politically charged agitation that might cost him white consumers. Sportswriter Dave Zirin and William Rhoden, author of *40 Million Dollar Slaves*, took Jordan to task for his apathy and unwillingness to do more with his platform. "Had he said 'jump,' had he said 'protest,' most athletes would have jumped; most would have protested. Instead, Jordan said, 'Be like Mike.'"[9] ESPN's record-breaking 10-part docuseries *The Last Dance* (2020) sparked a renewed interest in Jordan's refusal to be a leader for the black community. "America is quick to embrace a Michael Jordan, Oprah Winfrey, or Barack Obama so long as it's understood you don't get too controversial around broader issues of social justice," said former President Obama.[10]

The Jordan era coincided with hip-hop's Golden Era, lasting from the mid–1980s through the mid–1990s. Artists such as Public Enemy became black America's CNN, reporting on social injustices and giving a voice to the unheard not fortunate enough to "be like Mike." Ice Cube warned America of the violence exhibited during the 1992 LA uprising years earlier when he wrote "Fuck tha Police." Conscious rap and pro-black rhetoric were the norms during the Golden Era. This mindfulness was reminiscent of the social consciousness and cultural awareness displayed by black entertainers in the 1960s. However, by the dawn of the millennium that revolutionary spirit disappeared. As hip-hop moved into the mainstream artists became obsessed with bling, the pop charts, and the Grammys.[11] Simultaneously, contracts for black professional athletes ballooned to historic heights. Thanks to Jordan, nearly all the top black athletes were getting lucrative endorsement deals in addition to their salaries. It was also a great time for blacks lucky enough to achieve crossover success in Hollywood. Will Smith earned $20 million per picture in the early 2000s. To quote Drake and Future, "What a time, to be alive!"

The fatal shootings of Trayvon Martin and Michael Brown resulted in the next phase of the civil rights movement: Black Lives Matter. Social media created a new bully pulpit from which everyone could speak. Black celebrities could no longer ignore those echoes coming from the masses. The year of 2016 was the watershed moment when the pendulum swung towards the change that birthed today's celebrity activists. On August 26,

2016, the San Francisco 49ers played their third pre-season game against the Green Bay Packers. After the game reporters asked Colin Kaepernick, the 49ers' quarterback, why he sat during the national anthem. "I am not going to stand up to show pride in a flag or country that oppresses people of color," he replied. The next week Kaepernick, following the advice of Nate Boyer, a white U.S. Army Green Beret veteran, knelt during the anthem to avoid any confusion that his protest was anti-military. Kaepernick continued kneeling throughout the start of the 2016 regular season. Images of him on one knee with his huge Afro hairstyle blowing in the wind became viral sensations.

By taking a knee, Colin Kaepernick set off shockwaves that reverberated throughout the country. He became a hero for the young Black Lives Matter (BLM) movement and a pariah for individuals who believed that BLM promoted racism towards whites and anarchy. Donald Trump suggested that Kaepernick find another country if he was unsatisfied being in America.[12] At the end of the season, Kaepernick opted out of his contract with the 49ers. Despite leading the team to the Super Bowl three years earlier, he did not receive a single offer from any of the NFL's 32 teams. Howard Bryant noted how the NFL embraced former Baltimore Ravens linebacker Ray Lewis, who was found guilty of obstruction of justice in a 2000 criminal case involving the stabbing deaths of two black men. By contrast, the NFL blacklisted Kaepernick for speaking out against white supremacy. He has not taken a snap in an NFL game since 2016.[13]

Colin Kaepernick seemed like the most unlikely person to become the face of a movement. He was born in Milwaukee, Wisconsin, to a 19-year-old white mother and a black father of West African ancestry. After his mother put him up for adoption, he was taken in by Rick and Teresa Kaepernick, a white couple in Fond du Lac, Wisconsin. He moved to California with his adopted family when he was four. As a teenager Kaepernick was drafted by the Chicago Cubs to play baseball, but he chose to focus on football. For much of his career he was not outspoken. As a biracial man he was not bombarded with questions about having the chance to be the second black quarterback to win a Super Bowl. The media assigned to cover the game were more concerned with his tattoos than his skin color.

Kaepernick's kneeling surprised most people not in his inner circle. But his protest did not happen in a vacuum. He was one of many black celebrities to speak out in 2016. At the 58th Annual Grammy Awards ceremony, earlier in February, Kendrick Lamar was the star attraction. He came to the Grammys with 11 nominations—and left with five awards—for his album *To Pimp a Butterfly* (2015). The native of Compton, California, chose this occasion to deliver one of the most riveting live performances in television history. He and a group of black men slowly walked out on stage weighed down by the chains on their hands and feet. The members of Lamar's band were locked inside faux jail cells. He passionately began rapping the words to his singles "The Blacker the Berry" and "Alright," an unofficial anthem of the Black Lives Matter movement, in front of a giant bonfire. His emotional presentation ended with the stage going dark as he stood in front of a white outline of Africa's map with the word "Compton" written through it. Lamar's Grammy performance was infused with the black pride ingrained in him during an expedition to Cape Town and Johannesburg, South Africa just before recording his album.

A week before the Grammys a similar moment occurred at Super Bowl 50. Cam Newton, the Carolina Panthers' 25-year-old quarterback and the NFL's newly minted Most Valuable Player award recipient, set the tone for professional sports' biggest weekend by reminding the press that he was "a black quarterback."[14] Although all eyes were on Newton and his opponent Peyton Manning, a young black woman from Houston stole the show. Beyoncé, a special guest of the halftime concert's headlining act, Coldplay, used her three-minute set to debut her new song "Formation" and commemorate the 50th anniversary of women in the Black Panther Party. Queen Bey, as Beyoncé is known by loyal fans in her Beyhive, performed in the middle of the field surrounded by 50 black dancers dressed in black leather outfits and wearing black berets on top of their large Afros. She led the ladies into an X formation, in honor of slain human rights leader Malcolm X, and the performers raised their gloved fists in a manner that was reminiscent of John Carlos and Tommie Smith's famous Black Power salute.

The music video for "Formation" debuted online a day before the Super Bowl. The video included numerous references to New Orleans's Creole culture and Hurricane Katrina's effects on the city's black neighborhoods. It featured spoken interpolations from YouTube celebrity Messy Mya, a New Orleans rapper who was murdered in 2010, and Big Freedia, a black gay bounce artist. Bounce is an energetic form of music that originated in the city's housing projects. "Formation" was a long, blunt statement about race in America accompanied by a hooded black boy dancing in front of a line of police officers holding their hands up, graffitied walls reading "stop shooting us," and a Ford Crown Victoria police car sinking in the Mississippi River's waters.

Rudy Giuliani, President Trump's attorney, condemned Beyoncé's artistry as "outrageous" and "anti-police." Jonathan Thompson, the executive director of the National Sheriffs' Association, told *The Washington Post* Beyoncé was "inciting bad behavior."[15] The Miami Fraternal Order of Police called for a national police boycott of future Beyoncé concerts. This controversy was new for an artist known for her radio-friendly, crossover hit songs, fashion, blonde hair weaves, pretty face, and "bootylicious" figure.[16]

SNL satirized her cultural awakening with a sketch titled "The Day Beyoncé Turned Black" on the night before Lamar's Grammy moment. The vignette reenacted scenes from numerous disaster films where people flee from their homes and jobs in a futile attempt to survive the apocalypse. White people lost their minds as they ran through the streets in terror. A black bystander, played by Kenan Thompson, informed a confused white woman that Beyoncé had always been black, except for the time she acted in Steve Martin's film *Pink Panther* (2006). "Oh yeah, she was white in that," he said sarcastically.[17]

"Formation" was the lead single from Beyoncé's 2016 album *Lemonade*, which signaled a new direction in her image and musical content. The album dealt with the generational effects of slavery on black marriage which was manifested in the infidelity of her father and husband. *Lemonade's* release was accompanied by an hour-long film inspired by Julie Dash's 1991 independent film *Daughters of the Dust*. The film used an audio excerpt from "Who Taught You to Hate Yourself," a speech delivered by Malcolm X in 1962. Malcolm referred to black women as the most disrespected persons in America. He delivered the full speech at a funeral for Ronald Stokes, a 29-year-old black man, fatally shot on April 27, 1962, by white Los Angeles police officers while holding his hands up. Malcolm's excerpt foreshadowed a moving scene later in the film in which Beyoncé sang an a capella rendition of her song "Freedom," featuring Kendrick Lamar, to the grieving mothers of Trayvon Martin, Michael Brown, and Eric Garner.[18]

Beyoncé's new image was displayed again when she made history as the first black woman to headline the Coachella Valley Musical and Arts Festival, the premier music festival in America. Most festival attendees are middle- and upper-class whites due to the $450 price point of the tickets. Rather than give a safe performance, Beyoncé used the opportunity to present a two-hour spectacle of exuberant black excellence. Her mother, Tina Knowles, posted on Instagram that she was afraid that the audience would be confused by all the black culture. Beyoncé began her Coachella spectacle dressed like Queen Nefertiti, who ruled over Egypt during the wealthiest period of its history. She wore a black and gold headdress and matching cape with an emblazoned image of Nefertiti. Her headdress resembled the one that researchers discovered on a bust of Nefertiti in 1912. An interlude occurred seven minutes into the show to allow Beyoncé time to mark the occasion with an a capella rendition of "Lift Every Voice and Sing," the official "black national anthem" since 1919. Queen Bey acknowledged the historic moment with this unforgettable statement: "Ain't that 'bout a bitch?"

Beychella was probably the closest thing most of those white festival attendees will ever get to an HBCU homecoming weekend experience. A year later, Netflix began streaming *Homecoming*, a 137-minute documentary film based on the concert. Among the many highlights of *Homecoming* were salutes to black luminaires Maya Angelou, W.E.B. Du Bois, Marian Wright Edelman, Reginald Lewis, Audre Lorde, Nina Simone, Alice Walker, and Cornel West.[19] Special advanced screenings were held for students at Howard University, Morehouse College, and Spelman College. Three months later Beyoncé released *The Lion King: The Gift*, the soundtrack album for the remake of Disney's 1994 children's classic *The Lion King*. *Rolling Stone* called the soundtrack, featuring more than 20 artists from Ghana, Nigeria, Cameroon, and the United States, "Beyoncé's Love Letter to Blackness." The album's single "BROWN SKIN GIRL" inspired viral videos worldwide praising black femininity. She followed up that project with *Black Is King*, a visual album exclusive to Disney+ subscribers.

That's Just the Wave

As Kanye West went one way, the rest of "the culture" went in the opposite direction. The absolute contrarian whose *The Life of Pablo* album was initially titled *Waves*, Kanye was now going against the grain as usual and rejecting what he saw as the popular trend of overemphasizing race and being black. "Wake up, Mr. West. Wake up, culture. Everybody think they are so woke, but they are following the rules of what woke is supposed to be," he would tell radio host Big Boy.[20] Musical artists were not the only ones who awakened in 2016. Will (Smith) and Jada (Smith) were among a group of blacks in Hollywood who participated in the #OscarsSoWhite boycott of the 88th Academy Awards ceremony held on February 28 to spotlight the lack of black nominees. Chris Rock, the ceremony's host, delivered a scathing 10-minute opening monologue highlighting this subject.[21] *Grey's Anatomy* star Jesse Williams invigorated the crowd at the BET Awards on June 26 as he gave his Humanitarian Award acceptance speech. "We're done watching and waiting while this invention called whiteness uses and abuses us," said Williams.[22]

Jesse Williams's speech at the BET Awards was a prelude for what was to come at the ESPY Awards, ESPN's annual award ceremony, 17 days later. NBA all-stars LeBron James, Carmelo Anthony, Chris Paul, and Dwyane Wade had the spotlight at the beginning of the internationally televised event. These four players were among the highest-paid and most marketable athletes in the world. A week before the ESPYs, two black men, Alton Sterling in Louisiana and Philando Castile in Minnesota, were fatally shot by police officers. Neither Sterling nor Castile was violently resisting arrest when he was shot. Their murders struck a nerve in the majority-black NBA.

Accordingly, these four basketball superstars felt the need to use the ESPYs to speak on behalf of their slain brethren.

The ESPYs inspired black athletes in other professional leagues. Players on the Minnesota Lynx wore black T-shirts emblazoned with the phrase "Change starts with us, Justice & Accountability" on the front, with Philando and Alton's names on the back. Other players from the Phoenix Mercury, the Indian Fever, and the New York Liberty participated in similar acts of protest. The WNBA fined each team $5,000 for uniform infractions, and each player involved another $500. Two years later Minnesota Lynx star Maya Moore, the league's best player and a four-time WNBA champion, stepped away from the game to dedicate her next two seasons to criminal justice reform. Moore's efforts helped to overturn the wrongful conviction of Jonathan Irons, a 40-year-old black man serving a 50-year prison sentence.[23]

Tennis champion Serena Williams wrote a lengthy statement expressing her frustration with the growing number of unarmed blacks slain by police officers and posted the message, "I won't be silent," on her Facebook page. Williams, a dark-skinned black woman with natural hair, raised poor in Compton, has been the face of a majority-white, elite sport for the past two decades. She understands the double consciousness better than most celebrities. Williams has been criticized for her demeanor during matches, her flamboyant outfits, her "thick" body type, and her celebrations, such as Crip walking, at the 2012 Olympics.[24] The most egregious example was her confrontation with umpire Carlos Ramos at the women's final of the 2018 U.S. Open. Ramos's accusation that she cheated cost her the match and set off a firestorm. Racist images flooded the internet, depicting her as a big-lipped, big-hipped angry black woman verbally assaulting this helpless white man. In Williams's defense, other online images portrayed her as a victim being judged by a white man looking down on her from his elevated seat.

LeBron James spoke up in defense of Williams. Unlike his idol Michael Jordan, James views himself as an activist and a role model for black America. His awakening began in July 2010 when he and his childhood friends (Maverick Carter, Randy Mims, and Rich Paul) produced The Decision, an hour-long ESPN special, to announce which team he planned to sign with as a free agent. The live event was held at the Boys and Girls Club of Greenwich, Connecticut. James arrived late for the taping because he was out having a buffet dinner with Kanye West, who sat in the audience during the event. How ironic that Kanye was involved at a moment that would transform the way professional black athletes viewed their level of agency. LeBron James's decision to leave the Cleveland Cavaliers and take his talents to South Beach had two immediate effects.[25] It birthed a new age of player empowerment in the NBA and revealed the hidden racism found in James's so-called fans. He went from America's chosen one to a selfish and ungrateful villain. Cavaliers' owner Dan Gilbert penned a letter to Cleveland fans in which he came across as a slave owner upset that his prized possession fled from the plantation. The 25-year-old celebrity realized that he was little more than a commodity and entertainment source for many whites. Racist vandals spray-painted the word "NIGGERS" on a gate outside his home in Brentwood, California.[26]

The Decision was the watershed moment that birthed LeBron James's activism. As a new member of the Miami Heat, he organized a team photo with everyone wearing hoodies. They bowed their heads down to show solidarity for Trayvon Martin, the 17-year-old black teenager from Florida killed by a neighborhood watchman.[27] Two years later James wore a black T-shirt with the phrase "I can't breathe" across the front in white letters. Those were the final words spoken by Eric Garner, a black man in New York City who died in 2014 from a police chokehold. In the summer of 2020 James partnered with other NBA and WNBA players to form "More Than a Vote," an organization dedicated to fighting voter suppression and registering black voters for the upcoming presidential election.

LeBron James's activism has branched off to Hollywood. He was the executive producer for the 2020 Netflix miniseries *Self Made*, chronicling the business career of Madam C.J. Walker, a black hair care pioneer and the first self-made woman millionaire in America. He produced CNN's 2021 documentary *Dreamland: The Burning of Black Wall Street* about 1921 Tulsa Riot and *Josephine*, a limited series on Josephine Baker. After Fox News host Laura Ingraham advised him to "shut up and dribble," his production company, SpringHill Entertainment, released a three-part Showtime docuseries. Called *Shut Up & Dribble*, it chronicled the activism of black athletes since the 1960s. The stories of Craig Hodges and Mahmoud Abdul-Rauf were included in the docuseries. Hodges was Michael Jordan's teammate on the Chicago Bulls. When the team visited President George H.W. Bush at the White House following their 1991 championship, Hodges, a devout Muslim, struck a sour note by coming dressed in a dashiki and kufi. He gave the president a letter asking him to do more about the inner cities and black people. The Bulls released him the next season, and he was unable to find a job on another team. Rauf was fined, suspended, and became a target of ridicule in 1996 for refusing to stand for the national anthem at the start of games. Rauf, a devout Muslim, opted to pray rather than salute what he viewed as a symbol of injustice.

The Shop, a 30-minutes-per-segment series consisting of conversations held in a barbershop with celebrities debating sports, race, and politics, is James's latest endeavor. In one episode, he called the white NFL team owners, who blackballed Kaepernick, a bunch of slave masters. He described his first experiences and thoughts about attending a predominantly white private school to play basketball. "I'm not fucking with white people," he said.[28] Jamie Foxx was a guest on the second season's premiere episode. He explained how his generation, blindly benefiting from the sacrifices of past generations, viewed their obligation to uplift the race:

> We were almost on some white people shit like "this is going on! This is amazing. Did you see there were black people shot?" So, when you talk about the generation before you, there was a little bit of subliminal plantation thinking. Like, damn, if I make this move, I'm gonna fuck my money up. When you guys stood up [at the ESPYs], that sent shockwaves through everybody.[29]

I Can't Breathe

This new phase of social activism among the modern-day black celebrity reached its plateau in the summer of 2020. COVID-19 had celebrities in their homes quarantining, like the rest of Americans, and hosting Zoom dance parties and Verzuz battles on Instagram Live. After nearly three months in their homes, a new pandemic caught their attention, forcing them to take a stand. On May 5, the video of Ahmaud Arbery's fatal shooting came to light after more than two months. Arbery, a 25-year-old black man, was jogging through a neighborhood in Glynn County, Georgia, when two white men, Gregory McMichael (64) and his son Travis McMichael (34), riding in a truck stopped him. Gregory McMichael, a retired police officer, called 911 to report what he believed was a burglary suspect. Travis jumped out of the truck to confront Arbery. After a brief struggle, Travis shot him. In the police report, Gregory said Arbery reacted violently, thus causing Travis to kill him in self-defense.

Atlanta mayor Keisha Lance Bottoms called Arbery's murder a modern-day lynching. Jay-Z, Alicia Keys, Meek Mill, and Yo Gotti signed an open letter published in *The Atlanta Journal-Constitution* demanding justice. Kim Kardashian urged her Twitter followers to sign a petition calling for charges to be filed against the McMichaels. Just as #JusticeForAhmaud was trending, the country witnessed another tragedy. On May 25, ironically the Memorial Day holiday, a 46-year-old black man in Minneapolis was arrested for allegedly passing a counterfeit $20 bill in a deli. The man's name was George Floyd or "Big George" as friends called him due to his 6'4" stature. Derek Chauvin, a white police officer, handcuffed and pinned Floyd to the ground. Chauvin then knelt on Floyd's neck, with a smirk on his face and a hand in his left pocket, for an excruciating nine minutes and 29 seconds as Floyd, forced to become the narrator of his own horrific death, screamed out, "I can't breathe" and cried out for his departed mother—"Mama! Mama!"—before becoming unresponsive and pulseless for nearly four minutes.

By June 1 the demonstrations had spread from Minneapolis to every state and worldwide.[30] While Fox News emphasized the looting more than peaceful protests, President Trump fanned the flames of an already tense situation by chastising local government leaders for being too soft and calling the protestors thugs. He tweeted, "When the looting starts, the shooting starts," a phrase first used by Miami police chief Walter Headley in 1967 to excuse his officers' use of excessive force against young black protestors.[31] Trump warned of turning "vicious dogs" on protestors and deployed National Guardsmen in Washington, D.C., to reestablish law and order.[32] Peaceful demonstrators in DC were tear-gassed to clear a path for the president to take pictures holding a Bible in front of St. John's Church.[33]

Dave Chappelle delivered some of the most brilliant commentary on Floyd's murder in *8:46*, a 26-minute Netflix stand-up special offered for free on YouTube. "Who gives a fuck what Ja Rule [Jeffrey Atkins] thinks at a time like this?"[34] Chappelle's joke came in response to Don Lemon's criticism of black celebrities not doing more to fight racial injustice. Although Chappelle was trying to point out that he and other entertainers were insignificant compared to the masses marching in the streets, that did not deter his peers from getting involved. The traditionally light-hearted Kevin Hart displayed a vastly different side on *Straight from the Hart*, his bi-weekly Sirius XM podcast, devoting an hour to indignation over George Floyd's killing. Comedian Lil Rel Howery dedicated his opening monologue while guest hosting *Jimmy Kimmel Live* (2003–present) to police brutality and racial injustice. Tyler Perry and retired boxing champion Floyd Mayweather, Jr., paid Floyd's funeral expenses.[35]

Kareem Abdul-Jabbar and NFL star Von Miller penned op-eds for *The Los Angeles Times* and *Time*, respectively. A video of actress Keke Palmer asking a white National Guardsman at a rally to march with her went viral. T.I. called upon all blacks to participate in a national Blackout Day of economic boycotting on July 7, 2020. Retired NBA champion Stephen Jackson, a close friend of George Floyd, spoke at a rally in Minnesota. Boston Celtics forward Jaylen Brown drove 15 hours from Boston to Atlanta to join fellow NBA player Malcolm Brogdon at a rally. Kyrie Irving challenged his peers in the NBA to boycott the remainder of their season, paused for three months by COVID-19, to dedicate themselves to social justice causes. Although the season resumed in late July, the players used their platform to evoke change by playing on courts with "Black Lives Matter" written on them in all capital letters. The back of their jerseys replaced their last names with phrases like "I Am a Man," "How Many More," "Vote," "Anti-Racist," and "Say Her Name." Post-game interviews were used to further the cause. Irving paid the salaries of WNBA players Renee Montgomery and Natasha Cloud after they sat out their seasons to focus on activism.

On August 26, the fourth anniversary of Kaepernick's initial protest, Giannis Antetokounmpo and his Milwaukee Bucks teammates boycotted their game following the shooting of Jacob Blake, an unarmed 29-year-old black man in Kenosha, Wisconsin. Blake was left paralyzed from the waist down after police officers shot him in the back seven times as his three sons watched from the backseat of his vehicle. The remaining playoff games were postponed over the next 48 hours.[36] NBA players threatened to cancel the rest of the playoffs but changed their minds after meeting with the league's board of governors and a midnight phone conversation with Barack Obama.

The women in the WNBA wore white T-shirts, each with one of the letters to spell out Blake's name, and seven bullet holes in red ink. After the national anthem was played, they walked off the court and their games were canceled for that evening.[37] Naomi Osaka, the former number-one professional women's tennis player in the world, boycotted her upcoming semifinal match at the Western and Southern Open.[38] Osaka is a 24-year-old woman of Haitian and Japanese descent.[39] Earlier that summer, some of the NFL's most famous black players, including Super Bowl LIV Most Valuable Player and the league's highest-paid player Patrick Mahomes, filmed a public service announcement supporting Black Lives Matter.

The revolutionary fervor even spread to NASCAR. After William Darrell "Bubba" Wallace, Jr., the lone biracial driver in this very Southern white sport, spoke out and drove a car with a unique Black Lives Matter paint scheme, NASCAR prohibited spectators and vendors from displaying Confederate flags.[40] Two weeks later a noose, symbolic of the lynching ropes used to hang blacks from trees, was reported to be found in Wallace's garage stall.[41] NASCAR and the FBI released a statement, 24-hours later, refuting that Wallace was the victim of a hate crime. Months later Wallace left his racing team, owned by Trump supporter Richard Petty, and joined a new team started by Michael Jordan.

All this activism did come at a cost to the black celebrity. The NBA's viewership ratings declined. Several conservative commentators and talk radio callers expressed their exhaustion and displeasure with the protests and woke rhetoric. Nevertheless, a surprising number of white celebrities became allies to their black counterparts. Seth Rogen, Ashton Kutcher, and Billie Eilish reprimanded whites who prefer to say, "All Lives Matter." Justin Bieber told his 138 million Instagram followers that he, a beneficiary of black culture, was now committed to fighting systemic racism. Pastor Joel Osteen marched with George Floyd's family in Houston. Taylor Swift used her Twitter page to reprimand President Trump for his "looting and shooting" comment. Kim Kardashian and her sisters posted statements and videos on their social media pages. Kim urged her Instagram followers to donate money to the GoFundMe page for Floyd's family and sign a petition demanding the arrests of Chauvin and the three police officers who were with him. She also demanded justice for Breonna Taylor, a 26-year-old black woman in Louisville, Kentucky, killed while sleeping in her apartment on March 13, 2020, after police fired 20 rounds in her direction. None of the three police officers were charged with her murder.[42] While Kim was busy fighting on behalf of the black community, Kanye had gone silent.

Cancel Culture

It seemed like everyone had an opinion about the slayings of Floyd and Taylor except for the loquacious Kanye West, who was painfully mute for nearly 30 days. There were no tweets or viral Sunday Service benefit concerts. The only entries found online about Kanye during the first month of the protests were reports that he was threatening to sue a former bodyguard for $10 million for slander, his plans for a new Yeezy cosmetics line, and rumors of new music with Dr. Dre. If silence is complicity, Kanye West was guilty of being on the wrong side of history! When he was a guest on *The Breakfast Club* in 2015, Kanye asserted that his father instructed him not to voice an opinion on Trayvon Martin's death. Perhaps Ray West feared that the media would misconstrue his son's words. What was Kanye's reason for silence this time? In the previous chapter, I referenced my conversation with the Reverend Melvin Maxwell, the father of Mariah Maxwell, the lead vocalist in Kanye's Christian opera *Mary*. The Reverend Maxwell provided thoughts about Kanye's failure to address the recent police killings publicly:

> Kayne is sincere in his burden to get the Gospel of Jesus Christ out, but lost in the cause for social justice. He will have to learn that our work in social justice on the earth is part of the call to ministry. It is a holistic call that Christ demands advocacy and a fight for civil rights for the whole person, not a lukewarm dichotomy that keeps us in our comfort zones without disrupting the status quo. Kanye cannot be a disruptor in culture or for Christ in culture and then muzzle ministry when it gets risky to his wallet. Jesus is a radical revolutionary that disrupts wherever he goes, not creating chaos but order out of chaos. Kanye must learn following a crucified God puts a demand on him to confront social ills and to disrupt the status quo, especially wrapped in nationalism and white supremacy.[43]

Kanye West was not the only black celebrity known for speaking out over the years who was criticized for not getting involved in the demonstrations. Kendrick Lamar and J. Cole found themselves in this same predicament. Noname (Fatimah Warner), a rapper and activist from Chicago, tweeted about the irony in these artists remaining silent when they became wealthy from rapping about black people's plight. The sight of rappers like Lil Baby (Dominique Jones), DaBaby (Jonathan Kirk), and Roddy Ricch (Rodrick Moore, Jr.), who refrained from making socially responsible music in the past, marching with the protestors and dedicating new songs to the movement further magnified Noname's critiques. Other celebrities—Terry Crews, Virgil Abloh, and the rapper Trina (Katrina Taylor)—were chastised for speaking out against the demonstrations. Abloh and Trina were overly critical of the looting that took place during some protests.

Kanye and these other celebrities were the latest victims of cancel culture, a popular form of public shaming on social media. Individuals and corporations can be canceled for authentic wrongdoings. Bill Cosby, R. Kelly, Kevin Spacey, and Harvey Weinstein were canceled for rape allegations. Others have been canceled for making offensive or unpopular statements.[44] Novelist J.K. Rowling, political activist Noam Chomsky, *New York Times* opinion editor Bari Weiss, and several college professors published a piece in *Harper's* magazine titled "A Letter on Justice and Open Debate." Their letter, with 150 names, demanded an end to silencing dissent. President Trump shared his feelings on the subject in a speech delivered at Mt. Rushmore on July 4, 2020. He referred to it as "new far-left fascism demanding total submission from anyone who disagrees."[45] Rob Henderson, a doctoral student at the University of Cambridge, published "5 Reasons Why People Love Cancel Culture" in *Psychology Today*. According to Henderson, people cancel others because it increases their social status while reducing the status of their enemies. It also strengthens their social bonds with like-minded individuals and forces their so-called enemies to reveal themselves.[46]

No one is safe from cancel culture. Kanye's "big brother" Jay-Z learned this the hard way in 2019 after partnering with the NFL. One might ask how Jay-Z could get canceled. His track record includes producing documentaries on Trayvon Martin and Kalief Browder, paying the bails of Black Lives Matter activists, writing an op-ed in *The New York Times* on the failure of the war on drugs, and establishing a scholarship fund for disadvantaged black children. He mentored the late Nipsey Hussle (Ermias Asghedom) on entrepreneurship and financed the Free Meek campaign. Jay-Z co-founded the REFORM alliance with Van Jones and Meek Mill to tackle criminal justice reform. His pre–Grammy Roc Nation Brunch is an annual celebration of black excellence in the music industry.

None of these endeavors mattered to NFL safety Eric Reid and others who labeled Jay-Z a sellout due to his partnership with the NFL.[47] Jay-Z told NFL commissioner Roger Goodell that "we've moved past kneeling." In a large conference room surrounded by friends, business associates, and the press, he discussed a new venture that gave his company Roc Nation control over producing musical events for the league, including the Super Bowl Halftime Show. Roc Nation will also assist the league in community relations outreach initiatives. Some detractors accused the NFL of exploiting Jay-Z and using him as a puppet to appease black sports fans. But many perceived Jay-Z's "we're past kneeling" comment as a dismissal of Colin Kaepernick's protest. That comment infuriated Kaepernick's former teammate Eric Reid, Howard Bryant, and several others, including a middle-aged black woman I encountered at the annual meeting for the Association for the Study of African American Life and History (ASALH). She rhetorically asked, "What has Jay-Z done for black people? NOTHING!!!" Stephen A. Smith, who has also been accused of being a sellout, revealed on the *All the Smoke* podcast that Jay-Z was partially responsible for arranging Kaepernick's private workout for 26 NFL representatives in 2019. Thus, these accusations were ignorant.

I was invited to guest lecture at Howard University on November 21, 2019, weeks after Kanye had been on campus for their homecoming weekend. Many of the students attended his Sunday Service. At the end of my lecture I posed the question, "Should Kanye West be canceled?" Most students disagreed with silencing Kanye and others for harboring unpopular opinions. Cancel culture makes some black celebrities fearful of speaking out. Harold Varner III, one of five black professional golfers, asked ESPN's black golf analyst Michael Collins to tell audiences about the pressure black celebrities feel when the public expects them to speak on issues, immediately, with little time to process their thoughts. Michael Eric Dyson has severe gripes with today's "zero tolerance" policy. Dyson compares cancel culture to white supremacists stigmatizing blacks for their dissidence. He likes to remind anyone willing to listen that Malcolm X was murdered by fellow members of the Nation of Islam who were intolerant of his viewpoint.

Was it the fear of being canceled that drove Kanye to break his silence? He showed up at a Black Lives Matter rally in Chicago on June 4, 2020, wearing a facemask and hoodie. His surprise visit resulted in disorder as young marchers became more fascinated with his presence. Taylore Norwood, an organizer for the rally, attempted to restore order by reminding the crowd why they were marching. Kanye left shortly afterward to avoid being any more of a distraction. Hours later, it was announced that he had donated $2 million to help the families of George Floyd, Ahmaud Arbery, and Breonna Taylor with legal fees. A portion of that money would be set aside to support black-owned businesses nationwide. Kanye also established a 529 education plan to fund the college education for Floyd's 6-year-old daughter Gianna.[48]

I was conflicted by Kanye's insertion into the ongoing protests. I questioned the delay and his continued allegiance to a president who maligned demonstrators as thugs. Was his $2 million donation an attempt to buy back disgusted black fans? Was he shamed into speaking out after seeing so many of his famous peers, his wife, and the young people that he claimed to represent risking their health to be out on the streets protesting? He did not have much to risk by joining the movement. So many businesses supported the protests that it became trendy. Democratic House Speaker Nancy Pelosi and congressional members, adorned in kente cloth stoles, took a knee in support of the movement at the U.S. Capitol Visitor Center.[49] The NFL made a $250 million donation over 10 years to fight racial inequality. The politically apathetic Michael Jordan and his company, Jordan Brand, pledged $100 million over the next 10 years to nationwide organizations fighting for racial justice.[50] Jordan Brand also launched *Real Talk*, a new content series hosted by Angela Rye and dedicated to finding actionable solutions to racial inequality.

Kanye West was universally praised for his financial donations. Gianna Floyd posted a video on Instagram thanking him. DJ Akademiks (Livingstone Allen), the co-host of *Everyday Struggle* (2017–2020), joked that Kanye was not only allowed to return to the black family reunion, but he could work the grill at the cookout too. Some of the same hip-hop media figures who had canceled Kanye two years ago, such as Joe Budden and Wayno, were now willing to forgive him. On June 30, Kanye released "Wash Us in the Blood," which was supposed to be the first single from his 10th studio album, *Donda: With Child*. Arthur Jafa directed a music video for the song.[51] The video started with footage from a viral clip of Steven Pohorence, a white police officer in Fort Lauderdale, Florida, arguing with protestors at a George Floyd rally. Pohorence shoved one of the peaceful kneelers. Onlookers erupted in applause when a black female police officer came to their defense and reprimanded him.

The next three minutes of the video was a montage of clips from the Grand Theft Auto V video game mixed in with images of blacks suffering from COVID-19, protesting, rioting, fighting, twerking, doing donuts in their cars, and praising the Lord at church. Ahmaud Arbery was shown jogging moments before his death. There was also footage of a carefree Breonna Taylor dancing on TikTok.[52] Kanye's lyrics, which explicitly addressed racism and mass incarceration, invoked memories of the gospel hymn "Nothing but the Blood of Jesus," which declared that only Jesus's blood could wash away our sins and make us whole again. Kanye's next song,

"Donda," was released on July 12 to celebrate his late mother's 71st birthday. In the song, Dr. Donda West recites lyrics from KRS-One's "Sound of Da Police" in the form of spoken word over gospel music. "There could never really be justice on stolen land…. Overseer, overseer, overseer, officer, officer, officer," she said.[53]

Two weeks after the release of "Donda," Kanye appeared to be self-sabotaging the recent goodwill he amassed. While speaking at his first presidential campaign rally in Charleston, South Carolina, Kanye declared that Harriet Tubman freed blacks to go off and labor for future generations of white people. Weeks later reports began circulating of his ties to Jared Kushner and Trump operatives secretly working to get his name on the ballot as an independent candidate. Kanye admitted that he was running to siphon off votes from Democratic presidential nominee and eventual winner Joe Biden. He remained silent as professional athletes protested Jacob Blake's shooting. As TMZ and other outlets continued to make him look out of touch with reality, he sat down for a nearly two-hour interview with his close friend Nick Cannon for *Cannon's Class,* a podcast series filmed at Howard University's Founders Library.

Kanye denied the rumors that the GOP was funding his campaign, stating that he had more money than Trump and could not be bought. The purpose of the meeting with Kushner was to give him a copy of Claud Anderson's book *PowerNomics: The National Plan to Empower Black America* (2001). Anderson, who holds a Ph.D. in education, outlines a five-year plan for black economic freedom and empowerment in the book. Kanye did not specify if Kushner wanted this book to help his father-in-law develop an actual model to empower black people or solely to learn the talking points that would attract black voters concerned exclusively with finances.

Kanye blamed his tearful breakdown during the Charleston rally on his frustration with black liberals supporting Planned Parenthood and abortion, which he views as government-sanctioned genocide of unborn black babies. Regarding his comments about Harriet Tubman, Kanye continued to bemoan what he believes is black America's obsession with slavery and respectability politics. In his opinion, black Americans have been reared to be the nation's housekeepers. The housekeeper is trained to be respectful, act a certain way, and only speak at a certain volume in the master's house. Consequently, anything that disrupts order in "the Matrix" must be deemed crazy, problematic, and outside of the norm. Kanye's gift and curse have always been his fearless nature to say what he feels without thoroughly considering the impact of his words or how diverse audiences will receive them. As he reminded students at Howard University at their 2019 homecoming, he is the rare exception of black folks able to say and do almost anything without serious repercussions. If you believe Kanye, he is the second wealthiest black person in America behind investor Robert F. Smith. This extraordinary wealth adds to his feeling of invincibility.

Days after the second part of his Nick Cannon interview was uploaded on YouTube, Kanye went on a Twitter rant that got him temporarily banned from posting on the site. Twitter blocked his account because he shared the personal contact information of *Forbes* editor Randall Lane, whom he accused of being a white supremacist. At the heart of Kanye's rant was his ongoing feud with record labels for his music ownership. In January 2019, Kanye filed a lawsuit against Sony/ATV's EMI publishing company. He described his publishing deal as "servitude" because it was extended five times since 2005 and restricted him from retiring. His attorneys argued that the contract should have ceased in 2010 and have no longer been enforceable.[54] It is hard to ignore the racial undertones in the word "servitude." Before slavery was sewn into the fabric of American culture, black indentured servants were contracted to work for seven years.

A settlement was reached between Kanye and EMI out of court in February 2020. Seven months after the settlement, he filed a new lawsuit against Universal Music record labels Def Jam and Roc-A-Fella. He threatened to stop making new music until he was released from his contract and awarded his masters, or ownership of his music. Kanye tweeted pages from his Universal contract to show the world how he was being exploited and called himself the new Moses. God told him it was his mission to free other black musical artists from the bondage of slave contracts. His words resonated with other blacks in the music industry. Big Sean volunteered to let him review his contract. Hit-Boy (Chauncey Alexander Hollis), arguably the hottest hip-hop producer in 2020, told his 452,000 Instagram followers he supported Kanye's stance because he is tied to an oppressive publishing deal that he signed 14 years ago when was 19. Washington, D.C., rapper Wale (Olubowale Victor Akintimehin) expressed similar frustration over his contract.[55]

Kanye's fight was a civil rights issue. Black artists have been demanding the ownership of their masters for decades. Many of these black artists finished their careers penniless and received barely a fraction of the revenues still being generated by their art. Meanwhile white-owned record labels have continued to make millions from their music. A music publisher owns the rights to a song's lyrics and composition. The publisher collects royalties whenever the song(s) are performed live, used in commercials, or played in television shows and films.[56] Ray Charles became the first black artist to own his masters when he negotiated a recording deal with ABC-Paramount in 1959. Sam Cooke started his own publishing company in the 1960s to control the profits from his music. In 1993 Prince

(Prince Rogers Nelson) went to war with Warner/Chappell Music Publishing for the control of his masters.[57] Prince changed his name to an unpronounceable glyph nicknamed the Love Symbol. Two years later he began appearing with the word "slave" written on his cheek. Prince won ownership of the masters of future recordings after he was released from his label in 1996. He gained control of his masters in 2014 in exchange for releasing two new albums.[58]

Kanye's tweets also disparaged the Grammys and suggested that he would leave Adidas and Gap if they did not place him on the board of directors. While that demand might sound ridiculous, Jay-Z was placed on Square Inc's board after the company purchased his streaming service Tidal. This was about ownership and control. He questioned why Nike CEO Phil Knight, a white man, has a net worth of $46 billion while his top earner, Michael Jordan, is only worth $1.6 billion after 35 years with the company. Kanye called out the irony of Jordan's successors in the NBA today having "Black Lives Matter" and "vote" written on their jerseys as they risked their health in a man-made bubble to make white team owners and white corporate sponsors wealthier. He called for all black athletes in the NBA to empower themselves and use their wealth to become owners of the teams for which they labor. Once again Kanye was preaching freedom and control. He was not out on the block marching or retweeting hashtags. This was his form of activism on behalf of the black community. Suddenly, he did not seem like he had sold his *soul* for a seat at the white man's table. He had his own table with empty seats reserved for other black men and women.

Whether you agree with Kanye West or trust his sincerity, one thing can be said of him: he is free! After craving white validation and support for years, he is no longer beholden to those gatekeepers. Kanye West appears to have combined some aspects of Booker T. Washington's economic advancement philosophy with Du Bois's philosophy of agitation for racial equality. Kanye and his peers represent a 21st-century version of the Talented Tenth. Although it may sound Pollyannaish, when they use their platforms effectively for selfless means, they can genuinely uplift the race by creating change and opening doors for all black Americans. On April 20, 2021, Derek Chauvin was found guilty in the death of George Floyd. While I dare not overstate the influence of celebrity activism in the verdict, I cannot deny the role celebrities played in participating in the protests, posting viral videos, and tweeting support for the Floyd family's demand for justice.

In 2021 as Kanye West dealt with the election fallout and an impending divorce, his focus returned to music. Between July and August, he staged three listening parties for his forthcoming album, *Donda*. Forty thousand fans packed Atlanta's Mercedes-Benz Stadium for the first event that broke the Apple Music Global Livestream record with 3.3 million viewers. Kanye spent a two-week residence at the stadium to revise the album prior to the second event. For the final listening party, held at Chicago's Soldier Field, Kanye created a replica of his mother's Chicago home, set himself on fire to symbolize purification, offended some with special guests Marilyn Manson and DaBaby, and had Kim appear in a white Balenciaga dress to recreate their wedding.

Donda arrived on August 29th after numerous delays. The album, Kanye's tenth to top the *Billboard* 200, had the second-best release of 2021. Kanye became the first artist to chart 23 songs on *Billboard*'s Hot 100 in one week. *Donda*, running 108 minutes, is Kanye's longest album and features 33 guests including his mother, Larry Hoover Jr., and younger artists he has influenced. Freedom is one of the album's overarching themes. *Donda* opens with the exhilarating Jay-Z duet "Jail." Jail appears metaphorically throughout the album as a physical prison, mental slavery, a fractured marriage, celebrity, cancel culture, and self-destructive personal vices. *Donda*'s closing tracks "Come to Life" and "No Child Left Behind" remind listeners that God is the path to freedom. *Donda* received four Grammy nominations including Album of the Year.

There is little argument that Kanye West is an amazing musician, shrewd businessman, and innovative fashion designer. Countless fans, especially those outside the black community, are satisfied with those aspects of his career and persona. Does Kanye have an obligation to uplift the race? That is for you to decide. More importantly that is his decision to make.

Wake up, Mr. West!!! Oh, he's up!

Chapter Notes

Preface

1. Julius Bailey, *The Cultural Impact of Kanye West* (New York: Palgrave Macmillan, 2014), XIX–XX.

Introduction

1. An excerpt of Amiri Baraka speaking is featured in "Ain't Gonna Shuffle No More (1964–1972)," episode 11 of the PBS docuseries *Eyes on the Prize*. The episode aired on February 15, 1990.

2. Dave Chappelle shared a story of his first encounter with Kanye West on *The Tonight Show Starring Jimmy Fallon* in 2017.

3. *Vibe* staff, "Kanye West Receives Visit from Dave Chappelle Following Twitter Rant," *Vibe*, July 22, 2020, accessed August 21, 2020, https://www.vibe.com/2020/07/kanye-west-dave-chappelle-visit-following-twitter-rant.

4. Reelblack, "Dave Chappelle on Oprah (2006) | Complete Episode HD," February 8, 2019, video, https://www.youtube.com/watch?v=ILR9stCOUks.

5. *Ibid.*

6. Amy Zimmerman, "The Uncompromising Politics of Dave Chappelle," *Daily Beast*, November 8, 2016, accessed June 26, 2019, https://www.thedailybeast.com/the-uncompromising-politics-of-dave-chappelle.

7. Eric Lott, *Love & Theft: Blackface Minstrelsy and the American Working Class.* (Oxford, England: Oxford University Press, 2013).

8. Satire is a quintessential part of black comedy and humor. Satire is a literary work that spotlights human vices to be ridiculed or scorned. Satire, which appears in editorial cartoons, parody songs, late-night talk shows, sketch comedy series, and humorous media sources such as *The Onion* and *MAD*, is often offensive and disrespectful. A number of schools have banned Mark Twain's 1884 novel *The Adventures of Huckleberry Finn* for being racially insensitive and offensive. However, the novel was intended to satirize racist White southerners.

9. Seth Abramovitch, "Blackface and Hollywood: From Al Jolson to Judy Garland to Dave Chappelle," *Hollywood Reporter*, February 12, 2019, accessed June 26, 2019, https://www.hollywoodreporter.com/news/blackface-hollywood-al-jolson-judy-garland-dave-chappelle-1185380.

10. Reelblack, "Dave Chappelle on Oprah (2006) | Complete Episode HD," February 8, 2019, video, https://www.youtube.com/watch?v=ILR9stCOUks.

11. William David Chappelle was a bishop in the African Methodist Episcopal Church and the president of Allen University in South Carolina from 1897 to 1899. Bishop Chappelle, a former slave, took a group of black church leaders to the White House on March 13, 1918, to meet with President Woodrow Wilson to demand that he do something about the lynching of black Southerners.

12. Throughout her daytime series, Oprah Winfrey used her platform to improve race relations. One example was an episode in 1992, after the Los Angeles riots, when she featured educator Jane Elliott. Mrs. Elliott engaged Winfrey's unsuspecting audience in her controversial Blue Eyes-Brown Eyes exercise, which used eye color, rather than skin color, to illustrate racial bias.

13. *Ibid.*

14. Dunbar's poem expresses the invisible mask that African Americans are forced to wear to hide their pain and anguish as they interact with the (white) world.

15. Reelblack, "Dave Chappelle on Oprah (2006) | Complete Episode HD," February 8, 2019, video, https://www.youtube.com/watch?v=ILR9stCOUks.

16. Sammy Davis, Jr., appeared in Season 2, Episode 21 of *All in the Family*. The episode, titled "Sammy's Visit," was ranked by *TV Guide* as the 13th best television episode of all time.

17. Leslie Sammarco, "All In The Family, Sammy's Visit, S-2 E-21," July 12, 2017, video, https://www.youtube.com/watch?v=ku7hS6Y9kUY.

18. "Miles Davis: A candid conversation with the jazz world's premier iconoclast," *Playboy*, September 1962.

19. Nicolaus Mills, "Whites Said Marian Anderson Couldn't Sing In Their Hall. So She Sang at the Lincoln Memorial in a Concert for the Ages," *The Daily Beast*, April 21, 2019, accessed June 27, 2019, https://www.thedailybeast.com/whites-said-marian-anderson-couldnt-sing-in-their-hall-so-she-sang-at-the-lincoln-memorial-in-a-concert-for-the-ages?ref=scroll.

20. Suzanne E. Smith, *Dancing in the Street: Motown and the Cultural Politics of Detroit* (Cambridge, MA: Harvard Univ. Press, 2003), 149–151.

21. Dr. Shirley's family denounced the film's [mis]representation of their relative as estranged from his self-identity as a black man.

22. *Green Book*, Directed by Peter Farrelly (Universal City, CA: Universal Pictures, 2018).

23. Busing was a practice of transporting black and white students to predominantly segregated school districts to achieve school integration.

24. Wayne Brady was interviewed for the third season of TV One's docuseries *Unsung Hollywood*, episode 7.

25. Bryant Gumbel is a television journalist and sportscaster whom some in the black community consider to be a sellout due to his mild manner and genteel speech pattern.

26. *Ibid.*

27. W.E.B. Du Bois, "Strivings of the Negro People," *The Atlantic*, July 16, 2018, accessed June 30, 2019, https://www.theatlantic.com/magazine/archive/1897/08/strivings-of-the-negro-people/305446/.

28. David Levering Lewis, *W.E.B. Du Bois, 1868–1919: Biography of a Race* (New York: Henry Holt and Company, 1994).

29. W.E.B. Du Bois, *The Souls of Black Folk* (Chicago, IL: A. C. McClurg & Co., 1903).

30. Eric Liu, "Asian or American?" *Slate*, November 15, 1996, accessed May 18, 2020, https://slate.com/news-and-politics/1996/11/asian-or-american.html.

31. Adolph Reed, Jr., *W.E.B, Du Bois and American Political Thought: Fabianism and the Color Line* (Oxford, England: Oxford University Press, 1999).

32. Fred Montas, Jr., "Understanding Du Bois," *Dissent* 46, no. 1 (1999): 118.

33. Ernest Allen, Jr., "Du Boisian Double Consciousness: The Unsustainable Argument," *The Black Scholar* 33, no. 2 (2003): 26.

34. George Ciccariello-Maher, "A Critique of Du Boisian Reason: Kanye West and the Fruitfulness of Double-Consciousness," *Journal of Black Studies* 39, no. 3 (2009): 371–401.

35. Amanda Taylor was a guest speaker on *Inequality in America: A Call to Action*, a special airing on NBC4 in Washington, D.C., on the eve of the 57th anniversary of the 1963 March on Washington.

36. Lauren Wilkinson, *American Spy: A Novel* (New York: Random House, 2020).

37. The ESPN 30 for 30 film *Be Water* documents the struggle of martial arts legend Bruce Lee and Asian Americans to gain equality in America. *Be Water*, written and directed by Bao Nguyen (2020; London: Dorothy Street Pictures).

38. Jeannie Mai was interviewed for my podcast series, *Woke History*, on October 2, 2020.

39. Movieclips, "Selena (1997)—Twice As Perfect Scene (3/9)," June 27, 2017, video, 2:16, https://www.youtube.com/watch?v=HIBYaeYQF0k.

40. The National Liberation Front was the major nationalist movement in the Algerian War of Independence from France, 1954–1962.

41. Peter Hudis, professor of Humanities at Oakton Community College, talks about the philosophy of Frantz Fanon and how it is applicable in our contemporary

struggle against racism, police brutality, and inequality.

42. Ciccariello-Maher, 371–72.

43. J.A.M. Aiwuyor, "Kanye's Frantz Fanon Complex," *Our Legaci with J.A.M. Aiwuyor*, December 15, 2016, accessed May 29, 2020, https://ourlegaci.com/2013/12/02/kanyes-frantz-fanon-complex/.

44. "Unbought and unbossed" was Shirley Chisholm's campaign slogan when she ran for U.S. president in 1968.

45. An excerpt of Amiri Baraka speaking is featured in "Ain't Gonna Shuffle No More (1964–1972)," episode 11 of the PBS docuseries *Eyes on the Prize*. The episode aired on February 15, 1990.

Chapter One

1. BigBoyTV, "Kanye West Says 'WAKE UP CULTURE!' | Big's Quick Clips," November 1, 2019, video, 1:52, https://www.youtube.com/watch?v=MHE7UCOriA4.

2. Luke O'Neil, "Can Kanye West Solve America's Housing Crisis? Maybe...," *The Guardian*, August 5, 2019, accessed August 7, 2019, https://www.theguardian.com/music/2019/aug/05/kanye-west-housing-development-california.

3. Daniel White Hodge, "Yeezus is Jesuz: Examining the Socio-Hermeneutical Transmediated Images of Jesus Employed by Kanye West," *Journal of Hip Hop Studies* 6, no. 1 (2019): 54–77.

4. William Cowen, "Bono Explains Why Kanye's 'Black Skinhead' Is One of the Songs That 'Saved My Life,'" *Complex*, May 14, 2020, accessed May 21, 2020, https://www.complex.com/music/2020/05/bono-explains-why-kanye-black-skinhead-songs-that-saved-my-life.

5. The Adidas Yeezy 700 Wave Runner is a chunky running sneaker called a "dad shoe" because some consumers say it looks like a sneaker worn by their fathers to mow the lawn and complete yard work.

6. The Yeezy 350 V2 is a lifestyle sneaker that is characterized by its Primeknit design, bold stripes, and translucent midsole and outsole that is made from Boost. Adidas introduced Boost in 2013, as a revolutionary system designed to provide runners and walkers with softer cushioning and support for their feet.

7. Madeline Berg of *Forbes* refuted

Bloomberg's report, stating that Kanye was only worth $1.8 billion. She said the higher net worth was based on projected earnings.

8. Pamela N. Danziger, "Kanye West Gives Gap A Ten-Year Lifeline With Yeezy Partnership And Gets What He Always Wanted," *Forbes*. June 28, 2020. Accessed on July 6, 2020. https://www.forbes.com/sites/pamdanziger/2020/06/28/kanye-west-gives-gap-a-ten-year-lifeline-with-yeezy-partnership-and-gets-what-he-always-wanted/.

9. "Elon Musk: Kanye West Inspires Me," *BBC News*, March 12, 2018, accessed May 13, 2020, https://www.bbc.com/news/newsbeat-43369201.

10. Natalie Stone, "Inside Kanye West's Breakdown: Rapper Feels Like 'He's Under Spiritual Attack,' Source Says," *People*, November 22, 2016, accessed January 18, 2017, http://people.com/celebrity/kanye-west-feels-like-hes-under-spiritual-attack/.

11. *My Next Guest Needs No Introduction With David Letterman*, season 2, episode 1, "Kanye West," directed by Michael Bonfiglio, aired May 31, 2019, RadicalMedia, https://www.netflix.com/watch/81034499?trackId=1503589 5&tctx=3,3,93a5ae6d-7fda-4317-a605-ae4e92e14a48–76553935,fd9e806a-d944–4020–8dac-2d5dd1c45f8d_15283910X5 4XX1562094279732,fd9e806a-d944–4020–8dac-2d5dd1c45f8d_ROOT.

12. Janine Francolini, "5 Reasons Mental Health Is a Hidden Civil Rights Issue," *HuffPost*, December 7, 2017, accessed June 1, 2020, www.huffpost.com/entry/5-reasons-why-mental-heal_b_8992028?guccounter= 1&guce_referrer=aHR0cHM6Ly93d3c uYmluZy5jb20v&guce_referrer_sig=- AQAAAAOmuAHj3iMpDTJ4OIgxnjJ- wn35wCg2REYSBi5G6zWKzvKQpd1PM LxqjXGNUusdL-LsYSJg0SeeSEAJ5EZIY_ ueRxq3JgBe-cqpGeWIdQOUas.

13. "Black/African American," National Alliance on Mental Illness, accessed August 16, 2020, https://www.nami.org/Your-Journey/Identity-and-Cultural-Dimensions/Black-African-American.

14. Erin Aubry Kaplan, "Simone Biles and the New Black Power of 'No.'" *Politico*. July 29, 2021. Accessed on August 1, 2021. https://www.politico.com/news/magazine/2021/07/29/simone-biles-and-the-new-black-activist-athlete-the-one-who-says-no-501675.

15. Justin Tinsley, "Kanye, Bill Cosby, R. Kelly: When It All Falls down Celeb Culture Is and Always Has Been Insane, but This Week Is Just Surreal," *The Undefeated*, April 27, 2018, accessed July 02, 2019, https://theundefeated.com/whhw/bill-cosby-found-guilty-kanye-tweets-nas-kelis/.

16. The 13th Amendment ended American slavery in 1865. However, a loophole in the amendment indirectly enslaves prisoners by stripping them of their Constitutional rights. This loophole has allowed for racially biased systems of debt peonage, convict leasing, private prisons, and mass incarceration to flourish.

17. "Pinocchio Story" was originally a freestyle that Kanye performed at a concert in Singapore. Beyoncé encouraged him to include it on the album after she heard it.

18. Depireux, John, "Kanye West—808s and Heartbreak [Live @ Hollywood Bowl 2015]," May 28, 2017, video, https://www.youtube.com/watch?v=7T4SgKzsvYg.

19. The P-Funk Mothership is on exhibit at the National Museum of African American History and Culture in Washington, D.C.

20. Nina Simone, "Do What You Gotta Do," track 11 on *'Nuff Said!*, RCA Victor, 1968.

21. Marcus Garvey's movement attracted followers including Earl and Louise Little, the parents of Malcolm X. Garvey's outspokenness caused him to become the first black target of J. Edgar Hoover and the Federal Bureau of Investigation. He was convicted of mail fraud in 1923 and deported to Jamaica four years later. He died in London, England, in 1940.

22. James Turrell is an American artist affiliated with the minimalist art movement Light and Space. Thomas Schielke, "Light Matters: Seeing the Light with James Turrell," *ArchDaily*, June 04, 2013, accessed July 2, 2019, https://www.archdaily.com/380911/light-matters-seeing-the-light-with-james-turrell. Martin Gayford. "James Turrell and the Art of Light, Space, and Time," *MIT Technology Review*, May 27, 2016, accessed July 2, 2019, https://www.technologyreview.com/s/526566/enlightened-spaces/.

23. *My Next Guest Needs No Introduction With David Letterman*.

24. *Karen Hunter Show*, "Dave Chappelle's 8:46: The Breakdown and the

Breadcrumbs with Dr. Greg Carr," June 13, 2020, video, 101:03, https://www.youtube.com/watch?v=y85u-BVHJIE.

25. *Amos 'n' Andy* was America's first television series with an all-black cast. It was on the air from 1951–53 and in syndication until 1966 before the NAACP forced its banishment until 2012.

26. Timothy B. Tyson, *The Blood of Emmett Till* (New York: Simon & Schuster, 2017).

27. James H. Cone, *The Cross and the Lynching Tree* (Maryknoll, NY: Orbis Books, 2011).

28. Erik S. Gellman, *Death Blow to Jim Crow: The National Negro Congress and the Rise of Militant Civil Rights* (Chapel Hill: University of North Carolina Press, 2014).

29. *Democracy Now!*, "'George Bush Doesn't Care About Black People': Reflections on Kanye West's Criticism 10 Years After," August 28, 2015, video, 13:08, https://www.youtube.com/watch?v=lTuRPuhneAs.

30. *When the Levees Broke—A Requiem in Four Acts*, directed by Spike Lee (2006; New York City: HBO, 2016), DVD.

31. Kanye West founded his record label GOOD Music, which is stylized as G.O.O.D. Music, in 2004. G.O.O.D. means Getting Out Our Dreams.

32. Ned Martel, "On a Telethon Weekend, Restraint from an Unlikely Source," *The New York Times*, September 12, 2005, E7.

33. Sarah J. Jackson, *Black Celebrity, Racial Politics, and the Press: Framing Dissent* (New York: Routledge, 2014), 150.

34. *Ebony*'s editorial staff was most likely predominantly male in the 1960s. Gender bias should not be ignored when looking back at the magazine's decision to publish that article on Eartha Kitt.

35. Kwakiutl Lynn Dreher, "Don't Should On Me: The Black Actress 1940–1970 Lena Horne, Diahann Carroll, and Eartha Kitt" (PhD diss., University of California Riverside, 2001), 121.

36. Shirley Chisholm, "Remarks on Vietnam," *Congressional Record*, October 14, 1969, H30023–25.

37. Carolyn Lewis, "Mrs. Johnson Chides Eartha Kitt: 'Shrill Voice' Jars First Lady," *The Washington Post*, January 20, 1968, A1.

38. Jackson, 53.

39. *Ibid.*, 57.

40. ShaDawn D. Battle, "'Moments of

Clarity': Veiled Literary Subversions and De-Colonial Dialectics in the Art of Jay Z and Kanye West" (PhD diss., Wittenberg University, 2016).

41. George W. Bush, *Decision Points* (New York: Crown Publishers, 2010), 325.

42. Michael Eric. Dyson, *Come Hell or High Water: Hurricane Katrina and the Color of Disaster* (New York: Basic Civitas, 2007), 28–31.

43. Jamie Foxx featuring T-Pain, "Blame It," track 5 on *Intuition*, J Records, 2008.

44. The Moonman is the name of the VMA award.

45. Michael Jordan famously shrugged his shoulders after hitting a record six three-point shots in the first half of Game 1 in the 1992 NBA Finals against the Portland Trailblazers.

46. Taylor Swift revealed in her 2020 Netflix documentary, *Miss Americana*, that the VMA incident and Kanye's lyrics about her in his song "Famous" caused her tremendous emotional pain and years of hurt.

47. Kanye West refers to himself as a douche bag in his popular 2010 single "Runaway."

48. Daniel Kreps, "Kelly Clarkson, Pink, Katy Perry Lash Out at Kanye for Outburst," *Rolling Stone*, June 25, 2018, accessed December 16, 2019, www.rollingstone.com/music/music-news/kelly-clarkson-pink-katy-perry-lash-out-at-kanye-for-outburst-79211/.

49. Chris Good, "Obama Calls Kanye 'Jackass,'" *The Atlantic*, September 15, 2009, accessed July 9, 2019, https://www.theatlantic.com/politics/archive/2009/09/obama-calls-kanye-jackass/26563/.

50. David Cantwell, "Ray Charles and Country's Color Barrier," *Rolling Stone*, February 25, 2019, accessed March 9, 2019. https://www.rollingstone.com/music/music-country/ray-charles-modern-sounds-country-music-798729/.

51. Chris Molanphy, "The Controversy Over 'Old Town Road' Reveals Problems Beyond Just Race," *Slate*, April 12, 2019, accessed July 7, 2019, https://slate.com/culture/2019/04/lil-nas-x-old-town-road-billboard-country-charts-hot-100.html.

52. Omiseeke Natasha Tinsley, *Beyoncé in Formation: Remixing Black Feminism* (Austin: University of Texas Press, 2018), 45–50.

53. Julius Bailey, *The Cultural Impact of Kanye West* (New York: Palgrave Macmillan, 2014), 50.

54. *Ibid.*, 51.

55. Kanye put on his (superhero) cape and came to Beyoncé's defense again at the 2015 Grammy Awards ceremony. Beck, a white musician who performs a combination of alternative rock, country, hip-hop, and soul music, defeated her in the Album of the Year category.

56. W I Z A R D, "Kanye West TMZ FULL Interview," May 2, 2018, video, 30:27, https://www.youtube.com/watch?v=1LIGh91 mIoA.

57. J. Cole (Jermaine Cole) had released the song "False Prophets," which was full of subliminal shots at Kanye, two years earlier.

58. This quote was initially spoken by Rev. Martin Luther King, Jr.

59. Black Twitter is a collective of African American Twitter users who converse, across the globe, on a various topics. Black Twitter has taken the lead on popular hashtag campaigns like #BlackLivesMatter, #SayHerName, #DonLemonLogic, #OscarsSoWhite, #OscarsSoBlack, and #BlackGirlMagic.

60. To give someone a pound is a popular slang expression in the African American community for giving a fist bump as a form of greeting, acknowledgement, approval, or respect. In the film *Get Out* Chris (Daniel Kaluuya) attempts to give Logan (LaKeith Stanfield), the only other black person at the family gathering, a pound. Chris is stunned when Logan wraps his entire hand around his fist rather than bumping it.

61. Cancel culture is "a form of boycott in which someone has shared a questionable opinion, or again, has had problematic behavior called out on social media."

62. "TMZ Live: The Full Kanye West Episode," TMZ, June 17, 2019, accessed May 15, 2020, https://www.tmz.com/2018/05/02/tmz-live-kanye/.

63. *Ibid.*

64. "Why We Published The 1619 Project," *The New York Times*, December 20, 2019, accessed August 9, 2020, https://www.nytimes.com/interactive/2019/12/20/magazine/1619-intro.html.

65. Individuals who suffer from bipolar disorder experience manic symptoms, including an elevated mood, inflated self-esteem, racing thoughts, decreased

sleep, and excessive involvement in plea-
surable activities that could lead to dire
consequences.

66. Eliott C. McLaughlin, "Kanye West
Co-opts Confederate Flag: Publicity Stunt?"
CNN, November 6, 2013, accessed July 8,
2019, https://www.cnn.com/2013/11/04/
us/kanye-west-confederate-flag/index.
html.

67. Stereo Williams, "Kendrick Lamar,
Black Language and What White Fans
Don't Get About the 'N-Word,'" *Billboard*,
May 24, 2018, accessed July 8, 2019, https://
www.billboard.com/articles/columns/hip-
hop/8457834/kendrick-lamar-n-word-
white-fans.

68. Merch is a slang term for merchan-
dise. Kanye credits his close friend Che
Smith (Rhymefest) for his lessons on American history and African American studies. Kanye's late mother and father provided
black history lessons when he was a child.

69. John M. Coski, *The Confederate Battle Flag: Americas Most Embattled
Emblem* (Cambridge, MA: Belknap, 2006).

70. Jasmine Mans, "Poem-Footnotes for
Kanye," *Journal of Hip Hop Studies* 6, no. 1
(2019): 103–105.

71. Apartheid was government-
sanctioned racial segregation in South
Africa from 1948 until 1991.

72. Libby Torres, "Kanye's Africa Trip Is
Even More Embarrassing Than Melania's,"
The Daily Beast, October 18, 2018, accessed
July 9, 2019, https://www.thedailybeast.
com/kanye-wests-trip-to-africa-is-even-
more-embarrassing-than-melania-trumps.

73. Mya Abraham, "Kanye West Gets
Blasted By This Legend's Son Over Outlandish Comparison," *BET.com*, October 15,
2018, accessed July 18, 2019, https://www.
bet.com/music/2018/10/15/kanye-west-
tupac-bob-marley-fela-kuti-response.html.

74. Tucker Carlson, "Tucker Carlson:
Kanye West vs the Mob—Rapper Declares
Independence from Guilty Self-Righteous
Liberals," *Fox News*, October 31, 2019,
https://www.foxnews.com/opinion/tucker-
carlson-kanye-west-liberals.

75. Ta-Nehisi Coates, "I'm Not Black, I'm
Kanye," *The Atlantic*, May 7, 2018, accessed
July 31, 2019, https://www.theatlantic.com/
entertainment/archive/2018/05/im-not-
black-im-kanye/559763/.

76. Evelyn Brooks Higginbotham introduced the concept of respectability politics

in *Righteous Discontent: The Women's Movement in the Black Baptist Church, 1880–
1920* (1993). Respectability politics is a
form of moralistic discourse used by some
prominent figures, leaders or academics who are members of various marginalized groups. When these figures promote
respectability politics, this may serve as an
attempt to police some of their fellow group
members. Proponents of respectability politics may attempt to portray their personal
social values as being continuous and com-
patible with dominant values. They may
prefer not to challenge the mainstream for
its failure to accept the marginalized group
into the mainstream.

Chapter Two

1. Kanye West, "Gorgeous," track 2 on
My Beautiful Dark Twisted Fantasy, Def
Jam/Roc-A-Fella, 2010.

2. *Late Registration* was nominated for
eight Grammy Awards and won three.

3. Ann Powers, "Live: Kanye West's
Glow in the Dark Tour," *Los Angeles Times*,
April 18, 2008, accessed March 30, 2020,
https://www.latimes.com/entertainment/
la-et-kanye18apr18-story.html.

4. Noah Callahan-Bever, "The Day
Kanye West Killed Gangsta Rap," *Complex*,
April 20, 2020, accessed August 23, 2020,
https://www.complex.com/music/2015/09/
the-day-kanye-west-killed-gangsta-rap.

5. Joel Anderson, "Against Those Thugs,"
November 20, 2019, in *Slow Burn*, produced by *Slate*, podcast, 29:28, https://slate.
com/culture/2020/02/transcript-of-slow-
burn-season-3-episode-4.html.

6. Auto-Tune is an audio processor that
uses software to measure and alter the pitch
in vocal and instrumental recordings and
performances. Synth-pop or synthesizer
pop is a sub-genre of rock music and disco
popularized in the late 1970s and early
1980s.

7. Patrick Ryan, "Is Kanye West the
greatest artist of the 21st century?" *USA
Today*, February 9, 2016, accessed July 26,
2016, http://www.usatoday.com/story/
life/music/2016/02/09/kanye-west-new-
album/79814890/#.

8. Mark Beaumont, *Kanye West: God
& Monster* (London: Overlook Omnibus,
2015), 291.

9. Richard Lawson, "Kanye West's Harvard Lecture," *The Atlantic*, November 19, 2013, https://www.theatlantic.com/culture/archive/2013/11/kanye-wests-harvard-lecture/355227/.

10. Elahe Izadi, "Kanye West's Meeting with Donald Trump Was a Long Time Coming," *The Washington Post*, December 13, 2016, accessed October 16, 2019, https://www.washingtonpost.com/news/arts-and-entertainment/wp/2016/12/13/kanye-west-shows-up-at-trump-tower-to-discuss-life-with-donald-trump/.

11. Charlamagne tha God's one-hour-and-forty-five-minute interview with Kanye West was uploaded to YouTube on May 1, 2018.

12. President Barack Obama is the most beloved president in African American history. Nevertheless, he is not immune to criticism. Michael Eric Dyson, in his book *The Black Presidency: Barack Obama and the Politics of Race in America* (2017), criticized the president for failing to address race and issues primarily related to blacks as liberal white presidents had done before him. Jason L. Riley, a conservative black commentator on Fox News, argues in his book *False Black Power?* (2017) that black liberals have handicapped their progress by assuming that the election of Obama or any other black politician would end poverty or empower blacks fiscally.

13. Asian Americans and Asian immigrants were the victims of a racist practice in Hollywood called yellowface. Mickey Rooney appeared in yellow makeup to look like a person of Asian descent in the 1961 film *Breakfast at Tiffany's*.

14. "Sig Ep and Alpha Phi Draw Criticism after 'Kanye Western' Themed Raid," *Daily Bruin*, October 7, 2015, accessed July 13, 2019, http://dailybruin.com/2015/10/07/students-upset-after-sig-ep-hosts-kanye-western-themed-party/.

15. Yuval Taylor and Jake Austen, *Darkest America: Black Minstrelsy from Slavery to Hip-Hop* (New York: W.W. Norton & Company, 2012), 109–112.

16. *Ibid.*, 112.

17. Cary D. Wintz, *Encyclopedia of the Harlem Renaissance* (London, UK: Routledge 2004), 1210.

18. Donald Bogle, *Toms, Coons, Mulattoes, Mammies, and Bucks: An Interpretive History of Blacks in American Films* (New York: Bloomsbury Academy, 2013), 39.

19. Howard Thurman, *The Luminous Darkness: A Personal Interpretation of the Anatomy of Segregation and the Ground of Hope* (Richmond, IN: Friends United Press, 1989), 73–73.

20. Bogle, 39.

21. Todd Boyd, professor of Cinema and Media Studies at the University of Southern California, was interviewed in the 2004 documentary film *TV in Black: The First Fifty Years*.

22. Seth Abramovitch, "Oscar's First Black Winner Accepted Her Honor in a Segregated 'No Blacks' Hotel in L.A.," *The Hollywood Reporter*, February 22, 2016, accessed July 15, 2019, https://www.hollywoodreporter.com/features/oscars-first-black-winner-accepted-774335.

23. Kanye West and Jay-Z performed their hit "Niggas in Paris" 11 consecutive times for their final concert in Paris, France, during the 2012 *Watch the Throne* tour.

24. Kanye wanted to include the word *nigga* (or *nigger*) in each song title on the album.

25. Miles Davis and Quincy Troupe, *Miles, the Autobiography* (New York: Simon and Schuster, 2011), 125–133.

26. George Cole, "Miles Davis in Paris: The Love Lives on," *The Guardian*, December 10, 2009, accessed July 15, 2019, https://www.theguardian.com/music/2009/dec/10/miles-davis-paris-us-segregation.

27. Allison Keyes, "The East St. Louis Race Riot Left Dozens Dead, Devastating a Community on the Rise," *Smithsonian*, June 30, 2017, accessed July 15, 2019, https://www.smithsonianmag.com/smithsonian-institution/east-st-louis-race-riot-left-dozens-dead-devastating-community-on-the-rise-180963885/.

28. Jean-Claude Baker and Chris Chase, *Josephine: The Hungry Heart* (New York: Cooper Square Press, 2001).

29. Paul Robeson, the son of a runaway slave, became the third black student to attend Rutgers University where he won 12 varsity letters in football, basketball, baseball, and track. Robeson went on to earn a degree in law from Columbia University Law School before becoming a professional singer and film star. He countered black masculinity stereotypes with his cinematic

performances in films like *Emperor Jones* (1933). Similar to Josephine Baker, he had to travel abroad to escape racism. Robeson was blacklisted after visiting Russia and expressing communist sympathies.

30. M Ford, "Lena Horne Documentary 1996," July 19, 2016, video, 1:01:03, https://www.youtube.com/watch?v=AErWqNBhawI.

31. Hazel Scott demanded similar treatment from Hollywood executives in the 1940s.

32. Megan E. Williams, "'Meet the Real Lena Horne': Representations of Lena Horne in *Ebony* Magazine, 1945–1949," *Journal of American Studies* 43, no. 1 (2009): doi:10.1017/s0021875809006094.

33. Lena Horne was interviewed for a 1996 episode of the PBS series *American Masters*.

34. Diahann Carroll faced severe backlash from blacks for playing the lead actress in the NBC sitcom *Julia* about a middle-class single black mother in a predominantly white environment.

35. Donald Bogle, *Dorothy Dandridge: A Biography* (New York: Amistad, 1997).

36. "Richard Pryor: Icon," PBS, November 23, 2014, accessed July 17, 2019, https://www.pbs.org/video/richard-pryor-icon-full-episode/.

37. Mel Watkins, *On the Real Side: A History of African American Comedy* (Chicago: Lawrence Hill Books, 1999).

38. Glenda Carpio, *Laughing Fit to Kill: Black Humor in the Fictions of Slavery* (United Kingdom: Oxford University Press, 2008), 77.

39. Alan Siegel, "'Saturday Night Live' Was Dying. Then Eddie Murphy Showed Up," *The Ringer*, December 20, 2019, https://www.theringer.com/tv/2019/12/20/21029815/eddie-murphy-saturday-night-live-first-season-mister-robinson.

40. Bill Carter, "Bill Cosby Trying to Buy NBC From G.E.," *The New York Times*, October 29, 1992, accessed July 29, 2020, https://www.nytimes.com/1992/10/29/business/the-media-business-bill-cosby-trying-to-buy-nbc-from-ge.html.

41. Dominick Dunne, "How O.J. Simpson's Dream Team Played the 'Race Card' and Won," *Vanity Fair*, November 1995.

42. *O.J.: Made in America*, part I, directed by Ezra Edelman (2016; ESPN Films).

43. Carl E. Douglas was interviewed by Ezra Edelman in the 2016 docuseries *O.J.: Made in America*.

44. Excerpts from Muhammad Ali's interviews appear in the 2019 HBO documentary *What's My Name: Muhammad Ali*.

45. *Unforgivable Blackness: The Rise and Fall of Jack Johnson*, directed by Ken Burns (2004; Washington, DC: WETA, 2005).

46. Geoffrey C. Ward, *Unforgivable Blackness: The Rise and Fall of Jack Johnson* (New York: Vintage Books, 2006).

47. Bernice Tell, "'Separate Yet One': Booker T. Washington's Atlanta Compromise Displayed at Library," *Library of Congress Information Bulletin*, February 19, 1996, https://www.loc.gov/loc/lcib/9603/booker.html.

48. On September 11, 2012, the *Los Angeles Times* ran a front-page story headlined "HOW JACK JOHNSON TORTURED HIS WHITE WIFE." The article referred to him as a "beast" and a "black brute."

49. Joe Louis was praised for defeating German boxer Max Schmeling and sacrificing years of his career to serve in the U.S. Army during World War II. Nevertheless, his patriotism and "good negro" act did not prevent the Internal Revenue Service (IRS) from nearly bankrupting him.

50. Chris Mead, "Triumphs and Trials," *Sports Illustrated*, September 23, 1985, accessed June 23, 2020, https://web.archive.org/web/20081005055351/http://vault.sportsillustrated.cnn.com/vault/article/magazine/MAG1119926/index.htm.

51. Ibid.

52. Mark Kram, *Ghosts of Manila: The Fateful Blood Feud between Muhammad Ali and Joe Frazier* (New York: HarperCollins Publishers, 2001).

53. Howard Bryant, *The Heritage: Black Athletes, A Divided America, and the Politics of Patriotism* (Boston: Beacon Press, 2018), 74.

Chapter Three

1. Kanye West, "Hey Mama," track 16 on *Late Registration*, Def Jam/Roc-A-Fella, 2005.

2. BBC Radio 1, "Zane Lowe meets Kanye West 2015—Contains Strong Language," February 26, 2015, video, 43:51,

https://www.youtube.com/watch?v=4Rn0h DB6Z8k.

3. Jon Caramanica, "Behind Kanye's Mask," *The New York Times*, June 11, 2013, accessed May 11, 2020, https://www.nytimes.com/2013/06/16/arts/music/kanye-west-talks-about-his-career-and-album-yeezus.html?pagewanted=all.

4. Dr. Conrad Murray served two years of a four-year prison sentence for Michael Jackson's death.

5. David Drake, "Kanye West on the Day He Met Michael Jackson," *Complex*, June 1, 2018, accessed July 23, 2019, https://www.complex.com/music/2013/11/kanye-west-michael-jackson-juan-epstein.

6. Trey Alston, "The Colliding Worlds of 'Astroworld' and '808s & Heartbreak,'" REVOLT TV, August 17, 2018, accessed December 1, 2018, https://revolt.tv/stories/2018/08/07/travis-scott-astroworld-kanye-west-808s-heartbreak-album-comparison-0700bde6c3.

7. *i-D* staff, "Pharrell Williams: 'Faith Is about What You Feel,'" *i-D Magazine*, June 10, 2020, accessed June 11, 2020, https://i-d.vice.com/en_uk/article/m7jexy/pharrell-williams-interview-i-d-magazine.

8. Kanye West personally financed the second and third version of his music video for "Jesus Walks."

9. Rem Koolhaas is a noted Dutch architect and professor of Practice of Architecture and Urban Design at the Graduate School of Design at Harvard University in Cambridge, Massachusetts.

10. Travis Bean, "'Jesus Is King' Is Kanye West's '2001: A Space Odyssey,'" *Forbes*, September 29, 2019, accessed November 4, 2019, https://www.forbes.com/sites/travisbean/2019/09/29/jesus-is-king-is-kanye-wests-2001-a-space-odyssey/#50a2e0506ea5.

11. Timberland outdoor boots.

12. "From Jackson Street to Jackson 5 Blvd," J5 Collector, January 24, 2011, accessed July 25, 2019, http://j5collector.blogspot.com/2011/01/from-jackson-street-to-jackson-5-blvd.html.

13. Suzanne E. Smith, *Dancing in the Street: Motown and the Cultural Politics of Detroit* (Cambridge, MA: Harvard University Press, 2003), 45–48.

14. Joe Warwick, "The Motown Effect-Short Documentary, Motown and Civil Rights," March 12, 2011, video, 14:49, https:

//www.youtube.com/watch?v=VnRfy VQS_iA.

15. "The Jackson 5ive Episodes 1–12," August 30, 2017, video, https://www.youtube.com/watch?v=hVfchGfDxc8.

16. *The Wiz* was a soulful black retelling of *The Wizard of Oz* (1900).

17. *Michael Jackson's Journey from Motown to Off the Wall*, directed by Spike Lee (New York: Showtime, 2016).

18. *Ibid.*

19. Jackson won the Grammy Award for "Don't Stop 'Til You Get Enough."

20. Sara Tenenbaum, "I Know I Am Someone: Michael Jackson, *Thriller*, and American Identity" (Master's thesis, Brandeis University, 2008).

21. Jay-Z, "Come and Get Me," track 13 on *Vol. 3... Life and Times of S. Carter*, Def Jam/Roc-A-Fella, 1999.

22. Afrofuturism reimagines the future and science fiction through a black lens rooted in the African diaspora. Reynaldo Anderson, "Afrofuturism: The Digital Turn and the Visual Art of Kanye West," in *The Cultural Impact of Kanye West*, ed. Julius Bailey (New York: Palgrave Macmillan, 2014), 40.

23. Roberta Collier, "Kanye West Locks Down His African Roots," *Music in the World*, February 10, 2012, accessed July 30, 2020, https://blogs.longwood.edu/musicintheworld/2012/02/10/kanye-west-locks-down-his-african-roots/.

24. Tenenbaum, 44.

25. *Ibid.*, 46.

26. *Ibid.*, 66–67.

27. *Ibid.*, 72–77.

28. The Bad world tour set three Guinness World Records for being the highest-grossing tour, the most attended tour, and the most consecutive sold out shows in history. Jackson donated much of the tour's earnings to various charities such as the United Negro College Fund.

29. Michael Jackson began using the term "shamone" on the song "Bad" as a tribute to the black gospel and soul singer Mavis Staples, who initially used the phrase in a live performance of "I'll Take You There" in 1976.

30. *Bad 25*, directed by Spike Lee (Atlanta: Optimum Productions, 2012).

31. Robert Sam Anson, *Best Intentions: The Education and Killing of Edmund Perry* (New York: Vintage, 1988).

32. Excerpts from the music video for Michael Jackson's 1987 single "Bad."

33. Michael Jackson borrowed many of his dance moves from the black teenage dancers on the television series *Soul Train*, the kids dancing on the street, and urban contemporary dancers throughout his career. His legendary moonwalk, introduced on the 1983 *Motown 25* television special, was taught to him by Jeffrey Daniel, a black back-up dancer on *Soul Train* (1971–2006).

34. Michael Jackson's 1988 single "Man in the Mirror" resulted from his record label's desire to have an inspirational anthem on his 1987 *Bad* album that could compete with Whitney Houston's 1985 hit "Greatest Love of All." Gospel singers The Winans and the Andraé Crouch choir provided Jackson's song with the black church's sound.

35. Liberia Ganta, "Memory of Michael Jackson Uplifts Liberia," *The Washington Times*, July 2, 2009, accessed July 30, 2019, https://www.washingtontimes.com/news/2009/jul/02/king-of-pop-uplifts-liberia/.

36. Michael Jackson's song "They Don't Care About Us" from his 1995 album *HIStory: Past, Present, and Future, Book 1*, was accompanied by two Spike Lee-directed music videos. The first video was shot in Brazil, the second in an American prison. Brazil was the primary destination for African slaves during the Atlantic slave trade. In America, the prison system has become a new form of slavery. Thus, this video had powerful symbolism for blacks. Spike Lee, known for his pro-black stances, was the most successful black director of the period.

37. Michael Jackson, "Black or White," track 8 on *Dangerous*, Epic Records, 1991.

38. Joshua Bloom and Waldo E. Martin, *Black against Empire: The History and Politics of the Black Panther Party* (Oakland, California: University of California Press, 2016), 45–55.

39. Elizabeth Chin, "Michael Jackson's Panther Dance: Double Consciousness and the Uncanny Business of Performing While Black," *Journal of Popular Music Studies* 23, no. 1 (March 8, 2011), doi:10.1111/j.1533–1598.2010.01264.x.

40. *Ibid.*

41. *Ibid.*

42. *Ibid.*

43. Wesley Morris, "Why Is Everyone Always Stealing Black Music?," *The New York Times*, August 14, 2019, accessed August 9, 2020, https://www.nytimes.com/interactive/2019/08/14/magazine/music-black-culture-appropriation.html.

44. Mr. Wonder, "Rhythmless Nation—In Living Color," June 21, 2011, video, 1:41, https://www.youtube.com/watch?v=naSAQ-xuTvo&t=1s.

45. Tomi Obaro, "Lizzo Can Be Black And Corny At The Same Time," *BuzzFeed News*, September 8, 2019, accessed February 15, 2020, https://www.buzzfeednews.com/article/tomiobaro/lizzo-corny-truth-hurts-azealia-banks-white-gaze.

46. "BUSH 'OUT OF THESE TROUBLED TIMES ... A NEW WORLD ORDER,'" *The Washington Post*, September 12, 1990, accessed July 19, 2019, https://www.washingtonpost.com/archive/politics/1990/09/12/bush-out-of-these-troubled-times-a-new-world-order/b93b5cf1-e389-4e6a-84b0-85f71bf4c946/?utm_term=.a389b70bf43b.

47. "Whitney Houston Tells Diane Sawyer: 'Crack Is Whack,'" *ABC News*, December 4, 2002, accessed July 21, 2019, https://abcnews.go.com/Entertainment/whitney-houston-tells-diane-sawyer-crack-whack/story?id=131898.

48. Powers.

49. Ta-Nehisi Coates, "I'm Not Black, I'm Kanye," *The Atlantic*, May 7, 2018, accessed July 31, 2019, https://www.theatlantic.com/entertainment/archive/2018/05/im-not-black-im-kanye/559763/.

50. Kanye West owns a $14 million 1,400-acre ranch located 75 miles from Yellowstone National Park.

51. Jackson became more reclusive as his fame increased. At times he would wear disguises to walk out in public without being mobbed by fans.

52. Bhawgwild, "1993 Michael Jackson Interview (Oprah)," August 10, 2018, video, 52:48, https://www.youtube.com/watch?v=VFVm_3QJrEQ.

53. Isaiah 53:26 (KJV).

54. Jackson also blamed his accidental burning while filming a Pepsi commercial in 1984 for some of the surgical alterations to his appearance.

55. Toni Morrison, *The Bluest Eye* (New York: Holt, 1970).

56. The tragic mulatto trope is a biracial

person who suffers from depression, loneliness, or suicidal thoughts because he or she cannot fit in the white or black world.

57. Fnr Tigg, "MTV Reportedly Wants to Remove Michael Jackson's Name from Video Vanguard Award," *Complex*, July 27, 2019, accessed August 1, 2019, https://www.complex.com/music/2019/07/mtv-reportedly-wants-remove-michael-jackson-name-video-vanguard-award.

58. James Baldwin published the article "Freaks and the American Ideal of Manhood" in a 1985 issue of *Playboy* magazine. Baldwin discussed the public's treatment of Michael Jackson in the article.

59. In addition to purchasing the Beatles' catalog, Jackson acquired the catalog's international rights for Sly & the Family Stone in 1983.

60. Cancel culture is a form of public shaming on social media of celebrities and non-famous individuals who behave in a way or make comments that are not in tune with popular opinion or "acceptable" norms established by the masses.

61. Katt Williams mocked Jackson in his 2006 HBO standup special *The Pimp Chronicles*.

62. *i-D* staff, "Pharrell Williams: 'Faith Is about What You Feel,'" *i-D Magazine*, June 10, 2020, accessed June 11, 2020, https://i-d.vice.com/en_uk/article/m7jexy/pharrell-williams-interview-i-d-magazine.

Chapter Four

1. Kanye West's father speaking at the beginning of the music video for "Follow God."

2. Clout chasing is slang for engaging in an insignificant dispute with someone more famous for the sake of gaining popularity.

3. Lily Puckett, "Snoop Dogg on Kanye West: 'There's No Black Women in His Life,'" *The FADER*, May 18, 2018. https://www.thefader.com/2018/05/18/snoop-dogg-kanye-west-breakfast-club-interview.

4. Donuts is slang for rotating the rear or front of a vehicle around the opposite set of wheels in a continuous motion, creating a circular skid mark pattern.

5. Kanye West, "Follow God," track 3 on *Jesus Is King*, GOOD/Def Jam, 2019.

6. Portwood and Lucille Williams were

married for 72 years and had multiple great-grandchildren.

7. Donda West, *Raising Kanye: Life Lessons from the Mother of a Hip-Hop Superstar* (New York: Pocket Books, 2009), 15–17.

8. Elizabeth Clark-Lewis, *Living In, Living Out: African American Domestics and the Great Migration* (New York: Kodansha International, 1996), 150–151.

9. *Ibid.*

10. James Gribble Hochtritt, Jr., "An Absence of Malice: The Oklahoma City Sit-In Movement 1958–1964" (thesis, University of Oklahoma, 1994), 1.

11. Boss is a slang term in hip-hop for a highly successful individual, a leader, a trailblazer who does not conform to the norm.

12. Hannibal Johnson, *Black Wall Street 100: An American City Grapples with Its Historical Trauma.* (Fort Worth, TX: Eakin Press, 2020).

13. Chris Messer, "The Tulsa Race Riot of 1921: Determining its Causes and Framing" (thesis, Oklahoma State University, 2005), 8.

14. Biographical information on Dr. Donda West was gathered from her obituary.

15. Jeanne Theoharis, *A More Beautiful and Terrible History: The Uses and Misuses of Civil Rights History* (Boston: Beacon Press, 2019), 142–144.

16. Hochtritt, 6.

17. Hochtritt, 10.

18. West, 204.

19. Kanye West, "Never Let Me Down," track 8 on *The College Dropout*, Roc-A-Fella/Def Jam, 2003.

20. Kanye West appeared on *The Oprah Winfrey Show* on September 9, 2005. OWN, "Kanye West: 'Life Is in Color, and I Plan to Be Bright Red' | The Oprah Winfrey Show | OWN," June 23, 2016, video, 2:14, https://www.youtube.com/watch?v=IADsUFp4jbI.

21. Sajae Elder, "Kanye West Says He Is the 'Greatest Artist That God Has Ever Created' at Joel Osteen Service." *The FADER*, November 18, 2019, accessed December 25, 2019, https://www.thefader.com/2019/11/17/kanye-west-says-he-is-the-greatest-artist-that-god-has-ever-created-at-joel-osteen-service.

22. Randy Roberts and John Matthew Smith, *Blood Brothers: The Fatal Friendship Between Muhammad Ali and Malcolm X* (New York: Basic Books, 2016), 46.

23. Sean Michaels, "Kanye West Criticizes Hip-Hop Peers for Being Afraid of Gay People," *The Guardian*, February 10, 2009. https://www.theguardian.com/music/2009/feb/10/kanye-west-hip-hop-fashion.

24. West, 181.

25. West, 188.

26. *Ibid.*, 190–192.

27. *Ibid.*, 27.

28. As early as 1986 anthropologists John Ogbu and Signithia Fordham published their paper "Black Students' School Success: Coping with the Burden of 'Acting White.'" Ogbu and Fordham attributed some black students' poor academic achievement on fear of "talking" and "acting" white.

29. Michelle Obama, *Becoming* (New York: Crown Publishing Group, 2018).

30. Arienne Thompson, "Urkel Much? 4 Reasons Why Kanye Sounds like That," *USA Today*, August 31, 2015. https://www.usatoday.com/story/life/people/2015/08/30/real-kanye-please-stand-up/71435336/.

31. Brittany Lewis, "CODE SWITCH! Kanye West Talks About Using His 'White' Voice (VIDEO)," *Global Grind*, October 22, 2013. https://globalgrind.com/3879434/kanye-west-using-white-voice-video-radio-interview/.

32. Thurgood Marshall and the NAACP Legal Defense Fund used Dr. Kenneth and Mamie Clark's 1940s doll test in the 1954 *Brown v. Board of Education* case to prove that segregated schools were teaching black children to hate their complexion and race.

33. Todd Boyd, *Young, Black, Rich, and Famous: The Rise of the NBA, the Hip Hop Invasion, and the Transformation of American Culture* (Lincoln: University of Nebraska Press, 2008), 145–167.

34. Kobe Bryant's image in the black community evolved over the course of his career and life. He became very outspoken on social issues involving race and gender towards the end of his playing career and in retirement. Bryant's life was tragically cut short, at the age of 41, when he and his 13-year-old daughter, Gianna, died in a helicopter crash on January 26, 2020.

35. Nate Scott, "Kobe Bryant Fires Back at Jim Brown over African-American 'Culture' Comments," *USA Today*, December 12, 2013. https://ftw.usatoday.com/2013/12/kobe-bryant-jim-brown-arsenio-hall.

36. Hannah Smothers, "Kim Chose the Butt Model on 'The Life of Pablo' Cover," *Cosmopolitan*, October 6, 2017. https://www.cosmopolitan.com/entertainment/news/a53644/kim-chose-the-butt-model-on-the-life-of-pablo-cover/.

37. West, 36–44.

38. Dr. Donda West chaired the English Department at Chicago State University for six years.

39. West, 78.

40. During a conversation with Nick Cannon for the podcast *Cannon's Class* on September 1, 2020, Kanye West revealed that his parents originally had an agreement for him to split time with each of them every other weekend. But when his mother was offered more money to work for "a white company," she relocated to Chicago. This move resulted in him having a weaker relationship with his father.

41. West, 139.

42. James Melvin Washington, *Conversations with God: Two Centuries of Prayer by African Americans* (New York: HarperCollins, 1994).

43. Carol V.R. George, *God's Salesman: Norman Vincent Peale and the Power of Positive Thinking* (New York: Oxford University Press, 1993), 133–136.

44. Professor George describes Norman Vincent Peale's pragmatic, contemporary version of New Thought, which he called practical Christianity, as a theological tapestry displaying something of evangelical Protestantism, something of metaphysical spirituality, something of the American Dream uniquely blended. This orientation prompts the question: Was Kanye's banal narrative of chattel slavery as a burden of choice an emotionally disengaged misapplication of New Thought teachings?

45. West, 139.

46. West, 88.

47. Frantz Fanon, *Black Skin, White Masks* (New York: Grove Press, 1967).

48. "Adidas CEO Says Kanye West Is Very Important for Strategy," *Bloomberg*, May 3, 2018, accessed December 10, 2019, https://www.bloomberg.com/news/videos/2018-05-03/adidas-ceo-says-kanye-west-is-very-important-for-strategy-video.

49. Regina N. Bradley, "Kanye West's Sonic [Hip-hop] Cosmopolitanism," in *The Cultural Impact of Kanye West*, ed. Julius Bailey (New York: Palgrave Macmillan, 2014), 51–53.

50. Hugo Compain and Josh Arnold, "Kanye West and Vanessa Beecroft: the Collaboration in 9 Moments," *Vogue Paris*, January 9, 2019. https://www.vogue.fr/vogue-hommes/fashion/diaporama/kanye-west-vanessa-beecroft-collaboration-yeezy/40931.

51. Steppin' is a form of swing dancing that originated in Chicago's African American community during the 1970s.

52. Besides working with No I.D., Kanye West studied other greats like Detroit producer J Dilla (James Dewitt Yancey) and Wu Tang Clan's producer RZA (Robert Diggs).

53. Kanye's original stage name was Kanye The Influence.

54. Mark Beaumont, *Kanye West: God & Monster* (London: Omnibus Press, 2015), 35–40.

55. *Ibid.*, 47.

56. West, 103.

57. Erika Ramirez, "Kanye West's 'The College Dropout': An Oral History," *Billboard*, February 8, 2014, accessed June 1, 2020, https://www.billboard.com/articles/columns/the-juice/5893976/kanye-wests-the-college-dropout-an-oral-history.

58. West, 158.

59. Alondra Hernandez, "Donda West Died of Heart Disease after Surgery," *People,* January 10, 2008. https://people.com/celebrity/donda-west-died-of-heart-disease-after-surgery/.

60. Jon Caramanica, "Behind Kanye's Mask," *The New York Times*, June 11, 2013, accessed May 11, 2020, https://www.nytimes.com/2013/06/16/arts/music/kanye-west-talks-about-his-career-and-album-yeezus.html?pagewanted=all.

61. Kanye West, "Coldest Winter," track 11 on *808s & Heartbreak*, Def Jam/Roc-A-Fella, 2008.

62. Robert Kardashian passed away in 2003 from esophageal cancer.

63. Robert Kardashian died from esophageal cancer when Kim was 22.

64. Bruce Jenner underwent a gender transition in 2017. Today Caitlyn Jenner is considered the world's most famous transgender woman.

65. *The Brady Bunch* (1969–1974) was a popular sitcom on ABC about a blended middle-class white family.

66. Amaya Ribera, "*Keeping Up with the Kardashians: Season 1,*" *Popmatters,*

October 15, 2008, accessed December 11, 2019, https://www.popmatters.com/keeping-up-with-the-kardashians-season-1-2496113502.html.

67. In *The Great Gatsby*, East Egg represents the individuals who hail from old money, compared to the residents like Jay Gatsby, who belong to the nouveau riche.

68. *Forbes* reported in May 2020 that Kylie had forged her tax returns and was not a billionaire.

69. Robin Leach, an entertainment reporter from London, England, hosted the television series *Lifestyles of the Rich and Famous* from 1984 until 1995.

70. Mani-pedi is slang for receiving a manicure and a pedicure.

Chapter Five

1. *Empire*, season 1, episode 8, "The Lyon's Roar," written and directed by Danny Strong, first broadcast February 25, 2015, Fox.

2. Paris Hilton is the great-granddaughter of American hotelier Conrad Hilton.

3. Allie Gemmill, "Kanye West Didn't Even Know Kim Kardashian's Name When They Met," *Teen Vogue*, September 25, 2017, accessed November 3, 2019, https://www.teenvogue.com/story/kim-kardashian-kanye-west-relationship-beginning.

4. Sean P. Means, "Kanye's New Video Features Monument Valley and a Topless Kim," *The Salt Lake Tribune*, November 19, 2013, accessed November 3, 2019, https://archive.sltrib.com/article.php?id=57151614&itype=CMSID.

5. Kanye West participated in a panel discussion on business marketing and technology with Steve Stoute and Ben Horowitz.

6. Anna Wintour shared her thoughts on featuring Kanye West and Kim Kardashian on the May 2014 *Vogue* cover in her 2019 Masterclass.

7. Sarah Michelle Gellar (@SarahMGellar), Twitter post, March 21, 2014, 4:16 AM, https://twitter.com/SarahMGellar/status/447104444144955394.

8. Karen Attiah, "Opinion: Why Did It Take Vogue 125 Years to Have a Black Photographer Shoot a Cover?" *The Washington Post*, September 4, 2018, https://www.washingtonpost.com/news/act-four/

wp/2018/09/04/why-did-it-take-so-long-for-vogue-to-have-a-black-photographer-shoot-a-cover/.

9. Nathan Rabin, Yohana Desta, and Paul Chi, "The Monkey and the Metaphor: What Every King Kong Movie Is Really About," *Vanity Fair*, March 13, 2017, accessed on April 17, 2020, https://www.vanityfair.com/hollywood/2017/03/king-kong-skull-island-movies-metaphors.

10. The Costigan-Wagner Bill was proposed in the U.S. Congress in 1934 to criminalize the lynch mobs. The Dyer Anti-Lynching Bill, introduced 12 years earlier, was halted in the U.S. Senate by the Southern Democrats' filibuster.

11. The fear of little black boys mixing with white girls was the primary reason for school segregation and the severe backlash that resulted from the 1954 *Brown v. the Board of Education* U.S. Supreme Court decision.

12. Geoffrey C. Ward, *Unforgivable Blackness: The Rise and Fall of Jack Johnson* (New York: Vintage Books, 2006).

13. Peter Wallenstein, *Race, Sex, and the Freedom to Marry: Loving v. Virginia* (Lawrence: University Press of Kansas, 2014).

14. Sidney Poitier set a precedent for blacks when he won an Academy Award for Best Actor in 1964 for his role in *Lilies of the Field*.

15. Sidney Poitier and his first wife Juanita appeared on the cover of *Ebony* magazine's May 1959 issue. The cover read "Hollywood's First Negro Movie Star."

16. Betty Granger, "The Harry Belafontes at Home," *The Amsterdam- News*, April 27, 1957, 1.

17. Mark Hayward, "Harry Belafonte, Race, and the Politics of Success" (PhD diss., McGill University, 2000), 57.

18. *Ibid.*, 60–61.

19. Patrick Parr, Sam Sutton, Carly Sitrin, Bill Mahoney, Josh Gerstein, and Madina Touré, "'We Were Madly, Madly in Love': The Untold Story of MLK's White Girlfriend," *POLITICO*, April 1, 2018, https://www.politico.com/magazine/story/2018/04/01/martin-luther-king-junior-assassination-anniversary-interracial-relationship-217769.

20. The Masters Tournament is the marquee tournament in the Professional Golf Association (PGA).

21. Bill Russell, *The Second Wind: The Memoirs of an Opinionated Man* (New York: Ballantine Books, 1980).

22. Jasmine Mans, "Footnotes for Kanye," *The Journal of Hip Hop Studies* Volume 6, Issue 1 (2019): 105–107.

23. Jill Scott, "Commentary: Jill Scott Talks Interracial Dating," *Essence*, March 26, 2010, accessed April 19, 2020, https://www.essence.com/news/commentary-jill-scott-talks-interracial/.

24. Cultural appropriation occurs when members of a dominant culture take a disadvantaged minority group's culture without their permission and fail to provide proper recognition of that group.

25. Queer feminist Moya Bailey coined the word misogynoir.

26. Ezinne Ukoha, "How The Kardashians Keep Getting Away With Villainizing Black Men," *Medium*, April 13, 2018, accessed April 21, 2020, https://medium.com/@nilegirl/the-kardashians-keep-getting-away-with-villainizing-black-men-like-its-their-right-e898af98734a.

27. Harriet Jacobs, *Incidents in the Life of a Slave Girl* (Mineola, New York: Dover Publications, 2001).

28. Martha Hodges, *White Women, Black Men: Illicit Sex in the Nineteenth-Century South* (New Haven: Yale University Press, 1997), 130–131.

29. Joanna Bourke, *Rape: Sex, Violence, and History* (London: Virago Press, 2007), 219.

30. Winthrop Jordan, *White Over Black: American Attitudes Toward the Negro, 1550–1812* (Chapel Hill: University of North Carolina Press, 1968).

31. Miriam DeCosta-Willis, Reginald Martin, and Roseann Bell, *Erotique Noire— Black Erotica* (London, UK: Doubleday, 1992), xxxi.

32. "Helen Mirren Reveals What She Thinks Is 'Wonderful' about Kim Kardashian," *TODAY.com*, June 7, 2016, accessed April 21, 2020, https://www.today.com/series/love-your-body/helen-mirren-praises-kim-kardashian-making-it-ok-have-butt-t96846.

33. *Breaking the internet* is a slang expression for causing a large commotion on many social media and online news websites.

34. Kim Kardashian West (@KimKardashian), Twitter post, November 11, 2014, 9:15 PM, https://twitter.com/KimKardashian/status/532356049907355649.

35. Bethonie Butler, "Yes, Those Kim Kardashian Photos Are About Race," *The Washington Post*, November 21, 2014, accessed on April 1, 2020, https://www. washingtonpost.com/blogs/she-the-people/wp/2014/11/21/yes-those-kim-kardashian-photos-are-about-race/.
36. Matthew Rozsa, "What the Debate over Kim Kardashian Says about the Changing Face of Race in America," *The Daily Dot*, February 4, 2018, accessed on April 22, 2020, https://www.dailydot. com/via/kim-kardashian-race-changing-america/.
37. *Ibid.*
38. Kimberle Crenshaw, "Mapping the Margins: Intersectionality, Identity Politics, and Violence." *Stanford Law Review, 43* (6) 1991. 1241–1299.
39. Lauren Michele Jackson, *White Negroes: When Cornrows Were in Vogue... and Other Thoughts on Cultural Appropriation* (Boston: Beacon Press, 2019). Norman Mailer, *The White Negro: Superficial Reflections on the Hipster* (San Francisco: City Lights, 1957).
40. "Lauren Michele Jackson On 'White Negroes,'" *NPR*, November 10, 2019, accessed August 24, 2020, https://www. npr.org/2019/11/10/778015473/lauren-michele-jackson-on-white-negroes.
41. On July 9, 2016, Leshia Evans was at a rally protesting the recent murders of Alton Sterling and Philando Castile while in police custody.
42. *Double Jeopardy: To Be Black and Female* is a pamphlet written by Frances M. Beal in 1969 and published in *The Black Woman*, an anthology, in 1970.
43. Ryan Lizza, "Three Problems with the Melania Trump Plagiarism Admission," *The New Yorker*, July 10, 2017, accessed August 13, 2020, https://www.newyorker. com/news/news-desk/three-problems-with-the-melania-trump-plagiarism-admission.
44. "How Kim Kardashian Plans To Raise Her Bi-Racial Child," *HuffPost*, April 2, 2013, accessed April 28, 2020, https:// www.huffpost.com/entry/kim-and-kanye-baby-racial-identity_n_2966236.
45. The danger in whites adopting a color-blind attitude is that they refuse to see the problems that others encounter because of their color. Robin DiAngelo, author of *White Fragility: Why It's So Hard for White People to Talk About Racism* (2018), says this line of thinking and privilege prevents white people from having productive conservations on race. Such behavior runs counter to the notion of being an antiracist. Ibram X. Kendi, *How to Be an Antiracist* (New York: One World, 2019).
46. Janet Mock, "Kim Kardashian West & North West," *Interview*, November 25, 2019, accessed April 29, 2020, https://www. interviewmagazine.com/culture/kim-kardashian-west.
47. The CROWN Act (SB 188) is a state law that makes it illegal to discriminate based on an individual's hairstyle or texture.
48. Jennifer Latson, "The Biracial Advantage," *Psychology Today*, May 7, 2019, accessed May 8, 2020, https://www.psychology today.com/us/articles/201905/the-biracial-advantage.
49. Heidi Durrow, *The Girl Who Fell From the Sky* (Chapel Hill, North Carolina: Algonquin, 2011).
50. Steve Bradt, "'One-Drop Rule' Persists," *Harvard Gazette*, July 8, 2019, accessed May 1, 2020, https://news.har vard.edu/gazette/story/2010/12/one-drop-rule-persists/.
51. Latson.
52. Cablinasian refers to a person of Caucasian, black, American Indian, and Asian descent.
53. Howard Bryant, *The Heritage: Black Athletes, a Divided America, and the Politics of Patriotism* (Boston: Beacon Press, 2018), 96.
54. Howard Bryant, *Full Dissidence: Notes from an Uneven Playing Field* (Boston: Beacon Press, 2020).
55. Howard Bryant, "Why Black Athletes Run from Black Identity," *The Undefeated*, February 17, 2020, accessed May 16, 2020, https://theundefeated.com/features/ why-black-athletes-run-from-black-identity/.
56. Barack Obama, *Dreams from My Father: A Story of Race and Inheritance* (New York: Broadway Books, 2004), 80–83.
57. Robin Givhan, "Kamala Harris Grew Up in a Mostly White World. Then She Went to a Black University in a Black City," *The Washington Post*, September 16, 2019, accessed November 24, 2019, https://www.washingtonpost.com/ politics/2019/09/16/kamala-harris-grew-

up-mostly-white-world-then-she-went-black-university-black-city/?arc404=true.

58. People TV, "Halle Berry On Being Biracial At All-White School: We Got Called Oreos," August 8, 2017, video, 1:44, https://www.youtube.com/watch?v=_koseG_ulf.

59. James Melvin Washington, *Conversations with God: Two Centuries of Prayers by African Americans* (New York, NY: HarperCollins, 1994), xli.

60. Ruth Styles, "Prince Harry's New Girlfriend Meghan Markle's LA Home," *Daily Mail*, January 9, 2020, accessed April 29, 2020, https://www.dailymail.co.uk/news/article-3896180/Prince-Harry-s-girlfriend-actress-Meghan-Markles.html.

61. Kanye West, (Visionary Award acceptance speech, BET Honors, Washington, D.C., January 24, 2015).

62. Stephanie Marcus, "North West Verbally Attacked By Racist Woman On Plane," *HuffPost*, June 30, 2014, accessed April 29, 2020, https://www.huffpost.com/entry/north-west-racist-woman-plane_n_5543327.

63. Sheila Weller, "Are you white, or are you black?" *Glamour*, June 2005, 244–247, 259, and 267.

64. Other biracial actresses Maya Rudolph and Thandie Newton also played racially ambiguous characters on television and in films. Black female scholars have observed that biracial male actors like Dwayne "The Rock" Johnson and Vin Diesel encounter far less scrutiny for playing racially ambiguous characters in films.

65. Valeri M. Lo, "'We Can't Even Play Ourselves': Mixed-Raced Actresses in the Early Twenty-First Century" (PhD diss., University of Hawaii at Manoa, 2017), 56–75.

66. *Ibid.*, 85–93.

67. David Dennis, "'Fate of the Furious' Dwayne Johnson Has Been Wrestling for Years with the Politics of Race, pro Wrestling and Hollywood," *The Undefeated*, April 14, 2017, accessed August 16, 2020, https://theundefeated.com/features/the-rock-wwe-dwayne-johnson/.

68. Zeba Blay, "What The Conversation About Rashida Jones Blackness Is Missing," *HuffPost*, April 24, 2020, accessed May 2, 2020, https://www.huffpost.com/entry/rashida-jones-blackaf-blackness_n_5e9f62 34c5b6a486d080b5dd.

69. Rashida directed the third episode, "still…because of slavery," and used it to address a very serious issue, the adultification of black girls. Studies show that black girls, ages 5–14, are disproportionately deprived of their innocence and viewed as more adult-like than their white peers. This treatment has a lot to do with their body types, attire, and even how they dance. It will be interesting to see if North and her sister, Chicago, experience this stigma as they mature.

70. "TMZ Live: The Full Kanye West Episode," TMZ, June 17, 2019, accessed May 15, 2020, https://www.tmz.com/2018/05/02/tmz-live-kanye/.

71. Diana Dasrath and David K. Li, "Kim Kardashian files for divorce from Kanye West," *NBC News*. February 19, 2021. Accessed on May 26, 2021. https://www.nbcnews.com/news/us-news/kim-kardashian-files-divorce-kanye-west-n1258382.

Chapter Six

1. *Keeping Up with the Kardashians*, episode 228, "Chicago Loyalty," aired March 31, 2019 on E!.

2. BFF is an abbreviation of the phrase "best friend forever."

3. Rhymefest (@RHYMEFEST), Twitter post, February 12, 2016, 11:15 AM, https://twitter.com/RHYMEFEST/status/698178 615175987200?ref_src=twsrc%5Etfw %7Ctwcamp%5Etweetembed%7Ctw term%5E698178615175987200&ref_ url=https%3A%2F%2Fwww.billboard. com%2Farticles%2Fcolumns%2Fhip-hop%2F6875189%2Fkanye-west-co-writer-rhymefest-life-of-pablo-quits-says-rapper-needs-counseling.

4. Rhymefest (@RHYMEFEST), Twitter post, May 26, 2018, 12:06 PM, https://twitter.com/rhymefest/status/10004077772 88781824?lang=en.

5. Kim Kardashian West (@KimKardashian), Twitter post, May 26, 2018, 7:29 PM, https://twitter.com/KimKardashian/status/1000519257195663360?ref_src=tws rc%5Etfw%7Ctwcamp%5Etweetembed%7 Ctwterm%5E1000519257195663360&ref_ url=https%3A%2F%2Fwww.elle.com%2 Fculture%2Fcelebrities%2Fa20926809%- 2Fkim-kardashian-twitter-rant-defending-kanye-west-rhymefest%2F.

6. H.E.R. is an acronym for Hip-Hop in its Essence is Real.

7. Kanye West interview, WGCI Morning Show, Chicago, IL: WGCI, August 29, 2018.

8. In the African American community, "brothers" and "sisters" are terms of endearment used to describe men and women. Many assume that blacks belong to a large metaphorical family due to their African roots and collective experience coming out of slavery.

9. Kanye West interview, WGCI Morning Show, Chicago, IL: WGCI, August 29, 2018.

10. *Ibid.*

11. Kanye references his friend Virgil Abloh's Off-White collaboration with Nike and Louis Vuitton. He and Virgil, a Ghanaian American Illinois native, became rivals due to their success in the fashion industry. Kanye also references Kiki, a fictional woman in Drake's 2018 number-one hit single "In My Feelings." He and Drake were once close friends before their relationship soured and became a bitter feud.

12. Kanye West interview, WGCI Morning Show, Chicago, IL: WGCI, August 29, 2018.

13. Will Welch and Tyler Mitchell, "Inside Kanye West's Vision for the Future," *GQ*, April 15, 2020, accessed April 15, 2020, https://www.gq.com/story/inside-kanye-west-vision-for-the-future-cover-may-2020.

14. Teresa Wiltz, "Great African-American Entrepreneurs Who Made History," *The Root*, February 10, 2014, accessed January 3, 2020, https://www.theroot.com/great-african-american-entrepreneurs-who-made-history-1790868437.

15. Margena A. Christian, *Empire: The House That John H. Johnson Built (The Life & Legacy of Pioneering Publishing Magnate)* (Chicago: DocM.A.C. Write Publishing, 2018).

16. Robert "Scoop" Jackson was a guest on the *The Right Time with Bomani Jones* podcast on May 5, 2020.

17. Joshua K. Wright, "Be Like Mike?: The Black Athletes Dilemma," *Spectrum: A Journal on Black Men* 4, no. 2 (2016): 1. https://doi.org/10.2979/spectrum.4.2.01.

18. Zack O'Malley Greenburg, "Kanye West Is Now Officially A Billionaire—And He Really Wants The World To Know," *Forbes*, April 25, 2020, accessed April 25, 2020, https://www.forbes.com/sites/zackomalleygreenburg/2020/04/24/kanye-west-is-now-officially-a-billionaireand-he-really-wants-the-world-to-know/#ec276 577b9ec.

19. As of June 2020, the list of black billionaires in the United States included Shawn "Jay-Z" Carter, Michael Jordan, Robert E. Smith, Dave Steward, Kanye West, and Oprah Winfrey.

20. Melissa Repko, "Gap Stock Soars after Kanye West Touts Collaboration with His Fashion Brand Yeezy," *CNBC*, June 26, 2020, accessed June 26, 2020, https://www.cnbc.com/2020/06/26/gap-stock-soars-after-kanye-west-teases-possible-collaboration-with-gap.html.

21. Isabel Wilkerson, *The Warmth of Other Suns: The Epic Story of America's Great Migration* (New York: Vintage Books, 2011).

22. Robin F. Bachin, *Building the South Side: Urban Space and Civic Culture in Chicago, 1890–1919* (Chicago: University of Chicago Press, 2004), 247.

23. St. Clair Drake and Horace R. Cayton, *Black Metropolis: A Study of Negro Life in a Northern City* (Chicago: University of Chicago Press, 1993), 31.

24. Simon Balto, "'The Law Has a Bad Opinion of Me': Policing and Politics in Twentieth-Century Black Chicago" (PhD diss., University of Wisconsin-Madison, 2015), 26–28.

25. "A Crowd of Howling Negroes," *The Chicago Daily Tribune*, July 28, 1919.

26. William Tuttle, *Race Riot Chicago in the Red Summer of 1919* (Urbana: University of Illinois Press, 1970).

27. Katie Nodjimbadem, "The Long, Painful History of Police Brutality in the U.S.," *Smithsonian*, July 27, 2017, https://www.smithsonianmag.com/smithsonian-institution/long-painful-history-police-brutality-in-the-us-180964098/#8eKR9BK dZPjy18h2.99.

28. Bigger Thomas is the fictional black teen from Chicago's South Side in Richard Wright's 1939 novel *Native Son*. After Bigger accidentally kills a white woman, his life goes down a path of self-destruction.

29. Arnold Hirsch, *Making the Second Ghetto: Race and Housing in Chicago, 1940–1960* (Chicago: University of Chicago Press, 1988).

30. "Chicago Campaign," The Martin Luther King, Jr., Research and Education Institute, accessed May 21, 2018, https://kinginstitute.stanford.edu/encyclopedia/chicago-campaign.

31. "Dr. King is Felled by Rock," *Chicago Tribune*, August 6, 1966.

32. Xolela Mcpherson Mangcu, "Harold Washington and the Cultural Transformation of Local Government in Chicago, 1983–1987" (PhD diss., Cornell University, 1997).

33. Robert Pruter, *Chicago Soul* (Urbana: University of Illinois Press, 2007), and Aaron Cohen, *Move On Up: Chicago Soul Music and Black Cultural Power* (Chicago: The University of Chicago Press, 2019).

34. Peter Guralnick, *Sweet Soul Music: Rhythm and Blues and the Southern Dream of Freedom* (New York: Harper & Row, 1986), 2.

35. Aretha Franklin held a fundraiser for Jesse Jackson's 1984 presidential campaign.

36. The Fox series *Empire* (2015–2020) depicted a fictional black-owned record label. The company's CEO, Lucious Lyon, was inspired by Motown's Berry Gordy and other black record label executives.

37. Gene Demby, "Remembering the Woman Who Gave Motown Its Charm," *NPR*, October 15, 2013, https://www.npr.org/sections/codeswitch/2013/10/15/234738593/remembering-the-woman-who-gave-motown-its-charm.

38. Suzanne E. Smith, *Dancing in the Street: Motown and the Cultural Politics of Detroit* (Cambridge, MA: Harvard University Press, 2003), 141 and 153.

39. Otis Redding died in a plane crash on December 10, 1967.

40. Chipmunk soul refers to the musical sounds of the animated singers on the children's cartoon series *Alvin and the Chipmunks*.

41. Mark Anthony Neal, "Now I Ain't Saying He's a Crate Digger: Kanye West, 'Community Theaters' and the Soul Archive" in *The Cultural Impact of Kanye West*, ed. Julius Bailey (New York: Palgrave Macmillan, 2014), 3–10.

42. Alexis Petridis, "Pop, Prince and Black Panthers: the Glorious Life of Chaka Khan," *The Guardian*, February 15, 2019, accessed August 19, 2020, https://www.theguardian.com/music/2019/feb/15/pop-prince-and-black-panthers-the-glorious-life-of-chaka-khan.

43. "Touch the Sky" introduced the mainstream to Lupe Fiasco (Wasalu Muhammad Jaco), a devout Muslim emcee of West African descent from Chicago's West Side. For a brief stint in the 2000s, Lupe Fiasco, the son of a Black Panther, was one of hip-hop's most acclaimed artists for his ability to follow Kanye's original blueprint of blending conscious and commercial lyrics.

44. Kanye West also sampled Curtis Mayfield's "The Makings of You (Live)" for "The Joy," a bonus track on the *Watch the Throne* deluxe edition.

45. Marcus Baram, "Why Gil Scott-Heron Wrote 'The Revolution Will Not Be Televised,'" *Medium*, August 16, 2016, accessed August 19, 2020, https://medium.com/cuepoint/why-gil-scott-heron-wrote-the-revolution-will-not-be-televised-6e298f9d4e2.

46. *Ibid.*

47. Jon Caramanica, "Behind Kanye's Mask," *The New York Times*, June 11, 2013, accessed on May 11, 2020, https://www.nytimes.com/2013/06/16/arts/music/kanye-west-talks-about-his-career-and-album-yeezus.html?pagewanted=all.

48. Peter Guralnick, *Dream Boogie: The Triumph of Sam Cooke* (Boston: Back Bay Books, 2006), 51.

49. Sam Cooke and Muhammad Ali recorded a duet in 1964 titled "The Gang's All Here."

50. "A Change Is Gonna Come" was Cooke's version of Bob Dylan's 1962 protest anthem, "Blowin' in the Wind."

51. Sam Cooke's song "A Change Is Gonna Come" was introduced to many millennials and Generation Zers demonstrating in the 2020 protests over the police killings of George Floyd and Breonna Taylor.

52. Jacob Arnold, Lorena Cupcake, Meaghan Garvey, Michaelangelo Matos, and Steve Mizek, "A Celebration of House Music," *Chicago Magazine*, August 27, 2018, accessed December 31, 2019, https://www.chicagomag.com/Chicago-Magazine/August-2018/House-Music/.

53. Miles Raymer, "Who Owns Trap?" *Chicago Reader*, December 27, 2019, accessed January 3, 2020, https://www.chicagoreader.com/chicago/trap-rap-edm-flosstra

damus-uz-jeffrees-lex-luger/Content? oid=7975249.

54. Jeffrey Haas, *The Assassination of Fred Hampton: How the FBI and the Chicago Police Murdered a Black Panther* (Chicago: Lawrence Hill Books/Chicago Review Press, 2010).

55. Justin Zullo, "'We Get Free!': Chicago Hip-Hop, Juvenile Justice, and the Embodied Politics of Movement" (PhD diss., University of Wisconsin–Madison, 2015), 192–196.

56. Dan Hyman, "What the Controversy Over Spike Lee's 'Chi-Raq' Is Really About," *GQ*, March 10, 2017, accessed July 17, 2019, https://www.gq.com/story/chi-raq-controversy-spike-lee.

57. Viceland's 2014 docuseries *Noisey* was an eight-part series spotlighting Chicago's drill artists and gang culture's influence on the genre.

58. "Is Rap Rivalry To Blame In Teen's Shooting Death?" *HuffPost*, September 6, 2012, https://www.huffpost.com/entry/lil-jojo-dead-teen-chicag_n_1861326.

59. Justin Sink, "Kanye West to Talk Prison Reform, Gang Violence at White House," *Bloomberg*, October 9, 2018, accessed December 31, 2019, https://www.bloomberg.com/news/articles/2018-10-09/kanye-west-to-talk-prison-reform-gang-violence-at-white-house.

60. Miss2Bees. "Kanye West Asks Donald Trump to Pardon Larry Hoover," *The Source*, October 12, 2018, accessed February 9, 2019, https://thesource.com/2018/10/12/kanye-west-larry-hoover/.

Chapter Seven

1. Jay-Z and Kanye West, "New Day," track 6 on *Watch the Throne*, Def Jam/Roc-A-Fella, 2011.

2. Gerald Early was interviewed for *American Masters*, season 33, episode 2, *Sammy Davis, Jr.: I've Gotta Be Me*, aired February 19, 2019, PBS.

3. A. H. Weiler, "Stars 'Save the Children,'" *The New York Times*, September 19, 1973, accessed May 1, 2019, https://www.nytimes.com/1973/09/19/archives/stars-save-the-children.html.

4. Wil Haygood, "The Hug," *The Washington Post*, September 14, 2003, accessed April 22, 2019, https://www.washingtonpost.com/archive/lifestyle/magazine/2003/09/14/the-hug/0a2746a1-88fa-4738-9d96-4ee0e84c1118/.

5. Pernell Watson, "SAMMY DAVIS JR. A FRIEND OF NIXON," dailypress.com, August 14, 2019, accessed May 23, 2020, https://www.dailypress.com/news/dp-xpm-20020327-2002-03-27-0203261615-story.html.

6. *Ibid.*

7. Smack was a slang term for heroin.

8. Cape, a slang term that means to support or defend someone, especially when undeserving of such treatment.

9. Wil Haygood, *In Black and White: The Life of Sammy Davis Jr.* (New York: Alfred A. Knopf, 2003).

10. The benefits and disadvantages of the federal welfare program have been a complicated debate between liberals and conservatives for decades. While some liberals have defended modified welfare programs as a necessary aid, other liberals have supported conservative efforts to eliminate it. In her book *Getting Tough,* Julilly Kohler-Hausmann, documents campaigns by politicians in the 1970s to discredit welfare by casting beneficiaries as racialized deviants deserving imprisonment.

11. "Remarks by President Trump in Meeting with Kanye West and Jim Brown," The White House, October 11, 2018, accessed March 18, 2020, https://www.whitehouse.gov/briefings-statements/remarks-president-trump-meeting-kanye-west-jim-brown/.

12. *Ibid.*

13. Don Lemon shared his thoughts on Kanye West's White House visit on the October 10, 2018, episode of *CNN Tonight.*

14. The Faustian bargain is based on the medieval German legend of Johann Georg Faust who made a pact with the devil at the crossroads, exchanging his soul for power.

15. CyHi the Prynce (@CyhiOfficial), Twitter post, April 24, 2018, 12:29 AM, https://twitter.com/CyhiThePrynce/status/988636107788009472?ref_src=twsrc%5Etfw%7Ctwcamp%5Etweetembed%7Ctwterm%5E988636107788009472&ref_url=https%3A%2F%2Fwww.billboard.com%2Farticles%2Fcolumns%2Fhip-hop%2F8377040%2Fcyhi-the-prynce-kanye-west-trump-martin-luther-king-jr.

16. Olivia B. Waxman, "Was Martin Luther King, Jr., a Republican or a Democrat?" *Time*, January 23, 2020, accessed

January 24, 2020, https://time.com/5764282/martin-luther-king-jr-politics/.

17. Brian Rosenwald, *Talk Radio's America: How an Industry Took over a Political Party That Took over the United States* (Cambridge, MA: Harvard University Press, 2019), 5–6.

18. West, 148.

19. Slick Rick, "A Children's Story," track 3 on *The Great Adventures of Slick Rick*, Def Jam, 1988.

20. David W. Blight, *Race and Reunion: The Civil War in American Memory* (Cambridge, MA: Harvard University Press, 2002).

21. W.E.B. Du Bois and David Levering Lewis, *Black Reconstruction in America* (New York: Free Press, 1998), and Eric Foner, *Reconstruction: America's Unfinished Revolution, 1863–1877* (New York: Harper Perennial Modern Classics, 2014).

22. "Eleanor Roosevelt and the Tuskegee Airmen," Franklin D. Roosevelt Presidential Library and Museum, accessed March 21, 2020, https://www.fdrlibrary.org/de/tuskegee.

23. Elizabeth Hinton, *From the War on Poverty to the War on Crime: The Making of Mass Incarceration in America* (Cambridge, MA: Harvard University Press, 2016).

24. Gabriel Sherman, *The Loudest Voice in the Room: How the Brilliant, Bombastic Roger Ailes Built Fox News—and Divided a Country* (New York: Random House, 2014).

25. The Republican Party is nicknamed the Grand Old Party (GOP).

26. "Black Supporters of President Under Fire," *The New York Times*, October 17, 1972, 29.

27. Governor Lester Maddox was a proud symbol of segregation and white supremacy. Before his election to office, Maddox owned the Pickwick, a fried chicken restaurant in Atlanta. He gained national publicity by refusing to integrate his restaurant, chasing blacks out of the restaurant with an ax handle, and running on a platform for state rights and the preservation of the white race. Maddox, angry about being embarrassed by Jim Brown and Dick Cavett, stormed off the live television stage in disgust during a 1970 episode of *The Dick Cavett Show*.

28. Dave Zirin, "Understanding Jim Brown's Ugly Support of Donald Trump," *The Nation*, May 9, 2018, accessed June 21, 2019, https://www.thenation.com/article/archive/understanding-jim-browns-ugly-support-of-donald-trump/.

29. Dave Zirin, "Understanding Jim Brown's Ugly Support of Donald Trump." *The Nation*, May 9, 2018. Accessed on June 21, 2019. https://www.thenation.com/article/archive/understanding-jim-browns-ugly-support-of-donald-trump/.

30. Leah Wright Rigueur, "The Forgotten History of Black Republicans," *The Daily Beast*, February 12, 2015, https://www.thedailybeast.com/the-forgotten-history-of-black-republicans.

31. Gerald D. Jaynes and Robin M. Williams, eds., *A Common Destiny: Blacks and American Society* (Washington, D.C.: National Academy Press, 1989).

32. Uncle Tom, the protagonist of Harriet Beecher Stowe's 1952 novel *Uncle Tom's Cabin*, was based on Josiah Henson, a former slave in Montgomery County, Maryland. Henson fled his plantation in 1830 and found refuge in Canada, amid a free community of other former slaves. The fictional Uncle Tom is a deeply religious slave who is killed because he refuses to tell his master the whereabouts of runaway slaves. Over time the Tom character became wrongly associated with accommodating blacks who were willing to "sell out" to please whites. Folklorist Patricia Turner blames Tom's misrepresentation in 19th-century stage shows and early 20th century films for the negative archetype that exists now. An excellent example of this would be Christopher Darden, the black co-prosecutor in the 1995 O.J. Simpson murder trial. Simpson's attorney Johnnie Cochran and other members of the defense depicted Darden as an Uncle Tom.

33. Gina I. McNelley, "Black Republicans' Beliefs and its Affects on their Identity and Relationships," (PhD diss., United States International University, 1998), 51–54.

34. Clarence Thomas, "No Room at the Inn: The Loneliness of the Black Conservative," reprinted in *Policy Review* 58 (Fall 1991): 72–78.

35. Monique Judge, "After Skinnin' and Grinnin' for Trump, Steve Harvey Says He Should Have Listened to His Wife and Skipped Meeting," *The Grapevine*, September 6, 2017, accessed December 6, 2019, https://thegrapevine.theroot.

com/after-skinnin-and-grinnin-for-trump-steve-harvey-says-1800665192.

36. Cleve Wootson, "A Black R&B Artist Hoped Singing for Trump Would Build 'a Bridge.' It Derailed Her Career Instead," *The Washington Post*, January 18, 2019, accessed December 6, 2019, https://www.washingtonpost.com/nation/2019/01/18/black-rb-artist-hoped-singing-trump-would-build-bridge-it-derailed-her-career-instead/.

37. Ben Strauss, "Jason Whitlock to Young Black Conservatives: 'I'm Here to Tell You How' to Be Leaders," *The Washington Post*, October 30, 2018, accessed December 6, 2019, https://www.washingtonpost.com/sports/2018/10/30/jason-whitlock-young-black-conservatives-im-here-tell-you-how-be-leaders/.

38. Maya Rhodan, "Azealia Banks, Rihanna Feud Over Donald Trump," *Time*, January 30, 2017, accessed December 6, 2019, https://time.com/4653253/rihanna-azealia-banks-donald-trump/.

39. Ta-Nehisi Coates, "'This Is How We Lost to the White Man,'" *The Atlantic*, November 19, 2014, accessed December 6, 2019, https://www.theatlantic.com/magazine/archive/2008/05/-this-is-how-we-lost-to-the-white-man/306774/.

40. "Bill Cosby's Famous 'Pound Cake' Speech, Annotated," *BuzzFeed News*, July 9, 2015, accessed March 24, 2020, https://www.buzzfeednews.com/article/adamserwer/bill-cosby-pound-for-pound.

41. Michael Eric Dyson, *Is Bill Cosby Right?: Or Has the Black Middle Class Lost Its Mind?* (New York: Basic Civitas, 2006).

42. Kanye West, "Never Let Me Down," track 8 on *The College Dropout*, Def Jam/Roc-A-Fella, 2004.

43. Kanye West, Jay-Z, and Big Sean, "Clique," track 2 on *Cold Summer*, Def Jam/GOOD, 2012.

44. Kanye West references the 40 acres and a mule that newly freed slaves were promised by Union Army General William T. Sherman's Special Field Order No. 15 after the Civil War. Kanye West "All Falls Down," track 4 on *The College Dropout*, Def Jam/Roc-A-Fella, 2004.

45. Jane Wakefield, "Christchurch Shootings: Social Media Races to Stop Attack Footage," *BBC*, March 16, 2019, https://www.bbc.com/news/technology-47583393.

46. Tomi Lahren is a 28-year-old white political commentator on the Fox News Channel and the host of Fox Nation. She rose to fame by making controversial statements that went viral on social media.

47. Samuel Lovett, "Cardi B and Candace Owens engage in epic Twitter battled" *CNN*. March 17, 2021. Accessed on March 20, 2021. https://www.cnn.com/2021/03/17/entertainment/cardi-b-candace-owens-trnd/index.html.

48. Netflix Is A Joke, "8:46—Dave Chappelle," June 12, 2020, video, 27:20, https://www.youtube.com/watch?v=3tR6mKcBbT4.

49. "Racist Threats Case Filed by Stamford High Student Settled for $37,500," *News-Times*, November 17, 2009, https://www.newstimes.com/news/article/Racist-threats-case-filed-by-Stamford-High-107476.php.

50. Brexit or Vote Leave is a campaign for the United Kingdom (UK) to withdraw from the European Union (EU). An underlying reason for this withdrawal is anti–immigrant sentiment resulting from a growing population of darker immigrants in the UK and "Take Back Control" rhetoric spread on social media.

51. Thomas and Mary Edsall, *Chain Reaction: The Impact of Race, Rights, and Taxes on American Politics* (New York: Norton & Company, 1991).

52. Dahleen Glanton, "The Myth of the 'Welfare Queen' Endures, and Children Pay the Price," *Chicago Tribune*, May 20, 2019, accessed July 17, 2019, https://www.chicagotribune.com/columns/dahleen-glanton/ct-met-dahleen-glanton-welfare-queen-20180516-story.html.

53. Josh Levin, *The Queen: The Forgotten Life Behind an American Myth* (New York: Back Bay Books, 2020).

54. Lee Atwater's interview was published in the book *South Politics in the 1990s* (1999), edited by Alexander Lamis. Atwater is the subject of the 2008 documentary *Boogie Man: The Lee Atwater Story*.

55. On August 20, 2020, Steve Bannon was indicted on charges of conspiracy to commit wire fraud and money laundering in a scheme to defraud financial donors for Trump's wall on the border with Mexico. He was released from jail in less than 24 hours on a $5 million bond.

56. Sherman, xv–xvi.

57. Doug McAdam, "Putting Donald

Trump in Historical Perspective: Racial Politics and Social Movements from the 1960s to Today," in *The Resistance: The Dawn of the Anti-Trump Opposition Movement*, eds. Davis S. Meyer and Jacob S. Hacker (New York: Oxford University Press, 2018), 36–41.

58. Jose A. DelReal, "'Get 'Em out!' Racial Tensions Explode at Donald Trump's Rallies," *The Washington Post*, March 12, 2016, accessed January 30, 2020, https://www.washingtonpost.com/politics/get-him-out-racial-tensions-explode-at-donald-trumps-rallies/2016/03/11/b9764884-e6ee-11e5-bc08-3e03a5b41910_story.html.

59. David Duke, the former Grand Wizard of the Knights of the Ku Klux Klan, ran for U.S. president in 1988 and governor of Louisiana in 1991. His political career and its legacy are explored in Season 4 of *Slate's* podcast series *Slow Burn*.

60. The alt-right or alternative right is a far-right, white nationalist movement that was formed online in the 2010s under the leadership of Richard Spencer. Ben Jacobs and Warren Murray, "Donald Trump under Fire after Failing to Denounce Virginia White Supremacists," *The Guardian*, August 13, 2017, https://www.theguardian.com/us-news/2017/aug/12/charlottesville-protest-trump-condemns-violence-many-sides.

61. "Trump declines to condemn teen who killed two in Kenosha," *Al Jazeera*, August 31, 2020, accessed September 1, 2020, https://www.aljazeera.com/news/2020/08/trump-plan-condemn-teen-killed-kenosha-200831201450348.html.

62. President Trump called for ESPN to fire Jemele Hill after she called him a white supremacist in 2017. Hill was suspended by ESPN and moved out of a broadcast role a year later. Jessica Kwong, "Donald Trump Has Attacked Six Black Women in Three Days: 'Nasty,' 'Loser,' 'Racist Question' and 'Stupid Question,'" *Newsweek*, November 10, 2018, https://www.newsweek.com/donald-trump-attacked-black-women-racist-question-1209872.

63. The Squad is the nickname given to four women elected to the U.S. House of Representatives in 2018. The members of the group are Alexandria Ocasio-Cortez (NY), Ilhan Omar (MN), Ayanna Pressley (MA), and Rashida Tlaib (MI).

64. KUTV/ABC7 staff, "Trump Calls DC Mayor 'Incompetent' after Senator Says She Evicted Utah Soldiers from Hotel," *WJLA*, June 5, 2020, accessed June 6, 2020, https://wjla.com/news/local/president-donald-trump-utah-senator-mike-lee-national-guard-mayor-muriel-bowser-evicted-hotel.

65. Christina Binkley, "The Creation and the Myth of Kanye West," *WSJ Magazine*, March 25, 2020, accessed March 27, 2020, https://www.wsj.com/articles/the-creation-and-the-myth-of-kanye-west-11585139341.

66. Kanye raised these same talking points about classism replacing racism in America during a 2013 interview with Zane Lowe for BBC Radio 1.

67. Will Welch and Tyler Mitchell, "Inside Kanye West's Vision for the Future," *GQ*, April 15, 2020, accessed April 15, 2020, https://www.gq.com/story/inside-kanye-west-vision-for-the-future-cover-may-2020.

68. Kanye West said that his presidency would be a win for all Americans and God-loving people. It would feel like everyone's birthday, a time for celebration.

69. *The Black Eagle*, Joe Madison, July 14, 2020.

70. "Kanye West Qualifies for General Election Ballot in Oklahoma, Election Officials Say," July 16, 2020, accessed July 15, 2020, https://www.koco.com/article/kanye-west-qualifies-for-general-election-ballot-in-oklahoma-election-officials-say/33328337.

71. Mark Osborne and Beatrice Peterson, "Kanye West Announces 1st Presidential Campaign Event in South Carolina," *ABC News*, July 19, 2020, accessed July 24, 2020, https://abcnews.go.com/Politics/kanye-west-announces-1st-campaign-event-south-carolina/story?id=71864676.

72. Elana Lyn Gross, "Kanye West Will Now Appear on The Presidential Ballot in Eight States," August 26, 2020, accessed August 27, 2020, https://www.forbes.com/sites/elanagross/2020/08/26/kanye-west-will-now-appear-on-the-presidential-ballot-in-eight-states/.

73. Zach Montellaro, "Kanye spends nearly $6 million on presidential campaign," *POLITICO*, September 5, 2020, accessed September 6, 2020, https://www.politico.com/news/2020/09/04/kanye-

west-spending-millions-on-his-presi dential-campaign-409267.

74. Ben Jacobs, "Two People Linked to Kanye West's Campaign Have Ties to GOP," *New York*, August 4, 2020, accessed August 3, 2020, https://nymag.com/intelligencer/2020/08/two-people-linked-to-kanye-wests-campaign-have-ties-to-gop.html.

75. Danny Hakim and Maggie Haberman, "Republicans Aid Kanye West's Bid to Get on the 2020 Ballot," *The New York Times*, August 5, 2020, accessed on August 5, 2020, https://www.nytimes.com/2020/08/04/us/politics/kanye-west-president-republicans.html.

76. Randall Lane, "Inside Kanye West's 'Almost Daily' Chats With Jared Kushner—And Whether The White House Exploits His Mental State," *Forbes*, August 12, 2020, accessed on August 12, 2020, https://www.forbes.com/sites/randalllane/2020/08/12/inside-kanye-wests-almost-daily-chats-with-jared-kushner-and-whether-the-white-house-exploits-his-mental-state/.

77. Maegan Vazquez, "Kushner Claims Kanye West Meeting Was a 'Policy' Talk," *CNN*, August 13, 2020, accessed August 15, 2020, https://www.cnn.com/2020/08/13/politics/jared-kushner-kanye-west-policy-discussion-colorado/index.html.

78. Maya King and Alex Isenstadt, "Kanye Flops among Black Voters," *POLITICO*, August 12, 2020, accessed August 12, 2020, https://www.politico.com/news/2020/08/12/kanye-west-flops-among-black-voters-393860.

Chapter Eight

1. Kanye West, "God Is," track 8 on *Jesus Is King*, GOOD/Def Jam, 2019.

2. During a 2019 interview with Zach O'Malley Greenburg for *Forbes*, Kanye revealed that he looked to the Bible for inspiration when designing clothes and sneakers for his fashion label. The Yeezy Ararat, Yecheil, Yeezreel, Yeshaya, and Zyon are named after biblical terms.

3. A vlogger is a person who regularly posts short videos to YouTube and online platforms.

4. Elias Leight, "How Kanye West's 'Sunday Services' Began," *Rolling Stone*, October

31, 2019, accessed August 8, 2020, https://www.rollingstone.com/music/music-features/kanye-west-jesus-is-king-jason-white-choir-905199/.

5. *Ibid.*

6. In addition to performing with Kanye West, Mariah Maxwell sang backup for Beyoncé at Kobe Bryant's memorial service on February 24, 2020.

7. Rev. Melvin Maxwell was interviewed on June 5, 2020.

8. *Ibid.*

9. King Davis and Albert Thompkins, "Mental Health Education in African American Divinity/Theology Schools," The Institute for Urban Policy Research and Analysis, March 1, 2013, https://utexas.app.box.com/s/7lh30a2croaa9ja0hm2gj9knyvr9hk4e.

10. In December 2020 choir members sued Kanye West for $1 million in unpaid wages.

11. In the King James Version of the Bible, Revelation 19:1 reads: "And after these things I heard a great voice of much people in heaven, saying, Alleluia; Salvation, and glory, and honor, and power, unto the Lord our God."

12. Swag Surfing is a dance popular at HBCUs that involves large crowds moving with their arms downward as the entire crowd moves in the same direction to the rhythm of the beat.

13. Elias Leight, "Can Kanye West Save Gospel Choirs?" *Rolling Stone*, October 25, 2019, accessed December 6, 2019, https://www.rollingstone.com/music/music-features/can-kanye-west-save-gospel-choirs-893633/.

14. Peter Guralnick, *Sweet Soul Music: Rhythm and Blues and the Southern Dream of Freedom* (New York: Harper & Row, 1986), 2.

15. In 2013 Bishop Dr. Iona E. Locke delivered a lecture on gospel music's origins to students at Lincoln Center's Jazz Academy in New York, New York.

16. E. Franklin Frazier and C. Eric Lincoln, *The Negro Church in America. The Black Church Since Frazier* (New York: Schocken Books, 1976), and Albert J. Raboteau, *Slave Religion: The "Invisible Institution" in the Antebellum South* (Oxford: Oxford University Press, 2004).

17. Sterling Stuckey, *Slave Culture: Nationalist Theory & the Foundations of*

Black America (New York: Oxford University Press, 1988), 12, 24, and 36.

18. Tilford Brooks, *America's Black Musical Heritage* (Upper Saddle River, NJ: Prentice-Hall, 1984).

19. Eugene Genovese, *Roll, Jordan, Roll: The World the Slaves Made* (New York: Vintage, 1976), 148–150.

20. Howard Thurman, *The Negro Spiritual Speaks of Life and Death* (New York: Harper and Row, 1947), 12.

21. James H. Cone, *The Spirituals and the Blues* (Maryknoll, NY: Orbis Books, 1971), 13.

22. Michael Harris, *The Rise of Gospel Blues: The Music of Thomas Andrew Dorsey in the Urban Church* (New York: Oxford University Press, 1992).

23. Cheryl J. Sanders, "Resistance, Rebellion, and Reform The Collegiate Gospel Choir Movement in the United States," *The Journal of the Interdenominational Theological Center* Volume XXVII, Numbers 1 and 2 (Fall 1999/Spring 2000): 199.

24. Dwight Webster, "Gospel Music in the United States 1960s-1980s: A Study of the Themes of 'Survival,' 'Elevation,' and 'Liberation' in a Popular Urban Contemporary Black Folk Sacred Mass Music" (PhD diss., University of California, Berkeley, 2011).

25. Briana Younger, "How Kirk Franklin Revolutionized Gospel and Made Hip-Hop A More Spiritual Place," *The FADER*, November 8, 2017, accessed November 25, 2019, https://www.thefader.com/2016/05/19/kirk-franklin-gospel-hip-hop-chance-the-rapper.

26. Alice Marie Johnson and Kim Kardashian West, *After Life: My Journey from Incarceration to Freedom* (New York: Harper, 2019).

27. Cyntoia Brown, a 16-year-old forced into prostitution, was charged with the murder of a white man in 2004. Brown claims that she fatally shot him in self-defense. She was found guilty and sentenced to life imprisonment. Brown's sentence was commuted and she was freed on August 7, 2019.

28. Rodney Reed was on death row for the 1996 rape and murder of Stacey Stites, a white woman in Bastrop, Texas. Texas has the highest execution rate nationwide. In recent years new evidence has been found, including a statement in an affidavit that

charged Stites's fiancé Jimmy Fennell with bragging about killing his fiancée for cheating on him with a black man.

29. Lyrics are taken from a poem "When They See Us," delivered by Halim Flowers at Kanye West's Howard University Homecoming Sunday Service in 2019.

30. Walter McMillian was convicted for the murder of a white woman named Ronda Morrison in 1986. McMillian was exonerated in 1993 thanks to the efforts of Bryan Stevenson.

31. Kanye West, "We Don't Care," track 2 on *The College Dropout*, Def Jam/Roc-A-Fella, 2004.

32. ShaDawn Battle, "Moments of Clarity and Sounds of Resistance: Veiled Literary Subversions and De-Colonial Dialectics in the Art of Jay Z and Kanye West" (PhD diss., University of Cincinnati, 2016).

33. Kanye West, "New Slaves," track 4 on *Yeezus*, Def Jam/Roc-A-Fella, 2013.

34. Rupert Neate, "Welcome to Jail Inc: How Private Companies Make Money off U.S. Prisons," *The Guardian*, June 16, 2016, accessed April 4, 2020, https://www.theguardian.com/us-news/2016/jun/16/us-prisons-jail-private-healthcare-companies-profit.

35. 36 Talitha L. LeFlouria, *Chained in Silence: Black Women and Convict Labor in the New South* (Chapel Hill: University of North Carolina Press, 2016).

36. Joshua K. Wright, *Empire and Black Images in Popular Culture* (Jefferson, NC: McFarland & Company, Inc., 2018), 45.

37. "Flashing Lights" was the third single on Kanye West's *Graduation* album.

38. Tommy Curry, "You Can't Stand the Nigger I See!: Kanye West's Analysis of Anti-Black Death," in *The Cultural Impact of Kanye West*, ed. Julius Bailey (New York: Palgrave Macmillan, 2014), 132.

39. The *Oxford English Dictionary* defines *theodicy* as "the vindication of divine goodness and providence, given the existence of evil."

40. Angela M. Nelson, "Kanye West's 'Jesus Walks,' Black Suffering, and the Problem of Evil," *The Journal of Hip Hop Studies* Volume 6, Issue 1 (2019): 78.

41. Conã Marshall, "I'm so Self-Conscious: Kanye West's Rhetorical Wrestling with Theodicy and Nihilism," *The Journal of Hip Hop Studies* Volume 6, Issue 1 (2019): 88–89.

42. William R. Jones, *Is God a White Racist?: a Preamble to Black Theology* (Boston: Beacon Press, 1998).

43. Carter G. Woodson is the father of black history in America. He is the founder of Negro History Week (1926), which evolved into Black History Month (1976).

44. Kanye has a bad habit of evoking Harriet Tubman's name to make points about mental slavery. She never actually spoke those words, which have become incorrectly associated with her over the years.

45. On July 1, 1839, enslaved Africans seized a Portuguese slave ship, killed the captain and the cook, and demanded that the ship sail back to Africa.

46. The Most Unruly, "Kanye West and Jay Z: Making 'Watch The Throne,'" July 19, 2019, video, 26:38, https://www.youtube.com/watch?v=YogXo-1N1GI.

47. Philip S. Foner, *W.E.B. Du Bois Speaks: Speeches and Addresses 1890–1919* (New York: Pathfinder Press, 1970), 86.

48. The car was auctioned off with the proceeds going to help victims of the 2011–2012 East African drought ravaging Kenya, Ethiopia, and Somalia.

49. Dean Baquet, "On therapy, politics, marriage, the state of rap and being a black man in Trump's America: Jay-Z & Dean Baquet," *New York Times Style Magazine*, November 29, 2017, https://www.nytimes.com/interactive/2017/11/29/t-magazine/jay-z-dean-baquet-interview.html.

50. Heidi R. Lewis, "An Examination of Kanye West's Higher Education Trilogy," in *The Cultural Impact of Kanye West*, ed. Julius Bailey (New York: Palgrave Macmillan, 2014), 68–74.

51. Historian James Anderson discusses the impact of white financing and influence on early black education in *The Education of Blacks in the South, 1860–1935* (1988).

52. Joshua K. Wright, "Views from the Mecca: A History of Student Takeovers at Howard University," *Abernathy*, May 21, 2018, accessed November 23, 2019, https://abernathymagazine.com/views-mecca-howard-university/.

53. Elliot Williams, "How Kanye West's Howard Performance Sparked Debates on Campus and Beyond," *Washingtonian*, October 16, 2019, https://www.washingtonian.com/2019/10/15/how-kanye-wests-howard-performance-sparked-debates-on-campus-and-beyond/.

54. Jason Husser, "Why Trump Is Reliant on White Evangelicals," *Brookings*, April 6, 2020, accessed August 7, 2020, https://www.brookings.edu/blog/fixgov/2020/04/06/why-trump-is-reliant-on-white-evangelicals/.

55. Wadsworth, Nancy D. "The Racial Demons That Help Explain Evangelical Support for Trump," *Vox*, April 30, 2018, accessed August 7, 2020, https://www.vox.com/the-big-idea/2018/4/30/17301282/race-evangelicals-trump-support-gerson-atlantic-sexism-segregation-south.

56. Marisa Iati, "Southern Baptist Convention's Flagship Seminary Details Its Racist, Slave-Owning Past in Stark Report," *The Washington Post*, December 13, 2018, accessed August 7, 2020, https://www.washingtonpost.com/religion/2018/12/12/southern-baptist-conventions-flagship-seminary-admits-all-four-its-founders-owned-slaves/.

57. The Moral Majority was a conservative organization, founded by Rev. Jerry Falwell in 1979, closely associated with the Republican Party and Christian Right, an informal coalition of evangelical Christians and Roman Catholics who share conservative political values.

58. John Fea, Laura Gifford, R. Marie Griffith, and Lerone A. Martin, "Evangelicalism and Politics," *The American Historian*, accessed August 24, 2020, https://www.oah.org/tah/issues/2018/november/evangelicalism-and-politics/.

59. Merritt, Jonathan, "Southern Baptists Call Off the Culture War," *The Atlantic*, September 4, 2018, accessed August 7, 2020, https://www.theatlantic.com/ideas/archive/2018/06/southern-baptists-call-off-the-culture-war/563000/.

60. Tyler Burns, "How Kanye West embeds black gospel music in white evangelical theology," *Washington Post*, October 30, 2019, accessed November 25, 2020, https://www.washingtonpost.com/religion/2019/10/30/how-kanye-wests-jesus-is-king-embeds-black-gospel-music-white-evangelical-theology/.

61. Gaby Del Valle, "Chick-fil-A's many controversies, explained," *Vox*, November 19, 2019, accessed November 26, 2020, https://www.vox.com/the-goods/2019/5/29/18644354/chick-fil-a-anti-gay-donations-homophobia-dan-cathy.

62. Michelle Boorstein, "The Stunning

Difference between white and black evangelical voters in Alabama," *The Washington Post*, December 13, 2017, accessed November 27, 2020, https://www.washingtonpost.com/news/acts-of-faith/wp/2017/12/13/there-was-an-enormous-gap-between-black-evangelical-voters-and-white-evangelical-voters-in-alabama/.

Chapter Nine

1. Von Miller, former Super Bowl MVP for the Denver Broncos, penned an op-ed for *Time* on July 9, 2020.

2. In 1991, hip-hop, especially gangsta rap, began dominating the *Billboard* charts due to the introduction of SoundScan, which used point-of-sales data from cash registers in stores. Additionally, *Billboard* began its Hot 100 chart, which tracked the songs Americans were listening to and buying the most. Before this, the charts were based on radio stations' data and record-store inventories, which were often biased towards rock songs by white artists. Derek Thompson, "1991: The Most Important Year in Pop-Music History," *The Atlantic*, May 8, 2015, accessed August 22, 2020, https://www.theatlantic.com/culture/archive/2015/05/1991-the-most-important-year-in-music/392642/.

3. "Sway in the Morning (Ft. Kanye West)—Kanye West Sway in the Morning Interview [FULL TRANSCRIPT]," Genius, November 26, 2013, https://genius.com/Sway-in-the-morning-kanye-west-sway-in-the-morning-interview-full-transcript-lyrics.

4. "'The Drum Major Instinct,' Sermon Delivered at Ebenezer Baptist Church," The Martin Luther King, Jr., Research and Education Institute, accessed January 24, 2019, https://kinginstitute.stanford.edu/king-papers/documents/drum-major-instinct-sermon-delivered-ebenezer-baptist-church.

5. J.A.M. Aiwuyor, "Kanye's Frantz Fanon Complex," *Our Legaci with J.A.M. Aiwuyor*, December 15, 2016, accessed May 29, 2020, https://ourlegaci.com/2013/12/02/kanyes-frantz-fanon-complex/.

6. Sam Smith, *The Jordan Rules* (New York: Pocket Books, 1994).

7. David Halberstam, *Playing for Keeps: Michael Jordan and the World He Made* (New York: Three Rivers Press, 2000).

8. Joshua K Wright, "Be Like Mike?: The Black Athlete's Dilemma," *Spectrum: A Journal on Black Men* 4, no. 2 (2016): 1. https://doi.org/10.2979/spectrum.4.2.01.

9. David Zirin, *What's my name, fool? Sports and resistance in the United States* (Chicago: Haymarket Books, 2005), 79.

10. *The Last Dance*, "Episode V," written and directed by Jason Hehir, aired May 3, 2020, ESPN/Netflix.

11. *Bling* refers to ostentatious jewelry and a materialistic attitude that is associated with it.

12. In September 2017, President Trump, while speaking at a rally in Alabama to support incumbent senator Luther Strange, called Colin Kaepernick and any other (black) NFL player who "disrespected our flag" a son of a bitch deserving to be fired. Kanye West unsuccessfully offered to broker a peace deal and a White House summit between his buddy Trump and Kaepernick.

13. Howard Bryant, *The Heritage: Black Athletes, A Divided America, and the Politics of Patriotism* (Boston: Beacon Press, 2018), 15; Dave Zirin, *The Kaepernick Effect: Taking a Knee, Changing the World* (New York: The New Press, 2021).

14. After receiving backlash for his "black quarterback" statement before Super Bowl 50, Cam Newton changed his tune and told *GQ* magazine that America was "beyond" racism. Zach Baron et al., "Cam Newton on Everything, From Those Versace Pants to Race in America," *GQ*, August 15, 2016, accessed May 23, 2020, https://www.gq.com/story/cam-newton-versace-pants-race-and-football.

15. Niraj Chokshi, "Sheriffs: Beyoncé Is 'Inciting Bad Behavior' and Endangering Law Enforcement," *The Washington Post*, February 18, 2016, accessed May 23, 2020, https://www.washingtonpost.com/news/post-nation/wp/2016/02/18/the-beyonce-backlash-continues-sheriff-cites-super-bowl-show-after-shooting-near-home/.

16. "Bootylicious" was the second single on the Destiny's Child album *Survivor* (2001). Beyoncé was the lead singer of Destiny's Child before launching her solo career in 2003.

17. Saturday Night Live, "The Day Beyoncé Turned Black," February 14, 2016, video, 3:24, https://www.youtube.com/watch?v=ociMBfkDG1w.

18. Joshua K. Wright, *Empire and Black Images in Popular Culture* (Jefferson, NC: McFarland & Company, Inc., Publishers, 2018), 104–105.

19. Suyin Haynes, "Beyoncé's 'Homecoming' Is a Celebration of Black History," *Time*, April 17, 2019, accessed May 24, 2020, https://time.com/5572221/beyonce-homecoming-documentary-history/.

20. BigBoyTV, "Kanye West Says, 'WAKE UP CULTURE!' | Big's Quick Clips," November 1, 2019, video, 1:52, https://www.youtube.com/watch?v=MHE7UCOriA4.

21. "Chris Rock's Opening Oscar Monologue: A Transcript," *The New York Times*, February 29, 2016, accessed August 26, 2020, https://www.nytimes.com/2016/02/29/movies/chris-rock-monologue.html.

22. Megan Lasher, "Jesse Williams BET Awards Speech: Full Transcript," *Time*, June 27, 2016, accessed May 24, 2020, https://time.com/4383516/jesse-williams-bet-speech-transcript/.

23. Kurt Streeter, "Jonathan Irons, Helped by W.N.B.A. Star Maya Moore, Freed From Prison," *The New York Times*, July 1, 2020, accessed July 2, 2020, https://www.nytimes.com/2020/07/01/sports/basketball/maya-moore-jonathan-irons-freed.html.

24. *Crip walking* is a type of dance created by the Crips, a Los Angeles, California–based street gang.

25. The phrase "take my talents to South Beach" was inspired by a 17-year-old Kobe Bryant's 1996 announcement that he was skipping college and taking his talents to the NBA.

26. J.A. Adande, "LeBron's defaced gate brings racism into focus," *The Undefeated*, June 2, 2017, accessed August 27, 2020, https://theundefeated.com/features/lebrons-defaced-gate-brings-racism-into-focus/.

27. "Hoodies Up," November 14, 2017, in *30 for 30 Podcasts*, produced by ESPN, 33:11, https://30for30podcasts.com/episodes/hoodies-up/.

28. *The Shop*, "Episode 1," directed by Robert Alexander, written by Paul Rivera, aired August 28, 2018, HBO.

29. *The Shop*, "Episode 4," directed by Robert Alexander, written by Paul Rivera, aired March 1, 2019, HBO.

30. Zamira Rahim, "Thousands around the World Protest George Floyd's Death in Global Display of Solidarity," *CNN*, June 1, 2020, accessed June 2, 2020, https://www.cnn.com/2020/06/01/world/george-floyd-global-protests-intl/index.html.

31. Donald J. Trump (@realDonald Trump), Twitter post, May 29, 2020, 12:53 AM, https://twitter.com/realDonaldTrump/status/1266231100780744704. Barbara Sprunt, "The History Behind 'When The Looting Starts, The Shooting Starts,'" *NPR*, May 29, 2020, accessed June 1, 2020, https://www.npr.org/2020/05/29/864818368/the-history-behind-when-the-looting-starts-the-shooting-starts.

32. Lara Jakes and Helene Cooper, "Trump Orders Troops to Leave D.C. as Former Military Leaders Sound Warning," *The New York Times*, June 7, 2020, accessed August 24, 2020, https://www.nytimes.com/2020/06/07/us/politics/trump-military-troops-protests.html.

33. Tom Gjelten, "Peaceful Protesters Tear-Gassed to Clear Way for Trump Church Photo-Op," *NPR*, June 2, 2020, accessed August 24, 2020, https://www.npr.org/2020/06/01/867532070/trumps-unannounced-church-visit-angers-church-officials.

34. Netflix Is A Joke, "8:46—Dave Chappelle," June 12, 2020, video, 27:20, https://www.youtube.com/watch?v=3tR6mKcBbT4.

35. Clifford "T.I." Harris and other celebrities also spoke out after Rayshard Brooks, a 27-year-old black man in Atlanta, Georgia, was fatally shot by a white police officer in a Wendy's parking lot on June 12, 2020.

36. Multiple games and practices were canceled in professional baseball, football, soccer, and tennis.

37. WNBA players were partly responsible for Senator Kelly Loeffler's (R-Ga.) failed reelection campaign. Loeffler, a co-owner of the Dream, publicly denounced her players' support of the Black Lives Matter Movement. The players endorsed her black democratic opponent Rev. Raphael Warnock and wore t-shirts to games with "Vote Warnock" across the front. Their activism is documented in the 2021 ESPN film *144*.

38. Sean Gregory, "Why Athletes Are Boycotting Sports After Jacob Blake Shooting," *Time*, August 27, 2020, accessed August 28, 2020, https://time.com/5883892/boycott-nba-mlb-wnba-jacob-blake/.

39. Coco Gauff, a 16-year-old tennis protégé, delivered an emotional speech at a rally in her hometown of Delray Beach, Florida, on May 29, 2020. She expressed her outrage over George Floyd's killing and called upon black people to vote.

40. For decades the Confederate flag has been a familiar symbol at NASCAR races, primarily in the South.

41. Thirty-nine (white) NASCAR drivers demonstrated their support for Wallace by pushing his car to the front of the field at Alabama's Talladega Superspeedway. Andrew Lawrence, "Nascar Failed to Fight Racism for 72 Years. Don't Praise Its Support of Bubba Wallace Yet," *The Guardian*, June 23, 2020, accessed June 23, 2020, https://www.theguardian.com/sport/2020/jun/23/nascar-bubba-wallace-racism-talladega-wendell-scott.

42. Ta-Nehisi Coates and (photography) LaToya Ruby Frazier, "The Life Breonna Taylor Lived, in the Words of Her Mother," *Vanity Fair*, August 24, 2020, accessed August 24, 2020, https://www.vanityfair.com/culture/2020/08/breonna-taylor.

43. Rev. Melvin Maxwell was interviewed on June 5, 2020.

44. Nick Cannon was fired by Viacom CBS and stripped of his long-running series on MTV, *Wild 'n Out*, for making anti–Semitic comments in a botched attempt to promote the black community.

45. "Donald Trump Mount Rushmore Speech Transcript at 4th of July Event," *Rev*, July 7, 2020, accessed July 11, 2020, https://www.rev.com/blog/transcripts/donald-trump-speech-transcript-at-mount-rushmore-4th-of-july-event.

46. Rob Henderson, "5 Reasons Why People Love Cancel Culture," *Psychology Today*, December 1, 2019, accessed June 1, 2020, https://www.psychologytoday.com/us/blog/after-service/201912/5-reasons-why-people-love-cancel-culture.

47. Eric Reid is a former teammate of Colin Kaepernick. He has a habit of calling other black people sellouts if they do not support Kaepernick's protest in a manner that he approves. William C. Rhoden, "Jenkins vs. Reid: United in the Struggle but Torn Apart by Tactics," *The Undefeated*, October 24, 2018, accessed May 30, 2020, https://theundefeated.com/features/jenkins-vs-reid-united-in-the-struggle-but-torn-apart-by-tactics/.

48. Seth Cohen, "In a Surprise Response to Floyd Protests, Kanye West Shows That Actions Are Louder Than Words," *Forbes*, June 5, 2020, accessed June 5, 2020, https://www.forbes.com/sites/sethcohen/2020/06/05/in-a-surprise-response-to-protests-kanye-west-shows-that-actions-are-louder-than-words/.

49. Kente cloth is an indigenous textile made of interwoven cloth strips of silk and cotton, first worn by people in Ghana.

50. Rick Bonnell, "Hornets' Michael Jordan, Jordan Brand Pledge $100 Million to Support Racial Equality," *The Charlotte Observer*, June 5, 2020, accessed August 24, 2020, https://www.charlotteobserver.com/sports/charlotte-hornets/article243313501.html.

51. Arthur Jafa, a Howard University graduate, was the cinematographer for *Daughters of the Dust* (1991). Four days before the debut of "Wash Us in the Blood," 13 museums in seven countries streamed Jafa's 2017 visual essay *Love Is the Message; The Message Is Death*, set to music from Kanye's song "Ultralight Beam." The essay was a seven-minute montage of joyous and heart-wrenching clips from the black experience in America since emancipation.

52. TikTok is a popular video-sharing service created in China, often used for posting 15-second clips of people dancing or lip-syncing.

53. Kanye West, *Donda*, GOOD Music/Def Jam, 2020; KRS-One, "Sound of da Police," track 7 on *Return of the Boom Bap*, Jive, 1993.

54. Tosten Burks, "Kanye West Lawsuit Calls His Publishing Deal 'Servitude,'" *Spin*, March 04, 2019, accessed August 1, 2019, https://www.spin.com/2019/03/kanye-west-publishing-contract-lawsuit-servitude/.

55. Kanye's protest was also reminiscent of one by his adversary, Taylor Swift, who in 2019 used her Tumblr account to speak out on failed attempts to buy her masters from her manager Scott "Scooter" Braun. Swift claimed that Braun would not even allow her to use her own songs in a documentary about her career. Ironically, Braun was Kanye's manager from 2015 until 2018.

56. Dave Chappelle (47) asked Netflix to cease streaming episodes of *Chappelle's Show* because the contract he signed with Comedy Central at 28 left him without

additional payments for future licensing deals.

57. Prince was under a six-album contract to release one new album a year for a $10 million advance per album and 25 percent of royalties.

58. Julie Baumgold, "Why Prince Became a Symbol. (Literally.)," *Esquire*, April 25, 2018, accessed August 1, 2019, https://www.esquire.com/entertainment/music/a44218/prince-1995-esquire-gentleman/.

Bibliography

Abraham, Mya. "Kanye West Gets Blasted By This Legend's Son Over Outlandish Comparison." *BET.com*, October 15, 2018. Accessed July 18, 2019. https://www.bet.com/music/2018/10/15/kanye-west-tupac-bob-marley-fela-kuti-response.html.

Abramovitch, Seth. "Blackface and Hollywood: From Al Jolson to Judy Garland to Dave Chappelle." *The Hollywood Reporter*, February 12, 2019. Accessed June 26, 2019. https://www.hollywoodreporter.com/news/blackface-hollywood-al-jolson-judy-garland-dave-chappelle-1185380.

_____. "Oscar's First Black Winner Accepted Her Honor in a Segregated 'No Blacks' Hotel in L.A." *The Hollywood Reporter*, February 22, 2016. Accessed July 15, 2019. https://www.hollywoodreporter.com/features/oscars-first-black-winner-accepted-774335.

Adande, J.A. "LeBron's defaced gate brings racism into focus." *The Undefeated*, June 2, 2017. Accessed August 27, 2020. https://theundefeated.com/features/lebrons-defaced-gate-brings-racism-into-focus/.

Aiwuyor, J.A.M. "Kanye's Frantz Fanon Complex." *Our Legaci with J.A.M. Aiwuyor*, December 15, 2016. Accessed May 29, 2020. https://ourlegaci.com/2013/12/02/kanyes-frantz-fanon-complex/.

Alexander, Sophie, and Kim Bhasin. "Kanye West Vaults from Broke to Billions with Yeezy in Demand." *Bloomberg*, April 24, 2020. Accessed December 4, 2020. https://www.bloomberg.com/news/articles/2020-04-24/kanye-west-vaults-from-broke-to-billions-with-yeezy-in-demand.

Allen, Ernest, Jr. "Du Boisian Double Consciousness: The Unsustainable Argument." *The Black Scholar* 33, no. 2 (2003): 25–43.

Alston, Trey. "The Colliding Worlds of 'Astroworld' and '808s & Heartbreak.'" REVOLT TV, August 17, 2018. Accessed December 1, 2018. https://revolt.tv/stories/2018/08/07/travis-scott-astroworld-kanye-west-808s-heartbreak-album-comparison-0700bde6c3.

Arnold, Jacob, Lorena Cupcake, Meaghan Garvey, Michaelangelo Matos, and Steve Mizek. "A Celebration of House Music." *Chicago Magazine*, August 27, 2018. Accessed December 31, 2019. https://www.chicagomag.com/Chicago-Magazine/August-2018/House-Music/.

Attiah, Karen. "Opinion: Why Did It Take Vogue 125 Years to Have a Black Photographer Shoot a Cover?" *The Washington Post*, September 4, 2018. https://www.washingtonpost.com/news/act-four/wp/2018/09/04/why-did-it-take-so-long-for-vogue-to-have-a-black-photographer-shoot-a-cover/.

Bachin, Robin F. *Building the South Side: Urban Space and Civic Culture in Chicago, 1890–1919.* Chicago: University of Chicago Press, 2004.

Bailey, Julius. *The Cultural Impact of Kanye West.* New York: Palgrave Macmillan, 2014.

Baker, Jean-Claude, and Chris Chase. *Josephine: The Hungry Heart.* New York: Cooper Square Press, 2001.

Balto, Simon. "'The Law Has a Bad Opinion of Me': Policing and Politics in Twentieth-Century Black Chicago." PhD diss., University of Wisconsin–Madison, 2015.

Baram, Marcus. "Why Gil Scott-Heron Wrote 'The Revolution Will Not Be Televised.'" *Medium,*

August 16, 2016. Accessed August 19, 2020. https://medium.com/cuepoint/why-gil-scott-heron-wrote-the-revolution-will-not-be-televised-6e298f9d4e2.

Battle, ShaDawn D. "'Moments of Clarity': Veiled Literary Subversions and De-Colonial Dialectics in the Art of Jay Z and Kanye West." PhD diss., Wittenberg University, 2016.

Baumgold, Julie. "Why Prince Became a Symbol. (Literally.)" *Esquire*, April 25, 2018. Accessed August 1, 2019. https://www.esquire.com/entertainment/music/a44218/prince-1995-esquire-gentleman/.

Bean, Travis. "'Jesus Is King' Is Kanye West's '2001: A Space Odyssey.'" *Forbes*, September 29, 2019. Accessed November 4, 2019. https://www.forbes.com/sites/travisbean/2019/09/29/jesus-is-king-is-kanye-wests-2001-a-space-odyssey/#50a2e0506ea5.

Beaumont, Mark. *Kanye West: God & Monster.* London: Overlook Omnibus, 2015.

Binkley, Christina. "The Creation and the Myth of Kanye West." *WSJ Magazine*, March 25, 2020. Accessed on March 27, 2020. https://www.wsj.com/articles/the-creation-and-the-myth-of-kanye-west-11585139341.

Blay, Zeba. "What the Conversation About Rashida Jones' Blackness Is Missing." *HuffPost*, April 24, 2020. Accessed May 2, 2020. https://www.huffpost.com/entry/rashida-jones-black-af-blackness_n_5e9f6234c5b6a486d080b5dd.

Bloom, Joshua, and Waldo E. Martin. *Black against Empire: The History and Politics of the Black Panther Party.* Oakland: University of California Press, 2016.

Bonnell, Rick. "Hornets' Michael Jordan, Jordan Brand Pledge $100 Million to Support Racial Equality." *The Charlotte Observer*, June 5, 2020. Accessed August 24, 2020. https://www.charlotteobserver.com/sports/charlotte-hornets/article243313501.html.

Boorstein, Michelle. "The Stunning Difference Between White and Black Evangelical Voters in Alabama." *The Washington Post*, December 13, 2017. Accessed November 27, 2020. https://www.washingtonpost.com/news/acts-of-faith/wp/2017/12/13/there-was-an-enormous-gap-between-black-evangelical-voters-and-white-evangelical-voters-in-alabama/.

Bourke, Joanna. *Rape: Sex, Violence, and History.* London: Virago Press, 2007.

Boyd, Todd. *Young, Black, Rich, and Famous: The Rise of the NBA, the Hip Hop Invasion, and the Transformation of American Culture.* Lincoln: University of Nebraska Press, 2008.

Bradley, Regina N. "Kanye West's Sonic [Hip-hop] Cosmopolitanism." In *The Cultural Impact of Kanye West*, edited by Julius Bailey. New York: Palgrave Macmillan, 2014.

Bradt, Steve. "'One-Drop Rule' Persists." *Harvard Gazette*, July 8, 2019. Accessed on May 1, 2020. https://news.harvard.edu/gazette/story/2010/12/one-drop-rule-persists/.

Brooks, Tilford. *America's Black Musical Heritage.* Upper Saddle River, NJ: Prentice-Hall, 1984.

Bryant, Howard. *Full Dissidence: Notes from an Uneven Playing Field.* Boston: Beacon Press, 2020.

_____. *The Heritage: Black Athletes, a Divided America, and the Politics of Patriotism.* Boston: Beacon Press, 2018.

_____. "Why Black Athletes Run from Black Identity." *The Undefeated*, February 17, 2020. Accessed May 16, 2020. https://theundefeated.com/features/why-black-athletes-run-from-black-identity/.

Burks, Tosten. "Kanye West Lawsuit Calls His Publishing Deal 'Servitude.'" *Spin*, March 4, 2019. Accessed August 1, 2019. https://www.spin.com/2019/03/kanye-west-publishing-contract-lawsuit-servitude/.

Burns, Tyler. "How Kanye West embeds black gospel music in white evangelical theology." *The Washington Post*, October 30, 2019. Accessed November 25, 2020. https://www.washingtonpost.com/religion/2019/10/30/how-kanye-wests-jesus-is-king-embeds-black-gospel-music-white-evangelical-theology/.

Bush, George W. *Decision Points.* New York: Crown Publishers, 2010.

Butler, Bethonie. "Yes, Those Kim Kardashian Photos Are About Race." *The Washington Post*, November 21, 2014. Accessed April 1, 2020. https://www.washingtonpost.com/blogs/she-the-people/wp/2014/11/21/yes-those-kim-kardashian-photos-are-about-race/.

Callahan-Bever, Noah. "The Day Kanye West Killed Gangsta Rap." *Complex*, April 20, 2020. Accessed August 23, 2020. https://www.complex.com/music/2015/09/the-day-kanye-west-killed-gangsta-rap.

Cantwell, David. "Ray Charles and Country's Color Barrier." *Rolling Stone*, February 25, 2019. Accessed March 9, 2019. https://www.rollingstone.com/music/music-country/ray-charles-modern-sounds-country-music-798729/.

Caramanica, Jon. "Behind Kanye's Mask." *The New York Times*, June 11, 2013. Accessed May 11, 2020. https://www.nytimes.com/2013/06/16/arts/music/kanye-west-talks-about-his-career-and-album-yeezus.html?pagewanted=all.

Carpio, Glenda. *Laughing Fit to Kill: Black Humor in the Fictions of Slavery*. Oxford: Oxford University Press, 2008.

Carter, Bill. "Bill Cosby Trying to Buy NBC from G.E." *The New York Times*, October 29, 1992. Accessed July 29, 2020. https://www.nytimes.com/1992/10/29/business/the-media-business-bill-cosby-trying-to-buy-nbc-from-ge.html.

Chin, Elizabeth. "Michael Jackson's Panther Dance: Double Consciousness and the Uncanny Business of Performing While Black." *Journal of Popular Music Studies* 23, no. 1 (March 8, 2011).

Chisholm, Shirley. "Remarks on Vietnam." *Congressional Record*. October 14, 1969, H300 23–25.

Chokshi, Niraj. "Sheriffs: Beyoncé Is 'Inciting Bad Behavior' and Endangering Law Enforcement." *The Washington Post*, February 18, 2016. Accessed May 23, 2020. https://www.washingtonpost.com/news/post-nation/wp/2016/02/18/the-beyonce-backlash-continues-sheriff-cites-super-bowl-show-after-shooting-near-home/.

Christian, Margena A. *Empire: The House That John H. Johnson Built (The Life & Legacy of Pioneering Publishing Magnate)*. Chicago: DocM.A.C. Write Publishing, 2018.

Ciccariello-Maher, George. "A Critique of Du Boisian Reason: Kanye West and the Fruitfulness of Double-Consciousness." *Journal of Black Studies* 39, no. 3 (2009): 371–401.

Clark-Lewis, Elizabeth. *Living In, Living Out: African American Domestics and the Great Migration*. New York: Kodansha International, 1996.

Coates, Ta-Nehisi. "I'm Not Black, I'm Kanye." *The Atlantic*, May 7, 2018. Accessed July 31, 2019. https://www.theatlantic.com/entertainment/archive/2018/05/im-not-black-im-kanye/559763/.

_____. "'This Is How We Lost to the White Man.'" *The Atlantic*, November 19, 2014. Accessed December 6, 2019. https://www.theatlantic.com/magazine/archive/2008/05/-this-is-how-we-lost-to-the-white-man/306774/.

Cohen, Aaron. *Move On Up: Chicago Soul Music and Black Cultural Power*. Chicago: The University of Chicago Press, 2019.

Cohen, Seth. "In a Surprise Response to Floyd Protests, Kanye West Shows That Actions Are Louder Than Words." *Forbes*, June 5, 2020. Accessed June 5, 2020. https://www.forbes.com/sites/sethcohen/2020/06/05/in-a-surprise-response-to-protests-kanye-west-shows-that-actions-are-louder-than-words/.

Cole, George. "Miles Davis in Paris: The Love Lives On." *The Guardian*, December 10, 2009. Accessed July 15, 2019. https://www.theguardian.com/music/2009/dec/10/miles-davis-paris-us-segregation.

Collier, Roberta. "Kanye West Locks Down His African Roots." *Music in the World*, February 10, 2012. Accessed July 30, 2020. https://blogs.longwood.edu/musicintheworld/2012/02/10/kanye-west-locks-down-his-african-roots/.

Compain, Hugo, and Josh Arnold. "Kanye West and Vanessa Beecroft: the Collaboration in 9 Moments." *Vogue Paris*, January 9, 2019. https://www.vogue.fr/vogue-hommes/fashion/diaporama/kanye-west-vanessa-beecroft-collaboration-yeezy/40931.

Cone, James H. *The Cross and the Lynching Tree*. Maryknoll, NY: Orbis Books, 2011.

_____. *The Spirituals and the Blues*. Maryknoll, NY: Orbis Books, 1971.

Coski, John M. *The Confederate Battle Flag: America's Most Embattled Emblem*. Cambridge, MA: Belknap, 2006.

Cowen, William. "Bono Explains Why Kanye's 'Black Skinhead' Is One of the Songs That 'Saved My Life.'" *Complex*, May 14, 2020. Accessed May 21, 2020. https://www.complex.com/music/2020/05/bono-explains-why-kanye-black-skinhead-songs-that-saved-my-life.

Curry, Tommy. "You Can't Stand the Nigger I See!: Kanye West's Analysis of Anti-Black

Death." In *The Cultural Impact of Kanye West*, edited by Julius Bailey. New York: Palgrave Macmillan, 2014.

Danziger, Pamela N. "Kanye West Gives Gap a Ten-Year Lifeline with Yeezy Partnership and Gets What He Always Wanted." *Forbes*, June 28, 2020. Accessed July 6, 2020. https://www.forbes.com/sites/pamdanziger/2020/06/28/kanye-west-gives-gap-a-ten-year-lifeline-with-yeezy-partnership-and-gets-what-he-always-wanted/.

Davis, Miles, and Quincy Troupe. *Miles, the Autobiography*. New York: Simon & Schuster, 2011.

DeCosta-Willis, Miriam, Reginald Martin, and Roseann Bell. *Erotique Noire—Black Erotica*. London: Doubleday, 1992.

DelReal, Jose A. "'Get 'Em Out!' Racial Tensions Explode at Donald Trump's Rallies." *The Washington Post*, March 12, 2016. Accessed January 30, 2020. https://www.washingtonpost.com/politics/get-him-out-racial-tensions-explode-at-donald-trumps-rallies/2016/03/11/b9764884-e6ee-11e5-bc08-3e03a5b41910_story.html

Del Valle, Gaby. "Chick-fil-A's many controversies, explained." *Vox*, November 19, 2019. Accessed November 26, 2020. https://www.vox.com/the-goods/2019/5/29/18644354/chick-fil-a-anti-gay-donations-homophobia-dan-cathy.

Dennis, David, Jr. "'Fate of the Furious' Dwayne Johnson Has Been Wrestling for Years with the Politics of Race, Pro Wrestling and Hollywood." *The Undefeated*, April 14, 2017. Accessed August 16, 2020. https://theundefeated.com/features/the-rock-wwe-dwayne-johnson/.

Dickinson, Tim. "Charles Barkley: 'I Was a Republican Until They Lost Their Minds.'" *Rolling Stone*, June 25, 2018. Accessed March 7, 2020. https://www.rollingstone.com/culture/culture-news/charles-barkley-i-was-a-republican-until-they-lost-their-minds-191374/.

Drake, David. "Kanye West on the Day He Met Michael Jackson." *Complex*, June 1, 2018. Accessed July 23, 2019. https://www.complex.com/music/2013/11/kanye-west-michael-jackson-juan-epstein.

Drake, St. Clair, and Horace R. Cayton. *Black Metropolis: A Study of Negro Life in a Northern City*. Chicago: University of Chicago Press, 1993.

Dreher, Kwakiutl Lynn. "Don't Should On Me: The Black Actress, 1940–1970: Lena Horne, Diahann Carroll, and Eartha Kitt." PhD diss., University of California Riverside, 2001.

Du Bois, W.E.B. "Strivings of the Negro People." *The Atlantic*, July 16, 2018. Accessed June 30, 2019. https://www.theatlantic.com/magazine/archive/1897/08/strivings-of-the-negro-people/305446/.

_____. *The Souls of Black Folk*. Chicago: A. C. McClurg & Co., 1903.

Du Bois, W.E.B., and David Levering Lewis. *Black Reconstruction in America*. New York: Free Press, 1998.

Dunne, Dominick. "How O.J. Simpson's Dream Team Played the 'Race Card' and Won." *Vanity Fair*, November 1995.

Durrow, Heidi. *The Girl Who Fell from the Sky*. Chapel Hill, NC: Algonquin, 2011.

Dyson, Michael Eric. *Come Hell or High Water: Hurricane Katrina and the Color of Disaster*. New York: Basic Civitas, 2007.

_____. *Is Bill Cosby Right?: Or Has the Black Middle Class Lost Its Mind?* New York: Basic Civitas, 2006.

Edsall, Thomas and Mary. *Chain Reaction: The Impact of Race, Rights, and Taxes on American Politics*. New York: Norton & Company, 1991.

Elder, Sajae. "Kanye West Says He Is the 'Greatest Artist That God Has Ever Created' at Joel Osteen Service." *The FADER*, November 18, 2019. Accessed December 25, 2019. https://www.thefader.com/2019/11/17/kanye-west-says-he-is-the-greatest-artist-that-god-has-ever-created-at-joel-osteen-service.

Fanon, Frantz. *Black Skin, White Masks*. New York: Grove Press, 1967.

Foner, Eric. *Reconstruction: America's Unfinished Revolution, 1863–1877*. New York: Harper Perennial Modern Classics, 2014.

_____. *W.E.B. DuBois Speaks: Speeches and Addresses 1890–1919*. New York: Pathfinder Press, 1970.

Francolini, Janine. "5 Reasons Mental Health Is a Hidden Civil Rights Issue." *HuffPost*, December 7, 2017. Accessed June 1, 2020. www.huffpost.com/entry/5-reasons-why-ment

alheal_b_8992028?guccounter=1&guce_referrer=aHR0cHM6Ly93d3cuYmluZy5jb20v&g
uce_referrer_sig=AQAAAAOmuAHj3iMpDTJ4OIgxnjJ-wn35wCg2REYSBi5G6zWKzvK
QpdIPMLxqjXGNUusdL-LsYSJg0SeeSEAJ5EZIY_ueRxq3JgBe-cqpGeWIdQOUas.
Frazier, E. Franklin, and C. Eric Lincoln. *The Negro Church in America. The Black Church Since Frazier.* New York: Schocken Books, 1976.
Ganta, Liberia. "Memory of Michael Jackson Uplifts Liberia." *The Washington Times,* July 2, 2009. Accessed July 30, 2019. https://www.washingtontimes.com/news/2009/jul/02/king-of-pop-uplifts-liberia/.
Garbus, Liz, dir. *What Happened, Miss Simone?* RadicalMedia, 2015. https://www.netflix.com/title/70308063.
Gellman, Erik S. *Death Blow to Jim Crow: The National Negro Congress and the Rise of Militant Civil Rights.* Chapel Hill: University of North Carolina Press, 2014.
Gemmill, Allie. "Kanye West Didn't Even Know Kim Kardashian's Name When They Met." *Teen Vogue,* September 25, 2017. Accessed November 3, 2019. https://www.teenvogue.com/story/kim-kardashian-kanye-west-relationship-beginning.
Genovese, Eugene. *Roll, Jordan, Roll: The World the Slaves Made.* New York: Vintage, 1976.
Givhan, Robin. "Kamala Harris Grew Up in a Mostly White World. Then She Went to a Black University in a Black City." *The Washington Post,* September 16, 2019. Accessed November 24, 2019. https://www.washingtonpost.com/politics/2019/09/16/kamala-harris-grew-up-mostly-white-world-then-she-went-black-university-black-city/?arc404=true.
Gjelten, Tom. "Peaceful Protesters Tear-Gassed to Clear Way for Trump Church Photo-Op." *NPR,* June 2, 2020. Accessed August 24, 2020. https://www.npr.org/2020/06/01/867532070/trumps-unannounced-church-visit-angers-church-officials.
Glanton, Dahleen. "The Myth of the 'Welfare Queen' Endures, and Children Pay the Price." *Chicago Tribune,* May 20, 2019. Accessed July 17, 2019. https://www.chicagotribune.com/columns/dahleen-glanton/ct-met-dahleen-glanton-welfare-queen-20180516-story.html.
Good, Chris. "Obama Calls Kanye 'Jackass.'" *The Atlantic,* September 15, 2009. Accessed July 9, 2019. https://www.theatlantic.com/politics/archive/2009/09/obama-calls-kanye-jackass/26563/.
Granger, Betty. "The Harry Belafontes at Home." *The Amsterdam- News,* April 27, 1957.
Greenburg, Zack O'Malley. "Kanye West Is Now Officially a Billionaire (And He Really Wants the World to Know)." *Forbes,* April 25, 2020. Accessed April 25, 2020. https://www.forbes.com/sites/zackomalleygreenburg/2020/04/24/kanye-west-is-now-officially-a-billionaireand-he-really-wants-the-world-to-know/#ec276577b9ec.
Gregory, Sean. "Why Athletes Are Boycotting Sports After Jacob Blake Shooting." *Time,* August 27, 2020. Accessed August 28, 2020. https://time.com/5883892/boycott-nba-mlb-wnba-jacob-blake/.
Gross, Elana Lyn. "Kanye West Will Now Appear on the Presidential Ballot in Eight States." *Forbes,* August 26, 2020. Accessed August 27, 2020. https://www.forbes.com/sites/elanagross/2020/08/26/kanye-west-will-now-appear-on-the-presidential-ballot-in-eight-states/.
Guralnick, Peter. *Dream Boogie: The Triumph of Sam Cooke.* Boston: Back Bay Books, 2006.
_____. *Sweet Soul Music: Rhythm and Blues and the Southern Dream of Freedom.* New York: Harper & Row, 1986.
Haas, Jeffrey. *The Assassination of Fred Hampton: How the FBI and the Chicago Police Murdered a Black Panther.* Chicago: Lawrence Hill Books/Chicago Review Press, 2010.
Hakim, Danny, and Maggie Haberman. "Republicans Aid Kanye West's Bid to Get on the 2020 Ballot." *The New York Times,* August 5, 2020. Accessed August 5, 2020. https://www.nytimes.com/2020/08/04/us/politics/kanye-west-president-republicans.html.
Halberstam, David. *Playing for Keeps: Michael Jordan and the World He Made.* New York: Three Rivers Press, 2000.
Harris, Michael. *The Rise of Gospel Blues: The Music of Thomas Andrew Dorsey in the Urban Church.* New York: Oxford University Press, 1992.
Haygood, Wil. "The Hug." *The Washington Post,* September 14, 2003. Accessed April 22, 2019. https://www.washingtonpost.com/archive/lifestyle/magazine/2003/09/14/the-hug/0a2746a1-88fa-4738-9d96-4ee0e84c1118/

_____. *In Black and White: The Life of Sammy Davis, Jr.* New York: Alfred A. Knopf, 2003.

Haynes, Suyin. "Beyoncé's 'Homecoming' Is a Celebration of Black History." *Time*, April 17, 2019. Accessed May 24, 2020. https://time.com/5572221/beyonce-homecoming-documentary-history/.

Hayward, Mark. "Harry Belafonte, Race, and the Politics of Success." PhD diss., McGill University, 2000.

Henderson, Rob. "5 Reasons Why People Love Cancel Culture." *Psychology Today*, December 1, 2019. Accessed June 1, 2020. https://www.psychologytoday.com/us/blog/after-service/201912/5-reasons-why-people-love-cancel-culture.

Hernandez, Alondra. "Donda West Died of Heart Disease After Surgery." *People*, January 10, 2008. https://people.com/celebrity/donda-west-died-of-heart-disease-after-surgery/.

Hinton, Elizabeth. *From the War on Poverty to the War on Crime: The Making of Mass Incarceration in America.* Cambridge, MA: Harvard University Press, 2016.

Hirsch, Arnold. *Making the Second Ghetto: Race and Housing in Chicago, 1940–1960.* Chicago: University of Chicago Press, 1988.

Hochtritt, James Gribble, Jr. "An Absence of Malice: The Oklahoma City Sit-In Movement 1958–1964." Thesis, University of Oklahoma, 1994.

Hodges, Martha. *White Women, Black Men: Illicit Sex in the Nineteenth-Century South.* New Haven: Yale University Press, 1997.

Husser, Jason. "Why Trump Is Reliant on White Evangelicals." *Brookings*, April 6, 2020. Accessed August 7, 2020. https://www.brookings.edu/blog/fixgov/2020/04/06/why-trump-is-reliant-on-white-evangelicals/.

Hyman, Dan. "What the Controversy Over Spike Lee's 'Chi-Raq' Is Really About." *GQ*, March 10, 2017. Accessed July 17, 2019. https://www.gq.com/story/chi-raq-controversy-spike-lee.

i-D Staff, "Pharrell Williams: 'Faith Is About What You Feel.'" *i-D Magazine*, June 10, 2020. Accessed June 11, 2020. https://i-d.vice.com/en_uk/article/m7jexy/pharrell-williams-interview-i-d-magazine.

Iati, Marisa. "Southern Baptist Convention's Flagship Seminary Details Its Racist, Slave-Owning Past in Stark Report." *The Washington Post*, December 13, 2018. Accessed August 7, 2020. https://www.washingtonpost.com/religion/2018/12/12/southern-baptist-conventions-flagship-seminary-admits-all-four-its-founders-owned-slaves/.

Izadi, Elahe. "Kanye West's Meeting with Donald Trump Was a Long Time Coming." *The Washington Post*, December 13, 2016. Accessed October 16, 2019. https://www.washingtonpost.com/news/arts-and-entertainment/wp/2016/12/13/kanye-west-shows-up-at-trump-tower-to-discuss-life-with-donald-trump/.

Jackson, Lauren Michele. *White Negroes: When Cornrows Were in Vogue ... and Other Thoughts on Cultural Appropriation.* Boston: Beacon Press, 2019.

Jackson, Sarah J. *Black Celebrity, Racial Politics, and the Press: Framing Dissent.* New York: Routledge, 2014.

Jacobs, Ben. "Two People Linked to Kanye West's Campaign Have Ties to GOP." *New York*, August 3, 2020. Accessed August 3, 2020. https://nymag.com/intelligencer/2020/08/two-people-linked-to-kanye-wests-campaign-have-ties-to-gop.html.

Jacobs, Harriet. *Incidents in the Life of a Slave Girl.* Mineola, NY: Dover Publications, 2001.

Jakes, Lara, and Helene Cooper. "Trump Orders Troops to Leave D.C. as Former Military Leaders Sound Warning." *The New York Times*, June 7, 2020. Accessed August 24, 2020. https://www.nytimes.com/2020/06/07/us/politics/trump-military-troops-protests.html.

Jaynes, Gerald D., and Robin M. Williams, Jr., eds. *A Common Destiny: Blacks and American Society.* Washington, D.C.: National Academy Press, 1989.

Johnson, Alice Marie, and Kim Kardashian West. *After Life: My Journey from Incarceration to Freedom.* New York: Harper, 2019.

Jones, William R. *Is God a White Racist?: A Preamble to Black Theology.* Boston: Beacon Press, 1998.

Jordan, Winthrop. *White Over Black: American Attitudes Toward the Negro, 1550–1812.* Chapel Hill: University of North Carolina Press, 1968.

Judge, Monique. "After Skinnin' and Grinnin' for Trump, Steve Harvey Says He Should Have Listened to His Wife and Skipped Meeting." *The Grapevine*, September 6, 2017.

Accessed December 6, 2019. https://thegrapevine.theroot.com/after-skinnin-and-grinnin-for-trump-steve-harvey-says-1800665192.

Keyes, Allison. "The East St. Louis Race Riot Left Dozens Dead, Devastating a Community on the Rise." *Smithsonian,* June 30, 2017. Accessed July 15, 2019. https://www.smithsonianmag.com/smithsonian-institution/east-st-louis-race-riot-left-dozens-dead-devastating-community-on-the-rise-180963885/.

King, Maya, and Alex Isenstadt. "Kanye Flops Among Black Voters." *POLITICO,* August 12, 2020. Accessed August 12, 2020. https://www.politico.com/news/2020/08/12/kanye-west-flops-among-black-voters-393860.

Kram, Mark. *Ghosts of Manila: The Fateful Blood Feud Between Muhammad Ali and Joe Frazier.* New York: HarperCollins Publishers, 2001.

Kreps, Daniel. "Kelly Clarkson, Pink, Katy Perry Lash Out at Kanye for Outburst." *Rolling Stone,* June 25, 2018. Accessed December 16, 2019. www.rollingstone.com/music/music-news/kelly-clarkson-pink-katy-perry-lash-out-at-kanye-for-outburst-79211/.

Lane, Randall. "Inside Kanye West's 'Almost Daily' Chats with Jared Kushner—And Whether the White House Exploits His Mental State." *Forbes,* August 12, 2020. Accessed August 12, 2020. https://www.forbes.com/sites/randalllane/2020/08/12/inside-kanye-wests-almost-daily-chats-with-jared-kushner-and-whether-the-white-house-exploits-his-mental-state/.

Lasher, Megan. "Jesse Williams BET Awards Speech: Full Transcript." *Time,* June 27, 2016. Accessed May 24, 2020. https://time.com/4383516/jesse-williams-bet-speech-transcript/.

Latson, Jennifer. "The Biracial Advantage." *Psychology Today,* May 7, 2019. Accessed May 8, 2020. https://www.psychologytoday.com/us/articles/201905/the-biracial-advantage.

Lawrence, Andrew. "Nascar Failed to Fight Racism for 72 Years. Don't Praise Its Support of Bubba Wallace Yet." *The Guardian,* June 23, 2020. Accessed June 23, 2020. https://www.theguardian.com/sport/2020/jun/23/nascar-bubba-wallace-racism-talladega-wendell-scott.

Lawson, Richard. "Kanye West's Harvard Lecture." *The Atlantic,* November 19, 2013. https://www.theatlantic.com/culture/archive/2013/11/kanye-wests-harvard-lecture/355227/.

LeFlouria, Talitha L. *Chained in Silence: Black Women and Convict Labor in the New South.* Chapel Hill: University of North Carolina Press, 2016.

Leight, Elias. "Can Kanye West Save Gospel Choirs?" *Rolling Stone,* October 25, 2019. Accessed December 6, 2019. https://www.rollingstone.com/music/music-features/can-kanye-west-save-gospel-choirs-893633/.

_____. "How Kanye West's 'Sunday Services' Began." *Rolling Stone,* October 31, 2019. Accessed August 8, 2020. https://www.rollingstone.com/music/music-features/kanye-west-jesus-is-king-jason-white-choir-905199/.

Lewis, Brittany. "CODE SWITCH! Kanye West Talks About Using His 'White' Voice (VIDEO)." *Global Grind,* October 22, 2013. https://globalgrind.com/3879434/kanye-west-using-white-voice-video-radio-interview/.

Lewis, Carolyn. "Mrs. Johnson Chides Eartha Kitt: 'Shrill Voice' Jars First Lady." *The Washington Post,* January 20, 1968.

Lewis, David Levering. *W.E.B. Du Bois, 1868–1919: Biography of a Race.* New York: Henry Holt and Company, 1994.

Lewis, Heidi R. "An Examination of Kanye West's Higher Education Trilogy." In *The Cultural Impact of Kanye West,* edited by Julius Bailey. New York: Palgrave Macmillan, 2014.

Liu, Eric. "Asian or American?" *Slate,* November 15, 1996. Accessed May 18, 2020. https://slate.com/news-and-politics/1996/11/asian-or-american.html.

Lizza, Ryan. "Three Problems with the Melania Trump Plagiarism Admission." *The New Yorker,* July 10, 2017. Accessed August 13, 2020. https://www.newyorker.com/news/news-desk/three-problems-with-the-melania-trump-plagiarism-admission.

Lo, Valeri M. "'We Can't Even Play Ourselves': Mixed-Raced Actresses in the Early Twenty-First Century." PhD diss., University of Hawaii at Manoa, 2017.

Lott, Eric. *Love & Theft: Blackface Minstrelsy and the American Working Class.* Oxford: Oxford University Press, 2013.

Lovett, Samuel. "Trump Shares Candace Owens Interview Saying 'George Floyd Was Not a

Good Person."' *Yahoo! News*, June 6, 2020. Accessed June 7, 2020. https://www.yahoo.com/news/trump-shares-candace-owens-interview-131400391.html.

Mailer, Norman. *The White Negro: Superficial Reflections on the Hipster.* San Francisco: City Lights, 1957.

Mangcu, Xolela Mcpherson. "Harold Washington and the Cultural Transformation of Local Government in Chicago, 1983–1987." PhD diss., Cornell University, 1997.

Mans, Jasmine. "Footnotes for Kanye." *The Journal of Hip Hop Studies* Volume 6, Issue 1 (2019).

Marcus, Stephanie. "North West Verbally Attacked by Racist Woman on Plane." *HuffPost*, June 30, 2014. Accessed April 29, 2020. https://www.huffpost.com/entry/north-west-racist-woman-plane_n_5543327.

Marshall, Conā. "I'm So Self-Conscious: Kanye West's Rhetorical Wrestling with Theodicy and Nihilism." *The Journal of Hip Hop Studies* Volume 6, Issue 1 (2019).

Martel, Ned. "On a Telethon Weekend, Restraint from an Unlikely Source." *The New York Times*, September 12, 2005.

McAdam, Doug. "Putting Donald Trump in Historical Perspective: Racial Politics and Social Movements from the 1960s to Today." In *The Resistance: The Dawn of the Anti-Trump Opposition Movement*, edited by Davis S. Meyer and Jacob S. Hacker. New York: Oxford University Press, 2018.

McCune, Jeffrey. "'Ultralight Beam': The Gospel According to Kanye West." *The Journal of Hip Hop Studies* Volume 6, Issue 1 (2019).

McLaughlin, Eliott C. "Kanye West Co-opts Confederate Flag: Publicity Stunt?" *CNN*, November 6, 2013. Accessed July 8, 2019. https://www.cnn.com/2013/11/04/us/kanye-west-confederate-flag/index.html.

McNelley, Gina I. "Black Republicans' Beliefs and Its Effects on Their Identity and Relationships." PhD diss., United States International University, 1998.

Mead, Chris. "Triumphs and Trials." *Sports Illustrated*, September 23, 1985. Accessed June 23, 2020. https://web.archive.org/web/20081005055351/http://vault.sportsillustrated.cnn.com/vault/article/magazine/MAG1119926/index.htm.

Merritt, Jonathan. "Southern Baptists Call Off the Culture War." *The Atlantic*, September 4, 2018. Accessed August 7, 2020. https://www.theatlantic.com/ideas/archive/2018/06/southern-baptists-call-off-the-culture-war/563000/.

Messer, Chris. "The Tulsa Race Riot of 1921: Determining Its Causes and Framing." Thesis, Oklahoma State University, 2005.

Michaels, Sean. "Kanye West Criticizes Hip-Hop Peers for Being Afraid of Gay People." *The Guardian*, February 10, 2009. https://www.theguardian.com/music/2009/feb/10/kanye-west-hip-hop-fashion.

Mills, Nicolaus. "Whites Said Marian Anderson Couldn't Sing in Their Hall. So She Sang at the Lincoln Memorial in a Concert for the Ages." *The Daily Beast*, April 21, 2019. Accessed June 27, 2019. https://www.thedailybeast.com/whites-said-marian-anderson-couldnt-sing-in-their-hall-so-she-sang-at-the-lincoln-memorial-in-a-concert-for-the-ages?ref=scroll.

Miss2Bees. "Kanye West Asks Donald Trump to Pardon Larry Hoover." *The Source*, October 12, 2018. Accessed February 9, 2019. https://thesource.com/2018/10/12/kanye-west-larry-hoover/.

Mock, Janet. "Kim Kardashian West & North West." *Interview*, November 25, 2019. Accessed April 29, 2020. https://www.interviewmagazine.com/culture/kim-kardashian-west.

Molanphy, Chris. "The Controversy Over 'Old Town Road' Reveals Problems Beyond Just Race." *Slate*, April 12, 2019. Accessed July 7, 2019. https://slate.com/culture/2019/04/lil-nas-x-old-town-road-billboard-country-charts-hot-100.html.

Montas, Fred, Jr. "Understanding Du Bois." *Dissent* 46, no. 1 (1999).

Montellaro, Zach. "Kanye spends nearly $6 million on presidential campaign." *POLITICO*, September 4, 2020. Accessed September 6, 2020. https://www.politico.com/news/2020/09/04/kanye-west-spending-millions-on-his-presidential-campaign-409267.

Morris, Wesley. "Why Is Everyone Always Stealing Black Music?" *The New York Times*, August 14, 2019. Accessed August 9, 2020. https://www.nytimes.com/interactive/2019/08/14/magazine/music-black-culture-appropriation.html.

Morrison, Toni. *The Bluest Eye*. New York: Holt, 1970.

Neal, Mark Anthony. "Now I Ain't Saying He's a Crate Digger: Kanye West, 'Community Theaters' and the Soul Archive." In *The Cultural Impact of Kanye West*, edited by Julius Bailey. New York: Palgrave Macmillan, 2014.

Neate, Rupert. "Welcome to Jail Inc: How Private Companies Make Money Off US Prisons." *The Guardian*, June 16, 2016. Accessed April 4, 2020. https://www.theguardian.com/us-news/2016/jun/16/us-prisons-jail-private-healthcare-companies-profit.

Nelson, Angela M. "Kanye West's 'Jesus Walks,' Black Suffering, and the Problem of Evil." *The Journal of Hip Hop Studies* Volume 6, Issue 1 (2019).

Nodjimbadem, Katie. "The Long, Painful History of Police Brutality in the U.S." *Smithsonian*, July 27, 2017. Accessed December 6, 2020. https://www.smithsonianmag.com/smithsonian-institution/long-painful-history-police-brutality-in-the-us-180964098/#8eKR9BKdZPjy18h2.99.

Obama, Barack. *Dreams from My Father: A Story of Race and Inheritance*. New York: Broadway Books, 2004.

Obama, Michelle. *Becoming*. New York: Crown Publishing Group, 2018.

Obaro, Tomi. "Lizzo Can Be Black and Corny at the Same Time." *BuzzFeed News*, September 8, 2019. Accessed February 15, 2020. https://www.buzzfeednews.com/article/tomiobaro/lizzo-corny-truth-hurts-azealia-banks-white-gaze.

O'Neil, Luke. "Can Kanye West Solve America's Housing Crisis? Maybe…" *The Guardian*, August 5, 2019. Accessed August 7, 2019. https://www.theguardian.com/music/2019/aug/05/kanye-west-housing-development-california.

Osborne, Mark, and Beatrice Peterson. "Kanye West Announces 1st Presidential Campaign Event in South Carolina." *ABC News*, July 19, 2020. Accessed July 24, 2020. https://abcnews.go.com/Politics/kanye-west-announces-1st-campaign-event-south-carolina/story?id=71864676.

Parr, Patrick, Sam Sutton, Carly Sitrin, Bill Mahoney, Josh Gerstein, and Madina Touré. "'We Were Madly, Madly in Love': The Untold Story of MLK's White Girlfriend." *POLITICO*, April 1, 2018. Accessed December 18, 2019. https://www.politico.com/magazine/story/2018/04/01/martin-luther-king-junior-assassination-anniversary-interracial-relationship-217769.

Petridis, Alexis. "Pop, Prince and Black Panthers: the Glorious Life of Chaka Khan," *The Guardian*, February 15, 2019. Accessed August 19, 2020. https://www.theguardian.com/music/2019/feb/15/pop-prince-and-black-panthers-the-glorious-life-of-chaka-khan.

Powers, Ann. "Live: Kanye West's Glow in the Dark Tour." *Los Angeles Times*, April 18, 2008. Accessed March 30, 2020. https://www.latimes.com/entertainment/la-et-kanye18apr18-story.html.

Pruter, Robert. *Chicago Soul*. Urbana: University of Illinois Press, 2007.

Puckett, Lily. "Snoop Dogg on Kanye West: 'There's No Black Women in His Life.'" *The FADER*, May 18, 2018. https://www.thefader.com/2018/05/18/snoop-dogg-kanye-west-breakfast-club-interview.

Rabin, Nathan, Yohana Desta, and Paul Chi. "The Monkey and the Metaphor: What Every King Kong Movie Is Really About." *Vanity Fair*, March 13, 2017. Accessed April 17, 2020. https://www.vanityfair.com/hollywood/2017/03/king-kong-skull-island-movies-metaphors.

Raboteau, Albert J. *Slave Religion: The "Invisible Institution" in the Antebellum South*. Oxford: Oxford University Press, 2004.

Rahim, Zamira. "Thousands Around the World Protest George Floyd's Death in Global Display of Solidarity." *CNN*, June 1, 2020. Accessed June 2, 2020. https://www.cnn.com/2020/06/01/world/george-floyd-global-protests-intl/index.html.

Ramirez, Erika. "Kanye West's 'The College Dropout': An Oral History." *Billboard*, February 8, 2014. Accessed June 1, 2020. https://www.billboard.com/articles/columns/the-juice/5893976/kanye-wests-the-college-dropout-an-oral-history.

Raymer, Miles. "Who Owns Trap?" *Chicago Reader*, December 27, 2019. Accessed January 3, 2020. https://www.chicagoreader.com/chicago/trap-rap-edm-flosstradamus-uz-jeffrees-lex-luger/Content?oid=7975249.

Reed, Adolph, Jr. *W.E.B. Du Bois and American Political Thought: Fabianism and the Color Line.* Oxford: Oxford University Press, 1999.

Repko, Melissa. "Gap Stock Soars After Kanye West Touts Collaboration with His Fashion Brand Yeezy." *CNBC*, June 26, 2020. Accessed June 26, 2020. https://www.cnbc.com/2020/06/26/gap-stock-soars-after-kanye-west-teases-possible-collaboration-with-gap.html.

Rhodan, Maya. "Azealia Banks, Rihanna Feud Over Donald Trump." *Time*, January 30, 2017. Accessed December 6, 2019. https://time.com/4653253/rihanna-azealia-banks-donald-trump/.

Rhoden, William C. "Jenkins vs. Reid: United in the Struggle but Torn Apart by Tactics." *The Undefeated*, October 24, 2018. Accessed May 30, 2020. https://theundefeated.com/features/jenkins-vs-reid-united-in-the-struggle-but-torn-apart-by-tactics/.

Ribera, Amaya. "*Keeping Up with the Kardashians: Season 1.*" *Popmatters*, October 15, 2008. Accessed December 11, 2019. https://www.popmatters.com/keeping-up-with-the-kardashians-season-1-2496113502.html.

Rigueur, Leah Wright. "The Forgotten History of Black Republicans." *The Daily Beast*, February 12, 2015. Accessed September 13, 2019. https://www.thedailybeast.com/the-forgotten-history-of-black-republicans.

Roberto, Melissa. "Kim Kardashian and Kanye West Have Been Considering Divorce for Weeks: Reports." *Fox News*, July 23, 2020. Accessed August 7, 2020. https://www.foxnews.com/entertainment/kim-kardashian-kanye-west-considering-divorce-weeks-reports.

Roberts, Randy, and John Matthew Smith. *Blood Brothers: The Fatal Friendship Between Muhammad Ali and Malcolm X.* New York: Basic Books, 2016.

Rosenwald, Brian. *Talk Radio's America: How an Industry Took Over a Political Party That Took Over the United States.* Cambridge, MA: Harvard University Press, 2019.

Rozsa, Matthew. "What the Debate Over Kim Kardashian Says About the Changing Face of Race in America." *The Daily Dot*, February 4, 2018. Accessed April 22, 2020. https://www.dailydot.com/via/kim-kardashian-race-changing-america/.

Russell, Bill. *The Second Wind: The Memoirs of an Opinionated Man.* New York: Ballantine Books, 1980.

Ryan, Patrick. "Is Kanye West the greatest artist of the 21st century?" *USA Today*, February 9, 2016. Accessed July 26, 2016. http://www.usatoday.com/story/life/music/2016/02/09/kanye-west-new-album/79814890/#.

Sanders, Cheryl J. "Resistance, Rebellion, and Reform: The Collegiate Gospel Choir Movement in the United States." *The Journal of the Interdenominational Theological Center* Volume XXVII, Numbers 1 and 2 (Fall 1999/Spring 2000).

Scott, Jill. "Commentary: Jill Scott Talks Interracial Dating." *Essence*, March 26, 2010. Accessed April 19, 2020. https://www.essence.com/news/commentary-jill-scott-talks-interracial/.

Scott, Nate. "Kobe Bryant Fires Back at Jim Brown Over African-American 'Culture' Comments." *USA Today*, December 12, 2013. https://ftw.usatoday.com/2013/12/kobe-bryant-jim-brown-arsenio-hall.

Sherman, Gabriel. *The Loudest Voice in the Room: How the Brilliant, Bombastic Roger Ailes Built Fox News—and Divided a Country.* New York: Random House, 2014.

Siegel, Alan. "'Saturday Night Live' Was Dying. Then Eddie Murphy Showed Up." *The Ringer*, December 20, 2019. https://www.theringer.com/tv/2019/12/20/21029815/eddie-murphy-saturday-night-live-first-season-mister-robinson.

Sink, Justin. "Kanye West to Talk Prison Reform, Gang Violence at White House." *Bloomberg*, October 9, 2018. Accessed December 31, 2019. https://www.bloomberg.com/news/articles/2018-10-09/kanye-west-to-talk-prison-reform-gang-violence-at-white-house.

Smith, Sam. *The Jordan Rules.* New York: Pocket Books, 1994.

Smith, Suzanne E. *Dancing in the Street: Motown and the Cultural Politics of Detroit.* Cambridge, MA: Harvard University Press, 2003.

Smothers, Hannah. "Kim Chose the Butt Model on 'The Life of Pablo' Cover." *Cosmopolitan*, October 6, 2017. https://www.cosmopolitan.com/entertainment/news/a53644/kim-chose-the-butt-model-on-the-life-of-pablo-cover/.

Stone, Natalie. "Inside Kanye West's Breakdown: Rapper Feels Like 'He's Under Spiritual

Attack,' Source Says." *People*, November 22, 2016. Accessed January 18, 2017. http://people. com/celebrity/kanye-west-feels-like-hes-under-spiritual-attack/.

Strauss, Ben. "Jason Whitlock to Young Black Conservatives: 'I'm Here to Tell You How' to Be Leaders." *The Washington Post*, October 30, 2018. Accessed December 6, 2019. https:// www.washingtonpost.com/sports/2018/10/30/jason-whitlock-young-black-conservatives-im-here-tell-you-how-be-leaders/.

Streeter, Kurt. "Jonathan Irons, Helped by W.N.B.A. Star Maya Moore, Freed from Prison." *The New York Times*, July 1, 2020. Accessed July 2, 2020. https://www.nytimes. com/2020/07/01/sports/basketball/maya-moore-jonathan-irons-freed.html.

Stuckey, Sterling. *Slave Culture: Nationalist Theory and the Foundations of Black America*. New York: Oxford University Press, 1988.

Styles, Ruth. "Prince Harry's New Girlfriend Meghan Markle's LA Home." *Daily Mail*, January 9, 2020. Accessed April 29, 2020. https://www.dailymail.co.uk/news/article-3896180/ Prince-Harry-s-girlfriend-actress-Meghan-Markles.html.

Taylor, Yuval, and Jake Austen. *Darkest America: Black Minstrelsy from Slavery to Hip-Hop*. New York: W.W. Norton & Company, 2012.

Tenenbaum, Sara. "I Know I Am Someone: Michael Jackson, *Thriller*, and American Identity." Master's thesis, Brandeis University, 2008.

Thomas, Clarence. "No Room at the Inn: The Loneliness of the Black Conservative." Reprinted in *Policy Review* 58 (Fall 1991): 72–78.

Thompson, Arienne. "Urkel Much? 4 Reasons Why Kanye Sounds Like That." *USA Today*, August 31, 2015. https://www.usatoday.com/story/life/people/2015/08/30/real-kanye-please-stand-up/71435336/.

Thompson, Derek. "1991: The Most Important Year in Pop-Music History." *The Atlantic*, May 8, 2015. Accessed August 22, 2020. https://www.theatlantic.com/culture/ archive/2015/05/1991-the-most-important-year-in-music/392642/.

Thurman, Howard. *The Luminous Darkness: A Personal Interpretation of the Anatomy of Segregation and the Ground of Hope*. Richmond, IN: Friends United Press, 1989.

_____. *The Negro Spiritual Speaks of Life and Death*. New York: Harper and Row, 1947.

Tigg, Fnr. "MTV Reportedly Wants to Remove Michael Jackson's Name from Video Vanguard Award." *Complex*, July 27, 2019. Accessed August 1, 2019. https://www.complex.com/ music/2019/07/mtv-reportedly-wants-remove-michael-jackson-name-video-vanguard-award.

Tinsley. Justin. "Kanye, Bill Cosby, R. Kelly: When It All Falls Down." *The Undefeated*, April 26, 2018. Accessed July 2, 2019. https://theundefeated.com/whhw/bill-cosby-found-guilty-kanye-tweets-nas-kelis/.

Tinsley, Omiseeke Natasha. *Beyoncé in Formation: Remixing Black Feminism*. Austin: University of Texas Press, 2018.

Torres, Libby. "Kanye's Africa Trip Is Even More Embarrassing Than Melania's." *The Daily Beast*, October 18, 2018. Accessed July 9, 2019. https://www.thedailybeast. com/kanye-wests-trip-to-africa-is-even-more-embarrassing-than-melania-trumps.

Tuttle, William. *Race Riot Chicago in the Red Summer of 1919*. Urbana: University of Illinois Press, 1970.Tyson, Timothy B. *The Blood of Emmett Till*. New York: Simon & Schuster, 2017.

Ukoha, Ezinne. "How The Kardashians Keep Getting Away with Villainizing Black Men." *Medium*, April 13, 2018. Accessed April 21, 2020. https://medium.com/@nilegirl/the-kardashians-keep-getting-away-with-villainizing-black-men-like-its-their-right-e898af98734a.

Vazquez, Maegan. "Kushner Claims Kanye West Meeting Was a 'Policy' Talk." *CNN*, August 13, 2020. Accessed August 15, 2020. https://www.cnn.com/2020/08/13/politics/jared-kushner-kanye-west-policy-discussion-colorado/index.html.

Wadsworth, Nancy D. "The Racial Demons That Help Explain Evangelical Support for Trump." *Vox*, April 30, 2018. Accessed August 7, 2020. https://www.vox.com/the-big-idea/2018/4/30/17301282/race-evangelicals-trump-support-gerson-atlantic-sexism-segregation-south.

Wakefield, Jane. "Christchurch Shootings: Social Media Races to Stop Attack Footage." *BBC*,

March 16, 2019. Accessed February 19, 2020. https://www.bbc.com/news/technology-47583393.

Wallenstein, Peter. *Race, Sex, and the Freedom to Marry: Loving v. Virginia*. Lawrence: University Press of Kansas, 2014.

Ward, Geoffrey C. *Unforgivable Blackness: The Rise and Fall of Jack Johnson*. New York: Vintage Books, 2006.

Washington, James Melvin. *Conversations with God: Two Centuries of Prayer by African Americans*. New York: HarperCollins, 1994.

Watson, Pernell. "SAMMY DAVIS JR. A FRIEND OF NIXON." dailypress.com, March 27, 2002. Accessed May 23, 2020. https://www.dailypress.com/news/dp-xpm-20020327-2002-03-27-0203261615-story.html.

Waxman, Olivia B. "Was Martin Luther King, Jr., a Republican or a Democrat? The Answer Is Complicated." *Time*, January 17, 2020. Accessed January 24, 2020. https://time.com/5764282/martin-luther-king-jr-politics/.

Webster, Dwight. "Gospel Music in the United States 1960s–1980s: A Study of the Themes of 'Survival,' 'Elevation,' and 'Liberation' in Popular Urban Contemporary Black Folk Sacred Mass Music." PhD diss., University of California, Berkeley, 2011.

Weiler, A.H. "Stars 'Save the Children.'" *The New York Times*, September 19, 1973. Accessed May 1, 2019. https://www.nytimes.com/1973/09/19/archives/stars-save-the-children.html.

West, Donda. *Raising Kanye: Life Lessons from the Mother of a Hip-Hop Superstar*. New York: Pocket Books, 2009.

White Hodge, Daniel. "Yeezus Is Jesuz: Examining the Socio-Hermeneutical Transmediated Images of Jesus Employed by Kanye West." *Journal of Hip Hop Studies* 6, no. 1 (2019): 54–77.

Wilkerson, Isabel. *The Warmth of Other Suns: The Epic Story of America's Great Migration*. New York: Vintage Books, 2011.

Wilkinson, Lauren. *American Spy: A Novel*. New York: Random House, 2020.

Williams, Elliot. "How Kanye West's Howard Performance Sparked Debates on Campus and Beyond." *Washingtonian*, October 15, 2019. Accessed June 16, 2020. https://www.washingtonian.com/2019/10/15/how-kanye-wests-howard-performance-sparked-debates-on-campus-and-beyond/.

Williams, Megan E. "'Meet the Real Lena Horne': Representations of Lena Horne in *Ebony* Magazine, 1945–1949." *Journal of American Studies* 43, no. 1 (2009). doi:10.1017/s0021875809006094.

Williams, Stereo. "Kendrick Lamar, Black Language and What White Fans Don't Get About the 'N-Word.'" *Billboard*, May 24, 2018. Accessed July 8, 2019. https://www.billboard.com/articles/columns/hip-hop/8457834/kendrick-lamar-n-word-white-fans.

Wiltz, Teresa. "Great African-American Entrepreneurs Who Made History." *The Root*, February 10, 2014. Accessed January 3, 2020. https://www.theroot.com/great-african-american-entrepreneurs-who-made-history-1790868437.

Wintz, Cary D. *Encyclopedia of the Harlem Renaissance*. London: Routledge, 2004.

Woodson, Evan. "Strange Fruit on the Southern Plains: Racial Violence, Lynching, and African Americans in Oklahoma, 1830–1930." PhD diss., Oklahoma State University, 2013.

Wootson, Cleve. "A Black R&B Artist Hoped Singing for Trump Would Build 'a Bridge.' It Derailed Her Career Instead." *The Washington Post*, January 18, 2019. Accessed December 6, 2019. https://www.washingtonpost.com/nation/2019/01/18/black-rb-artist-hoped-singing-trump-would-build-bridge-it-derailed-her-career-instead/.

Wright, Joshua K. "Be Like Mike?: The Black Athlete's Dilemma." *Spectrum: A Journal on Black Men* 4, no. 2 (2016): 1. https://doi.org/10.2979/spectrum.4.2.01.

_____. *Empire and Black Images in Popular Culture*. Jefferson, NC: McFarland Inc., 2018.

_____. "Views from the Mecca: A History of Student Takeovers at Howard University." *Abernathy*, May 21, 2018. Accessed November 23, 2019. https://abernathymagazine.com/views-mecca-howard-university/.

Younger, Briana. "How Kirk Franklin Revolutionized Gospel and Made Hip-Hop A More Spiritual Place." *The FADER*, May 19, 2016. Accessed November 25, 2019. https://www.thefader.com/2016/05/19/kirk-franklin-gospel-hip-hop-chance-the-rapper.

Zimmerman, Amy. "The Uncompromising Politics of Dave Chappelle." *Daily Beast,* November 8, 2016. Accessed June 26, 2019. https://www.thedailybeast.com/the-uncompromising-politics-of-dave-chappelle.

Zirin, Dave. *The Kaepernick Effect: Taking a Knee, Changing the World.* New York: The New Press, 2021.

_____. "Understanding Jim Brown's Ugly Support of Donald Trump." *The Nation,* January 18, 2017. Accessed September 13, 2019. https://www.thenation.com/article/archive/understanding-jim-browns-ugly-support-of-donald-trump/.

_____. *What's My Name, Fool? Sports and Resistance in the United States.* Chicago: Haymarket Books, 2005.

Zullo, Justin. "'We Get Free!': Chicago Hip-Hop, Juvenile Justice, and the Embodied Politics of Movement." PhD diss., University of Wisconsin–Madison, 2015.

Index